NATO In Transition:

The Future of the Atlantic Alliance

NATO in Transition:

The Future of the Atlantic Alliance

Timothy W. Stanley

Published for the
Council on Foreign Relations
by **FREDERICK A. PRAEGER,** *Publishers*
New York • Washington • London

The Council on Foreign Relations is a non-profit institution devoted to the study of political, economic and strategic problems as related to American foreign policy. It takes no stand, expressed or implied, on American policy.

The authors of books published under the auspices of the Council are responsible for their statements of fact and expressions of opinion. The Council is responsible only for determining that they should be presented to the public.

For a list of Council publications see pages 415-417.

FREDERICK A. PRAEGER, *Publishers*
111 Fourth Avenue, New York 3, N.Y., U.S.A.
77-79 Charlotte Street, London W.1, England

NATO IN TRANSITION: THE FUTURE OF THE ATLANTIC ALLIANCE

Published in the United States of America in 1965
by Frederick A. Praeger, Inc., Publishers

FIRST EDITION

Library of Congress catalog card number: 65-15650
Printed in the United States of America
by Capital City Press, Inc., Montpelier, Vermont

This book is respectfully dedicated to my father with admiration for his unfailing kindness, humor and courage

Preface

In attempting to examine dispassionately the political chemistry of an alliance in transition, I have discovered that the classic problem of the author as critic has a counterpart in the difficulties of the bureaucrat turned scholar. The latter is expected to criticize, to explore, and to suggest the imaginative new solutions which the former instinctively rejects as unrealistic or unworkable. In attempting to combine the functions of both academician and sometime practitioner, I am conscious of having done full justice to neither. Nevertheless, this book also has an educational role—not the least aspect of which has been the author's own education.

The Council on Foreign Relations made possible a sabbatical away from the daily pressures of pruning back the "trees," which enabled me, figuratively speaking, to explore the forest and to compare notes with knowledgeable people in and out of the governments of several NATO countries.

During the period between the completion of the first draft at the end of my leave of absence, and the reading of the proofs, much has happened to affect the book's substance. The American election campaign, for example, brought forth a spate of political and journalistic commentary on defense issues. Much of it has been artificial, oversimplified and misleading. I hope that this book will at least demonstrate that the underlying problems have been with us for a long time, and that there are no ready or simple solutions to any of them. But at the same time, I have tried to express my belief that the discord and disarray of the alliance have been greatly exaggerated, for it is far easier to discover and criticize defects than to evaluate accomplishments. I believe that common sense and goodwill can not only preserve those achievements which are still vital to the future, but also adapt them to the new challenges of a world in transition. During the periodic updatings of the manuscript that were necessary after the original cut-off date, I found additional evidence of this underlying continuity, notwithstanding many apparent surface changes; for the basic insights obtained in 1962-1963 seemed if anything even more valid in 1964.

It is important to underscore that this book is a private scholarly endeavor written while on leave from government as a Visiting Research Fellow at the Council on Foreign Relations in New York, and that it is based entirely upon sources in the public domain. It is in no sense intended to reflect U.S. policies or the views of any U.S. government agency or official; any similarity is therefore coincidental. Having thus exonerated the Defense Department for any errors of omission or commission which the book may contain, I should express my thanks to that agency for granting me an extended leave of absence, and in particular to Paul H. Nitze and Henry S. Rowen for their encouragement and help in connection with the project.

The members of the Council Study Group listed below have contributed a great deal to this book, individually and collectively, by sharing with me their extensive experience. Their discussions of, and not infrequent disagreements over, the major issues affecting NATO were most helpful in sharpening my own ideas and providing a sounding board for them. But the responsibility for the book is entirely mine and it does not represent the views or have the endorsement of any members of the Study Group or of the Council on Foreign Relations. But I do wish to express my appreciation to all the members, many of whom travelled long distances at considerable personal inconvenience to attend the six discussion meetings, and especially to our able

Chairman, John N. Irwin II, with whom it was first my privilege to work when he was Assistant Secretary of Defense (International Security Affairs).

The group was composed of John N. Irwin, II, Chairman, Stephen R. Petschek, Rapporteur, Robert Amory, Maj. Gen. C. Stanton Babcock, Francis M. Bator, Robert R. Bowie, Maj. Gen. David A. Burchinal, William A. M. Burden, W. Randolph Burgess, Russell Fessenden, William T. R. Fox, Brig. Gen. Henry C. Huglin, Milton Katz, Col. William R. Kintner, Klaus Knorr, Ben T. Moore, Paul H. Nitze, Robert E. Osgood, David H. Popper, Isidor I. Rabi, Henry S. Rowen, Thomas C. Schelling, Brig. Gen. Richard G. Stilwell, Robert Strausz-Hupé, Albert Wohlstetter, and Arnold Wolfers.

I owe special thanks to Philip E. Mosely, former Director of the Council's Study Program, for wise counsel and encouragement about the project; and similarly to W. Phillips Davison and David W. MacEachron. Robert W. Valkenier was a tactful and patient but hard-working and effective editor; and Albert P. Toner also labored valiantly in Washington to help me render the jargon of the defense business into English. Finally, I want to thank the many others at the Council who assisted in many ways —not least by providing a pleasant and intellectually stimulating environment in which to work. This includes the librarians and in particular, Lorna Brennan and her staff who typed the several drafts of the manuscript and handled the materials for the Study Group, and Mrs. Carole W. Parsons who served as my secretary and valued research assistant.

So many other individuals were helpful in various ways during the preparation of the book that I cannot acknowledge some without slighting others. Moreover, during a two month trip through Europe, I interviewed many officials of NATO, other international organizations, and of the U.S. and other member governments. They stated their personal views very frankly on the understanding that our discussion was not for attribution. I must therefore record my indebtedness to them collectively and anonymously. Last but not least, I owe apologies to my family for the many inconveniences endured on account of this project, and especially to my wife—with whom I have shared both the difficulties and the lasting benefits of an "Atlantic" alliance!

TIMOTHY W. STANLEY

Contents

NATO In Transition:
The Future of the Atlantic Alliance

Introduction

On a spring morning in 1949 the representatives of ten nations solemnly foregathered in Washington's Departmental Auditorium to create the North Atlantic Treaty Organization. The cruel winter of 1948-49 and the most destructive war in history were behind. But in the aftermath, Europe's dreary economic prospects had moved the United States to initiate the Marshall Plan. Much of Eastern Europe and, most recently, Czechoslovakia had fallen under Communist control. The Berlin blockade, then in its tenth month, revealed how much Western Europe lay at the mercy of Soviet power—which was augmented by Communist political strength within several key countries.

The peoples of the Atlantic world seemed to have surmounted one threat to Western civilization only to face another. They were afraid. That fear brought into being one of the farthest-reaching collective efforts ever undertaken by a group of sovereign nations.

Many things can be said about the intervening years of developments within the alliance. The dominant fact is that its peoples are no longer afraid. America and Europe share in a material prosperity undreamed of before World War II and together they dispose of unimagined military power. Economic prosperity has been matched by European political resurgence; yet, paradoxically, these very factors have permitted the development of factionalism and national differences which raise concern about the future of the alliance.

The Soviet Union has also acquired an unprecedented destructive potential. Its declared intentions and ideology are different only in degree rather than in kind. Ideologically, the peoples of Western Europe are even less favorably disposed toward communism. Intellectually they recognize the reality of the Soviet threat. But somehow the sense of imminent danger that had molded so much of NATO's institutions is now lacking.

On the available evidence, NATO and the Atlantic alliance in its broadest sense deserve much of the credit for the feeling of security which permitted Europe's political and economic *risorgimento*. Ironically it is NATO's very success which raises the vital question to which this book is addressed: "Has the unity of purpose which characterized so much of the alliance's history outlived its usefulness?"

I shall attempt to demonstrate in the following chapters that the answer should be "No!" America and Europe still have a common task. But since the whole world, like the alliance, is in transition, the task may require some redefinition. Moreover both the strategic concepts and the instruments for meeting the military challenge require some refashioning.

These problems present the familiar triad of economic, political and military aspects, each with endless ramifications. Books have been written about each one separately, but our modern world has made the three into a seamless web. I have therefore—and perhaps overambitiously—sought to treat the whole, at least in general outline, although the main focus is upon the military and strategic aspects.

This is a book about the Atlantic alliance. I hope it can also be a book *for* the alliance in the sense of being useful to interested citizens in various member countries. But since it is written by an American, I should like to address a few preliminary thoughts to the American reader—not so much the fellow specialist as the intelligent and perhaps troubled fellow citizen.

Although the foundation for America's role in world affairs was laid over many decades, our country's broad involvement on the world scene has come within the span of a single generation beginning with World War I. In that conflict and its aftermath we made many mistakes. And although we thought that our purposes were good ones, we tended to discover the wrong lessons in reviewing our failures. During the 1930s we made a virtue of minding our own business. As a result, the America of 1939 stood at first on the sidelines of World War II, troubled and unsure, leaving the British alone to prepare for "their finest hour." In retrospect, this is not a pose America can be proud of. Yet the war effort and the succeeding ten years brought much which we can view with pride. Even in the much-needed learning process a great deal was accomplished; and on the whole it can be said that despite its lack of experience our country has demonstrated a sense of responsibility commensurate with its enormous power.

In the first postwar decade two major tides were running: the expansion of the Communist bloc and the painful, sometimes bloody disengagement of the colonial powers from their major overseas possessions. Almost overnight dozens of new nations came into being. It fell to the United States to try to modulate this tide of disengagement—not a happy role, to be sure, but on balance it met with success.

During the 1950s it was America's task to stem the other tide by building almost singlehandedly the free world's defenses against Communist expansion. For the most part this, too, was accomplished, albeit at a cost of over 150,000 U.S. casualties and hundreds of billions of dollars.

It is conceivable that the historian a century hence may regard these accomplishments as illusory, like the story of the man who threw matches out of a subway-car window to keep the tigers away. When his sanity was challenged, he retorted, "You haven't seen any tigers around, have you?" But this evaluation seems unlikely; for, if the future historian has access to the surviving Kremlin archives, he should be able to document both the prevalence of tigers and their fear of matches!

It is true that no final victory has yet been won. Nor is it clear that there will be one in the years to come. But given the Communist advantages of aggressive and totalitarian power, it is no mean tribute to American leadership that the non-Communist world has not lost.

What of the future? Must we settle for a "draw?" Certainly not —although partially as a result of our past success, the future challenges will be more subtle and less easily identified. If we are to secure the future for posterity there are new tides which America and Europe must jointly help the world to channel.

This task will require flexibility as well as firmness, forbearance as well as forcefulness, and patience along with determination. It will demand understanding, tact, and the sophistication to respond to an international kaleidoscope more often gray than black and white. I have no doubt that America and Europe can meet these challenges. But the outcome depends on the most unpredictable of all factors, the human will. If this book serves to help focus our collective will by analyzing what *can* be done, it will have fulfilled its purpose.

PART I

The Task of America and Europe

1

The Communist Challenge in a World of Change

> The policy of Peaceful Coexistence is . . . a form of intense economic, political, and ideological struggle between the proletariat and the aggressive forces of Imperialism in the world arena.
>
> KHRUSHCHEV

The current turmoil in the Communist world encourages the West to overemphasize change at the expense of forgetting the continuity which communism has displayed throughout the ups and downs of its development. Yet, despite Khrushchev's ouster and the repercussions of the Sino-Soviet dispute, the threat of Communist expansion remains.

A threat, in military parlance, is a combination of capabilities and intentions. The Soviet Union at present disposes of hundreds of intercontinental nuclear delivery vehicles and even more shorter range missiles and bombers, plus thermonuclear warheads which have been tested to about 50 megatons and which could be made still larger. This strategic capability is reinforced by as many as 150 army divisions, 3,000 naval vessels, and 12,000 or more operational aircraft.[1]

Russia has a strong industrial-technological foundation though the economy has some weak spots, such as agriculture, but on the

[1]The Institute for Strategic Studies, *The Military Balance 1963-1964* (London: 1963), pp. 3-6.

whole it provides an adequate base for an expanding production of both military and nonmilitary goods. Russia's gross national product has been growing at an annual rate of over 5 per cent, and it has risen from a third of the U.S. total in 1955 to more nearly one-half by 1960. More recently the growth rate has slowed significantly, but over the longer term the Soviet Union's economic potential remains high. The loyalty and zeal of the Soviet people are open to different estimates; but on balance the downgrading of terror as an instrument of control has strengthened the ability of the system to direct the energies of the population through more subtle means.

If the capabilities are formidable, the declared goals of communism appear to be unchanged—although they are not an infallible guide to current intentions. Soviet leaders have reiterated that the long-range goal remains "the triumph of Socialism and Communism on a worldwide scale."[2] This was a program for action, as shown by the injunction to the Party Congress that the transition from capitalism to socialism can only come about through revolution.[3] Subsequent pronouncements have been more ambiguous, under the impact of the Moscow-Peking polemics, but the underlying message remains. The West cannot afford to mistake constant shifts in Soviet means for a change in ends. We ignore at our peril Khrushchev's definition of peaceful coexistence as "a form of intense struggle in the world arena."

Three recurrent themes, however, lend some support to the

[2] This statement, issued in the name of the World Communist Leaders Meeting, was published in *The New York Times,* December 7, 1960. It is compared with Khrushchev's speech of January 6, 1961, together with commentary, by Charles Burton Marshall in *Two Communist Manifestoes* (Washington: Washington Center of Foreign Policy Research, 1961).

[3] Text of some of the 22nd Party Congress material is printed in *The New York Times,* October 18, 1961. In September 1962 at the United Nations, Soviet Foreign Minister Gromyko affirmed that "the foreign policy of the Soviet state" is governed by the 22nd Party Congress program—with specific reference to "wars of liberation." Subsequent statements have muted, but never repudiated, this theme. The views of a number of specialists are collected in Arnold Wolfers, ed., *Changing East-West Relations and the Unity of the West* (Baltimore: The Johns Hopkins Press, 1964).

contention that the Communist leopard is changing his spots. The first is that the governing hierarchy now has such a stake in the system that maintaining the *status quo* takes priority over ideological goals. The second is that because the Soviets are concerned with their own human survival, they will therefore avoid a thermonuclear war which could destroy all that they have built at such costs. Finally there is the argument that the Sino-Soviet split may eventually lead the Russians to make common cause—or at least reach a settlement—with the West.

There is an element of truth in all three themes, but none offers more than the long-term hope of a change in the Communist system. Important as it is that Western policy encourages evolution in this direction, policy must nevertheless be based upon realities rather than on hopes. It is worthwhile, therefore, to examine some of the current influences in the direction of change.

Internal Evolution

This theme of domestic change has been in the category of "famous last words" almost since the 1917 revolution. Fridtjof Nansen, a Norwegian Nobel Peace Prize winner noted for his relief work in Russia, reported after a trip in 1922: "Our troubles with Russia are over: Lenin is returning to capitalism."[4] One could find many such examples of the wish being father to the thought. Millions around the world reacted with relief and bright anticipation to the wartime dissolution of the Comintern, Stalin's adherence to the Atlantic Charter, and Khrushchev's homely anecdotes about Soviet life while he toured the United States during the "spirit of Camp David."

The course of internal developments in Russia over the past several years does show some signs of evolution toward a society in which rewards and punishment are more evenly balanced, in which the legal system is acquiring a growing role in protecting individual rights, and where there is a real, if subtle, impact of the

[4] Quoted in Bertram D. Wolfe, "Communist Ideology and Soviet Foreign Policy," *Foreign Affairs*, October 1962, p. 152.

desires and interests of the people upon the party hierarchy. The seeds of change were greatly nourished by Khrushchev's speech to the Twentieth Party Congress denouncing the cult of the individual. This denunciation—which surely must stand as one of the remarkable events of our times—confirmed Stalin's absolute dictatorship in these words: "Whoever opposed his concept . . . was doomed to removal and to subsequent moral and physical annihilation. Many thousands of honest and innocent Communists have died as a result of all kinds of slanderous confessions."

The relationship of the internal dictatorship to errors of judgment in external affairs was revealed: "Information concerning the threat of German armed invasion was coming in. However, because the leadership was conditioned against such information, such data was dispatched with fear and assessed with reservation." The inhumanity of the regime was exposed as "rude violations of the nationality policy, mass deportations from their native places of whole nations, not dictated by any military consideration."

One must bear in mind that this was a strictly private discussion; for as the speaker stated: "We cannot let this matter get out of the party, especially not to the press . . . we should not give ammunition to the enemy; we should not wash our dirty linen before their eyes."[5]

The admissions in this speech both support and refute the hopeful implications of internal evolution. One explanation is that Khrushchev was engaged in a bitter internal struggle for power and that only by the strongest accusations against the Stalinists could he capitalize on the fears and hopes of the people and thus emerge in control. On the other hand, Khrushchev must have known that even the most naïve in his audience could well conclude that the crimes, injustices, and failures attributed to Stalin were in reality defects of the whole system, in which Khrushchev himself had played a major part. That he could run this risk without incurring serious disaffection at home, although the revelations

[5] The full text is contained in *The Anti-Stalin Campaign and International Communism—A Selection of Documents* (New York: Russian Institute of Columbia University, 1956).

split the international Communist movement, suggests that the system has become so solidly rooted that its subjects can conceive of no alternative. Indeed the system has outlasted both members of the original post-Stalin team of Bulganin and Khruschev, only to produce another—and probably temporary—alphabetical tandem in Brezhnev and Kosygin.

Whoever the ultimate rulers prove to be, they may find that in dealing with the practical problems of Soviet life, they are tied to a dreary treadmill of outworn ideological clichés from which escape is impossible. Improvements in living standards and a relaxation of tensions at home may well sap some of the remaining vitality of the ideology. There is certainly a connection between internal developments and the external dynamics of the Communist system, and these dynamics involve both the Communist revolutionary ideology and the use of power in all its forms to promote Soviet national interests. But the interconnection is difficult, if not impossible, to predict. If internal preoccupations are causing the Russians to pay mere lip service to the goal of worldwide communism, such a conclusion is hard to square with recent crises provoked by the Soviet Union, ranging from several minor harassments involving Berlin to the dangerous confrontation over Cuba.

Survival

This brings us to the second theme: Soviet interest in survival. There seems little doubt that as their awareness of the consequences of a nuclear war has grown, the Soviet leaders are determined to avoid such a conflict and have modified their doctrine accordingly. Khrushchev repeatedly warned the Communist movement not to expect victory through a major war, not only because it is dangerous but because victory could be achieved without it.

But the Communist recognition of the dangers of nuclear war has been explicitly coupled with Khrushchev's famous announcement about "just" wars: "There will be liberation wars as long as imperialism exists, as long as colonialism exists. Wars of this kind are revolutionary wars. Such wars [citing Algeria, Viet-Nam,

Cuba as specific examples] are not only justified, they are inevitable."[6]

The Communist party platform has warned the faithful as to what peaceful coexistence does *not* mean: "Specifically, it does not imply renunciation of the class struggle, as the revisionists claim." In one of those unconscious ironies at which the Communists are so adept, disarmament is described as a "fighting slogan, an effective factor in the fight against imperialism," while elsewhere Khrushchev was asserting that we "sincerely want disarmament, which is not a tactical move."[7]

What does the Communist doctrine of the 1960s hold out to the West? One answer was in the statement of the 1960 meeting of the leaders of 81 Communist parties: "The degree of bitterness and the forms of the class struggle will depend on the resistance put up by the reactionary circles." In other words, whoever does not wish to be embraced by the Socialist camp had best give up peaceably; otherwise he will be dealt with by whatever degree of violence is necessary to overcome his resistance.

That the Soviet leaders are now exempting general and limited wars from their spectrum of violence does not imply accommodation. The most that can be said for the Communists' genuine interest in survival is that it has caused a revision in tactics. This development does, however, have encouraging aspects. The Soviets are unlikely to provoke a deliberate nuclear conflict; and Western firmness may be an effective deterrent wherever a confrontation of military power can be made credible. Moreover, Kremlin power politics obviously involves the conflicting ideas of

[6] Speech by N. S. Khrushchev, "For New Victories of the World Communist Movement," delivered on January 6, 1961, at a meeting of Communist leaders in Moscow. The text was released via the Soviet Home Service on January 19, 1961, and is reprinted as Appendix III to the Hearings before the Senate Judiciary Committee, Internal Security Subcommittee, 87th Cong., 1st sess., entitled "Analysis of the Khrushchev Speech of January 6, 1961."

[7] January 6, 1961, speech, cited; also compare the 22nd Party Congress statements with Khrushchev's speech at the World Congress for General Disarmament and Peace (reprinted as a U.S.S.R.-sponsored advertisement in the *New York Herald Tribune,* Sunday, July 22, 1962, p. 20).

personalities, factions, and interest groups with varying degrees of sincerity in their approach to *détente* and arms control. Although such differences are hardly subject to external manipulation, the West should be able to use its strength and flexibility to deter the rash while encouraging the moderates.

Sino-Soviet Relations

It remains to examine the implications for the West of the Sino-Soviet conflict. The reality of that conflict now seems established, although its cause and future course are less clear-cut. Some analysts believe that whatever the theoretical positions adopted by the two contestants, the real issue is "pecking order," since a totalitarian movement permits but one true leader. Although both the Russians and the Chinese initially tended to garb their differences in the ideological terminology of "inter-party relations," something very like the bourgeois concept of conflicting national interests seems to be involved.

Red China has its own special interests: "liquidating" the Chiang Kai-shek regime and capturing Taiwan; extending its control into Southeast Asia's rice bowl; and driving the U.S. Seventh Fleet from its coast, as well as controlling access to the Indian subcontinent and perhaps eventually neutralizing Japan and dominating Indonesia.[8]

Soviet national interests, narrowly defined, are less involved in the Far East. The Russians are also concerned with avoiding a confrontation with the West which could lead to dangerous conflicts or interfere with their other objectives. If revolutionary wars of liberation are to be the key to Communist strategy, it is logical to expect that Mao will not take a back seat to Moscow in the very area where he has had the most experience.[9] Communist China

[8] The September 1962 issue of *Current History* is a useful symposium on Communist China. See in particular Bernard B. Fall's article on "Red China's Aims in South Asia." More recent developments are discussed in Harold Hinton's article in *Changing East-West Relations and the Unity of the West*, cited, p. 76.

[9] Mao Tse-tung, after all, is considered in China as communism's greatest

still resents the Soviet caution displayed during the Indo-China War, when Soviet interests in the Communist party of France tended to conflict with the military objectives of Chou En-lai and Ho Chi Minh. This conflict was further evidenced by the U.S.S.R.'s desire to supply the Pathet Lao forces in Laos and co-operate in reaching a political settlement in the area.

The Chinese Communists re-established hegemony over most of the lands bordering on the Soviet Union after their victory in the Chinese Civil War. It is possible that the Kremlin worries about the relatively empty Siberian spaces and the enormous, expanding population just to the south.[10]

Additional differences are apparent in the degree of military risks which the two countries are willing to run, and inevitably doctrinal competition has emerged between the technologically advanced state and the underdeveloped, relatively primitive one. Nevertheless it is unlikely that such tactical experts as Mao and Khrushchev's heirs would scrap the teachings of the Communist movement and fail to combine against common enemies wherever they could do so without endangering their respective positions in their intramural rivalry. It seems likely therefore that relations between Moscow and Peking will continue to fluctuate unevenly in the near term between limited reconciliation and ill-concealed hostility. Over a longer period, however, a further deterioration in the relationship seems inevitable.

Whether the Sino-Soviet competition for allegiance of the underdeveloped world in Asia, Africa, and Latin America should be a source of comfort for the West remains to be seen. It gives the two Communist giants opportunities for a "one-two" punch.

---

living tactician, and his works on guerrilla conflict rank almost with Clausewitz's as contributions to military theory. Most of his writings are contained in *Mao Tse-tung, Selected Works* (New York: International Publishers, 1955).

[10] For a useful historical analysis see Howard Boorman's "The Borderlands and the Sino-Soviet Alliance," in *Moscow-Peking Axis* (New York: Harper & Row, for the Council on Foreign Relations, 1957), Ch. 4. See also the articles in *Problems of Communism*, especially the survey by H. Gelman in the Spring 1964 issue.

On the other hand, the mutual competition further strains the resources of both countries.

In the long term, one of the most significant impacts of the Sino-Soviet split may prove to be its explosion of the myth of monolithic solidarity. The effect of "polycentrism" on other satellites, especially in Eastern Europe, has already proved unsettling, and it has released pent-up nationalistic tendencies.

The West can take some comfort in the greater sobriety of the stronger of the Communist partners, even though the threat posed by Communist China to its neighbors may become greater by virtue of the reduction in Moscow's ability to control situations. However, if the "hard" line advocated by Peking should threaten to dominate the world Communist movement, Khrushchev's successors might find it necessary to take larger risks as the price of maintaining leadership.

On balance there may well be more hopeful signs than ominous ones in the flux which currently permeates the Communist world; but the very uncertainties caused by this turmoil appear to counsel a Western policy of firmness combined with flexibility.[11] Caution is also indicated in any effort to exploit and inflame the internal rivalry, lest such action merely work to close the breach.

The Non-Communist World

It is very well to say that the Communist goal is a world order which conflicts with natural diversity and independence and that it must therefore be resisted. But the confrontation can be looked at in another way. For all of the non-Communist nations share the goal of a peaceful world in which peoples everywhere are free to pursue their destinies in accordance with their own way of life. This must be a world which can accommodate inevitable

[11] A group of expert advisers were polled at one of the study group meetings connected with this book, and significantly none saw Russia seeking a real détente with the West, let alone active cooperation, as a result of the Sino-Soviet conflict. The replies were divided between those foreseeing no change in Russia's aggressiveness toward the West and those predicting a slight lessening of aggressiveness at best.

change without major violence; a world in which individual freedom, dignity, and equality are advancing along with standards of living, and in which the ideal of government by consent can be perfected.

Communism stands in the way of such a world order. It is the free world which has the positive approach to the future. This is the way the cold war ought to appear—but it does not. For one thing, the non-Communist world has been unable to decide who "we" are in relation to the Communist "they." This is not an easy question. In the last analysis it must include all of the world's peoples who wish to pursue their future independent of Communist control. But this is the outer circle, too nebulous a basis for combined action. Within it there are concentric circles; and at the center are North America and Europe. Thus defined, "we" can pass to the offensive against closed and totalitarian societies *if* we can make meaningful to all the rights of man in an open society. If actions support this promise, the free world will be the true revolutionaries, and the determinism of Marxism-Leninism will be exposed as obsolete in the present and irrelevant to the future. The task outlined above must take into account not only developments within the Communist bloc but also the evolving world power structure.

The Elements of Power in the 1970s

To the traditional elements of national power—geography, population, natural resources, and industrial capacity—technology must be added as a vital measure of both military and economic capabilities in the modern age. The significance of the geographic factor has been changed by the strategic advantages of geographic space in the nuclear and missile era,[12] and by the ease with which

[12] The values of "space" are suggested by the fact that a 50-megaton explosion can cause severe blast damage up to 14 miles radius from ground zero, first degree burns out to 70 miles, local fallout up to 500 miles down wind, and under certain conditions retinal burns out to 250 miles. If a 25-plus megaton groundburst weapon will produce 20 pounds per square inch overpressure (PSI) against targets at a distance of 21,000 feet or about 4

modern technology permits the bypassing of such traditional obstacles as oceans, mountains, or even the polar ice caps.

Traditionally, population was measured as an asset in terms of potential military and industrial manpower. Now raw numbers must be modified in terms of the health, education, and inherent skills of the labor force, as well as its levels of employment and productivity. Mao Tse-tung has reminded us, however, that raw manpower still has some relevance by pointing out that a major nuclear war would leave "30 million Americans and 50 million Russians but 200 million Chinese!"

Population is also relevant because its explosive expansion depresses living standards, promotes local and international instabilities, and generates pressures for *Lebensraum*. Table 1 shows the ranking of the fifteen most populous countries in 1960-61 and as projected for 1970. It suggests that the world of 1970 can be divided into two superpopulated areas with over one-half billion inhabitants each (China and India); two areas of one-fifth to one-quarter billion population (the U.S.S.R. and the United States); three areas of one-tenth billion (Pakistan, Indonesia, and Japan); and several areas of 30 million to 50 million. Brazil stands alone between the last two groupings.

The major powers should not be seriously restricted by shortages of natural resources, measured in terms of basic commodities like coal, iron, and petroleum. But by 1970, consumption in the United States may exceed the available domestic supply of such critical industrial materials as chromite, manganese, tungsten, tin,

---

miles, this means that each such weapon used in pattern bombing could cover an area of nearly 50 square miles with 20 PSI. Warning time—another function of distance—is also vital in the absence of a secure second-strike capability. Against a missile averaging Mach 25 before re-entry (over 12,500 miles an hour) a missile based at Chicago has four minutes less reaction time than one at Dallas—and even seconds can be decisive both for active defense and retaliation. The recuperative ability of a society is also affected by its geographic dispersal in relation to the attack pattern. These and other computations in this book are based on data from the Defense Department-AEC pamphlet, *The Effects of Nuclear Weapons* (Washington: GPO, June 1957), No. 39-3, as updated by AEC releases, especially that of October 31, 1961, and revised in 1962.

TABLE 1

Fifteen Countries with Largest Populations—1960 and 1970

(In millions, rounded to nearest million)

	Country	Approximate 1960-61 Population[a]	Estimated 1970 Population[b]	1970 Rank
1	Communist China	647	799	1
2	India	435	504	2
	(European NATO members, total)	(278)	(299)	—
3	U.S.S.R.	218	254	3
4	U.S.A.	180	204	4
5	Indonesia	96	109	6
6	Pakistan	94	114	5
7	Japan	93	109	7
8	Brazil	71	88	8
9	Federal Republic of Germany	56	59	9
10	Great Britain	53	54	10
11	Italy	50	54	11
12	France	45	47	12
13	Nigeria	35	40	14
14	Mexico	35	45	13
15	Spain	30	33	15
	(World Population, total)	(3 billion)		(3.5 billion)

[a] *United Nations Statistical Yearbook, 1962* (New York: United Nations, 1963).

[b] *The Future Growth of World Population,* United Nations, Population Studies No. 28, 1958, Table II, Appendix C (median assumption).

and bauxite.[13] The same is generally true for Europe, which is a net importer of many industrially important materials;[14] and to a lesser extent the Soviet Union faces the same prospect. As many key natural resources at or close to home become depleted, there

[13] National Planning Association, *The Future of Industrial Raw Materials in North America* (Washington: Author, 1961).

[14] Dewhurst, Coppock, Yates and Associates, *Europe's Needs and Resources* (New York: Twentieth Century Fund, 1961), see especially p. 881.

will be continuing competition for economically usable reserves in other parts of the world, which will clearly have political consequences.

Land and water are, of course, among the world's prime natural resources. Notwithstanding the problems of food production in some of the more populated areas, it seems safe to say that while land resources may some day be inadequate to sustain the world's population as it mounts by the billions, this point will not be reached during the next several decades. Likewise, the major powers of the 1970s should not be significantly affected by water shortages; and it is unlikely that desalination, despite recent technological progress, will make the world's deserts bloom.[15] Nevertheless conservation and allocation of water will be a major domestic problem in many areas; and often, as with the Jordan and Indus Rivers, it will constitute a source of major international friction.

The industrial base and infrastructure of a country is the key to its economic progress and the extent to which it can translate its other resources into national power. Although dozens of indicators must be examined in any thorough analysis, there are nevertheless a few key criteria which can provide a very crude yardstick. Table 2 gives some estimates of production in 1970 of coal, steel, food grain, and electric power for the larger countries. Perhaps the best single measure of a country's economic strength is gross national product, for which some estimates for 1970 are also included in the table. Notwithstanding the lack of comparability between the products of different economies, these figures suggest that Europe and America will still have the predominant share of the world's wealth, followed by Russia and (at a sizable lag) Communist China. The gross national product of all other countries will be quite small in comparison. But in per capita terms a number of smaller countries will move to the top of the list, while China and India will be near the bottom.

One additional intangible must be mentioned, which might be called the national will or public morale. Without it resources are

[15] A realistic survey is contained in "The Economic Realities of Water Desalting," George A. Boehn, *Fortune*, January 1962, p. 97.

TABLE 2

Estimates of Economic Indicators for 1970
(Middle of the range)

	Coal	Steel	Food Grains	Electric Power Output	Gross National Product
	(Millions of tons)			(Billions of KWH)	(U.S. $ billions at 1955 prices)
United States	575	135	200	1,100	650
Europe	456	154	103	720	300
Total	1,031	289	303	1,820	950
U.S.S.R.	600	145	230	900	340
Communist China	600	30	450	100	120
Total	1,200	175	680	1,000	460
Japan	70	38	26	190	45
India	105	16	130	80	72
Total	175	54	156	270	117
Pakistan, Indonesia, Brazil, total	–	–	–	–	60

Note: The primary sources for these production estimates for the United States and Europe are the studies cited in notes 13 and 14 above, plus *The New York Times*, October 20, 1961; for the Soviet Union, *The New York Times Magazine*, January 21, 1962. Estimates for Asian countries are from Saburo Okita, "Japan's Economic Prospects," *Foreign Affairs*, October 1960, pp. 123-131; "Statistiques Relatives à L'Economie de . . . Chine, 1949-1959," *La Documentation Française* (Paris: Secrétariat Général du Government), May 1960; and from various issues of the *U. N. Economic Bulletin for Asia and the Far East* and *India Economic Newsletter*.

The U. S. dollar at 1955 prices is used for GNP to improve comparability, but since relative price weighting has not been employed, purchasing power is not comparable. Also, the conversion of local currencies on the basis of official exchange rates tends to give a low dollar figure. In addition to the sources already listed, these projections are based on data in: Hitch and McKean, *The Economics of Defense in the Nuclear Age* (Cambridge: Harvard University Press, 1960), Ch. 6.; The International Monetary Fund, *International Financial Statistics;* and William W. Hollister, *China's GNP and Social Accounts 1950-1957* (Glencoe, Ill.: The Free Press, 1958). Where estimates vary widely, the middle of the range was used as a basis for projection.

meaningless. With it even a very poor people can give a military accounting of themselves quite out of proportion to their material assets. One must thus add something to Japan for the energies (misguided though we think them) which were demonstrated in World War II and perhaps discount something from India.

In Chapter 3 we shall explore in detail the East-West military balance, with particular reference to strategic forces and the dangers of nuclear proliferation. The growing consequences of nuclear conflict will, however, place a great premium on non-nuclear strength. Table 3 gives some current order-of-magnitude comparisons with respect to key indicators of this strength for the major powers and groupings. It is worth noting that NATO has more men under arms than the Soviet Union and the European satellites. If non-Communist Asian forces are included, the total exceeds that of the entire Communist bloc even when China's 2.5 million men are added. That figure, however, represents only slightly over 1.3 per cent of China's current military manpower pool, compared with 4.5 per cent for the United States and nearly 4 per cent for the West as a whole.

NATO spends nearly twice as much as the Communist bloc on defense, and the quality of its forces is much higher as, however, is their cost. If, as Secretary McNamara has suggested,[16] the smaller-size bloc divisions are adjusted for comparability with NATO units, the number of active divisions available to NATO plus those in non-Communist Asia is about equal to that of the bloc. NATO has a clear edge in quantity and quality of naval vessels, plus an over-all qualitative edge in air power, although the bloc may have a greater total of aircraft.

Communist China has an almost limitless supply of manpower, but the economic base may be lacking for equipping adequately a force much larger than that now maintained. It also lacks the sea and air power, as well as logistic support, for projecting military

[16] Remarks to the Economic Club of New York, November 18, 1963, Dept. of Defense Press Release, November 18, 1963, pp. 12-14.

TABLE 3

Some Rough Indicators of Conventional Military Power

	Active Armed Forces		Current Defense Budget			
	Millions of men	*As % of male pop. 15-64*	*U.S. $ Billions*	*Army Divisions*[a]	*Active Fleet Ships*[b]	*Air Squadrons*[c]
United States	2.7	4.5	52	16	850	200
Other NATO	3.1	—	20	74	1,150	250
Total	5.8	3.8	72	90	2,000	450
U.S.S.R.	3.3	6.4	31	120-150	1,000	350
Com. China	2.5	1.3	7	100-120	100	100
Other bloc	1.7	—	2	80- 90	100	100
Total	7.5	2.6	40	300-360	1,200	550
India	.6	—	1.8	15	30	35
Japan	.2	0.8	.7	13	50	20
Indonesia	.4	—	.4	15- 25[d]	70	30
Other Asia[e]	.8	[f]	1.2	50	200	55
Total Non-Communist Asia	2.0	—	4.1	93-103	350	140

[a]Based on a 12,000-13,000 man division but varies widely as to combat support, readiness, and percentage of actual manning.

[b]Including all major combatant-type vessels but excluding small coastal ships, Soviet trawlers and junks.

[c]Based upon a squadron of about 12 aircraft; but with wide variance as to quality, readiness, and modernization of equipment. Includes all tactical units of all services but not reserve and administrative aircraft of the major powers.

[d]An approximation, since the army is organized only in battalions.

[e]Australia, New Zealand, Pakistan, Taiwan, South Korea, Philippines, Thailand.

[f]Ranges from 1% for most to 9% for Korea and 19% for Taiwan.

Source: The Institute for Strategic Studies, *The Military Balance, 1963-64* (London: Author, 1963), Tables I-III, and data on individual countries, pp. 3-31.

force beyond the contiguous land areas. An upsurge in the Chinese economy during the next decade could, however, make possible a major increase in the military threat to Southeast Asia. But if India, Japan, and Indonesia cooperated with other non-Communist nations of Asia, their combined military potential could be a match for China alone—assuming, of course, that the embryonic Chinese nuclear capability remains checkmated by the United States.

Much will depend in this balance upon the degree of support (and military and technical assistance) rendered to Communist China by Russia, and to the other Asian countries by the United States and Europe.

The rising curve of military technology could make the world a rather frightening place to live in during the 1970s. Nuclear weapons (including fusion, fission, and the so-called "neutron" devices) are the obvious examples,[17] but there may be equally dangerous possibilities in chemical and biological warfare or even in concentration of energy utilizing the laser principle.[18] Man's future may be decided ultimately by the extent of the gap between the technological curve and the companion curve of man's ability to control his scientific creations. If the rate of diffusion of the most destructive weapons to the less responsible powers is slow, if the world's inherent instabilities can be kept in reasonable balance, and if the growing moral awareness finds effective political expression, the impact of military technology on the world of 1970 may be considerably less than during the preceding decades. But these are important "if's" which make it particularly relevant to consider the power structure of the next decade.

[17] It is believed technically feasible to make nuclear "bullets" out of isotopes like Californium, which have such a low critical mass that fission would occur on impact. Fortunately, the half-life is only a few days, so that constant replenishments would be needed. Nevertheless even the theoretical possibilities of a fractional kiloton "six shooter" applied, say, to Latin American or Middle Eastern politics are hardly reassuring. See Herman Kahn, *On Thermonuclear War* (Princeton University Press, 1960), p. 494.

[18] General Curtis LeMay, as Air Force Chief of Staff, has referred to "beam-directed energy weapons" in several public speeches. See, for example, *The New York Times,* March 29, 1962, p. 2.

The World Power Structure of the 1970s

No matter what the criteria of measurement, except of course for raw manpower, the United States and Russia seem certain to remain the dominant military powers. Communist China will be well behind the Soviet Union in terms of gross military force inasmuch as it will lack the sophisticated weapons common to the United States, Europe, and Russia. But it could become a dangerous threat to Asia, especially since it has begun to add nuclear potential to its capacity for mischief.

Europe, taken collectively in terms of NATO membership, *could* come third. But political developments during the next few years will have a considerable impact on the cohesiveness of the alliance and its ability to project power and influence into other areas. Without prejudging these important uncertainties, let us assume that "Europe" can be aggregated in terms of populations, national products, and military capabilities. One hears with increasing frequency talk of Europe's becoming a "third force"—a world power in its own right. Even without counting strategic nuclear forces, which "Europe" now lacks except for the relatively small British and French bomber commands, the data in Table 3 suggest that European NATO powers will be behind the United States in most of the key indicators of military strength. Given the complex technology and infrastructure required by modern strategic warfare, there seems almost no chance that "Europe"—let alone its separate components—could join the United States and Russia in the ranks of the "super-powers" in the coming decade.

Nevertheless Europe, certainly, and Communist China, probably, will both be ahead of the only other potential contenders, India and Japan. Hence the first two might be styled "great powers" and the last two as merely "potential powers." In the case of India this depends upon some optimistic assumptions about the success of current development plans, i.e., that there will be sufficient assets left over from the struggle for individual and national survival to attain and project power in international affairs. All of the other Asiatic countries together barely equal

Japan's projected GNP, so that, except for manpower assets, they are not in the picture. Indonesia, despite its large population and natural wealth, is so dispersed over a vast ocean area and so ethnically diverse that great power status by 1970 is most doubtful, although its potential for trouble-making will be large and its resources will make it a sought-after prize. Pakistan will also have a large population—and a fairly high content of the "national will" element mentioned previously; but its GNP is so low as to eliminate it from the first rank. The remaining possibility is Brazil, which by 1970 will contain nearly one-half (88 million) the population of Latin America. Should a regional federation emerge with Brazil as the leader, and should Brazil conquer its chronic problems of one-crop dependency, inflation, and an underdeveloped interior, the picture might change. But if, as it is often stated, Brazil is now where the United States was before World War I, even modern technology cannot manage to telescope fifty years in ten, given the low GNP per capita and its extreme maldistribution.

In abstract terms, therefore, the world power structure of the 1970s might be depicted as an unequal and roughly hexagonal pattern comprising: the United States and Russia, Europe and Communist China, and India and Japan. Around this nucleus can be grouped other nations which will tend to be as much the objects as the subjects of power. Many of them constitute what might be called target areas, in the sense that the conflicting interests and objectives of the larger states will be directed there for both positive and preclusive reasons. The foremost are: Southeast Asia (including Indonesia, the Philippines, Taiwan, and South Korea), the Middle East (including Iran and Egypt), Africa, and Latin America. It is also conceivable that in the 1970s international organizations such as the United Nations will have to be considered as power factors in their own right. The U.N. is not only a forum, an arena, and a sounding board, but also it has shown itself capable of executive action in a number of trouble spots.

The structuring of international power a decade hence will of course derive from patterns that have grown up since World War II. The colonial and imperial relationships of the nineteenth century were already fading when, at the end of the war, communism leaped forward to embrace much of the Eurasian land mass and a third of the world population. For the ensuing fifteen years world politics became frozen into the conflict between an apparently monolithic Sino-Soviet bloc and an Atlantic alliance, supported by other collective security pacts, and centered around American military power and assistance. The so-called neutrals, especially the Afro-Asians, assumed a posture of "nonalignment." (Just as a youthful America might be said to have ridden to maturity in the wake of the British navy, today's newly independent nations have done so on the contrails of America's Strategic Air Command!) In the 1950s, in short, the geometric pattern of world power was triangular: the United States and its NATO and other allies, the Sino-Soviet bloc, and the self-styled neutrals.

In the 1960s we appear to be in transition. The Communist bloc has split into competing Russian and Chinese factions. The common bond of the Afro-Asians in nonalignment is not so compelling in a depolarized world. Even NATO may be in some danger of beginning a parallel process of fragmentation.

General de Gaulle apparently believes that the phase of opposing ideological camps has passed and that the Soviet threat has receded sufficiently to restore France to its nineteenth-century role in power politics. French recognition of Communist China is, therefore, only in part a rejection of American leadership, a bid for economic and trade advantages, and a device for regaining some of France's former position in Southeast Asia. It is equally a classic balance-of-power move. From the time of Richelieu, French diplomacy has looked to Franco-Russian alliances, as well as to Britain, as a counter to German power. What is more natural, therefore, than for the latter-day emulators to look to an entente with China as a counter to Russia and a riposte for a growing Washington-Moscow dialogue? To De Gaulle the fact that China has a Communist regime may be less relevant than the coincidence that France and China are the "outcast" nuclear aspirants of their respective alliances. Gaullist tactics do not, of course, preclude a simultaneous rapprochement with Moscow.

If further fragmentation develops within East or West, or both, the 1970s could produce any number of possible power alignments. The worst case would consist of a badly disunified and quarreling West beset by a strong Sino-Soviet alliance—which could well be revived by such a tempting prospect of free world disorder. The best of all possible worlds, by contrast, would be the reverse situation of Western unity and cohesion facing a faction-ridden Communist camp.

One of the more bizarre configurations could find the "have" nations of the developed northern hemisphere, including Russia and Japan, on the defensive against the "have nots" of the southern hemisphere, led by Communist China and perhaps including India, Indonesia, and even Latin America and Africa. In such an unpleasant world the technological and economic superiority of the north would be pitted against the impoverished two-thirds of the world's exploding population.

Still another possibility would be a "spheres of influence" contest, with Europe perhaps reasserting its former role in Africa, Russia in the Middle East, the United States in Latin America and the Pacific, and China in Southeast Asia, and with Japan and India standing uneasily on the sidelines. Or, failing even a tacit recognition of primary areas of interest, world power politics might become a general melee in which Russia, China, the United States and the several nations of Europe all competed for influence in Africa, Latin America and the Middle East, while Japan, India, and Indonesia struggled with each other and with Communist China for predominance in Asia.

These possibilities may seem farfetched indeed—and in some respects they reflect more a backward glance than a future forecast. But if the world cannot learn from the past, we may, as the aphorism goes, be condemned to repeat it.

Whatever the shape of the future, two things are sure: man can still exercise considerable influence upon it; but the world's inherent characteristics are turbulence and instability. The number of sovereign political entities has doubled since the interwar period and will total well over 120 by 1970. Relatively few of them have either the traditions or the institutions for the peaceful transmission of power. Simply as a matter of statistics, there will be numerous coups d'état, assassinations, plots, insurrections, feuds and crises—all with potential international implications.

The year 1964 opened with a month in which the United States and Panama were enmeshed in a major dispute over the canal; Cuba was threatening the naval base at Guantanamo; still another coup jeopardized the counterinsurgency effort in Viet-Nam; the Communists stepped up activities in Laos; Cambodia threatened to seek Chinese bases; Indonesia continued guerrilla operations against Malaysia; France broke relations with the Republic of China and began dealings with Communist China; India and Pakistan pursued their endemic rivalry; the Arab League threatened war against Israel over the diversion of the Jordan River; Greece and Turkey neared the brink of open conflict over Cyprus—where Russia threatened to intervene; an American jet was brutally shot down while off course over East Germany; and, in Africa, Somali and Ethiopian troops fought over border issues while tribal massacres swept several central areas, Zanzibar fell to Communist-oriented rebels, and native troops revolted in Kenya.

That was one month that was—and there are many others to come. If Russia and China are rivals within the Communist bloc, both still propound a doctrine of revolutionary struggles and try to pour oil on as many fires elsewhere as they can. The day may come when Russia will in fact cooperate responsibly in building international stability. But the day has not yet arrived; nor does it seem close at hand. China may need another generation, or two, to reach even the level of sobriety attained by Communist Russia. And it is always possible that the two powers will resume cooperation for the common ends of world communism.

Japan, constrained by the legacy of World War II and neutralist in orientation, is only now beginning to face up to the need for taking greater international responsibility. India is too beset by internal problems and instabilities to contribute much beyond the moralistic nonalignment that was Nehru's trademark and may or may not survive him. And, as we have seen, there are no other major contenders. Thus by default the burden of leadership, example, economic and technical assistance and, where necessary, the military power to keep the peace—through the U.N. or otherwise—must be borne by the other two non-Communist power centers, America and Europe.

If they drift apart and become competitors, they may partially offset each other and accelerate rather than help control the world's inherent instabilities. But if Europe moves toward internal unity and an effective partnership with North America, and if the two areas work in harness rather than at cross-purposes, there will be an enormous potential for advancing world peace and progress. Neither America nor Europe, even should it become united, can alone meet the challenges and uncertainties of the world in the 1970s. Separately there is much which they cannot even hope to accomplish. But together there is little they cannot do if the will is present. The cement of fear can and must be replaced by the bonds of hope.

In summary, then, the task of America and Europe appears to be twofold: first, to preserve their common military security thoughout the Atlantic area; and second, to develop the political and economic cohesion to contain the Communuist challenge elsewhere while building a stable and progressive world order for the future. Success in both tasks will depend critically upon the extent of Europe's internal unity on the one hand and its partnership with America on the other, and to these companion themes we now turn.

2

European Unity and Atlantic Partnership

The remedy . . . is to recreate the European family, or as much of it as we can, and to provide it with a structure under which it can dwell in peace, in safety and in freedom. We must build a kind of United States of Europe.

WINSTON CHURCHILL at Zurich in 1946

It is currently fashionable to mark General de Gaulle's famous press conference of January 14, 1963, as a symbolic setback to Europe's halting struggle toward unity. But this event was neither the beginning nor the end of that evolutionary process. To understand the present, and thus make even tentative judgments about the future, it is essential to comprehend the past. However far back history can be traced, for our purposes here, it suffices to pick up the thread at the end of World War II.

Sir Winston Churchill's Zurich proposal for European unity was several years ahead of his contemporaries. According to *The New York Times*,[1] Paris was shocked and London was cool. Even as a private citizen, Churchill was not ahead of his own vision as Prime Minister. Six years before, during the darkest hours of the war, he had proposed an immediate and full union of the French and British peoples. Interestingly enough, he reportedly had the text of this offer drafted by the Frenchman Jean Monnet who was later to be acclaimed as a champion of European unification.

[1] *The New York Times*, September 20, 1946.

Almost two decades later, there is confusion as to whether a "United States of Europe" still may lie just around the next corner or whether it remains a totally visionary concept. In 1962 top officials of the Kennedy administration spoke of "a partnership between the United States on the one hand and a great European power on the other."[2] Journalists have filled columns with interpretations of the challenges and opportunities which a united Europe would pose for the United States and the free world. As subsequent events showed, such anticipation underestimated the realities of time and political geography. At least one U.S. legislator argued even during the halcyon days of 1962 that emphasis on the European Common Market was "the wrong group, pursuing the wrong goal, at the wrong time."[3]

On the other hand, there are unifying dynamics at work on the continent. If one travels about Europe to discuss its future with knowledgeable citizens and government leaders, one finds of course that "homo Europiensis" has not yet evolved. Britons, Germans, Italians, Belgians, Dutchmen, and even the French not greatly changed in their customary attitudes, are going about their national endeavors almost as usual. But the "almost" is important: for while any imminent unity in Europe was shown to be a myth by the ease with which General de Gaulle blocked British membership in the Common Market, there are signs of continuing vitality in the concept.

For one thing, there is a striking similarity of ideas expressed in the several capitals. The very words, *mutatis mutandis*, are often the same, in Bonn and in Rome, in Paris and in Brussels—to the point that they seem unconsciously cut from a common pattern. The theme is simple, and it echoes "historical inevitability." Europe, so runs this theme, will unite because it must. A chemical

[2] McGeorge Bundy, Special Assistant to the President for National Security Affairs, in an address to the Economic Club of Chicago, December 6, 1961.

[3] Remarks of Representative Henry Reuss (D., Wisc.), *Congressional Record*, May 17, 1962. He argued instead that a wider free world economic community was needed.

reaction has been started which must culminate in a true European Community. The several economies, in a seamless web, will inevitably demand a supranational center of political decision. Walter Hallstein, the President of the Commission of the European Economic Community, has phrased it this way: "Economic integration is a political process and therefore changes the social condition of man . . . integration has set in motion a process which can have only one direction—forward."[4]

Europe's commitment to the concept of community is not always apparent from across the Atlantic; but it is there nonetheless, even though its ultimate form—confederation, federal union, or alliance of fatherlands—and its timing are far from clear. It may be well to recall that various forms of "unity" have been experienced by portions of Europe long before the twentieth century. Two thousand years ago, the writ of Rome ran throughout most of the territory now covered by the Common Market—and beyond from Scotland to Armenia. Europe's common heritage from Rome is well known. Sometimes overlooked, however, is the Frankish Empire of Charlemagne, which by about A.D. 800 included France, Germany, Italy, and the Low Countries. Barbarossa's Holy Roman Empire some 400 years later was primarily Germanic in scope, although its outposts included key areas of Burgundy and Belgium-Netherlands. Subsequent efforts by France under Napoleon in the nineteenth century to unify—or rather, dominate Europe by force—were in the long run unsuccessful, as was Hitler's Third Reich in the twentieth. Certainly the Nazi legacy was far more divisive than cohesive.

Paris, Brussels and Strasbourg

The origins of the present movement are to be found in the aftermath of World War II, with the idealistic recognition that, as Churchill phrased it, Europe "cannot afford to drag forward . . . the hatreds and revenges which have sprung from the injuries of

[4] European Economic Community, *Economic Integration as a Factor of Political Unification,* June 28, 1961, No. 8026/5/VII/1961/5.

the past." In place of the nation-state system which had caused two world wars in a generation, many of the shaken survivors sought in the concept of European federation a better vehicle for their hopes, and a chance to regain collectively in world influence what the war had lost them as nations. This feeling reinforced the unification concepts which had been advanced by a few European intellectuals before the war.

Further impetus developed when the economic consequences of the war caught up with Europe during the winter of 1946-47. Frantic and piecemeal efforts to cope with fiscal, agricultural, production and commercial crises proved inadequate. By early 1947 it was becoming evident that the visions of world peace through big power cooperation in the postwar United Nations were pipe dreams.

The Marshall Plan

The result was the Marshall Plan, conceived in the spring of 1947 and launched publicly by Secretary Marshall's commencement address at Harvard. One of its key features was the insistence that the recovery program must be a joint one. European nations would agree among themselves on their over-all needs, decide what portion could be met from their own combined resources, and determine the allocation of the American assistance designed to fill in the gap. It was no accident that the legislation which gave effect to the Marshall Plan—after a year of the most intensive examination by legislative and executive branch committees and citizens groups —was called the Economic Cooperation Act of 1948.

One of the motivating desires in the U.S. approach was to get Europe on its own feet as rapidly as possible, and to relieve the American taxpayer of a continuing burden. The Marshall Plan itself was visualized by its authors as a temporary shot in the arm, to last at most three or four years. A united Europe, it was believed, would make more rapid progress toward economic recovery than a fragmented group of economies shackled by tariffs, export and import quotas, and monetary restrictions. The

Europeans responded almost immediately by establishing a Committee of European Economic Cooperation to work with the United States in establishing the European Recovery Program, which was followed a year later by permanent machinery in the form of the Organization for European Economic Cooperation (OEEC). The accomplishments of these groups in establishing the working principles and tools of economic interdependence have properly been acclaimed as one of history's major examples of international cooperation. But a combination of Britain's traditional reluctance toward continental commitments and the generally sluggish state of the war-weakened economies led to a deliberate dragging of feet as far as economic integration was concerned. American efforts persisted, however, and included less than subtle threats to terminate U.S. assistance. By 1949-50 the European Payments Union was operating under the OEEC to liberalize payments, and a parallel reduction in trade restrictions was under way.

In retrospect it would appear that OEEC deserves a generous share of the credit for breaking down the traditional barriers of economic nationalism and facilitating Europe's startling postwar recovery. The Marshall Plan requirement of "cooperation" led to OEEC's role in the division of U.S. aid and hence to a most searching examination of the economies and policies of the participants by an international body—something which would have been inconceivable in Europe before the war.

Defense

Meanwhile, the cold war had rapidly progressed to the point that the West was increasingly concerned about the dangers of overt Soviet aggression. This threat was always available to back up the subversive efforts of the Communist parties in Western Europe, which were then in control of roughly a third or more of the electorates in France and Italy. In Greece and Turkey special assistance had preceded the Marshall Plan by several months. The Truman Doctrine explicitly involved the United States for the first time in countermeasures against Communist pressures in Europe.

Talk about a Western defensive alliance had begun as early as 1946 among British and Canadian leaders. In March 1947, as disillusionment grew with the United Nations' inability to provide international security, Britain and France signed at Dunkirk a treaty of alliance and mutual assistance directed against any revival of German aggression. The Rio Treaty, though limited to the Western Hemisphere, gave further momentum to the concept of regional defensive treaties sanctioned by the U.N. Charter when the treaty was signed in September of that year.

The Czechoslovakian coup in February 1948 helped to crystallize the idea of European unity by dramatizing the need for collective security measures. A few weeks before, British Foreign Secretary Ernest Bevin had proposed a form of European union, to be backed by American power. It now found a ready response from France, Belgium, the Netherlands and Luxembourg—the latter three having already planted a small acorn of economic integration by constituting themselves as the "Benelux" customs union in the previous fall. Accordingly, representatives of Britain, France, and Benelux met on March 4, 1948; and in less than two weeks they drew up and signed the Brussels Treaty, "to strengthen . . . the economic, social, and cultural ties by which they are already united . . . coordinate their efforts to create in Western Europe a firm basis for European economic recovery . . . afford assistance to each other . . . in maintaining international peace and security and in resisting any policy of aggression."

The operative section from a defense standpoint was Article IV, which provided that if any of the parties "should be the object of an armed attack in Europe" the others "will, in accordance with the provisions of Article 51 of the Charter of the United Nations, afford the party so attacked all the military and other aid and assistance in their power."

This major stepping stone toward European unity—and toward NATO, for the Brussels partners recognized the need for American military support—was almost immediately followed by the imposition of the blockade on Berlin. The Consultative Council (the only organ established in the Brussels Treaty) accordingly set up a Western Union defense organization with international commanders for land, air, and naval forces and with a headquarters under Britain's Field Marshall Montgomery at Fontainebleau outside Paris.

This evidence of European action to achieve greater unity, plus the growing awareness of the Soviet threat and of the relationship between European and American security, led to a trans-Atlantic dialogue during the spring of 1948 which culminated in the Vandenberg Resolution. This remarkable document, containing only 274 words, managed to devote 24 of them to repeated references to the United Nations or its charter. The significance of the resolution, however, was in the emphasis on *other* means of promoting U.S. security, specifically, "regional and other collective arrangements."

The "sense of the Senate" that the United States should exercise its right of self-defense in association with such arrangements brought an end to 160 years of a declared national policy of isolation. Pursuant to this evolution in American thinking, the United States and Canada agreed to a common defensive pact with the Brussels powers. Following a decision to invite Denmark, Iceland, Italy, Norway, and Portugal to accede, this concept quickly became the North Atlantic Treaty, signed in Washington on April 4, 1949. Greece and Turkey subsequently joined in 1952, and the Federal Republic of Germany in 1955.

Just as Marshall Plan economic aid had galvanized the OEEC, the military assistance provided by the United States under the Mutual Security Program began to give reality to the Atlantic defense organization. At first, NATO overlapped with the Western European Union (WEU) defense organization which had grown out of the Brussels Treaty. But by 1951, under the impetus of the Korean War, as NATO scrambled desperately to improve its defenses, WEU dismantled its nascent defense activities and turned them over to NATO.

The WEU Council of Ministers has continued to hold periodic discussions, and its assembly still meets. But the momentum of European unity passed into other channels, and WEU remained largely dormant until it was revived in connection with German rearmament.

The Community Idea

Meanwhile another European organization had emerged on the political side which was to have a secondary but useful role in the movement toward European unity. The International Committee of the Movements for European Unity (which, as this title suggests, had mushroomed after the war) convened a "Congress of Europe" in The Hague in May 1948. Out of this Congress there eventually grew the Council of Europe—a term first proposed by Winston Churchill two years before. Its statute, signed in London a year later, was intentionally vague, referring to greater unity among its members "for the purpose of safeguarding and realizing the ideals and principles which are their common heritage and facilitating their economic and social progress." This formulation reflected the predominance of OEEC and NATO on economic and military affairs as well as Britain's self-imposed inability to tie its interests too closely to the Continent—a disinclination which was strongly reinforced by Commonwealth links.

Nevertheless, the Council's Consultative Assembly gradually assumed the title, though not the powers, of a European Parliament. Its members are selected by the various national parliaments, but in Strasbourg they sit not as national delegations but individually as elected political leaders and collectively as "Europeans."

A number of conventions have been established under Council auspices, dealing with human rights, cultural exchanges, social security, and the like. Noteworthy is the acceptance by the member governments (all of Western Europe, except Spain, Portugal, and Switzerland) of any individual's right to complain against them for violation of the Human Rights Convention. The Council has thus done quiet and useful work through its many functional committees and the several conventions which have been adopted in preparing the way for the widespread acceptance of an international, i.e., a "European" consensus in national parliaments.

During the Council's emotional debates in May 1962, the Irish Minister of Foreign Affairs noted the organization's thirteenth anniversary, and after citing its many accomplishments, observed that Rome was not built in a day and the evolution of Switzerland was the fruit of several centuries of negotiation and conciliation. The Council of Europe, he stated, could rightfully claim credit for its part in the spectacular development of opinion in favor of European unity. Paul Henri Spaak also gave a major policy address on the problems of Britain and the neutrals in connection with the Common Market. By thus supporting the Council's role as a sounding board for the broadest kind of problems, he hoped to dispel the feeling that "l'Assemblée était quelquefois un peu découragée, qu'elle doutait de son utilité"[5] Nevertheless, this suggestive reference tends to confirm the dry notation of one author that "the Council's activities have not electrified Europe."[6] But all in all, the Council has kept alive and added to the momentum of "community" in Europe. It has bridged the gaps between such functional organs as OEEC, and regional groupings like Scandinavia's Northern Council, and Benelux (or its abortive extension, "Fritalux"). It has, in short, provided much of the social and political infrastructure, if such a term may be used, for Europe's evolution.

The Schuman and Pleven Plans

Against this background of an international but not supranational OEEC, Western European Union, and Council of Europe, the first major step toward true economic integration came with the Schuman Plan in May 1950. For its time this was a truly revolutionary proposal—so much so, in fact, that the sincerity of its proposers

[5] Council of Europe, Consultative Assembly, Fourteenth Ordinary Session, First Part, Second Sitting, May 15, 1962, Document A 71.072.

[6] Ben T. Moore, *NATO and the Future of Europe* (New York: Harper & Row, for the Council on Foreign Relations, 1958), p. 139.

was initially subjected to considerable skepticism. Foreign Minister Robert Schuman proposed in the name of the French government to place Franco-German production of coal and steel under a common high authority, within the framework of an organization open to the participation of the other countries of Europe.[7] Not only did the plan deal with the very lifeblood of an industrial economy, but it envisaged a Franco-German partnership hardly a decade after France was last invaded by Germany. Furthermore, the implication of supranational authority was contained in a reference to decisions being binding on members. The possibility of accessions to the organization further suggested a nucleus for Europe. Schuman's statement thus contained two of the dominant themes of European unification: first, to make any war between France and Germany "not merely unthinkable but materially impossible"; and second, to provide "the first step in the federation of Europe." As William Diebold has described it, "this was a drastic change in the direction of French policy. . . . Yet there was a clear basic logic. France could not prevent the growth of German strength; to try to delay that growth would weaken France's position; the possibility that remained was to find a new framework. . . ."[8]

Instrumental in the formulation of the Schuman Plan was the extraordinary Frenchman, Jean Monnet (later to become the President of the Coal and Steel Community's High Authority), who has guided, cajoled, negotiated, and directed the unification movement, sometimes as a leading actor, sometimes from the wings or the orchestra pit, and sometimes from the audience. Monnet's "theory of change" has been explained in terms of a man climbing a mountain on a path with an infinite number of views from an infinite number of points. The man at the bottom lacks the view

[7] The background and evolution of the European Coal and Steel Community are described at length in William Diebold's authoritative work *The Schuman Plan* (New York: Praeger, for the Council on Foreign Relations, 1959). See also European Community Information Service, *Political Unity in Europe, a Selection of Key Documents* (Brussels: Author, 1961), p. 5.

[8] Diebold, cited, p. 11.

not only of a man at the top, but of someone part way up. "To change his view, you must get him to start moving up, however slowly. As soon as he has moved, he will have a different view, perhaps a better one, and the improvement will induce him to take another step."[9]

This pragmatic determination to get moving, even without a clearly defined ultimate goal, has been the key to the subsequent success of the Schuman Plan. Behind the scenes preparatory work, conducted against the background already discussed, enabled the plan to find acceptance in principle with the German, Italian, and Benelux governments, notwithstanding its controversial nature. Less than a month after the publication of the Schuman proposal, the six countries issued a communiqué reflecting their intention to pool coal and steel resources and to begin detailed negotiations.

Reaction in Britain foreshadowed, almost to the very words, the arguments that were to rage there a decade later over joining the Common Market. Parliamentary debates focused on the supranational High Authority, with its clear overtones of delegating a degree of political sovereignty. The Labor government argued that " . . . a political federation, limited to Western Europe, is not compatible either with our Commonwealth ties, our obligations as a member of the wider Atlantic community, or as a world power."[10] The Conservative opposition, led by Anthony Eden, pointed out the risks of being left outside, including the possibility of German domination of a Franco-German partnership in which Britain would have the mere "status of observer." The Tories, however, officially concurred that foreign control of British coal and steel was unacceptable.

In any event, Britain declined to join the Coal and Steel Community, but for some ten years maintained a peculiar form of association with it which involved consultation and representation, but not participation. Only in 1962 did Britain formally seek mem-

[9] John Brooks, "The Common Market," *The New Yorker,* September 22 and September 29, 1962.

[10] House of Commons, *Parliamentary Debates,* Weekly Hansard, No. 159, June 26, 1950.

bership, as part of the process of joining the larger European Economic Community.

The exciting prospects of these European developments received both a shock and a stimulus from the Korean War. The North Korean attack across the 38th parallel on June 25, 1950, was the first overt military aggression by a Communist state. Intelligence reports in the ensuing months showed that it represented careful planning and a deliberate policy choice which had been approved, if not dictated, in the Kremlin. This opened up the ominous possibility of other attacks, perhaps even in Europe. The West reacted by resisting the North Korean aggression with American forces, acting under U.N. auspices, and by a major program of rearmament. American defense appropriations, which had reached a postwar low of about $13 billion for fiscal 1950, jumped to $48 billion in the following year, while the manpower on active duty more than doubled in the same period, from 1.4 to 3.2 million men.[11] Deliveries to Europe under the Mutual Defense Assistance Program were expedited, and NATO hastened its organizational and planning efforts. During the summer and fall of 1950, the NATO Council adopted a forward strategy and, recognizing the inadequacy of available means in relation to requirements, began to consider the possibility of a German contribution. To make this event as palatable as possible, the United States proposed an integrated force under centralized command, and offered to provide an American commander plus additional U.S. ground forces.

Meanwhile, the negotiations for the Coal and Steel Community proceeded slowly. Not only did the numerous vested interests begin to harden in opposition to the feared impact of the Community, but a bombshell was dropped when Secretary Acheson's proposal to create a German army of ten divisions leaked to the press just prior to the meeting of British, French, and American foreign ministers in September 1950. The French had hoped that the Coal

[11] See the Semiannual Report of the Secretary of Defense, January 1 to January 30, 1951 (Washington: GPO, 1951).

and Steel Community could pave the way for Franco-German co-operation on a wider scale before the emotionally charged problem of German rearmament had to be faced publicly. But events forced the pace to quicken too rapidly. Accordingly, as with the Schuman Plan, the French courageously faced the facts and sought a new framework along quite parallel lines. This was the Pleven Plan proposed by the French Prime Minister to the National Assembly in October 1950. It envisaged a European army which would include German units, but sufficiently integrated so that they could never operate as a national military force.

The winter of 1950-51 was a hectic one. The Inchon landings and subsequent U.N. advance into North Korea had been set back by massive Chinese intervention. The President of the United States was under severe congressional attack from conservative critics, especially for his proposal to assign additional ground troops to Europe. This so-called "Great Debate" had hardly ended (with a compromise which was in essence a victory for the administration),[12] when the recall of General MacArthur precipitated a second major domestic crisis. The sensational crime disclosures of one Senate Committee kept millions television bound, while others were mesmerized by the rapid rise of Senator McCarthy and the "ism" that soon bore his name. In Europe, the chronic political crises in France had brought down the Pleven government, and "instability" was the word of the day.

As NATO hastened to mend its meager defenses, General Eisenhower took over as Supreme Allied Commander, Europe (SACEUR) and soon afterwards activated the alliance's international headquarters (SHAPE). In February 1951 the French called a conference to consider the European army proposal, which rapidly took shape under the label of the European Defense

[12] The U.S. commitment to Europe's defense was recognized and the dispatch of additional forces approved. But the President promised that future deployments would be submitted for legislative approval. See S. Res. 99 and S. Con. Res. 18, 82nd Cong., 1st sess., and "Assignment of Ground Forces to Duty in the European Area," Hearings before the Senate Foreign Relations and Armed Services Committees, 82nd Cong., 1st sess., 1951.

Community (EDC). By April, the treaty establishing the European Coal and Steel Community was signed after long and tortuous negotiations; and the process of parliamentary ratification began.

It is difficult to trace the interaction of these and other events in this brief summary. But the cumulative momentum of the Schuman and Pleven Plans and the Coal and Steel and the Defense communities which they engendered appreciably quickened the pace. The United States backed the European army concept as early as August 1, 1951, when General Eisenhower supported the proposal in a major speech to the English-Speaking Union in London. While some French elements dragged their feet, or sought to spin out negotiations as a delaying tactic, there was a surprising overall acceptance of supranationalizing even defense—the very essence of sovereignty.

In recognition of the fact that military affairs of the economic heartland of Europe could hardly be managed in a political vacuum, consideration was given to a European Political Community, and parliamentarians from the Six began discussions looking to a draft treaty. In February 1952 the French Assembly approved the Defense Community idea in principle. A few days later the Pleven Plan was further endorsed by the North Atlantic Council, and supporting protocols were worked out at the Lisbon meeting, where a force goal of fifty divisions was set for NATO. The actual treaty establishing EDC was approved by the participating governments in May, with ratification expected to follow in due course.

The blueprint for European unity which had emerged during 1952-53 therefore revolved around three interlocking communities, each composed of France, Italy, West Germany, and Benelux. This was "little Europe"—the hard core of the Continent, since Britain had made abundantly clear that it could not integrate with the movement. Britain, however, was tied to France by the Dunkirk Treaty, to the Six (less Italy and Germany) through the Brussels Pact, and to Europe as a whole through the OEEC and the

Council of Europe. Britain and the United States were both intimately involved in European defense through NATO.

Parliamentary approval of the European Coal and Steel Community (ECSC) had been proceeding at a fairly rapid rate, and Italy completed the process when its lower house voted affirmatively by a large margin on June 17th, 1952. The Community became operative in July 1952, set up its institutions in Luxembourg during the ensuing months, and by February 1953 had taken the first administrative actions to establish a common market in coal and steel. The top administrative body was the High Authority with Jean Monnet serving as President. It was composed of members from the participating nations who had a supranational responsibility. The legislative branch consisted of a Common Assembly, drawn from and chosen by the parliaments of the Six, which could compel the High Authority to resign on a vote of censure. A seven-judge Court of Justice was granted the sole judicial power, including the constitutional role of upholding or quashing decisions of the High Authority. But perhaps the most significant feature was the Council of Ministers, who were national representatives (usually the foreign ministers) and whose task was to conciliate the inevitable clashes between the national interests of the members and the interests of the Community as a whole as represented through its institutions, notably the High Authority. A rough analogy might be imagined had the U.S. Constitution provided for an interim stage in which the balance between powers delegated and powers reserved would be worked out by a conference of the governors.

The Defense Community likewise was to have an executive, styled a "Commissariat," and a Council of Ministers as a balance wheel. The Political Community envisaged a directly elected European legislature which would, in time, supplant the ECSC assembly and exercise control over both the military and economic executives, while expanding the latter's area into a true Common Market for all products. The pattern of functional federalism had thus reached its peak.

Agony and Reappraisal

Then, in effect, the roof appeared to sag, if not to cave in. In retrospect it is clear that too much was attempted too soon. The near-miraculous acceptance of federal institutions among the Six had disguised the friction which the pace of developments had produced. Invisibly, like static electricity, French resistance was stored up, until finally it was discharged in several lightning-like bursts. First, major modifications were demanded by France in both the Political and Defense Community treaties. Britain, unwilling to join, was asked for and gave certain assurances designed to assuage French fears about being left "alone on the continent with a resurgent Germany." But the fears and emotions revolving around Germany nevertheless gathered strength despite, or perhaps because of, American pressures, which were strongly applied. The intimation was that if an agonizing reappraisal was necessary, the United States might withdraw its newly made commitments to Europe.

The tensions of the cold war also had eased. The Korean truce had been in effect for over a year. Stalin had died, and Soviet policy appeared to be taking a more moderate line on some matters, although the Soviet Union's nuclear tests and the French losses in Indo-China showed that communism remained a major threat. The latter experience, however, served as an irritant to French pride and made doubly distasteful the prospective merger of armed forces into a European army. The net effect was that on August 30, 1954, the French Assembly declined to ratify the European Defense Community by a majority of fifty-five votes. This also meant the official death of the Political Community proposal, which had, in any case, been virtually shelved some months earlier as opposition to it grew.

Looking backward, it is surprising not that these ambitious ventures failed in 1953-54, but that they came so near to success. Almost a decade later, De Gaulle and Adenauer still found it necessary to exchange symbolic pilgrimages to bury formally the enmity between their countries. The French syndrome has been accurately described in the context of a dilemma of the pro-Europeans. "In their effort to bind Germany tightly to Europe and prevent the rise of German nationalism they had proposed a degree of integration that was unacceptable to their own nationalists."[13]

The demise of the EDC-EPC complex left unsolved the problem of Germany's rearmament and future ties, for, in anticipation of the EDC, almost complete sovereignty had been returned to Bonn and the occupation statute was replaced by contractual agreements in May 1952. Furthermore, at the time, the French vote appeared to be a serious setback for European unity. In retrospect, however, it was not that much of a disaster. The Coal and Steel Community continued to operate effectively and quietly, taking good care not to add to the atmosphere of crisis. The build-up of NATO continued. Its institutions were strengthened while its membership expanded with the accession of Greece and Turkey. The general health of the European economies was improving rapidly, and the OEEC functioned smoothly. If its trade liberalization program did not come up to expectations, less spectacular but equally important gains were made by two OEEC subsidiaries (the European Payments Union and the European Productivity Agency) in the monetary and financial field and in improving the productivity of European industry. The two other significant bodies, Western European Union and the Council of Europe, likewise remained as going entities—although the direction was sometimes obscure. The task faced by Europe and the United States after the EDC collapse was to rebuild a structure out of the available timbers which could accommodate the central problem of Germany.

Operation Salvage

Fortunately, Western statesmanship proved equal to the salvage task. In rapid succession there were conferences in London and Paris, followed by a special Ministerial Meeting of the North Atlantic Council. The end result, known as the "Paris Agree-

[13] Moore, cited, pp. 52-53.

ments," was an interlocking series of accords, declarations, protocols, amendments, and exchanges of letters which is a monument to the legal and political professions.

In brief, France and Germany resolved a number of disputes bilaterally (e.g., on the Saar). The 1952 conventions between the occupying powers and Germany were further amended to provide for a German defense contribution and to restore complete sovereignty to the Federal Republic. The occupation powers made a tripartite declaration regarding maximum self-government in Berlin consistent with its special status. The dormant Brussels Treaty was revived, and its five original members invited Germany and Italy to accede. The resulting seven powers then revised the treaty to make it into an instrumentality for controlling German rearmament, although limits were also placed on the forces of other powers. (Their agreed peacetime forces, as contemplated by the EDC treaty, were incorporated by reference.) Britain undertook to maintain the equivalent of four divisions and a tactical air force on the Continent. The treaty "notes" in great detail the unilateral declarations by Germany not to manufacture atomic, biological, and chemical weapons and to accept limitations on other forms of armament. Finally, all of the foregoing agreements were in effect blessed formally by the fourteen members of NATO, to which organization Germany then acceded.[14]

In a 1962 debate in the House of Lords, the Earl of Avon, Anthony Eden, suggested a parallel between France's "parliamentary travail" over the EDC in 1954 and that of Britain over the EEC. In retrospect, he concluded that everything then had worked out for the best. "What we did was to say . . . if we cannot get agreement on a small European Army, the problem behind it is German rearmament. Let us have German rearmament where it is safest, not in a European Army but in NATO. . . . It was a fortunate solution and one extremely advantageous for the future of

[14] The documents are printed in the Appendices to *NATO—Facts About the North Atlantic Treaty Organization* (Paris: NATO Information Service, 1962).

the world."[15] Thus Germany's place as an equal member of the Western alliance was at least temporarily settled—although, as we shall see, the "German problem" remains at the root of Europe's difficulties a decade later.

Messina and Rome

The Coal and Steel Community (ECSC) proved itself as an experiment beyond even the hopes of its founders. Despite a mild recession in 1953-54, steel output rose from 42 million metric tons before the Common Market to 53 million tons by 1955. Coal production likewise climbed during the years of heavy demand. The dire predictions of disaster for the high-cost producers were not borne out; and those who feared such a large dose of supranationalism were surprised at how painless it had been. In the analogy of Jean Monnet, Europe had climbed a few steps up the mountain—and the view was different! The setback which the more ambitious EDC-EPC blueprint had received led to a retracing of steps back to the ECSC pilot plant.

The foreign ministers of the Six met at Messina, Italy, in June 1955 to concentrate once more on economic matters. A committee of experts was named under the chairmanship of Belgium's Paul Henri Spaak—another of the great European leaders—to draw up recommendations for extending the Common Market principle. So strong had the sentiments for further progress become that the Spaak Committee report of a year later was adopted almost verbatim as the starting point for detailed drafting of a treaty. In this consensus, too, Jean Monnet played a role, resigning from the ECSC High Authority to head an Action Committee for a United States of Europe, which acted as a high-powered "European" lobby. The technicians and experts then settled down to a long ten months of negotiations in Brussels, which led to the Treaty Establishing the European Economic Community. Signed in the Italian capital—hence its better known name, the Treaty of Rome

[15] House of Commons, *Parliamentary Debates*, Weekly Hansard, No. 568, August 2, 1962.

—on March 25, 1957, the documents created the European Atomic Energy Community (Euratom) and the European Economic Community or EEC, better known as the Common Market. Ratification followed swiftly and the new communities went into effect in 1958.

Although the treaty with its protocols and appendices is an enormous and complex volume of documentation, the essence is simple. The Six agreed to set up a single large market by eliminating internal trade barriers over a specified period. But going beyond a mere free trade area, EEC is designed to become a true customs union with a common external tariff. With an eye to ultimate economic union, the treaty also provided for rules of fair competition and common policies with respect to agriculture, transport, economic and fiscal policy, and labor and social policy. The machinery which had worked satisfactorily for Coal and Steel was duplicated for each of the two new Communities as well. Each had a Commission empowered to make binding supranational decisions and a Council of Ministers sitting as national representatives. A new "European" Parliament succeeded in 1958 to the functions of the ECSC Assembly. Now it serves as the legislative body for all three executives, as the Court of Justice does with respect to judicial functions. Eventually, the three executives (the Common Market and Euratom Commissions and the ECSC High Authority) will certainly merge too, although the subject is sensitive for bureaucratic and geographic reasons, since the two Commissions with their staffs are in Brussels, while the High Authority remains in Luxembourg, which is fighting any prospect of losing it. The matter remains under active discussion.

The over-all mechanism is a delicate and ingenious balance of interests. The Councils of Ministers review, and can disapprove, acts of the Executives, but the "federal" government has the initiative and serves as the guardian of the constitution's mandates. The secret of the initial success of the EEC has been a highly effective dialogue between the Commission and the Council. The initial requirement of Council unanimity was designed to yield progressively to majority rule on specific areas, as has already happened in the ECSC. The Parliament provides some democratic controls through its theoretical ability to vote no confidence in the Executives. The legislators are still members of their national parliaments, but plans for the more distant future have been drawn up pursuant to the Treaty whereby the Parliament could be elected directly by European voters. The decisions of the judiciary are binding, not only on the member states, but upon individuals and business entities and without entailing national action to give them effect. Enforcement is largely carried out by national authorities, with direct supervision in some cases from the Commission.

A guarantee of progress was in effect built into the Treaty, by virtue of its transition periods, of three stages of four years each in tariff cuts and quota eliminations. The Common Market is in one sense a product of an upswing in European prosperity that made the necessary changes politically palatable. But it is not really a chicken-or-egg question as to whether the prosperity was in turn produced by the lowered tariffs under the EEC, for the lead time was insufficient for modernization or elimination of inefficient producers to have had much effect. What did happen was an unexpected modification of business decisions in anticipation of the reductions, and this in turn accelerated the economic effects. There was also an inflow of capital from other countries, whose manufacturers wanted to get a foothold inside the market. The interaction of the business cycle and the Community's economic impact permitted the stages within the twelve-year adjustment period envisioned by the Rome Treaty to be accelerated so that by the end of 1962 Europe had reached the point in tariff reductions it had originally planned for 1965.

When the Community reached the end of Stage I on January 1, 1962, further progress became automatic. The Commission alone can delay the schedule, and then only with unanimous consent. This rule means that any member can veto delay, but cannot in theory impede progress.[16]

[16] EEC Information Memo of January 1962, "Into Stage Two," p. 7221. Other publications of the Community describe the working of its institu-

Despite the Community's economic and organizational momentum, the detailed implementation of plans depends upon a politically powerless group of international bureaucrats. However able and dedicated they may be, their organization will atrophy without the lifeblood of political support from the member countries. And the Treaty of Rome's only reference to political goals is to establish "the foundations of an even closer union among the European peoples—a somewhat lesser commitment even than the one made in Philadelphia 170 years previously. If the political promise is tacit rather than explicit, it is widely understood nonetheless. Walter Hallstein has made a point of saying in almost all of his many speeches about the Common Market: "We are not in business—we are in politics." De Gaulle, on the other hand, has made it clear that he also understands—and opposes—the development of political supranationalism via the economic route. This conflict in views has helped bring the Community to its present impasse, which developed initially over British membership.

Britain and the Six

Since 1957 a key issue of European unification has been the relationship of the Common Market to Europe outside the Six. The main problem has been Great Britain, which has maintained an ambivalent attitude, but with the over-all bias away from continental involvement. Britain declined full membership in the ECSC, vetoed any expansion in the supranational features of the Council of Europe or the OEEC, and stood aside from the proposed European Defense and Political Communities. On the other hand, Britain had "associated" itself from the beginning with the Coal and Steel Community, taken an active part in the Council of Europe and OEEC, and cooperated with the backers of the EDC, later applying its guarantees of a continued presence on the continent to the revised WEU and NATO arrangements. Although

---

tions and the timetable established by the treaty. See, e.g., "ECSC," "Euratom," "The European Parliament" and "The European Community" which are revised periodically.

British representatives met with the Six at Messina and kept in close touch with the Spaak Committee and the subsequent drafting of the Treaty of Rome, the traditional problems of Commonwealth ties and preferences (particularly in agricultural products), the age-old tradition of independence from the Continent, and the special relationship with America combined to keep Britain out.

The period 1957-58 was marked by serious negotiations between Britain and the Six. The widening gap between the growth rates of Britain and the Common Market in production and trade made it increasingly clear that the United Kingdom faced serious competition and was not in the best position to cope with it. Finally, following the breakdown of these discussions, conducted under OEEC auspices, Britain took the leadership in forming the European Free Trade Association (EFTA), which became known as the Outer Seven.[17] Norway, Denmark, Sweden, Austria, Switzerland, and Portugal were the other members. All of them for reasons of geography or tradition had remained outside the mainstream of the continental unification movement.

EFTA had a combined GNP of over $100 billion by 1960 (more than half from Britain), compared to the EEC total of about $165 billion, but its growth rates have been substantially less. The Community's average rate of growth in GNP (at constant prices) was 5 per cent from 1955 to 1960 compared with EFTA's 3 per cent. In per capita terms, the rates were 4 per cent and 2.4 per cent, respectively, which meant that EFTA was growing only 60 per cent as fast as the Community.[18] Furthermore, during the 1950s Britain's exports had increased by only 30 per cent, compared to a 115 per cent jump by the Six. In 1951 the British had more than one-fourth of the world's export trade in manufactured goods, a share which

[17] Useful data on the relationships between EFTA and the EEC are contained in Emile Benoit's *Europe at Sixes and Sevens* (New York: Columbia University Press, 1961). EFTA was created by the Stockholm convention of November 1959.

[18] Data are from Statistical Office of the European Communities, *Basic Statistics for Fifteen European Countries* (Brussels: Author, 1961), Table 14.

had dropped to about 16 per cent ten years later. These economic facts sharpened Britain's awareness that it needed the expanded markets of the Continent, and, perhaps even more, that its competitiveness must improve. Although EFTA has a tariff reduction program among members (and has brought them down by nearly 50 per cent), there was never an intention to develop the free trade area into a customs union with a common external tariff, nor any thought of political unification.

Paradoxically, British fears of merging its national traditions and sovereignty into a European federation were somewhat eased by De Gaulle's accession in France, which both improved French political stability and dampened the prospects for the extreme federalists on the Continent. His accession also permitted the implementation of those reforms in the French economy which were necessary before France could proceed with the timetable of the Rome Treaty.

The end result of a long and bitter period of internal doubts was Prime Minister Macmillan's historic statement of July 31, 1961. He told the Commons that "it is both our duty and our interest to contribute towards . . . strength by securing the closest possible unity within Europe." Macmillan also agreed that the issue was political as well as economic—an admission required by the fact that two weeks previously, the heads of state of the Six had pointedly announced their decision to "give shape to the will for political union already implicit in the treaties."[19] Britain thus had reached a turning point as a matter of national policy; and on August 9, 1961, it formally requested negotiations with the Six for admission to the Treaty of Rome pursuant to Article 237.

The hard bargaining that occupied the next year and a half concerned the Commonwealth relationship, the interests of Britain's EFTA partners (all of which subsequently either applied for EEC membership or sought some kind of associate status), and agriculture. The latter was especially difficult for Britain, not only be-

[19] Both statements are abstracted in the European Community Information Service Pamphlet, *Political Unity in Europe* (Brussels: Author, 1961).

cause of its specialization and heavy subsidy on farm products, but because of Britain's reliance on Commonwealth imports, many of which could not compete against a high EEC common tariff. The problem was also acute politically and emotionally, as well as economically, for many Commonwealth farmers are former servicemen from England set up in Australia and New Zealand under special programs. (In the latter country the Common Market's transitional period was sometimes referred to as a "transition to oblivion" as far as New Zealand was concerned.) Gradually, however, after months of negotiation, many of the apparent obstacles were solved in principle, if not in detail. The temporary break-off of negotiations in the early morning of August 5, 1962—almost exactly a year after Britain's first initiative—came over the financial regulations covering the thorniest issue of all: the proposed common agricultural policy. *The Economist* complained at the time, with considerable prescience, that ". . . the French have pursued a closely calculated policy of insisting on the last pound of flesh of national interest in every instance where they could hope to carry their partners with them, and always provided that their insistence could be presented as fidelity to the letter and principle of the Treaty of Rome."[20]

The French Veto

Nevertheless patience, exhaustive staff work, and man-killing schedules carried the resumed talks over (or around) one agenda hurdle after another during the fall of 1962. Cautious optimism began to spread on both sides of the Atlantic that an historic marriage of Britain with the Continent might soon be celebrated. As the remaining issues dwindled in number, the talks recessed for a much-needed breather.

Then, catching the entire world—including the principals themselves—quite by surprise, came the icy wind of De Gaulle's January 1963 press conference. Britain, said the General, was not yet ready

[20] *The Economist*, August 18, 1962, p. 594.

for entry, for it remained "insular, maritime, linked through its trade markets and food supply to very diverse and often very distant countries. . . . In short the nature, structure, and economic context of England differ profoundly from those of the other states of the continent."[21]

The meaning was clear; and it remained only for the formal *coup de grâce* to be delivered at the Brussels negotiations. Two weeks later the French foreign minister brought the talks to a close with the blunt proclamation that "L'Angleterre n'a pas la possibilité d'entrer." The companion issues—the membership status of the neutrals (especially Austria and Finland), the applications of other EFTA associates, and the Commonwealth arrangements—also lost their immediacy.

Much nonsense was written during 1962 about the supposed imminence of a United States of Europe—as though it was going to spring full grown from Macmillan's anticipated signature of accession to the Rome Treaty. At most, such an offspring might have subsequently been conceived as a result of the marriage. The then prevailing mood of great anticipation of an imminent flowering of the grand design reflects in part the news media's self-stimulating search for drama, and in part wishful thinking by politicians.

A similar self-hypnotism by government leaders and pundits alike has clouded the attempts to explain De Gaulle's action. Some attributed it to the Skybolt affair; some to the Nassau meeting and the U.S.-U.K. agreement on Polaris; some to Gallic impatience at the slow pace of the technocrats' negotiations at Brussels; others blamed the General's well-known resentment of "les anglo-saxons," or his desire for a "Gaullist" dominated Continent. The full truth will probably never be known, for even among the General's intimates there are few who pretend to understand him completely. But several key facts do stand out.

[21] The text released by the French press service in New York appeared in most U.S. papers the following day, January 15, 1963, and has been widely reprinted in various publications.

The negotiations were quite close to succeeding in a technical sense. That is, Britain's formal marriage to the Continent was approaching, even though this would have been merely the beginning of a long and difficult adjustment by all concerned.[22] It was no longer possible for France to fight the battle with the tactic that *The Economist* had called the "the last pound of flesh in the name of the Rome Treaty." It had become necessary to grasp the political nettle—and the carefully staged ceremonial press conference was an ideal vehicle for the DeGaulle style. It seems inescapable that De Gaulle simply did not want Britain to enter the Common Market—at least on the terms which had been so laboriously outlined. The "why" of his decision is less clear.

Certainly the Skybolt-Nassau-Polaris matter provided some ammunition for Gaullist complaints about Britain's special relationship with America (and perhaps even of the latter's potential unreliability as a source of weapons). But the political-military complex of problems which centered on Nassau has been played up out of all proportion to its true significance for Britain and the Common Market. An excuse it may have been, but not a reason, because the French course of nuclear independence had long since been charted.

Had De Gaulle felt that French interests required Britain to join the Common Market in 1963, any personal "anglo-saxon" syndrome would surely have been suppressed. Nor do some of the more charitable explanations which are sometimes advanced seem convincing. For example, it has been argued that De Gaulle was merely trying to ensure that the foundations of "Europe" would be solid by raising the hurdles to membership; thus, if Britain

[22] At the request of the European Parliament, the Common Market Commission prepared a report on the history of the EEC negotiations with Britain, which notes that solutions had been found or were in sight on most of the important issues, but that special difficulties remained in a few areas. Not surprisingly, the Gaullists abstained in the otherwise unanimous resolutions relating to this report. A summary of the report was released by the EEC on March 5, 1963, and is reprinted in *The Atlantic Community Quarterly*, Summer 1963, Vol. 1, No. 2, p. 282.

could nevertheless overcome them, the British people would be irrevocably committed to full participation. True, the famous press conference statement praised Britain's record and closed on the hopeful note of England's having taken "the *first* steps along the path that one day, perhaps, will bring it to make fast to the continent." But such Olympian vagueness is often just part of the Gaullist trappings which disguise an immediate tactical objective –in this case, to prevent the laying of the cornerstone of a type of Europe which De Gaulle did *not* want. It was not so much that Britain's entry would have complicated, and in some ways set back, the progress achieved by the EEC; for it remains doubtful how much store De Gaulle sets on that progress, except where basic French economic interests are directly involved. Rather it was that the whole character of the association of the Six would have been changed by Britain's overseas ties and the collateral applications from EFTA. And at the heart of the matter was the fact that the larger and possibly looser grouping would have diluted the *French* influence. The tightly knit Europe of fatherlands which De Gaulle envisages as being less dependent on the United States would have been passed by; and American influence on the Continent might even have increased.

But, it might be asked, if this is the case, why did De Gaulle wait so long? Why this particular timing since all of the foregoing implications of the Brussels negotiations were clear as much as a year before? Several answers suggest themselves.

First, it had become clear that the U.K.-EEC negotiations would not necessarily fall of their own weight; on the contrary, the "supranationalists in Europe" seemed to be gaining momentum as the talks progressed. Second, his cool appraisal of the European political situation may have convinced De Gaulle that the timing was right–that the opposition to his move would be unable to muster any decisive censure,[23] and perhaps also, the Nassau imbroglio seemed to offer a useful smoke screen. Third–and certainly

[23] An attempt to censure the break-off of negotiations in the European Parliament ended in an even vote: 38 for, 38 against. Same, p. 283.

most important—the Adenauer era was drawing to a close in Germany. The Paris-Bonn alignment was and is the centerpiece of De Gaulle's strategy in Europe, although the results to date must be somewhat disappointing to him. The bilateral consultation called for in the Franco-Germany treaty of cooperation is in some ways contrary in spirit to the Rome Treaty's emphasis upon the European community as a whole. The "Atlantic and European" caveats in the rider which the Bundestag attached during the ratification of the Franco-German treaty showed that all of "der Alte's" authority was needed to help De Gaulle put this keystone into place. Had the political transition in the Federal Republic taken place in an atmosphere of emerging British partnership with the Continent, the special German alignment with France might have been placed in serious doubt.

The foregoing paragraphs perhaps sketch a less than generous view of De Gaulle's underlying motives and tactics; but if the alliance is to cope with De Gaulle, it must match his own realism. At least, the General's actions and their success have stripped away a number of illusions about the readiness of Europe to unite. They have also revealed the basic incompatibility between the Gaullist grand design and that envisaged by the late President Kennedy.

The issue of what kind of Europe will—or should—emerge from the movement toward unity long antedates De Gaulle and may well survive him. He has rendered the service of highlighting the interdependence of that issue with the question of the "Atlantic" relationship between Europe and North America. In fairness, we cannot assign to France all responsibility for the setback to European unity. For had Britian not been a brooding and indecisive Hamlet on the stage of Europe for so long, De Gaulle might never have gotten to play the murderous role of Macbeth! And in this composite Shakespearean drama, there were many other European devotees of unity who, Romeo-like, allowed themselves to be frustrated by other peoples quarrels. Even the United States found itself playing an anxious King Lear, desperately seeking reassurance as to the loyalty of his European daughters before settling his dowry!

European and Atlantic Relationships

The theme of an earlier Council on Foreign Relations' study of these problems is that American policy has been inconsistent with respect to Europe: "We have steadfastly sought to further a European union for economic but not for defense purposes. To bolster the security of Western Europe we have fostered not European Union but the Atlantic Alliance."[24]

This criticism suggests that the economic, military, and political aspects of the Atlantic relationship ought to be symmetrical. But symmetry was not possible. In the case of defense, Europe's weakness required intimate American military involvement with Europe on a multilateral basis, as well as military assistance, while a comparable economic relationship was not necessary (or for that matter possible) for Europe's recovery. European economic unity began by making a virtue of necessity, imposed by the Marshall Plan insistence on cooperation. It continued during a decade of growth and prosperity by making a virtue of good fortune. European defense on the other hand lacked the essential element of intra-European confidence. Public opinion surveys have suggested that Europeans consider the United States a far more reliable ally in case of Soviet aggression than any other member of NATO.[25]

A decade ago, only a U.S. military guarantee to, and active participation with, the European nations individually and collectively could have provided the security which permitted Europe's recovery. A bilateral pact with, and assistance to, an embryonic European organization such as Western European Union—or even EDC—would hardly have been effective. The essence of security is confidence, and it is hard to place confidence in an untried entity. NATO's progress since its inception has been extraordinary in many ways. Whether it can evolve sufficiently to meet the new problems of the mid-1960s is the major question addressed

[24] Moore, cited, p. 1.
[25] See for example, *Sondages Revue Française de l'Opinion Publique*, 1958, No. 1 & 2, pp. 49-50.

in this book. As the preceding historical review suggests, once OEEC had fulfilled its dual purpose of channeling U.S. aid and stimulating European economic cooperation, the main emphasis shifted to functional integration as embodied in the European Common Market. This produced a period of stagnation in the OEEC, which, while much broader in its European membership than the EEC, had no formal trans-Atlantic tie and lacked the stimulus of a dynamic mission. In recognition of the growing importance of coordinating Atlantic policies on trade, finance, and aid to less developed areas, the OEEC was reborn as the Organization for Economic Cooperation and Development, or OECD, which symbolically dropped the "European" in its title and added "development" to "cooperation."

The United States and Canada, which had been associates of the OEEC, became full members of the new group, giving the Atlantic world an economic organ for the first time. The OECD held its first Council meeting at the ministerial level in November 1961. It began by setting the goal of a 50 per cent growth in real GNP for its members during the decade. Utilizing the extensive staff and knowledge inherited from the OEEC, the new organization has developed considerable technical competence through its secretariat and permanent staff of experts. But since the OECD lacks any supranational authority, much of its work is done through meetings of the key ministers of the member countries and through numerous international committees and working groups. Persuasion, disclosure, and discussion have proved reasonably effective tools in harmonizing fiscal, economic, and trade policies on an informal basis, but the organization lacks the authority as well as the power to act formally.

To the extent that an Atlantic community exists organizationally, it is composed of NATO in the military field, and OECD in the economic. "Europe" is represented by two potentially competitive economic entities (the three European Communities of the Six[26]

[26] The European Economic Community (EEC or Common Market) and the European Atomic Energy Community (Euratom) were established by the Treaty of Rome in 1957, while the European Coal and Steel Community

on one hand, and the European Free Trade Association on the other), one cultural and quasi-political organ (the Council of Europe), and one politico-military agency (WEU). A key question therefore is whether the Atlantic and European orientations of these various bodies are essentially competitive or complementary in nature.

The pace and direction of the European and the Atlantic movements are schematically suggested in Fig. 1, which reveals that both have moved upward in roughly parallel courses, but with the latter somewhat behind (although more stable) in recent years. Both ended 1964 with a large question mark. The chart is designed merely to illustrate broad directional trends and no quantitative significance is intended. To speculate on these question marks and attempt some projections requires us to consider some alternative political patterns.

Patterns for the Future

At one extreme might be what could be described as a non-Atlantic pattern, in which Europe (whatever its ultimate form) and America would go their separate ways, with perhaps a division of the non-Communist world into spheres of influence and responsibility. Under such a pattern, existing organs, including NATO, could be allowed to atrophy. They might even be formally dissolved. There are some who believe that General de Gaulle has been merely articulating publicly the premise upon which virtually all countries have been acting but lack the honesty to admit openly, namely, that all forms of supranationalism are a myth and that the nation is the only authoritative expression of society's will and power. If national interest is in fact the supreme criterion and is likely to remain dominant, then alliances can exist only to express a limited and perhaps temporary common interest. Belief in an

(ECSC) was established several years earlier. Collectively, the three comprise a "European community," although this term must be pluralized for accuracy inasmuch as the three components are still separate entities.

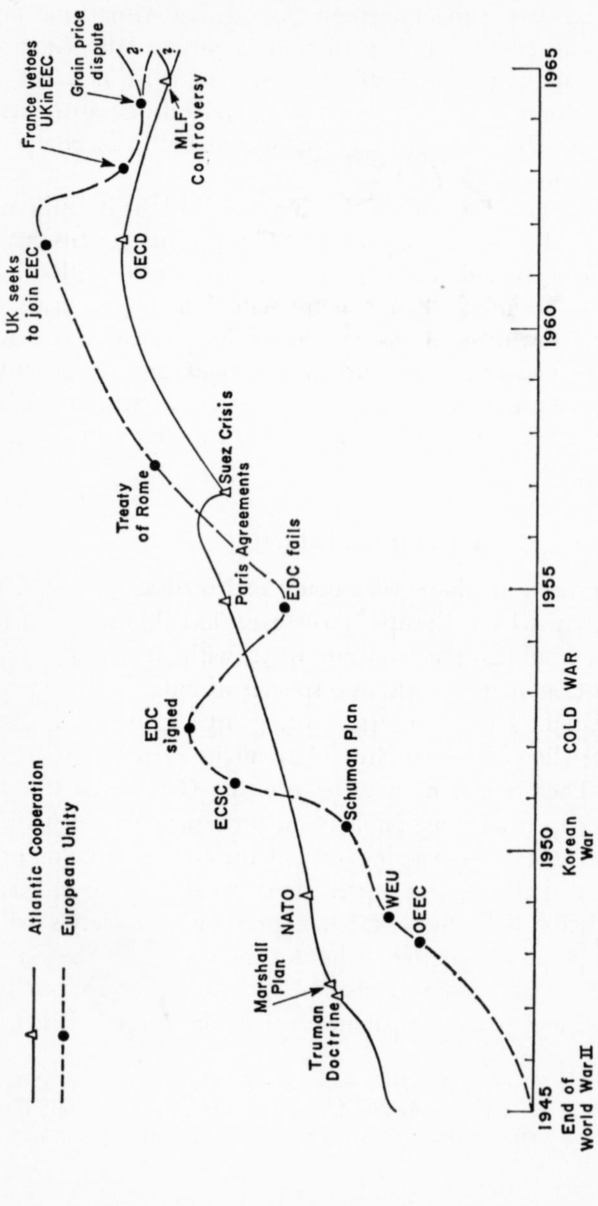

Fig. 1 Chronological Trends in European and Atlantic Cooperation

underlying community of tradition and purpose is, in this view —which is held by a number of individuals—merely a delusion.

It is here that the cynic and the idealist part. To the former, the non-Atlantic pattern is merely a recognition of the true state of affairs. By freeing itself from the illusory entanglement with Europe, America could regain its independence of action with respect to Communist China, Cuba, and other areas of particular concern. And as Europe's counterpart of the American neo-isolationist, the Gaullist presumably sees analogous advantages.

The idealist, on the other hand, disputes the aforesaid premise. While conceding that there are many potential and actual conflicts of national and regional interests, he believes that we have come too far and sacrificed too much to abandon now the concept of community—be it of the world as a whole, as in the U.N., or of a region like the Atlantic area. He opposes efforts to redefine national interests in narrow parochial terms, disregarding their longer term implications. Moreover, he sees a positive benefit in retaining as goals those objectives which are impractical for short-term achievement. For it is only within a framework of such long-range goals that contemporary conflicts can be better adjusted. And in this, the idealist is joined by the realist who holds that the shrinking globe and destructiveness of modern weapons have produced a set of interlocking interests which reinforce each other at least as much as they compete. Thus America and Europe are both involved, willy-nilly, in what the other does or does not do outside their common geographic area, as well as within it. In sum, the arguments for an Atlantic pattern seem far more persuasive than those against. Three in particular seem to me decisive.

First, any de-coupling of the American strategic deterrent would surely leave Europe more or less at the mercy of the Soviet Union for the many years it would take, at the very least, for Europe to evolve an effective strategic defense of its own, which would in any case involve some wasteful duplication of resources among the most powerful non-Communist nations.

Second, an independent, uncommitted "Europe" may be too big

a politico-military-economic entity to be unleashed in a tense and divided world to wander in search of its own destiny.

Third, in the power relationships that are forecast for 1970, Europe's energies are needed to work with the United States rather than for neutral or contrary objectives. The evident dynamism of the democratic European system is too valuable an asset in the global challenge with communism to allow it to remain exclusively regional in focus.

Assuming then that there must be a pattern which links Europe and North America, a number of variations merit consideration. One pattern would emphasize the development of Pan-Atlantic relationships, and point toward a coalescence of political-economic and military interests by Europe and America with Japan and other nations outside the North Atlantic area in the British Commonwealth and Latin America. If one looks far enough ahead, this possibility cannot be rejected. The relationships between what former Secretary of State Christian Herter terms "Atlantica"[27] and the rest of the non-Communist community is one of the vital questions of the 1960s. The classic arguments for free trade support the need for close ties among the industrialized nations; and, since many of their markets depend upon economic development in the poorer countries, coordinated aid policies undertaken by as many countries as possible may also be desirable. America's payments imbalance highlights the importance of fiscal cooperation. It is for these reasons that Japan has become a full member of the OECD, and a case can be made for including other non-Atlantic countries as well. At the very least, the Atlantic nations cannot afford to turn inward and must not ignore the needs and aspirations of others.[28]

Yet, however intriguing a Pan-Atlantic confederation may be

[27] See the article of this title in the January 1963 *Foreign Affairs*, pp. 299-309.

[28] Congressman Henry Reuss' book, *The Critical Decade: An Economic Policy for America and the Free World* (New York: McGraw-Hill, 1964), makes an effective argument along these lines. See also the U.S. Senate Foreign Relations Committee Staff Studies, *Problems and Trends in Atlantic Partnership* I and II—especially I, Senate Document No. 132, 1962, pp. 29-30.

from an intellectual point of view, the practicalities are something else again. Britain and a number of other European states stood quite aloof from the evolving unity of the Continent until its apparent success compelled them in that direction. There is no evidence that Japan, or India, or Brazil would be ready at present to add responsibilities and wider horizons of an ambiguous and necessarily loose nature to their domestic preoccupations. And even if other countries were interested, there does not appear to be a consensus within "Atlantica" ready to accept a formal wider-than-Atlantic pattern of organization other than the United Nations itself.

The Atlantic Pattern: Three Alternatives

Our process of elimination has discarded the non-Atlantic pattern as undesirable, and the Pan-Atlantic as impractical, but there are still many forms which relations between Europe and America could take. At one extreme would be arrangements leading to a true federation.

It is surprising that among the relative handful of supporters for Atlantic Union now, there are a number of men whose very familiarity with the foibles of human political behavior has led them to reject any lesser goal. Their skepticism in effect, has brought them full circle to embrace Atlantic political integration as an article of faith. This apparent paradox might be explained as follows: Human inertia can be overcome only by the greatest of challenges, not minor ones. Since an act of political will is all that is required to begin Atlantic Union, the very magnitude of the concept may be the most effective means of generating it. Had the Constitutional Convention not been so motivated, it might still be in session haggling over the details of gradualism.

A somewhat similar line of reasoning may have led Henry Cabot Lodge to make his proposal for a group of "Wise Men" whose views would be binding (on a special interim committee) unless specifically repudiated by governments in order to "put the burden of effort on those seeking to divide the free world instead of on those seeking to unite it."[29] The emotional and intellectual appeal of federalism remains strong; but its political appeal seems to have dropped sharply from the peak achieved just after World War II. It is possible that those who dismiss Atlantic Union as unrealistic will be proved as wrong as the Englishman who, only two years before George Washington's inauguration, described the prospect of a united America as the "idlest and most visionary notion ever conceived." Conceivable as a true "Atlantica" may be, its creation does not seem likely; and we must proceed with our analysis accordingly.

The concept of an Atlantic partnership has become everybody's favorite refuge, for it is broad enough to cover views as divergent as those of De Gaulle and the late President Kennedy. Yet, since we have argued that some form of Atlantic cooperation is both the minimum necessary and the maximum practicable at the present time, "partnership" does at least provide a convenient point of departure.

During 1962 and 1963, much attention was focused on what became known as the "twin pillar" approach to partnership (also known as the "dumbbell" configuration). This was shorthand for an equal relationship between America on one hand, and a united Europe on the other. President Kennedy's July 4, 1962 address at Philadelphia—a symbolic date and place—promised that "the United States will be ready for a declaration of interdependence . . . to discuss with a United Europe the ways and means of forming a concrete Atlantic partnership. . . ."[30]

This echoed the thought widely expressed in Europe that, as Walter Hallstein put it, "We need the European Community . . . as one pillar of the Atlantic Partnership."[31] If Europe were to form a whole comparable to the American federation, wrote another European "the two federations could cooperate like twin sisters."[32]

[29] Henry Cabot Lodge, preface to Pierre Uri, *Partnership for Progress* (New York: Harper & Row, for the Atlantic Institute, 1963), p. xxiii.

[30] *The New York Times*, July 5, 1962.

[31] Speech at Columbia University, New York, March 2, 1963, reprinted in *The Atlantic Community Quarterly*, Summer 1963, Vol. 1, No. 2, p. 143.

[32] Bernard Baudry, *Euro-America* (Paris: Plon, 1962), p. 16.

The assumptions underlying this approach were, first, that partnership can exist only between equals; second, that Europe could be an equal only by uniting; and third, that before it could unite it must free itself of "American hegemony" and gain a greater measure of independence.[33] To this line of reasoning, the Kennedy administration added the tactical consideration that European unification seemed to have gathered irresistible momentum through the Common Market, which the United States could not have halted even if it had wanted to. Every American administration since World War II (whether wisely or not) had strongly promoted European unity. To have withdrawn support as the project seemed to be approaching success might have jeopardized the partnership concept by arousing European suspicions that the United States was seeking "to drown the European baby in the Atlantic bath."

Hence, U.S. efforts were directed at supporting Britain's application to join the Common Market and developing, through the Trade Expansion Act, the tools for fashioning a sound economic basis for American-European cooperation. The Trade Expansion Act may go down in history as one of President Kennedy's greatest achievements. Not only does it authorize the President to reduce tariffs by 50 per cent over five years (and to eliminate them entirely in certain categories in reciprocal negotiations with the EEC), but it provides for adjustment assistance to U.S. firms. Perhaps of greatest significance, Congress gave up to the President its theretofore jealously guarded prerogatives over tariffs, thereby in effect raising international trade from the state and local to the national level of decision. With these measures, it was hoped, the United States could ensure that the emerging European entity would be liberal and outward-looking, as opposed to protectionist and parochial—a suitable pillar, in short, for the Atlantic partnership which it was assumed would follow eventually.

President Kennedy was therefore careful in spelling out his

[33] This viewpoint is well expressed in Altiero Spinelli's "Atlantic Pact or European Unity," *Foreign Affairs*, July 1962, pp. 542-552.

grand design to assure the Europeans that "we do not regard a strong and united Europe as a rival but as a partner." For their part, the advocates of a United States of Europe advanced the twin themes of European unification and "pursuing the organization of an equal partnership." But the key was the sentence: "It is essential that the European Community should be able to deal *as a unit* with the powerful United States and the other countries of the world."[34]

The alternative approach placed less emphasis upon the construction of the European *partner* and more upon establishing the *partnership* itself. This approach was reflected in the several declarations of the Atlantic unity, notably the Declaration of Paris, which expressed the conviction that "our survival as free men, and the possibility of progress of all men, demand the creation of a true Atlantic Community within the next decade." It also called upon governments to undertake without delay such measures to establish this community as a Commission to draw up a charter, a High Council, Consultative Assembly, and Court of Justice.[35]

Officially, advocates of both approaches denied that European unification and Atlantic partnership were in conflict.[36] But privately, most Americans tended to accept the former as an unavoidable means to the latter; while many Europeans gave lip service to Atlanticism as a means of gaining American support for their primary goal—creating a single European "great power."

[34] See Action Committee for a United States of Europe, "Declaration on a Unified Europe," December 18, 1962, (reaffirming a similar statement of June 26, 1962) which is reprinted in the *Atlantic Community Quarterly*, March 1963, p. 98.

[35] The "Declaration of Paris" of January 20, 1962, was sponsored by the Atlantic Convention of NATO Nations (a meeting of leading private citizens from the NATO countries), and grew out of earlier meetings of the Atlantic Congress. The main points of the Paris document were incorporated in the "Second Declaration of Atlantic Unity" in April 1962, and were endorsed by the NATO Parliamentarian's Conference in November. See the *Atlantic Community Quarterly*, Summer 1963, p. 275.

[36] There have been many books and articles on this general subject. In addition to those already cited, Christian A. Herter's *Toward an Atlantic Community* (New York: Harper & Row, for the Council on Foreign Re-

There were nevertheless a large number of issues which were glossed over. What, for example, was to happen in NATO or in the OECD, if the Six (with or without Britain) insisted upon reaching prior agreements among themselves on important military or economic matters before they could be addressed within the broader framework? A glance at Table 4 reveals the overlapping membership of European and Atlantic organizations.

Even if Britain and its EFTA associates had gained membership in the EEC, there would still have been half a dozen associates and independents or neutrals within the geographic area of Western Europe. At present no blueprint for a United Europe seems likely to include Sweden, Switzerland, Austria and Finland (the four neutrals); or Greece (although it is a Common Market Associate) Turkey and Iceland (all members of NATO) or Spain, with which the United States has vital defense arrangements. Western European relationships with an Eastern Europe which is also in transition involves a dimension often ignored in Western blueprints.

Nor, for that matter, did it ever become clear whether the basic assumptions of the "twin pillar" advocates were valid. It is not necessarily true that a partnership is impossible without equality of size and power or that it is easier to negotiate a satisfactory arrangement with two major parties than it is with a larger num-

lations, 1963), and *Building the Atlantic World*, by Robert Strausz-Hupé, James E. Dougherty and William R. Kintner (New York: Harper & Row, for the University of Pennsylvania Foreign Policy Research Institute, 1963) are particularly valuable. Other recent comment is contained in Kurt Birrenbach's *The Future of the Atlantic Community* (New York: Praeger, 1963) and George Lichteim's *Europe and America: The Future of the Atlantic Community* (London: Thames and Hudson, 1963). Two of the leading articles are Lord Franks' "Cooperation is not Enough" in the October 1962 *Foreign Affairs* and "A Community of Free Nations," the second of Senator Fulbright's three Clayton Lectures delivered at Tufts University, April 30, 1963. H. Field Haviland, Jr.'s "Building an Atlantic Political Community" in *International Organization*, Summer 1963, is a useful review of the various concepts and problems, as is that publication's special supplement, *The Atlantic Community: Progress and Prospects*, now available as a book. (New York: Praeger, 1964).

TABLE 4

Membership of Western Organizations

Countries	OECD	*The Atlantic Institute*	*Atlantic Treaty Association*	NATO	*Council of Europe* (CE)	*Western European Union* (WEU)	*European Communities* ECSC	EEC	EURATOM	EFTA
Belgium	•	•	•	•	•	•	•	•	•	
France	•	•	•	•	•	•	•	•	•	
German Fed. Rep.	•	•	•	•	•	•	•	•	•	
Italy	•	•	•	•	•	•	•	•	•	
Luxembourg	•	•	•	•	•	•	•	•	•	
Netherlands	•	•	•	•	•	•	•	•	•	
Canada	•	•	•	•						
Denmark	•	•	•	•	•					•
Greece	•	•	•	•	•			§		
Iceland	•	•	•	•	•					
Norway	•	•	•	•	•					•
Portugal	•	•	•	•						•
Turkey	•	•	•	•	•					
United Kingdom	•	•	•	•	•	•	*		*	•
United States	•	•	•	•						
Austria	•	•			•					•
Irish Republic	•				•					
Sweden	•	•			•					•
Switzerland	•	•								•
Spain	•									
†Cyprus					•					

* The United Kingdom has a special association with the ECSC, and an agreement for co-operation with Euratom.
§ Associate member. † Joined in 1961. *Source: The Atlantic Community Quarterly*, Vol. 1, No. 2, p. 297

ber. On the contrary, bilateral confrontations sometimes make it harder to compromise than negotiations where there are many and each knows it must yield in some measure.

These issues became less imminent but not necessarily irrelevant with General de Gaulle's January 1963 press conference. There, in one swoop, he cast a negative vote on the admission of Britain to the EEC, struck a blow at the Commission of the Common Market (the leading symbol of supranationalism on the Continent), made explicit his opposition to American influence in Europe, and paved the way for his concept of a Paris-Bonn axis. He made it clear, morever, that any real flowering of the EEC into a true political federation would have to be reckoned as "A.D.," for After-de Gaulle).

He thereby exposed quite clearly the differing concepts about the future which had been concealed within the "partnership" concept and had only partially been brought to the fore by the two approaches outlined above. As Senator Fulbright, the Chairman of the powerful Senate Foreign Relations Committee, put it:

> The fundamental issue is one between two different conceptions of the future organization of the West and the world. The Gaullist design . . . seeks to reshape Europe as an essentially national entity . . . strong enough to participate as a great power . . . in the traditional patterns of rivalry and balance. The Atlantic conception on the other hand is built on the premise that . . . the nation-state can no longer serve as the ultimate unit of law and human association.[37]

The essential problem for 1965 is how to pick up the pieces of the original grand design and reshape them to accord with the facts of international life. It may be that the Atlantic concept can again help rescue Europe from the consequences of a French veto, as did NATO and the WEU mechanism after the collapse of the

[37] Clayton Lectures, cited; the quotation is from the summary in *Atlantic Community Quarterly*, Summer 1963, p. 113.

EDC. Or it may be that the EEC can step carefully enough around the thorny issues of agricultural policy, French intransigence and a cycle of national elections to resume some forward political progress, while keeping the door at least ajar for future efforts to achieve British membership. Alternatively, the events of 1963-64 may have revealed inherent defects in the "twin-pillar" approach, and opened up the possibility of a tri-legged arrangement among the Six, Britain and its EFTA partners, and North America.

We cannot be precise about the possibilities until we have explored the central issues of strategy, nuclear control and defense which are analyzed in detail in Part II. And in any case it may be too soon to judge accurately the practicality of specific alternatives. But we can postulate some broad political assumptions within which to consider the alliance's major military task: preserving the security of the Atlantic area. The foregoing review suggests a number of guidelines for softening the potential conceptual conflicts between "Atlantica" and "Europa":

First, the United States cannot attempt to dictate the details of intra-European arrangements. But if it can solve the riddle of exerting leadership without dominating, America has every basis for insisting that these arrangements *not* produce the type of Europe which would:

> a) jeopardize the *U.S.* interest in European security—an interest which has led America into two world wars and brought forth an enormous economic and military investment during the cold war;
>
> b) seek to become a "third force" or a competitive power which might settle its own relationships with the Eastern bloc apart from those of the West as a whole;
>
> c) become inward-looking and protectionist—ignoring or shirking the Western responsibility toward the less developed areas of the world.

And Europe, of course, has quite parallel claims which it is entitled to make on the United States.

Second, the United States must face frankly the unpleasant fact that De Gaulle's design simply does not meet these criteria. Therefore, it should not hesitate to make known its official opposition. But it need not always identify De Gaulle with France, nor allow France to speak for Europe by over-responding to the many provocations which De Gaulle seems determined to inflict. Those who disagree with him should seek to isolate De Gaulle as much as possible by continuing and developing the many trans-Atlantic ties, bilateral as well as multilateral. In particular, the United States should so conduct itself as to minimize any legitimate European dissatisfactions with American leadership—for these merely add to the malaise of "third force-ism."

Third, the West cannot afford to wait and see what kind of a Europe will emerge as a potential equal partner for America. Rather, it must first establish the mechanics of the partnership and the infrastructure of an Atlantic Community to the extent possible, by proceeding to take such practical measures as are both sound and attainable. Pending developments in Europe, collectively and individually, America will have to work closely both with the Six, and with Britain and other members of the Atlantic world.

If a working blueprint can be established along these lines, on the basis of NATO and the OECD, which is firm in concept yet flexible in development, Europe's inevitable internal adjustments need not be seriously disruptive. That is, arrangements among the Six, or between them and the British, can safely evolve in accordance with their normal dynamics if they occur within an immutable Atlantic framework.

It hardly needs saying that the foregoing criteria are far easier to propound in theory than to implement in practice. Europe's preoccupation with internal evolution will not make it easy to obtain a focus on Atlantic restructuring. Moreover, many Europeans will fear an adverse impact—the "smothering" effect mentioned earlier—of an Atlantic emphasis. It is a characteristic of human nature that creative efforts often have exclusive tendencies. Clubs and associations are often distinguishable by those that they keep out as well as those who are members. In a period of declining concern with the Soviet threat, "Europe" has too often been defined negatively in terms of a counterpoise to, and independence from, American hegemony. Such sentiments lend support to Gaullist concepts, even in quarters not otherwise sympathetic.

America therefore cannot be obstructionist vis-à-vis European aspirations. Nor, even if it were so inclined, should the United States push for the immediate establishment of major new organizations. The important thing is to set the direction and establish the framework of assumptions for the Atlantic Community—of which Europe, however constituted, must be an essential part. This will require leadership of a high order; and a willingness to pave the way by suitable adjustments in the American role.

We shall return in Part III to this theme and its relationship to the tasks of building a stable world order, after we have examined in Part II the military facts bearing on the task of defense.

PART II

The Defense of the Atlantic Area

3

Strategy for the West

Strategy is simple, but it is not thereby easy.

VON CLAUSEWITZ

On August 6, 1945, the strange cloud that rose over Hiroshima meant that one long war was near an end. But it ushered in a new era of unimagined dangers, as if the gods were re-enacting the punishment of Prometheus for stealing their secret fires. Einstein brooded over the possible suicide of humanity. A macabre war of the future was foretold, in which the survivors might envy the dead. Clerics wondered whether man's folly had at last transcended the protective limits of providence, while statesmen and soldiers tried to ride out the storm and reach a new equilibrium.

The early pronouncements of world leaders on the atomic bomb reflected a sense of humility and awe, although Stalin sought to minimize the significance of a weapon which he did not yet possess. Some Western military leaders initially shared in the fear that another war might blast mankind to perdition; but for the most part, their professional instincts cautioned against the popular belief that nuclear weapons could "outlaw" war or had invalidated all previous weapons and tactics. As the cold war intensified during the late 1940s atomic energy came to be viewed merely as an order-of-magnitude increase in firepower. The greater the explosive effect of the atomic bomb, wrote one expert, the more effective it will be as a tactical weapon.

In 1949 the Russian test of an atomic device focused widespread attention upon civil defense. The Korean War and the military build-up it occasioned led to further examination of military strategy in the nuclear age. In 1952 General Bradley could still say that "if any enemy wanted to disperse its force so that its soldiers walked 100 yards apart, they could march across Europe tomorrow in the face of the greatest atomic power on earth," and the Secretary of the Army cautioned that atomic weapons were not all-powerful "wonder drugs."

The cycle of official thinking was challenged anew by the perfection of thermonuclear fusion techniques which made possible the hydrogen bomb. To Churchill, for example, the import of the American H-bomb tests was "laden with doom." The Russians also appeared to be impressed, for they now possessed the ability to make such weapons of their own. Once more, however, awe and fear gradually adjusted to the demands of effective military power.[1]

The enormous expenditures involved in the development of nuclear weapons systems led to a search for "security at acceptable cost," which produced the Eisenhower administration's New Look, envisaging an "increased reliance upon atomic weapons of all types and hydrogen attack upon cities." The press quickly attached the label of massive retaliation to John Foster Dulles' reference to "places and times of our own choosing." Subsequently, Secretary Dulles was criticized for policy inflexibility, but unfairly so. The doctrine bearing this label originated in his statement that "*local defenses* must be reinforced by the further deterrent of massive retaliatory power"; and Mr. Dulles was among the first to recognize that American policies would have to adjust to the emergence of a major Soviet nuclear capability.

[1] Comments of various leaders on atomic weapons will be found in *Vital Speeches*, October 15, 1945 (Truman); October 1, 1945 (Attlee); July 1, 1946 (Bunche); December 1, 1945 (Eisenhower); May 1, 1952 (Bradley); June 1, 1952 (Pace) and *The New York Times*, August 7-10, 1945; September 25, 1946 (Stalin); March 2, 1955 (Churchill). Representative U.S. military comments are contained in articles in the *Saturday Evening Post*, September 1, 1949 (Bradley); *Combat Forces Journal*, November 1950 (Gavin); and *Vital Speeches*, February 15, 1952 (McLain).

During the 1950s the planning problem was further complicated by growing agitation for nuclear disarmament, an end to weapons testing, and renunciation of the use of atomic weapons. Soviet sponsored "peace" and "ban the bomb" petitions won millions of adherents around the world. Britain's Labor Party strongly attacked the government's decision to manufacture hydrogen weapons, and the Oppenheimer case in the United States generated emotions that have split the scientific community ever since.

As the moral and political debate intensified, military experts divided ranks over the need for a greater capacity to fight local wars in peripheral areas. The emergence of a Soviet nuclear capability increased the danger that the use of tactical nuclear weapons would escalate out of control. It thus undermined the airpower advocates' claim that the forces and organizations needed for general war could handle local conflicts as well—or, as one of them expressed it, that "the dog we keep to deal with the cat will be able to deal with the kittens."[2]

The military debate over strategy and doctrine also extended to the relative priority of preparations for various types of conflict, represented by force-level and budget decisions. By the end of President Kennedy's first two years, the consensus appeared to support his contention that the United States must improve the range of choices between "nuclear holocaust and surrender." In practice, this meant "graduated options" and a greater emphasis on non-nuclear forces.

Thus, the advent of hydrogen bombs produced a renewed cycle of respect followed by a rationalization of deterrence through the balance of terror. More recently, the distinction between "deterrence" and "defense" has been recognized, for there are obviously many challenges which cannot be met by nuclear response. The increased emphasis on conventional forces is therefore accompanied by new efforts to mitigate disaster if nuclear deterrence should fail.

[2] Sir John Slessor, *Strategy for the West* (New York: William Morrow, 1954), p. 122.

The Doctrinaires and Their Doctrines

The labelling of ideas can be misleading or unfair, but the ship of Western strategy will be buffeted by winds from many quarters over the coming decade; and it is helpful to understand something about the strategic ideas before attempting to set a course. For convenience in identifying them, I shall label several opinion groups: the unilateral disarmers, the mutual disarmers, the arms controllers, the nuclear abolitionists, the deterrers, and the defenders.

The beliefs of the unilateral disarmers stem from two different sets of assumptions: either that there are no alternatives between pacifism and perdition (and that, of these, the former is of course preferable); or that even if the West were to disarm completely, the Communists would not in fact seek to dominate the world. The latter cannot be demonstrated conclusively one way or the other. But there is little in either the theory or the practice of communism to date which suggests that either the Russians or the Chinese would respond in kind to pacifism. On the contrary, history shows that the removal of risks to the expansion of an imperialistic system makes that expansion almost inevitable. Pacifism is a perfectly respectable moral choice for an individual. But until humanity loses its aggressive and rebellious tendencies, its adoption as national policy in the West could leave the world to the questionable mercies of competing Russian and Chinese factions.

With respect to the former assumption, the unilateral disarmers view the world situation in terms of C. P. Snow's choice between the "*either* of accepting a restriction on nuclear armaments . . . *or* the certainty of disaster."[3] He believes that "within at the most ten years some of those bombs are going off; that is a certainty." Such an approach leads naturally to the rhetorical "Red or Dead" type of question.

But this is not the correct way to state the choice. Rather, it is

[3] *Science*, January 27, 1961.

a question of what risks of how many people being killed one is willing to run to avoid the risks of totalitarian domination. There are those who claim that since it is now physically possible for mankind to destroy itself, this unhappy outcome will eventually occur. But this fatalistic view is a distortion and misapplication of a theory of probability which postulates that everything which can happen eventually will happen. It also assumes that if we choose "red" rather than "dead," the latter alternative is ruled out. Logically, in fact, we could be first red and then dead in a Communist civil war over the spoils resulting from their victory.

A thermonuclear war could be fought under a variety of circumstances in which the total casualties could range from thousands to some 300 million. Even the formidable upper figure is only about 10 per cent of the human race. Longer term fallout casualties and the indirect consequences of such a war (disease, floods, contamination of food supplies and the like) might raise the total to 25 per cent. The destruction (or shortened life span) of one-quarter of the human race staggers the imagination; but even that catastrophe is not wholly unprecedented, for the Black Death reduced Britain's population by almost one-half and the syphilis epidemic of the sixteenth century reportedly wiped out nearly one-third of Europe's population in a decade. The point is that one-fourth of the human race is not the whole of it, nor is it necessarily the beginning of the end of all life on the planet. Thus there appears to be more editorial license than scientific method in statements about the nuclear "extinction" of the human race which abound in the literature of peace groups. The physical scientists who sometimes lend support to such assertions tend to become "political" scientists in these matters. Their failure, says one commentator, "is not their lack of prescience but their acting frequently as if they had it."[4]

There is a particular horror about nuclear death. The 150,000

[4] Albert Wohlstetter, "Scientists, Seers and Strategy," *Foreign Affairs*, April 1963, p. 478. His larger monograph of the same title, to be published soon, effectively rebuts the scientists' claims to a special wisdom.

deaths caused by the two atomic weapons used thus far in war seem to blot out any general awareness that the so-called cold war has to date killed an equivalent number of Americans; that automobile accidents in the United States over four or five years will exact a comparable toll; that, statistically, cigarette smoking may be responsible for millions of premature deaths over the next decades. When it was estimated that up to forty million Communist Chinese might die in one winter without massive wheat imports, foreign policy considerations tended to take precedence over humanitarian concerns. In the ideal world, perhaps, the human life span will come to be regarded everywhere as sacred. Meanwhile, the real world has to live with automobiles, tobacco, starvation, the radiation from fallout and other sources, and the risks of nuclear war—and do the best it can to reduce the consequences by realistic and attainable steps, such as the atmospheric test ban.

Judge Learned Hand, in applying a familiar maxim of human behavior to a legal issue, suggested that the actions taken must be weighed against the gravity of the evil to be prevented as discounted by the probability of its occurrence. Large as the evil of thermonuclear war is, the probability of its occurrence is quite low. How much greater than zero the probability is, can be debated inconclusively, for we are dealing with a unique phenomenon which cannot be determined actuarially. However, it appears that most people (and governments) rate the probability as low. Moreover, since the occurrence is not a result of random chance but is affected by the actions of men and governments, it can be reduced to a probability range which will be very small, even if it will never be zero.

President Kennedy once said that a "nuclear sword of Damocles" hangs over everyone's head "by the slenderest of threads, capable of being cut at any moment by accident, miscalculation or madness." This is persuasive rhetoric; but we ought to examine more closely these three ways in which the thread might be severed. A deliberate nuclear attack on the United States by the Soviet Union approaches madness. "Miscalculation" of this magnitude seems unlikely, for the Soviets are well aware of the disastrous consequences to them of even the most favorable circumstances of a nuclear war. During the next ten years the probability of a madman emerging in complete control of a major nuclear power is generally agreed to be remote, although to judge by European reactions to some Goldwater campaign pronouncements in the U.S., it is not zero either. Both sides seem determined to steer clear of measures which could provoke the other to extreme desperation. Madness or irresponsibility at a lower level which could lead to an accidental or unauthorized detonation, is perhaps somewhat more likely. But—"Dr. Strangelove" and similar fiction notwithstanding—the consequences are a good deal less, for the surveillance and command and control measures now being taken by the major nuclear powers increase the assurance that a major nuclear exchange would *not* be triggered by a single unexplained detonation. But since this is less true of smaller potential nuclear powers, the future level of risks in this category will depend in part on the success of efforts to discourage nuclear proliferation.

Miscalculation would seem more likely to occur as a result of escalation in a local or limited conflict. But in the past decade, few of the major cold war crises (which averaged about one a year) produced an imminent confrontation of Western and Soviet armed force such as the 1962 Cuban crisis. It is more than chance that no shots have been *exchanged* between the regular military forces of the United States and the Soviet Union since 1918-19. The numerous cold war incidents that have occurred—shooting down of aircraft, blockades, assassinations and various provocations—might have created a dozen *casi belli* in former times. That they have not done so since World War II suggests that the thread on Damocles' sword may be stouter than is commonly assumed.

My somewhat optimistic views are based on the consideration that in most of the cold war's crises—Hungary, Suez, Lebanon, the Offshore Islands, Berlin, Southeast Asia, and Cuba—power has been exercised responsibly and with restraint, with every effort to avoid putting the opposition into a desperate corner. And from what could be judged, maintenance of tight control was a major objective of both sides. The indisputable fact of the West's enormous nuclear power may have contributed greatly to its achievement. It was also important that most operations were managed centrally by a single *political* authority at the highest level; for this reduced enemy fears of recklessness and hence the risks of desperate nuclear pre-emption. Centralized political control also enabled the strategic power, which was inevitably in the background, to render affirmative support to national objectives.

Future projections are difficult, for mutual restraint may further reduce the risk of major war and of its actual consequences if it should occur. At the same time, the potential consequences are increasing with each new development in weapons technology; and, more importantly, nuclear proliferation could multiply the incidence of dangerous situations. But the continuing though slow evolution of Russian society, outlined in Part I, makes the Armageddon of an inevitable showdown—at least with the Soviet Union—less likely. Also, it exposes the thin logic of "preventive" war, which could be justified, if at all, only on the certainty that war is inevitable and that choosing the time is more desirable than waiting for the enemy. Surrender and preventive war are, in fact, two sides of the same coin of inevitability.[5]

At the least, it can be said that we are not dealing with categorical alternatives of the either-or variety, and that man can still exercise a good deal of influence over the degree of risks. He has not yet been removed from control of developments, however much he may come to rely on the assistance of machines. The Strategic Air Command's "fail-safe" procedures were distorted in a recent novel of this title, which depicted men as helpless to countermand a mechanical error. The book contains a number of serious errors of fact; and other sensational accounts of a thermonuclear war of

[5] This is one of the few points on which Herman Kahn agrees with Bertrand Russell. See Herman Kahn, *Thinking About the Unthinkable* (New York: Horizon Press, 1962), p. 235.

the future also distort the ease with which events can get out of control].[6]

The mutual disarmers, for the most part, are somewhat less categorical about the imperatives and risks than are the unilateralists, and they do not postulate mandatory pacifism. But by definition they are more optimistic about the prospects of mutual disarmament, and their number includes advocates of a variety of approaches. There are serious and responsible advocates of world peace through world law, such as Grenville Clark and Louis Sohn. Proponents of unilateral initiatives by the West, and particularly by the United States, such as Charles Osgood and Arthur Waskow, hope that small conciliatory steps would be followed by voluntary reciprocal actions on the other side, giving the arms race a reverse thrust. Others, like Seymour Melman, seek new, nonmilitary areas of conflict and competition, in other words a "peace race" instead of an arms race. Finally, there are the traditional advocates of disarmament through negotiation, persuasion and compromise. Certainly the vast majority of mankind applauds and supports the objectives of disarmament. The "disarmers" differ only in the emphasis to be placed on disarmament as a means to world peace and on the risks to be accepted in the process.

Few people today subscribe to the prevalent theory of the 1930s that armaments *per se* are responsible for the tensions and dangers of war. Rather, it is recognized that pre-existing tensions and conflicts tend to cause arms races which, in turn, lead to greater tensions and to military conflicts. After all, the conflict known as the "cold war" results from Western resistance to the determination of the Communist bloc to pursue certain goals—in other words, from the interaction of incompatible national objectives and policies. If the basic Western-Soviet incompatibility continues gradually to lessen, disarmament prospects should grow apace.

Since World War II, disarmament has become a tool and an arena for diplomacy. Both East and West compete by propaganda

[6] The *Time* magazine issue of January 18, 1963 lists several of the major errors in the implications of *Fail-Safe*.

and political measures for the "hearts and minds of men." After several years of artful dodging to avoid being pinned with the donkey's tail of "general and complete disarmament" (GCD) by the Soviet Union, the United States officially accepted the GCD goal. As an objective, it is of course unexceptionable; but viewed as an absolute, unattainable. In the absence of world government with absolute police powers, man will continue to adopt whatever means are at hand, or can be created, as instruments of force. The "GCD and nothing else" slogan has been used by the Soviet Union as a means to mobilize pressures against NATO's security measures and to evade the more immediately demanding step-by-step controlled disarmament proposals of the West.

In recent years a number of strategists, acknowledging the "game" aspects of disarmament negotiations, have developed proposals involving disarmament as an integral part of the over-all East-West conflict, rather than as an illusory solution to it. They are not properly included in the "disarmer" group, although many of the ideas overlap. It makes sense to consider disarmament measures which would enhance the prospects for a favorable evolution in communism's basic orientation. Unfortunately there is little hard evidence as to whether reducing military pressures is more effective from this standpoint than maintaining or increasing them.

The "arms controllers" include persons in all of the other schools of thought; for in its broadest sense, arms control embraces any measure, unilateral, bilateral or multilateral, which seeks to reduce the likelihood of conflict and of the consequences if war should occur. The nuclear test-ban treaty concluded in 1963 is a good example. No disarmament or reduction in stockpiles is involved; nevertheless, by limiting the types of tests which can be conducted, the treaty does slow down the nuclear arms race and might increase the stability of the East-West balance. Confidence-building measures, such as observation posts, overlapping radars, or President Eisenhower's "open skies" proposal, also fall into the arms control category. The proposed "bomber bonfire" would be a confidence-building and limited-disarmament measure, as well as arms control

—a measure especially aimed at reducing the risks that surplus strategic weapons might find their way into irresponsible hands in other countries. The Polaris submarine, because of its invulnerability and lack of need for immediate firing, might be said to contribute to arms control. So does a strategic doctrine which avoids immediate attack on population centers. In short, arms control seeks to mitigate the risks of the existing conflicts and tensions pending longer range remedies for their underlying causes, which in turn may permit a degree of true disarmament.

The atomic abolitionists overlap to some degree with the "deterrers" group. For they recognize, like Leo Szilard, that "as long as there is no agreement providing for arms control and Russia remains in possession of large stockpiles of bombs, America has no choice but to maintain a strategic atomic striking force. However, it should maintain such a force only as a protection against America or her allies being attacked with bombs."[7] In most cases, therefore, the abolitionists are really advocating a doctrine of "no first use" of atomic weapons.

This group includes those who reluctantly point to the bright side of the "balance of terror" by proclaiming that thermonuclear weapons have, in effect, made major war outlaw itself. A great deal of sentiment favors the legal "ratification" of this alleged self-outlawing effect of modern weapons. For example, the United Nations General Assembly has voted to outlaw the use of atomic bombs in war and to make their use an international crime and a violation of the United Nations Charter. These proposals would involve a renunciation of strategic bombing as a general deterrent, and "a single basic break between all conventional and all nuclear weapons," with the latter existing only "to deter their use by the Russians at each level."[8]

The goal—at least as far as nuclear weapons are concerned—is

[7] Leo Szilard, "Are we on The Road to War?," *Bulletin of the Atomic Scientists,* April 1962, p. 5.

[8] Michael Brower, "Nuclear Strategy of the Kennedy Administration," *Bulletin of the Atomic Scientists,* October 1962. The writer makes this suggestion after reviewing and criticizing current policies.

therefore one of mutual deterrence and stability in the nuclear arms race. This approach raises a number of problems concerning defense, which its proponents would meet through various combinations of conventional armaments, arms control, world law and peace initiatives. While some of these problems will be discussed subsequently in this chapter, the point is that nuclear abolitionists are interested first and foremost in reducing the danger of nuclear warfare rather than in deterring aggression or in effective defense against it. This viewpoint is particularly widespread in Europe, where it poses difficulties for a consensus on NATO strategy.

It should be added that a small but growing group of those who are concerned with defense have come to believe that NATO's essential interests can best be preserved by primary reliance on non-nuclear means. Reduction of nuclear armaments to the role of deterring the other side from using them is thus seen by them as a logical corollary to an over-all strategy rather than as an end in itself.

Finally, I lump together all of the other schools of thought into the category of "defenders" (a varied group, indeed) because they believe that none of the preceding attitudes can alone meet the problems of today's world, and that, however desirable and important measures to control the risks of the arms race may be, the basic problem is still to defend the vital interests of the United States and its allies. This of course includes preserving our civilization, so that their differences with the nuclear abolitionists and the disarmers concern means more than ends. Even so, the latter perform the useful function of a "conscience," and they apply valuable intellectual resources to the formidable problems of international security. These views, moreover, appear to be gaining a greater measure of respectability. Even those who once referred—with some justification—to the "Hogwash" conferences, now concede that the Pugwash and similar East-West exchanges have planted valuable politico-scientific seeds among the Soviet leaders.

In my view, however, none of the aforementioned views can be the basis of a realistic strategy for the West in the kind of world which reason postulates for the late 1960s. Beyond the next few years, it is impossible to make intelligent predictions. It may well be that ideas which fail utterly in meeting today's problems of defense may be a good deal more applicable in ten years. But let us approach that possibility only after we have crossed some of the intervening bridges.

The analysis must therefore proceed on the premise that nuclear weapons and arms competition are unpleasant but inescapable facts of life. They will not be dispelled by wishing, nor will nuclear weapons be voluntarily proscribed. Khrushchev himself used to point out that even if a war started on a purely conventional basis, the side which was losing would find it impossible to keep a non-nuclear pledge. Although such escalation should not be regarded as certain, the other side could hardly afford to rely upon such a guarantee.

As long as nuclear arsenals exist they will continue to dominate the power struggle, even though hopefully they will never be employed. We cannot solve our problems by disregarding reality. In Herman Kahn's masterful "defense of thinking," it is hard to disagree with his conclusion that, "in our times, thermonuclear war may seem unthinkable, immoral, insane, hideous, or highly unlikely, but it is not impossible. To act intelligently we must learn as much as we can about the risks. We have to do the best we can with the tools and abilities we have."[9]

If we are going to think about the problems of defense and develop a strategy for the West in the thermonuclear-missile age, a number of separate aspects must be considered. First, there is strategic nuclear warfare in its offensive and defensive contexts. Second, there are limited wars and the relative emphasis to be placed upon tactical nuclear weapons and conventional forces. Third, there are lesser forms of aggression and provocation which must be dealt with, whether they come under the heading of sub-

[9] Kahn, cited, pp. 19-31.

limited wars, guerrilla warfare, or subversion. Fourth, there is the whole area of "passive" defense, which is closely related to strategic nuclear warfare and includes civil defense, evacuation, and the mobilization-recuperation base. Fifth, there are arms control demands and possibilities. Sixth, there is the relativity of defense measures to the attitudes, actions, and capabilities of the other side. Finally, there is the effect of time and the march of technology. We shall give some consideration to each of these in the following sections, but with the primary emphasis here on strategic warfare.

The Strategic Nuclear Options

A number of schools of thought debate the strategic use of nuclear weapons. The elements of the actual choices, however, are not always made clear. There is the matter of target system: cities and industry versus military forces. There are the circumstances of employment: first use or no first use, and conventional or nuclear environment. There is the element of maximum control versus no control at all—to which Thomas Schelling's analogy of a driver in a game of "chicken," who demonstratively throws his steering wheel away, is uncomfortably descriptive. And there is the question of the size of the strategic force—obviously dependent to a large extent on the other three. These four elements can be combined in various ways, but it may be helpful to arrange them into four groupings.

At one extreme are those who believe, with the "abolitionists," that nuclear weapons should be used primarily to deter the use of such instruments by an enemy—in effect, to outlaw nuclear warfare, or at least to resort to it only in retaliation, e.g., a no first use doctrine. A somewhat similar view, variously termed "minimum," or "finite" deterrence, holds that the dangers of war can be reduced by a stabilization of what Albert Wohlstetter aptly terms the "delicate balance of terror," by limiting the number of weapons and, in order to make the nuclear warfare so disastrous that it will not occur, targeting them only on major cities, where populations serve as hostages. In short: no first use, controlled use, cities only, and by implication small strategic forces.

A second strategy, now largely outdated, combines such notions as "cities-plus," "massive retaliation" and "optimum mix." The last term envisages a combination of military and civilian targets, with priority, of course, on enemy striking power, while industrial areas, transportation centers, and cities serve as bonus targets for the bomber force. This goes beyond minimum deterrence in that the threat of retaliation against the entire politico-military-economic structure of a country is intended to deter a wide range of aggressive or provocative actions. In short: probable first use, little control, cities and military targets, large strategic forces. But this massive retaliation threat was most credible against the lesser forms of provocation only so long as the United States had a virtual monopoly on nuclear weapons. Even then, it did not suffice to prevent the Korean War or bring it to a successful conclusion, or to prevent the Communist conquest of much of Indo-China. And as the Soviets acquired the ability to devastate American cities in return, their own potential became a shield behind which piecemeal conquests could be obtained.

A third strategy belongs to the advocates of as nearly pure "counterforce" targeting as possible. They argue that the role of the military is to prevail over enemy military forces and dictate the terms of the peace treaty. Their strategy therefore endeavors to disarm an enemy by force rather than to destroy his civilization. In other words: tight control, avoidance of cities, relatively large strategic forces, and preferred first use, though this is not essential.

Finally, as a modification of the first and third strategies, the doctrine of "controlled, selective response" seems to be emerging as the official policy of the United States. Here, too, the emphasis is on destroying as much as possible of an enemy's striking power, but the concept significantly prescribes what targets should not be hit. This is sometimes called a "no-cities" strategy, since enemy cities would probably not be attacked initially, unless U.S.

population centers had been struck. The concept also stresses passive defenses to limit damage to U.S. and allied civil society. This alternative, the evolutionary product of inadequacies in each of the other three taken alone, has also been called a "damage limiting" strategy. It features tight control, coverage of all feasible military targets, secure reserves for retaliating against cities, medium-sized forces and preferred first use of strategic nuclear weapons.

The Evolution of U. S. Strategy

The massive retaliation-optimum mix strategy which served the United States reasonably well for several years was eventually superseded for a number of reasons. First, it offered only an all-or-nothing option. Once launched, U.S. forces had either to return to base or execute massive preplanned attacks, in which case little could be done to alter their size and direction. By contrast, as Secretary McNamara has pointed out, "our new policy gives us the flexibility to choose among several operational plans, but does not require that we make any advance commitment with respect to doctrine or targets."[10]

A second factor concerned the American casualties to be expected from Soviet retaliation. One dramatic, if somewhat oversimplified, account of the evolution toward a new strategy describes the results of a nuclear war under the maximum devastation doctrine of the late 1950s:

> Over and over again the war games were played. Each time the number of dead fluctuated. Each time the amount of damage varied [with changes in the basic assumptions], but given the strategies used, the general outcome was always the same. If the Soviet Union struck first, we lost. If America struck first, we tied "or even won." In the tying and the winning, however, most

[10] Address to the Fellows of the American Bar Foundation Dinner, Chicago, Illinois, February 17, 1962, Dept. of Defense Press Release, p. 7.

> of us died . . . the difference in strategy was the difference between life and death for America . . . when the United States destroyed Soviet cities and the enemy did the same in reply, more than 100 million Americans died—even when we struck first.[11]

Using a no-cities strategy, however, the casualties were often ten times lower, while the military outcome remained roughly the same or favored the United States.

The vulnerability factor also made the old strategy increasingly undesirable. During the time when it was thought that a large missile gap was developing in favor of the Soviet Union, the Commander of SAC reportedly stated that there were only fifty SAC home bases within the United States.[12] The Soviets would have had a fair chance of destroying all the planes that were on the ground at these installations with about 200 missiles. Massive retaliation was in essence a first strike concept, for it did not contemplate having to strike with a badly damaged force following a Soviet nuclear attack. Although this appears to have been a dangerous doctrinal lag in the mid-1950s,[13] measures were under way by the end of the decade to reduce vulnerability by hardening, dispersal, and by an acceleration in the missile program.

The pure counterforce theory (sometimes implying a first disarming strike) has traditionally been an air force doctrine, although it has been shared at various times by planners in the other services. It requires a high degree of assurance that the enemy could be disarmed completely. In other words, the objective is surgical removal of an enemy's nuclear striking potential, but without necessarily killing his body politic in the process. In terms of costs and numbers of weapons, this is the most expensive strategy; and more importantly, it is increasingly infeasible. Given Soviet

[11] Richard Fryklund, *100 Million Lives* (New York: Macmillan, 1962), p. 13.

[12] Speech by General Power; see *The New York Times*, January 20, 1960.

[13] A thorough discussion will be found in Albert Wohlstetter's "The Delicate Balance of Terror," *Foreign Affairs*, January 1959, pp. 211-235.

submarine-launched missiles, their efforts to harden ICBMs, and the mobile missiles able to reach Western Europe, more than a few missiles seem likely to survive. A massive blanket attack might reduce the number, but the civil damage and casualty by-products would be enormous. And if such an attack were not completely successful, even a few surviving enemy missiles could deal a devastating retaliatory blow. Moreover, there would be little incentive not to direct them against major cities in the West, if Soviet cities had been destroyed as a by-product of the Western attack.

As to the *second* strike situation, following an enemy surprise attack, counterforce advocates rely upon the increased survivability of U.S. forces from hardening (as with Minuteman) and mobility (as with Polaris) to eliminate the enemy's remaining strike potential. But the largest part of the enemy force would already have been launched and–in the absence of antimissile defenses–would accomplish its mission–whether to attack U.S. forces or to devastate the country as a whole.

A preplanned counterforce strategy, based on a "go-no-go" option, provides too little flexibility. Virtually all U.S. forces might have to be used, leaving nothing for retaliation against enemy cities if necessary. Finally, a strategy and force structure which has its primary utility in a first strike situation may seem dangerously provocative to an enemy. It might lead Russia to take the all-or-nothing gamble of a pre-emptive strike in a period of extreme crisis.

If the massive retaliation and counterforce-disarming strike strategies are too inflexible or infeasible, Herman Kahn's fictional (but not inconceivable) Doomsday Machine is the *reductio ad absurdum* of concentrating exclusively on deterrence by threat of civil destruction. The "Doomsday" terminology has, however, misdirected attention from this application. More illustrative, perhaps, would be a suicide pact, analogous to the arrangements suggested by Leo Szilard and others, whereby the United States and the Soviet Union each agreed to allow the other to maintain, in foolproof underground caverns beneath their major cities, a small force which could not be prevented from detonating multi-megaton bombs upon electronic confirmation that their own cities had been destroyed. This, in a sense, is the fantastic situation depicted at the end of the novel *Fail-Safe*, in which the whine of disintegrating telephones informed the Soviet Premier and the President of the United States that Moscow and New York had both been destroyed. Here is the ultimate in mutual deterrence—an automatic guarantee that action by *either* side would totally and symmetrically destroy the urban centers of both. Fantastic though this may sound, it is more or less what is advocated by the "countercity only" advocates. And as the number of protected strategic missiles grows on both sides, the theoretical capability for such symmetrical destruction will increasingly be present. There have been proposals by no less a person than the late President Kennedy's science advisor, for example, to limit each side to, say, 200 missiles, presumably of the "city-busting" variety. It has also been suggested that some of the missiles be located in major cities to further insure against their use. The cities themselves might then gain some security as hostages from *nuclear* attack, but not necessarily from anything else—e.g., attack by nonlethal incapacitating agents. And the effectiveness in all other situations would vary inversely with the degree of threat to these cities. The deterrent would be inapplicable to all provocations other than a massive nuclear assault upon the United States. The somewhat differing situations of North America and Europe have inclined the former to think more in counterforce terms, and the latter in terms of countercity or minimum deterrence forces—a divergence which, as we will see later, is a major facet of NATO's nuclear problems.

Fortunately, the Soviet Union's declaratory policy of a first and massive use of nuclear weapons has not been matched by their forces. When they were confronted by substantial tactical superiority in connection with the Cuban blockade, they had very little recourse but to back down, for it was hardly believable that they would risk the destruction of their cities by threatening ours in defense of their investment in Cuba.

Voices are still heard occasionally arguing the merits of a particular concept or weapons system on the ground that it is not accurate or destructive enough for counterforce. Being therefore less provocative, it is advertised as the invulnerable ideal of a minimum deterrence system.

Apart from the deterrence gap which such a strategy would leave there are even more serious objections to minimum deterrence. It virtually guarantees the *maximum* amount of loss of life or damage if such an attack should occur. Such a strategy could hardly be the basis for a credible defense of Western interests. In effect, it says to an enemy: "You are at liberty to do anything you choose other than to drop nuclear weapons on our cities. You may land as many divisions as you can on our coasts, or, more to the point, engage in a massive attack upon Western Europe or any of our allies, and you run no risks of being met with strategic nuclear warfare, for this would be catastrophic for us as well as for you." In its pure form, therefore, minimum deterrence is also self-deterrence.

Few strategists advocate minimum deterrence in its extreme form—at least for the United States as the major nuclear power of the West. Most would attempt to extend the guarantee of U.S. cities to cover at least the major urban centers of our allies. Others would want enough striking power to attack, in addition to cities, any important enemy military targets that remained vital after the Soviets had gotten off an initial blow. This finite deterrence variant does have some appeal. It brings the principle of diminishing returns to the arms race, and permits a levelling-off in defense expenditures on strategic systems by recognizing the marginal value of procuring weapons beyond those necessary to pose a threat to the opponent's civil society and to cover vital military targets. As we approach the 1970s, with both sides having a high proportion of invulnerable missiles, it may be the wave of the future. But for the present, any effort to make a "finite" determination of strategic force levels independent of the enemy's force size discounts too much the dynamics of military technology. In addition to the damage-limiting criterion, the coercive psychological and political potential of a maximum, rather than minimum, coverage of enemy targets is also an important factor.

Out of the deficiencies of the minimum deterrence, massive devastation, and disarming counterforce approaches taken alone, there has emerged a strategy which combines a number of different elements. Sometimes referred to as a "no-cities" or "controlled response" doctrine, it might be more accurately described as a controlled and restrained damage-limiting option. Secretary McNamara stated its underlying premise as follows:

> To the extent feasible, basic military strategy in a possible general nuclear war should be approached in much the same way that more conventional military operations have been regarded in the past. That is to say, principal military objectives, in the event of a nuclear war stemming from a major attack on the alliance, should be the destruction of the enemy's military forces, not of his civilian population. The very strength and nature of the alliance forces make it possible for us to retain, even in the face of a massive surprise attack, sufficient reserve striking power to destroy an enemy's society if driven to it. In other words, we are giving a possible opponent the strongest imaginable incentive to refrain from striking our own cities.[14]

In one sense then, the new strategy is a reaction against the

[14] Remarks at the University of Michigan commencement exercises, Ann Arbor, Michigan, Saturday, June 16, 1962, Dept. of Defense Press Release, June 16, 1962, p. 9. A further elaboration of McNamara's views is contained in "Our New Strategy, The Alternatives to Total War," by Stewart Alsop in *The Saturday Evening Post,* December 1, 1962, p. 13. The best elucidation of the Kennedy administration's defense policy is contained in William W. Kaufmann's *The McNamara Strategy* (New York: Harper & Row, 1964), especially Chs. 2 and 3.

massive civil destruction implicit in either the spasm-type of all-out response or the minimum deterrence city-busting doctrine. It seeks deliberately to avoid hitting the cities of the enemy in order to restrain him from attacking ours. It also carries a significant counterforce emphasis: an attempt would be made on either a first or second strike basis to destroy as much as possible of the enemy's military power, and thus end the exchange with a favorable balance of surviving strength. At the same time, there must be provision to deter the enemy from attacking our relatively defenseless cities, even after war has started. Conceptually, two forces are therefore required: one would attack military targets, while the other, sufficient to destroy the enemy's population centers, would be held in reserve to deter him from attacking our own. The reserve, of course, must have a high degree of survivability such as the Polaris or hardened Minuteman systems provide.

Maintaining these options, once a nuclear attack has been initiated by either side, also requires a perfection of command, control, communications and reconnaissance techniques. In this connection, Mr. McNamara has mentioned "alternate command posts at sea and in the air, with communications links to all elements of our strategic force" able to "survive an attack and apply the surviving forces in consonance with national security objectives."[15] It must be recognized, however, that there is always a lead-time gap between the evolution of theory and the actual creation of the means to implement it.

This strategy also depends upon the enemy's ability and incentive to play the game by the same rules, an important question which will be considered subsequently. Finally, there must be some sure way of telling whether an enemy has, in fact, observed the rules and refrained from attacking nonmilitary targets. For this purpose, an elaborate bomb alarm system has been devised, which will automatically flash to various headquarters an indication that a nuclear device has been exploded. From the pattern of such

[15] Chicago Speech, February 17, 1962, cited, p. 6.

signals it should be possible to deduce the nature of the enemy's attack and direct the American response accordingly.[16]

The debates that continue to be waged in the Pentagon are directed less at the underlying concept described above than at the respective roles and missions of the services in carrying it out. But there are questions about what level of strategic forces for the future can justify their cost in terms of potential effectiveness. The balance between offensive and defensive systems is always difficult to strike, especially in the technologically complex field of missile defenses. There are disagreements about the rate of build-up of Soviet forces and their vulnerability. In essence, these and other related questions are concerned with both the feasibility and utility of attempting to maintain strategic superiority in the decade ahead. Because the answers are so vital to the security of the alliance as a whole, it is appropriate to examine the problem in some detail.

The Elements of Strategic Superiority

Strategic comparisons are too often expressed in pure numbers of missiles and bombers, or in terms of the relative vulnerability of forces. Actually, the situation is a great deal more complex. Who strikes first, against what targets, and with what results is of prime importance. One must estimate how many bombers and missiles the attacker will attempt to launch, assuming that he will keep some in reserve and that others may not be in a ready status. How many of those launched will actually reach the defender's targets will depend upon many factors. One concerns the reliability of the attacker's delivery systems, since some elements will malfunction at the start and others will abort during the mission. Some missiles may be targeted so as to knock out air defense for the bombers, and some of the latter may be used in a feint. Medium-range

[16] Fryklund, cited, p. 15, describes one of the hypothetical wars as follows: "Bomb alarm signals in American cities verify that the enemy has aimed at military targets, not population centers. So word is flashed to the bombers: 'Use your "A" target list; do not destroy Soviet cities."

bombers depend upon refueling, either at staging bases or from airborne tankers, introducing still another variable.

Next, it is necessary to determine how many delivery units can actually arrive over target. This depends upon the over-all capability of the defender's air defense system, the state of his alert, and such factors as warning time and the effectiveness of decoys and electronic countermeasures. Most important is the extent to which the first-wave attack renders the radars, ground controls, and interceptor forces of the defender incapable of dealing with subsequent waves. This battle of offense and defense will involve air-to-air, air-to-ground, and ground-to-air combat of enormous complexity. It puts a large premium on effective defense against missiles, for even an ability to "kill" one in three incoming missiles would require the attacker to program many more delivery units. He could not be sure in advance which of his missiles would be destroyed, leaving a major target undamaged.

At present, radar-directed interceptors and ground-to-air missiles are reasonably effective against the manned bombers at most altitudes, especially if they use nuclear warheads. One such anti-aircraft warhead can eliminate a large number of incoming bombers. The great problem is that enemy nuclear missiles might destroy these unhardened defenses before the bombers came within range, or create a nuclear environment in which radars and controls would not function properly. But at least the chances are good of preventing the enemy from having a "free ride."

After years of doubt that the Army's Nike-Zeus would prove effective enough to justify its enormous costs, the Defense Department is going ahead with the research on a more advanced version to be called "Nike-X." At the same time the Russians are improving their own air defense missiles, some of which have reportedly already been deployed. Submarine-launched missiles present a special defense problem to which there is as yet no really good solution. In any case, the side that first gets a truly effective anti-missile system into operation will achieve a breakthrough of strategic importance, and acquire a meaningful option of stressing active defenses (as against further increasing the number of offensive missiles).

Each element of an attacking force which gets through air defenses must next be assessed in terms of probability of a "kill." Because some warheads may not function as planned, impacts will be at varying distances from the target. Accuracy is usually measured in terms of "circular error probable" (CEP). From the ground or air burst of a weapon of given yield one must take into account nuclear radiation, thermal effects, and blast; from the last it is possible to determine the overpressure in pounds per square inch (PSI) at a given radius from ground zero.

It is obvious that the size of the warhead is important, for the blast varies with the warhead yield. But it is less commonly understood that missile accuracy is a most significant measure of strategic power, especially against small targets. One missile of high accuracy can do the work of several less accurate ones. Consequently, the technological race also involves refinement of accuracy as well as the yield of warheads in relation to their weight.

In estimating the effects of the attack, the vulnerability of the defender's target system will be a vital consideration. Are his targets dug in and reinforced? How many PSI can they stand? What fallout and blast protection does the population have? What survival equipment is available? How reliable was the attacker's intelligence–i.e., were the targets actually in the place where the attackers believed them to be? How good is his post attack surveillance and assessment of bomb damage, e.g., if the target is an airfield, were the planes in fact destroyed on the ground or did they get away before the strike?

Most important of all, what type of targets did the attacker select? Did he try to knock out the defender's striking power by attacking his delivery systems? Or did he seek maximum destruction of cities, industrial centers, communications, and the like? Or both?

These questions oversimplify the thousands of variables which must be worked into any attempt to conduct war games involving such a situation. For instance, what about weather conditions, and the effect of human and mechanical errors? By using mountains of data and making assumptions where necessary, it is possible to get an approximation of the results of the attacker's strike. But the best that can be expected is a range of numbers which will vary according to the assumptions. Even slight changes in the data used can strongly influence the results. If one assumes that the enemy's objective is to knock out the defender's retaliatory forces, one might conclude that so many missiles, airfields, and aircraft were destroyed; or, if the targets are assumed to be cities as well, the list would include a number of urban areas totally destroyed, more with heavy damage, and so many million casualties.

But even after these calculations, the task is not half done. One must now subtract for the damage caused by the enemy's first assault. Assuming that the defender retaliates, he now becomes the attacker, and similar measurements must be applied in estimating the effectiveness of his response. The counter-strike damage has to be applied to what the original attacker had in reserve, got back from his first bomber strikes, or readied in the meantime by reloading missile launchers or correcting launch-pad failures. Theoretically, at the end of the first exchange, a rough balance sheet of surviving power can thus be drawn up. But unfortunately for the analyst, the relatively simple case where the attacker completes his strike and the defender retaliates is quite unlikely. It would be more realistic to expect continuous and overlapping exchanges of weapons from both sides, complicating the calculations still further.

Nonetheless, war games can be and are run on such matters, presumably in the Soviet Union as well as in the West. Decision makers on both sides must operate with at least order-of-magnitude guesses about the outcome of a thermonuclear war, even though, contrary to widespread opinion, these uncertainties make detailed computer calculations of relatively little value.[17]

Of all the unknowns, the most important, and in some ways the least predictable, is the reaction of the enemy. The cold war consists of confrontations between East and West. It may involve two military police stations at Checkpoint Charlie in Berlin, aircraft formations over the Taiwan Straits, or a naval blockade, as in the case of Cuba. A basic imperative for each side is to calculate the consequences of each succeeding step on the escalation ladder. If tanks face each other at the Berlin wall, one side may reinforce them; if shooting starts, the other may throw in an infantry company. The riposte may take the form of a battalion or a regiment, and so on up the line. Neither side may desire or expect that the higher levels of violence will be reached. But every response—be it political, diplomatic, psychological, or military—is governed not only by the immediate levels of contact but by the ultimate in escalation, general nuclear war. The chance of reaching the ultimate may be, as we have seen, very small indeed; but the extent to which one side's bluff may be called depends significantly upon it. Chess experts need not play the whole game to know who has the advantage; they can often foresee the outcome after a few moves. Diplomats used to say that a protest note was only as strong as the divisions behind it. And this truism has by no means been completely outmoded by the atomic age.

Any president of the United States, confronted with a major crisis, say in Berlin, has more flexibility if a greater range of military actions is open to him. A president whose only effective choice was to initiate massive thermonuclear attacks on cities could do little but capitulate if his bluff were called. But if he had the option first of using other than nuclear forces, and then of threatening a limited and controlled use of nuclear weapons, backed by strategic superiority, his chances of successful diplomatic resolution—or, if

[17] For some simplified accounts, see Fryklund, cited, Chs. 1-3, and Herman Kahn, *On Thermonuclear War* (Princeton University Press, 1960), Ch. X.

necessary defending vital Western interests at the lowest possible level of violence—would be materially enhanced. The will to take the first step is, in short, a product of both tactical and strategic power in all their forms.

Of course, there is no assurance that the enemy will play the game this way. He might threaten massive retaliation with "100-megaton" weapons and, if his bluff were called, and the confrontation escalated, either yield, or initiate an irrational and suicidal strike. But in calculating each move an enemy cannot ignore the probable outcome of a nuclear exchange on a counterforce basis, so that it is worthwhile to examine the calculations involved. Some readers will find such analysis unpleasant, not to say repugnant or immoral. To them I can only repeat that it reflects the present facts of life of the nuclear age. Ignoring these facts will in no way solve the problems they pose or promote the responsible statesmanship which the world requires if it is to learn to live less dangerously.

The Significance of Numbers

It may be worthwhile to examine on a quantitative basis a hypothetical exchange in which attacker and defender both attempt to limit the damage to enemy population and civil society in the hope of avoiding the destruction of his own. Even for an artificial and oversimplified model, the assumptions are too involved for discussion here; and of course, no attempt can be made to predict the possible outcome of an actual nuclear conflict. But in order to show that, in the calculus of deterrence, relative numbers are meaningful, it may be useful to follow the analytical method outlined above.

Judging from the experience of the small number of nuclear powers there seems to be a progression in stages of sophistication about atomic weapons. Initially, there is a fascination with the warhead itself and its yield. Then attention becomes focused on the problems of carrying the bomb. Next there is concern about penetrating enemy defenses. Finally, the vulnerability problem dawns, and the distinction is made between striking with an undamaged force and striking with one that has been damaged by an enemy attack. From the concern with its own vulnerability, a country eventually comes to address the significance of the protection which the enemy is providing to his own target system. Finally there comes concern over controlled and limited use—usually when the interaction of two strategic forces and their respective defenses is assessed in terms of both civil and military damage.

In the early and middle 1950s, American comparisons were made mainly in terms of numbers of warheads and vehicles and usually in the context of a one-sided nuclear war, or with at most a few one-way missions to deliver the small Communist stockpile. Then the pendulum swung the other way and stressed the first-strike/second-strike distinction, and the relative vulnerability of the respective forces. One recent book, for example, presents a table showing the outcome of all-out war purely in terms of broad categories of vulnerable and invulnerable target systems and first and second strikes, without any reference to the size of the forces concerned.[18] The current gap in understanding appears to reflect a widespread belief that numbers are irrelevant, and that once a country has obtained a significant number of invulnerable delivery units, anything else is senseless "over-kill" capacity—a term being used with growing frequency, but rarely with any understanding of the factors involved. It is true that the existence of a very large number of *completely* "invulnerable" missiles on both sides could and presumably will introduce greater stability in the U.S.-U.S.S.R. relationship. (In certain other respects it might be unstabilizing.) And it is also true that a point can be reached (as it may have been in the United States) at which weapons stockpiles are approaching the foreseeable needs of even the worst combination of contingencies. In the late 1940s, however, a strategic stand-

[18] Henry A. Kissinger, *The Necessity for Choice* (New York: Harper & Row, 1960), pp. 30-40, esp. p. 34. This was, however, written on the assumption of a missile gap in favor of the U.S.S.R.

off was forecast for the 1950s; and in the 1950s, it was predicted for the early 1960s. In 1963, Secretary McNamara told Congress that we are "approaching an era when it will become increasingly improbable that either side could destroy a sufficiently large portion of the other's strategic nuclear force . . . to preclude a devastating retaliatory blow."[19] That era may indeed have arrived for Western Europe, and it is probably imminent for the U.S.; but the march of technology always has managed to postpone it many times. Nevertheless, Soviet efforts to reduce vulnerability will further increase their second-strike capability. A higher priority on missile defenses may produce a significant improvement in defenses against an attack or counterattack. But the controlled counterforce option makes a decision to deliver it against NATO cities extremely difficult.

In our hypothetical example only 10 per cent of the forces are made absolutely invulnerable; and, on the assumption of effective surprise, the bombers which could be launched between warning and the actual attack are included in that figure. This is probably too small in terms of the actual East-West situation. But at the present stage of technology, vulnerability of most strategic forces (except for missile-launching submarines actually at sea) is relative, not absolute. This relativity is taken into account in the respective figures for target system vulnerability. These terms, and a more detailed explanation of the methodology used to derive Table 5, are contained in the explanatory note facing the table.

Table 5 assumes constant values (as in the preceding discussion) for both sides in all categories but three: size, vulnerability, and

[19] Statement of the Secretary of Defense before the House Subcommittee on Dept. of Defense Appropriations, February 6, 1963, p. 27. This document of over 150 pages is an extraordinary unclassified blueprint for U.S. defense programs and an unprecedented compendium of information. For the first time in history the basic objectives, assumptions, concepts and alternatives underlying U.S. defense policy are spelled out in detailed relationship to programs and budgets. The 1964 version is almost as comprehensive. In fact the annual testimony may become *the* authoritative Defense "white paper."

first or second strike. *A*, as the attacker, is about to launch a surprise first strike against the defender, *D*. Cases are considered where *A* has three times the number of delivery units as the defender, twice as many, an equal number, one-half as many, and one-third as many. Then the relative vulnerability for each side is considered at three levels: namely, 0.5 (where two of the attacker's own delivery vehicles are required to eliminate one of the defender's, indicating a fair degree of hardness and dispersal), 1, and 2—the latter permitting each attacking vehicle to neutralize two units of the defender's strategic forces, which are thus relatively vulnerable.

It can be observed from Table 5, that under the assumptions postulated, the side which starts with a two- or three-to-one numerical advantage ends the exchange with its advantage maintained or improved, irrespective of who attacked first. The extent of that advantage, of course, increases or decreases with the respective vulnerabilities and the advantages of getting in the first strike. Vulnerability, in short, changes the outcome only in degree, except where the starting numbers are equal.

Another noteworthy conclusion is that a numerically inferior country cannot gain anything by making a counterforce attack on a country which is superior by these margins, provided that the latter has taken the precaution of protecting at least a part of its forces. The adverse balance against the inferior attacker merely worsens in the example under discussion. However, the superior country can multiply its initial advantage by a factor of as much as ten in a well-executed counterforce attack, if the defender is even moderately soft. That is why counterforce is the preferred strategy of the stronger side, while the weaker is in the unhappy position of having to rely upon massive retaliation against cities.

Changing the assumptions and numerical values will of course change the results of the table considerably. One could, for example, construct a case where a weaker power reverses the strength ratio by a surprise attack against a much larger force

TABLE 5

Results of a Hypothetical Counterforce Exchange

RATIO OF INITIAL STRENGTH (1 = 500 delivery units)	*Attacker Vulnerability* (V^A)	RATIO OF SURVIVING DELIVERY UNITS — *Defender Vulnerability* (V^D): 0.5 (Relative invulnerability)	1 (Moderate vulnerability)	2 (Considerable vulnerability)
A = 3, D = 1, Attacker Much Stronger	0.5 (Relative invulnerability)	A (5 : 1)	A (30 : 1)	A (30 : 1)
	1 (Moderate vulnerability)	A (4.5 : 1)	A (30 : 1)	A (30 : 1)
	2 (Considerable vulnerability)	A (3.6 : 1)	A (30 : 1)	A (30 : 1)
A = 2, D = 1, Attacker Considerably Stronger	0.5 (Relative invulnerability)	A (2.5 : 1)	A (4.5 : 1)	A (30 : 1)
	1 (Moderate vulnerability)	A (2 : 1)	A (4 : 1)	A (19 : 1)
	2 (Considerable vulnerability)	A (1.5 : 1)	A (3 : 1)	A (18 : 1)
A = 1, D = 1, Attacker and Defender Equal	0.5 (Relative invulnerability)	D (1.4 : 1)	D (1 : 1)	A (2 : 1)
	1 (Moderate vulnerability)	D (1.6 : 1)	D (1.3 : 1)	A (1.6 : 1)
	2 (Considerable vulnerability)	D (1.6 : 1)	D (1.3 : 1)	A (1.3 : 1)

TABLE 5 (*Cont'd*)

Results of a Hypothetical Counterforce Exchange

RATIO OF INITIAL STRENGTH (1 = 500 delivery units)	*Attacker Vulnerability* (V^A)	RATIO OF SURVIVING DELIVERY UNITS — *Defender Vulnerability* (V^D): 0.5 (Relative invulner- ability)	1 (Moderate vulner- ability)	2 (Considerable vulner- ability)
A = 1 D = 2 Defender Considerably Stronger	0.5 (Relative invulnerability)	D (3.4 : 1)	D (3.1 : 1)	D (2.6 : 1)
	1 (Moderate vulnerability)	D (3.4 : 1)	D (3.1 : 1)	D (2.6 : 1)
	2 (Considerable vulnerability)	D (3.4 : 1)	D (3.1 : 1)	D (2.6 : 1)
A = 1 D = 3 Defender Much Stronger	0.5 (Relative invulnerability)	D (5 : 1)	D (5 : 1)	D (4 : 1)
	1 (Moderate vulnerability)	D (5 : 1)	D (5 : 1)	D (4 : 1)
	1 (Considerable vulnerability)	D (5 : 1)	D (5 : 1)	D (4 : 1)

Analysis of a Hypothetical Counterforce Exchange

For this example, it is necessary to make some arbitrary assumptions in assigning values for the numerous variables outlined in the text. The selections made could be challenged on several grounds, but they are are at least within a realistic range.

Let us assume that country *A* makes a surprise attack on country *D*—for defender. The attacker's total number of striking units (*A*) might be reduced by a reserve of 0.25*A* (including pre-launch failures and units not in a ready status), so that $0.75A$ are scheduled for launch. Attrition (losses to air defenses), post-launch aborts, and allocation to suppression of air defenses or to feints, might cause an over-all reduction of one-half (0.5). Applying to this a reliability-accuracy factor of 0.8 gives a net "on target" of 0.3 ($0.75 \times 0.5 \times 0.8$) of *A*'s total strength. This is conservative from the attacker's viewpoint, but necessarily so.

The defender's target system vulnerability (V^D) can be expressed as the number of military striking units incapacitated by each on-target delivery unit, taking into account multiple bombs in a single delivery unit and the possibility of a single hit knocking out several aircraft or missiles on a base, as well as the likelihood that some of the well-hardened sites may require a targeting ratio of 3 or more to 1 to assure a high probability of destruction. Thus, a V^D of 2 would permit 600 attacker's delivery units to take out 1,200 strategic military targets, and a V^D of 0.5 would require two attacking units on target for each one of the defender's.

We might further assume that 10 per cent of the defender's striking units (*D*) are so hardened or mobile as to be untargetable, or are launched successfully in the few minutes warning available. The remaining 90 per cent are reduced by the damage from the attacker's strike, as indicated above; and the balance (less a 25 per cent reserve, pre-launch failures that can be repaired, etc.,) are used in strikes against the attacker's remaining vital military forces. Here also an attrition rate of 0.5 and a 0.8 reliability factor are applied. If we similarly assume that the invulnerable one-tenth of *A*'s forces is included in *A's* reserve of $0.25A$, the remaining $0.15A$ is reduced by the defender's counterattack, weighted by the attacker's target system vulnerability (V^A). If we then take account of usable units from recycling aircraft and reloading undamaged missile launchers, assumed to be one-tenth of the initial launch, we can arrive at a ratio of surviving striking units for each side at the end of the first exchange. We could then proceed to estimate the results of succeeding exchanges in like fashion. However, for our purposes, the initial strikes will suffice.

Table 5 is a matrix which uses constants for all factors but initial strength and attacker and defender vulnerability. Because the results are affected by the use of small numbers, it is assumed that the initial strength ratios are expressed in units of 500 delivery vehicles. The table shows the surviving delivery units as a ratio favoring one side or the other, as of the end of the initial strike and counterstrike.

So that the reader can better follow the derivation of the surviving ratios, let us go through the case where *A* has a favorable initial ratio of 3 to 1, and both *A* and *D* are relatively invulnerable (0.5), i.e., the top left hand box of the table. Of its 1,500 vehicles, *A* keeps a reserve of 0.25 or 375 (of which 150 are invulnerable) and launches 1,125; of those launched, 450 are assumed to be over target, and to destroy one of *D*'s delivery vehicles for every two launched—a total damage of 225.

Of *D*'s original 500, 50 are assumed invulnerable, and 450 are targeted, leaving him with 225 plus the 50, or 275. He keeps 0.25 or about 69 in reserve and launches 206, of which 0.4 or 82 arrive over target. They destroy 41 of

A's remaining vulnerable forces, leaving *A* with 334. Then if *A* can recycle 10 per cent of his initial launch, or 113, his surviving total is 447. *D* has his reserve of 69, plus 10 per cent of his launch to recycle (21), making a surviving total of 90 delivery units. The ratio after the first exchange is therefore roughly 5 to 1 in favor of *A*, as shown in the table.

The implications of the table and some additional qualifications are discussed in the text.

which is extremely vulnerable. Or, if its own forces were sufficiently secure, it could concentrate its attack upon the vulnerable *portions* of the larger enemy force and thus gain a more favorable ratio. Many other qualifications also apply, so that there is no magic to the particular ratios derived in Table 5. But the example does support the proposition that within limits, relative numbers are relevant to strategic superiority. And they will remain relevant until a very large part of the forces of both sides are almost completely invulnerable and the over-all size is proportional to the target system. Finally, it should be recognized that significant improvements in the air defense and especially missile defense capabilities of either side could affect the strategic balance as much as the size and vulnerability of the offensive forces and further enhance the relevance of numbers.

So far, we have been discussing only the surviving force ratio on the assumption that both sides were constrained to play the counterforce game. But since this is at best uncertain, we must also consider casualties and civil damage—which are even more relevant criteria of war outcomes in terms of "winning" or "losing." If, in the foregoing example, *D* used the invulnerable and surviving portion of its forces to retaliate against *A*'s population centers, the damage could be staggering. It would be of small comfort that *A*'s remaining force ratio was very favorable or that *A* could destroy an even larger proportion of *D*'s society. We shall examine the implications of this for the current East-West strategic balance below. Nevertheless, in terms of the calculus of deterrence, the option of a partially disarming strike available to the superior force is worth something, even though it cannot preclude retaliation.

The Current Strategic Balance

Britain's authoritative Institute for Strategic Studies publishes an annual analysis of the East-West military balance. For 1963-1964, it credits the United States with 630 long-range B-52 bombers, some carrying long-range air-to-ground missiles, 90 of the newer B-58s, and about 600 medium-range B-47 jet bombers, (which are, however, being phased out), serviced by a KC-135 fleet of aerial tankers numbering close to 600. Britain, in addition, contributes some 180 V-bombers to NATO's strategic delivery capability, and France will shortly have several dozen light bombers supported by tankers.

In intercontinental ballistic missiles, the United States reportedly entered 1964 with over 126 liquid-fueled Atlas and 108 Titan missiles, plus about 200 solid-fueled and hardened Minuteman missiles, and 10 nuclear-powered submarines, each with 16 Polaris missiles—a total of 160. Additional missiles are deployed in Europe, although the Royal Air Force's obsolescent Thor squadrons (60 missiles) and the 45 Jupiters in Italy and Turkey have been, or are in process of being, phased out. Several hundred of the Navy's carrier-borne attack aircraft are capable of making devastating nuclear strikes, as are many of the tactical fighter-bomber squadrons in NATO.[20]

According to published summaries, by 1965 the United States

[20] Institute for Strategic Studies, *The Military Balance, 1963-1964* (London: 1963). These figures are generally consistent with those cited in official testimony and speeches. (Many of the major speeches and congressional testimony are conveniently abstracted in Michael Brower's "Nuclear Strategy of the Kennedy Administration," *Bulletin of the Atomic Scientists*, October 1962). The annual Defense Department's Armed Forces Day Speakers Guide (Washington: Dept. of Defense, Office of Public Affairs) is also a useful compendium. Secretary McNamara's January 27, 1964 statement to the House Armed Services Committee on the 1965 Defense budget is, like the 1963 statement cited above, particularly valuable. The 1964 testimony indicated (p. 36) that the U.S. would have 630 B-52's and 600 Minuteman missiles by July 1964—a considerably larger number of missiles than that cited by the ISS. The Secretary later announced that the U.S. has 750 ICBMs on launches, while Russia "has less than one-fourth that number in operation." *The Washington Post,* April 15, 1964, p. 1.

will have over 1,500 long-range missiles (rising to 1,700 by 1968) plus some 700 bombers capable of intercontinental attacks, of which only about one-fourth will require in-flight refueling.[21] Many of the planes can carry several nuclear weapons as bombs and/or air-to-ground missiles such as Hound Dog. Thus the mid-1960s should see the United States with a long-range strategic delivery force of about 2,500 vehicles. Former Deputy Defense Secretary Gilpatric has said the United States has "tens of thousands" of nuclear delivery vehicles, when tactical systems are included, with more than one warhead for each vehicle.[22] More recently, Mr. Khrushchev has referred to a U.S. ability to deliver 40,000 nuclear bombs on Russia, which may or may not be an exaggeration.

As for the Soviets, they are credited in *The Military Balance 1963-1964* of the Institute for Strategic Studies with about 100 operational ICBMs of the first and second liquid-fueled generations, about 200 long-range Bison and Bear bombers, capable of carrying winged missiles, plus small numbers of newer models, and about 1,000 medium-range Badger aircraft, for which there are relatively few tankers or other refueling facilities. They also muster a formidable force of perhaps 750 medium-range ballistic missiles (MRBMs) which, while posing a major threat to Europe, cannot attack the United States from Russian territory. The Russians also deploy a large number of submarines, of which perhaps twenty are nuclear powered. Some of them undoubtedly are capable of launching missiles, although at present these appear to be shorter-range versions which cannot be launched submerged. But within a very few years, a much less vulnerable Soviet counterpart of the Polaris can be expected.

The current East-West strategic balance, mainly the forces of the United States and the U.S.S.R., is summarized in Table 6,

[21] Deputy Secretary of Defense Gilpatric, Speech of May 2, 1962, and Secretary McNamara's February 6, 1963 testimony. See also Kaufmann, cited, p. 283.

[22] Speech to the Business Advisory Council, Hot Springs, Va., October 21, 1961 (Dept. of Defense Press Release, October 21, 1961).

which suggests that the United States now has an edge of three-to-one in intercontinental delivery units.

TABLE 6
*Some Estimates of Comparative Strategic Strength**
Early 1964

Category	*Western Alliances*	*Communist Bloc*
ICBMs (over 2,500 mile range)	475	100+
Fleet Ballistic Missiles	192	100
IRBMs and MRBMs (600-2,100 mile range)	—	800
Long-range bombers (over 5,000 mile range)	630	200
Medium-range land-based bombers (over 2,000 miles, excluding carrier air-based aircraft)	780	1,400
Carrier-based bombers (over 2,000 mile range)	600	—
Carriers (including Commando and Escort carriers)	38 (37)	—
Cruisers	33 (25)	19 (2)
Escorts	742 (358)	124 (248)
Nuclear Submarines	33	23
Conventional submarines	219 (42)	446 (55)
Active Forces: (a) Armies	5,696,300	6,035,000
(b) Navies	1,211,269	661,800
(c) Air Forces	1,658,775	771,000

Figures in brackets denote ships in reserve.
*Reprinted, with permission, from Table III, *The Military Balance 1963-1964,* The Institute for Strategic Studies, London.

However, if one adds Soviet medium-range missiles and bombers, the NATO-Soviet ratio is more like five-to-four; and if a larger proportion of satellite air forces are included, it may approach parity in potential delivery vehicles, though not in quality or in numbers, variety and yield of nuclear weapons.

As we shall see in Chapter 4, this fact—and especially the medium-range missile threat to Europe—is behind some of

NATO's current problems. Yet, unless the West is very foolish and General de Gaulle's views come to dominate, the Soviets should be unable to separate the United States and Europe strategically. This means that, at least for counterforce calculations, the Soviet Union must consider the intercontinental balance and the long-range power of the United States.

Looking to the future, the Soviets will certainly increase the numbers and quality of their strategic weapons. No accurate predictions can be made, of course, but assuming no order-of-magnitude increase in the Soviet defense effort, even to hold the West to the three-to-one ratio against them will cost the Soviet Union considerable effort. To reduce their inferiority even to two-to-one would mean still greater sacrifices in agricultural and industrial investment, as well as in consumer production.

These figures constitute a rather sharp reversal of the gloomy predictions of several years ago to the effect that by now a missile gap would exist in favor of the Soviet Union. A word of explanation might therefore be in order. In the first place, predictions about future Soviet missile strengths had to be based on speculation in the light of what the Soviets appeared capable of doing, since there was no way to predict what they would, in fact, do. Even the lowest of these estimates tended to put them ahead of the force structure programmed for the United States. But then two things happened: the Soviet Union failed to produce anything like the number of missiles anticipated, while the United States, in effect, accomplished a breakthrough with solid propellant missiles so that, its Polaris and Minuteman systems became operational ahead of schedule. Thus, the long-range missile gap turned out to favor the United States. The revised estimates also reflect improved Western intelligence, presumably including data from the U-2 project which came in until the Summit Meeting in 1960.[23] Top officials have subsequently spoken with sufficient assurance about the missile balance to imply continuing confidence in intelligence on

[23] See David Wise and Thomas B. Ross, *The U-2 Affair* (New York: Random House, 1962), pp. 57, 263.

Soviet missile strength. Hanson Baldwin, for example, has reported that "intelligence data on Soviet missiles . . . are considered quite reliable by Washington."[24]

Having already examined a hypothetical situation in this chapter, we can now apply the foregoing figures to the real world. The approximate three-to-one advantage in intercontinental missiles existing in favor of the United States is the ratio examined in Table 5. What would happen if the Soviets made a massive attack, aimed primarily at major urban centers, in the hope of causing sufficient destruction and casualties to render the United States incapable of a retaliatory strike?

There is little doubt that from 3,000 to 5,000 megatons could be delivered and that this total could destroy many of the major urban areas of the United States even without one hundred-plus megaton "monsters." Certainly, 75 per cent or more damage could be done to the more than fifty so-called standard metropolitan areas. In the absence of more than a token civil defense effort, immediate blast-thermal-radiation casualties might run as high as 80 million to 100 million, with another 24 million to 40 million dying of fallout and indirect consequences in subsequent weeks. This total of about three-fourths of the population is consistent with some published estimates of civil defense studies and with the Secretary of Defense's testimony.[25]

In an all-out general war in which Soviet medium-range missiles were targeted on European cities, the additional casualties in NATO Europe might be as high as, or probably higher than, those in the United States. It is no exaggeration to say that the Soviet

[24] *The New York Times,* July 26, 1962.

[25] See, for example, Fryklund, cited, p. 5; Arthur T. Hadley, *The Nation's Safety and Arms Control* (New York: Viking Press, 1961), p. 34, who estimates that 75-80 per cent of the U.S. population would be casualties in a 5,000-megaton attack. However, Herman Kahn in *On Thermonuclear War,* cited, p. 35, gives somewhat lower estimates of 50-80 million casualties. Secretary McNamara (February 6, 1963 statement, cited, p. 30) merely refers to "tens of millions"; before the Senate Foreign Relations Committee, however, he quoted the President's figure of 300 million Americans, Europeans, and Russians. *The New York Times,* August 14, 1963.

Union would have destroyed the United States and the major nations of Europe as going entities, although depending on the pre-attack preparations, a partial recuperation might take place over a period of many decades. Just how long is a matter of continuing debate among the experts. Herman Kahn, who is admittedly optimistic, estimates that the United States could, with proper preparations, recoup the loss of 50 major metropolitan areas and up to 20 million dead in 10 years. The extreme pessimists, on the other hand, measure post-attack time in centuries. Of course, the key question is what preparatory measures will have been taken. We shall return to this point briefly in the next section.

Now what can the Soviet planner expect in return for this wholesale destruction? He has left a substantial portion of U.S. striking power intact by concentrating on cities. U.S. forces are already dispersed, protected, and mobile; and assuming that there is a surviving command and control system, to which much attention continues to be devoted, the United States might still have roughly two-thirds of its original force intact. This would be more than sufficient to eliminate virtually all Soviet residual striking power and deliver devastating retaliatory damage to Soviet cities. Their lower population density and greater passive defense preparations might limit Soviet casualties from the 5,000-plus megatons delivered to 50 or 60 per cent of the population, or over 100 million. Thus, the initial exchange would end with comparable and appalling damage on both sides. Counting European casualties, up to 300 million lives might have been sacrificed and the United States would still retain a preponderance of the surviving nuclear power, which is not a result to tempt the Soviet planner.

What if the Soviets took the other option, and concentrated on U.S. striking power in the hope of eliminating as much as possible, while deliberately avoiding U.S. cities? In this hypothetical counterforce exchange, discussed previously, the attacker starts with a ratio of three-to-one against him. Even with the advantages of striking first, the attacker could wind up the initial exchange on the short end of the five-to-one ratio given in Table 5. A Defense

Department spokesman has pointed out that the destructive power which the United States could bring to bear, even after a Soviet surprise attack upon our forces, would be as great as—perhaps greater than—the total undamaged force which the enemy could launch against the United States in a first strike.[26] This is such a clearly losing proposition that it is difficult to see the Soviet Union making any kind of a rational attack on the United States. If, nevertheless, it did so on a counterforce basis, the blast casualties on both sides would be relatively low—mainly in populated areas adjoining air bases and missile installations—and it is not always possible to separate civil and military targets. However, the fall-out and collateral damage from several thousand megatons of fission products delivered in this exchange could cause a range of from 2 million to 25 million casualties on each side (depending, of course, on whether the attacker used air bursts and small-yield weapons, and particularly on the fallout protection available). This is a shocking figure in human terms, but distinctly a less awful result than the hundreds of millions of casualties from a "city-busting" war. If the Soviet Union tried a "mix"—that is, attacked both civilian and military targets, it lacks the numbers to insure complete success in either category, and the consequences would be somewhere between those discussed in the two examples given. (Of course, not many megatons would have to be diverted from military targets to the largest cities in order to produce heavy civil damage.) In short, the Soviets have no good strategic options.

A surprise attack by the United States would be contrary to all American traditions and concepts of morality, as well as explicitly against its current policies. But it has, through its overseas commitments, especially to Europe, a stated policy of first use of nuclear weapons, if necessary, in response to Soviet aggression. And the use might have to be strategic. As the late President Kennedy pointed out in an interview with Stewart Alsop, "in some circumstances we might have to take the initiative,"[27] although he

[26] Deputy Secretary of Defense Gilpatric, Hot Springs speech, cited.
[27] Stewart Alsop, "Kennedy's Grand Strategy," *Saturday Evening Post*, March 31, 1962.

clearly did not have in mind an unprovoked initiative. We cannot afford to guarantee that, where its vital interests are threatened, the United States will never launch the first nuclear strike, for example, if the Soviet forces should start to overrun Western Europe. In strategy, ambiguity is usually too important an asset to remove it entirely and thereby enable enemy planners to concentrate only on one range of possibilities. In practice, we have seen that Soviet planners must always consider the theoretical possibility of such a U.S. first strike in weighing the escalation risks from various actions.

Applying the same assumptions discussed previously to the case of U.S. initiative, the five hundred-plus delivery units which could be expected to reach Soviet targets could easily destroy several hundred cities with total casualties running from 60 to 80 per cent of the population (depending on whether the attack sought to maximize fallout, and on Soviet shelter facilities and the amount of warning received) and many military targets, e.g., in the rejected "optimum mix" type of attack. One writer has calculated that in a maximum destruction effort, using all U.S. forces, the United States could deliver 18 to 20 kilo-megatons (i.e., 18,000 to 20,000 megatons) on the Soviet Union.[28] While the United States could thus vastly reduce the amount of retaliatory power left in the Soviet Union, some delivery capability would be left in mobile or specially hardened systems. Since there would be no incentive for the Soviets to do other than seek maximum devastation, several large-yield weapons could be delivered on U.S. cities, causing a casualty range somewhere between that for the Soviet first strike against cities and the first strike against military forces. Western Europe would probably be much more severely damaged. This result would be so disastrous for the West that a U.S. strike of this type could serve no rational purpose whatever. Moreover, a policy of deliberately initiating a nuclear attack on cities would be beyond the bounds of any conceivable morality

[28] Hadley, cited, p. 33.

—an act which would make the Nazi extermination of the Jews pale in comparison.

Russia's extremely large-yield weapons are probably not especially effective for counterforce purposes, although they may have some terror value as an instrument of blackmail and intimidation, i.e., from a minimum deterrence standpoint. The blast from a 27-megaton bomb is only 3 times as great and its point-target effectiveness 9 times (rather than 27 times) as great as a 1-megaton bomb.[29] However, large-yield weapons produce thermal effects which could incinerate whole areas, extremely heavy fallout, and electromagnetic and other results of an unpredictable nature.[30] Khrushchev himself once noted that his 50-megaton and 100-megaton weapons may be too large to use in Europe, because of the fallout consequences for the Soviet Union. Nevertheless, such weapons might conceivably be used in a last-gasp response by a dying dictator who had seen his country obliterated in a massive and indiscriminate enemy attack.

In the last analysis, the least disadvantageous, and the only remotely rational use of strategic nuclear weapons is in a controlled and limited counterforce context. Threatened or implied use may be something else again, although to be credible, the threat normally must bear some relationship to rational use, unless the threatener is deliberately playing up the possibility of an irrational response. Returning again to our hypothetical example, we now have the attacker starting with a favorable three-to-one ratio. Assuming even moderate Soviet vulnerability, the United States

[29] Blast increases with the cube of the yield, and the probability of damage to a point target or area coverage goes up with the two-third power of the yield. See the U.S. Department of Defense and U.S. Atomic Energy Commission, *The Effects of Nuclear Weapons* (Washington, GPO, 1962), revised edition, p. 127.

[30] An AEC Press Release of October 31, 1961, described the effects of very high yield nuclear detonations. Some of the data has been incorporated into the revised edition of the weapons effects handbook cited in footnote 29. Also, it is possible that the yields could be made even higher. There has been speculation that the 58-megaton bomb tested by the Soviets was intended to demonstrate the possibility of a 500-megaton explosion or larger.

could emerge with an extremely favorable ratio of surviving forces. But this would still not enable American cities to escape destruction if the Soviet Union chose to use its surviving forces for that purpose. However, that would be a suicidal choice, for Russian cities could be destroyed ten times over in retaliation. Thus, the United States would have achieved a decisive superiority of power, for the purpose of forcing an end to the war and dictating a favorable settlement, though not perhaps an unconditional surrender.

We noted at the outset that force size was one major element of the various strategic alternatives. In rejecting the "overkill" approach, and what I termed "minimum deterrence," (cities only) and the "full first strike" theory (or "pure" counterforce), Secretary McNamara has adopted the term "damage limiting." It describes a force capable of striking back not only against cities but also against all remaining enemy missiles and aircraft, so as to limit the damage he can do with them. Obviously the "damage limiting" approach is applicable to either a first or second nuclear strike situation–although in different degrees. It thus is broad enough to include the coercive and psychological aspects I have incorporated into the "controlled and limited" counterforce concept.[31]

Looking ahead, one imagines the uses of nuclear weapons for demonstrative purposes (as distinct from a disarming or counterforce attack) to raise the level of violence and signal determination. Obviously such an act would entail grave risks, and would be used only as a next-to-last step and in defense of the most vital interests, such as Berlin. But superiority of strategic power would be an essential ingredient of the ability to initiate even such a "limited" strategic war.[32]

This Western advantage of flexibility in strategy and superiority

[31] See Secretary McNamara's January 27, 1964, House Armed Services Committee statement, cited, pp. 29-32.

[32] The limited employment of strategic weapons in conjunction with bargaining is discussed in some detail in *Limited Strategic War*, edited by Klaus Knorr and Thornton Read, Princeton Studies in World Politics (New York: Praeger, 1963).

in quality and quantity of strategic weapons can to some degree be used to support a firmer and more forward strategy in the cold war, should this become necessary. But one cannot push luck too far. Whatever the theoretical "outcome," there are situations in which a major power might feel compelled to fight, no matter what the consequences. The United States could not, for example, demand that the Soviets evacuate Eastern Europe under threat of initiating a "limited counterforce" attack. The risks of irrational reaction or miscalculation leading to a desperate Soviet effort to get in a first strike would be altogether too high. Then, too, there are always possibilities of serious error in the execution of such an attack. There can be no absolute certainty, and anything less is inadequate when one is dealing with millions of human lives. Even a "clean," no-cities, nuclear war would be terrible at best, with serious collateral damage owing to the proximity of civil to military targets. And there can be no assurance ahead of time that such a conflict would stay "clean."

Some people believe that the Pentagon is full of militarists who would like to wage a "preventive" war. Nothing could be further from the truth. The moral considerations are a most important factor; and American officers are not, on the whole, any less sensitive to their bearing on questions of nuclear war than other citizens. Also the military profession is by nature a conservative one. The British did not risk their fleet at Jutland, despite the opportunities for a decisive engagement, because if they lost, the right arm of the Empire would be gone. Since military power is the ultimate protection of the state, those who wield it are among the last to risk its destruction. Only a Hitler could override this innate military conservatism. We must all hope he was the last of his kind.

The Strategic Implications of Interdependence

There are two strategic implications of the interdependence which Part I postulated as the essential relationship between America and Europe. The first is that the two sides of the Atlantic must be indivisible from the standpoint of defense. According to Article 5 of the North Atlantic Treaty, an armed attack against one shall be considered an attack against all, although the commitment was only to take such action as each party deemed necessary. That this commitment implied "all for all" was taken for granted until the emergence of a Soviet ability to visit nuclear devastation on American cities began to arouse doubts about the American guarantee. As suggested in Chapter 4, these doubts and any resulting tendencies toward de-coupling American power from Europe must be resolved; for if they set in motion a separatist trend, or if the political factors which motivate the Gaullist views come to dominate, Europe may in fact become the "hostage" which the Soviets already claim it is. If American strategic power were ever withdrawn from protecting Europe, that area would be at an overwhelming military disadvantage against the Soviet Union. But, as long as the two are indissolubly linked, then not just America, but NATO as a whole will possess the strategic superiority described in the preceding section. Russia itself then becomes communism's hostage to the West!

There should be only one nuclear strategy for the defense of interdependent partners—and it should be global rather than regional; for the potential enemy disposes of continental power, from the Mediterranean to the Pacific. This does not mean that Europe cannot come to play a more active and responsible role with respect to nuclear power. On the contrary, adjustments in the *status quo* are necessary and desirable. NATO should have a common strategic approach developed through group consultation, and not imposed by the Americans alone. The strategic monologue must become an effective dialogue.

The controlled and restrained counterforce or damage-limiting option outlined in this chapter appears to be the optimum strategy for the West as a whole, for the next several years at least. While it has the flexibility to accommodate forces with different missions and alternative targeting policies, it nevertheless should be based upon the rock of strategic indivisibility. But whether or not adjustments in this concept prove necessary as a result of trans-Atlantic dialogue, Europe and America cannot afford to be defended by different strategies which would weaken and divide the forces at their disposal and could lead to strategic independence rather than interdependence. We shall discuss the ways and means of managing strategic power in the interest of both America and Europe in the next chapter.

The second implication is that neither America nor Europe can be engaged in major hostilities anywhere in the world without the other also being potentially involved. Britain shares American commitments in CENTO and elsewhere via Commonwealth links; and both Britain and France share them in SEATO. This is the logical result of the free world's alliance system. Europeans can cite Suez as a failure of this system; and the United States can point to frequent differences with France and Britain in various Asian conflicts. The 1962 Cuban crisis particularly exposed the problem. Some Europeans complain that the unilateral American actions could have involved them in a nuclear war without consultation, and claim that they backed the United States after the fact only because they had no other choice. There could perhaps have been more advance consultation; however the issue was not Cuba, but an attempt by the Soviets to alter the balance of missile power. Had they succeeded in that blackmail of the United States, on the next occasion, say in Berlin, the entire alliance would have suffered. As Lord Home put it in discussing Cuba, "if America is threatened, we are threatened."[33] By the same token, when the Suez adventure engendered Soviet threats against Britain and France, the United States reportedly reacted by alerting SAC, notwithstanding its firm opposition to the invasion, for it too was thereby threatened.[34]

This interdependence outside the Atlantic area is necessary for two reasons. First, serious limited conflict in which a major Com-

[33] *The New York Times Magazine,* November 25, 1962.

[34] See Herman Finer, *Dulles Over Suez* (Chicago: Quadrangle Books, 1964), p. 421.

munist power is involved could escalate; it is the strategic nuclear deterrent which provides the ultimate restraint. To be effective, a seamless umbrella of nuclear power must cover the West's vital interests. Second, apart from the escalation problem, there may be political requirements for solidarity in order to rally support from the non-Communist community as a whole. Unfortunately the postwar period has been marked by the absence of such cooperation between America and Europe on a number of occasions. In part the explanation lies in the so-called colonial issues and U.S. support of U.N. activities on several controversial matters. But it also reflects the gradual withdrawal of effective French and British military power from Asia, Africa, and the Middle East, and the resulting pressures on the United States to fill the gap by assisting local forces and providing defensive alliances.

In the long term, NATO must resolve the political differences which have marred its reactions to non-Atlantic crises, but discussion of this difficult task is best deferred to Part III. In the long term too, if America and Europe are to meet the over-all challenge by working in harness, Europe must participate extensively in global military planning and activities. For the present, Britain is already finding it difficult to maintain and modernize its forces east of Suez, partly because of the emphasis on expensive nuclear forces. French preoccupation with the *force de frappe*, to be discussed in the next chapter, likewise handicaps its efforts, although the over-all modernization program now underway may eventually bear some fruits in terms of mobility. In any case, there are higher priorities for the European members of NATO within their own continent. Consequently, during the next several years the main burden of non-European defense will have to be borne by the United States. However, America ought to consider this role as one of defending NATO and the free world, as opposed to purely national interests. Since Europe is inherently involved in what the United States does, American leadership is all to the good; but it must be exerted in an atmosphere of NATO consultation and as far ahead of events as possible.

Other Elements of Security

Because the West's strategic nuclear superiority will not be effective in all situations, and since the prospects in a nuclear war—especially for Europe—are already bad and are getting worse, deterrence requires a spectrum of capabilities, including the ability to fight at whatever level is needed if deterrence fails. Fortunately, a growing number of competent authors on both sides of the Atlantic are addressing themselves to such topics as limited war, counterguerrilla warfare, mobility and civil defense; for these must be recognized as important components of the over-all strategy for the West. A subsequent chapter deals with the tactical defenses of Europe in considerable detail; but elsewhere the requirement for expanded limited war forces, as noted above, falls mainly upon the United States.

Limited Conflicts Outside of NATO

The United States has taken a number of major steps in the past two years to increase the strength, conventional firepower, and mobility of its nonstrategic forces. These have included a doubling in the number of ready combat divisions in the army's Strategic Reserve; an increase in troops deployed in Europe; expansion in sealift and airlift capacity; a modernization of weapons and ammunition, and a build-up in antiguerrilla forces and in the marines. The U.S. active fleet has increased by more than seventy vessels and its tactical air forces by over a dozen wings.[35]

These actions have brought about a significant increase in local war capability. Restrictions which have hampered the development of army aviation are also being eased—to the point that the army reportedly has the world's third largest air force, following only that of the U.S.S.R. and the U.S. air force!

But there are still some logistic weaknesses. For example, if the

[35] Secretary McNamara's February 1963 statement to the House Defense Appropriations Subcommittee, cited, contained a wealth of detail on all of these points. See especially his discussion of the General Purpose Forces, pp. 51-81. The Secretary's speech to the Economic Club of New York, November 18, 1963, (Dept. of Defense Press Release), explains the rationale for the non-nuclear buildup. See also Kaufmann, cited, Chs. 2, 8 and Epilogue.

United States should be involved in simultaneous limited conflicts in the Far East, and, say, in Iran, it would be extemely difficult to support both. Mobilization measures might be required, introducing considerable delays. Even a three or four division operation in Iran could severely tax the available airlift and sealift. Prepositioning of supplies and the earmarking and training of advance detachments to implement various contingency plans could reduce these weaknesses; and some measures along these lines are under consideration. The creation of the Strike Command which integrated the army's STRAC (Strategic Army Corps) with elements of the air force's Tactical Air Command, is a significant step toward an effective, mobile fire brigade force. It has recently taken over contingency planning responsibility for areas of the world not covered by other unified commands. This reorganization is important from the NATO standpoint because the need for an immediate response, as in Lebanon, has sometimes required the United States to withdraw combat and support troops and supplies from the NATO area. To some extent this may be unavoidable, but the less the reliance on forces committed to NATO to meet responsibilities in other areas, the better.

It is difficult to assess the role of nuclear weapons in limited wars. Once it would have been very difficult for the United States to conduct a major non-nuclear operation, when bomb racks and shackles, for example, were fittted to nuclear rather than high-explosive bombs, and adequate non-nuclear ordnance was not always available at the places needed. The Kennedy administration's defense budgets provided for a sizable increase in production of new and more effective types of non-nuclear ordnance and for modification of tactical aircraft to enable delivery of heavier loads.[36] Secretary of Defense McNamara believes that the United States has sufficient active forces—and that they continue to be further strengthened—for the initial stages of conflict without resorting to nuclear weapons in areas *other* than Europe.[37]

[36] Dept. of Defense Speakers Guide, 1962, cited, footnote 20, p. 5.
[37] February 6, 1963, House Subcommittee statement, p. 55.

While this ability to meet challenges at the non-nuclear level is all to the good, it would not be appropriate to go to the other extreme of being unable to back up conventional forces with the threat of tactical nuclear weapons—or psychologically inhibited from using them if necessary. Such an ability is important, both to limit the enemy's options of escalating the conflict and to maintain at least a small element of ambiguity about U.S. intentions. For example, the possibility that the United States might resort to tactical nuclear weapons should induce enemy caution in massing forces, for instance in a Communist Chinese invasion of Formosa. It might also be necessary to employ nuclear weapons in an air defense role, to prevent an enemy from attaining air superiority. The rising challenge of Communist China—and the delicate nuances of its split with Russia—may require more rather than less American-European consultation and cooperation.

Counterinsurgency

Another category of conflict that is currently receiving a great deal of emphasis is variously known as sub-limited warfare, counterinsurgency, countersubversion or counterguerrilla warfare. The classic example of such activity is Viet-Nam, where the responsibility for supporting the local government has fallen almost exclusively to the United States. British advice has already been useful, drawing on the experiences in Malaya, and this area may be one in which greater coordination of tactics and equipment with our European allies would be productive—given a harmonization of objectives (General de Gaulle, however, currently seems to want to fish in these waters for motives of his own, rather than assisting in a common effort). The West's experience has shown that types of equipment developed for other kinds of warfare are, in many cases, inapplicable for fighting in Southeast Asia. Western rifles are sometimes too heavy for small Asian soldiers. Light, high-speed boats have special applicability to the many waterways in guerrilla infested areas; lightweight communications are in great demand; and new techniques are needed for surveillance and identification of personnel. This area also could furnish opportunities for effective use of nonlethal chemical warfare, in the interest of controlling escalation and limiting casualties. In these and many other areas, cooperative research, development and test programs could be worked out with allied countries indigenous to the areas concerned, and those members of NATO with relevant experience.

Passive Defense

There is considerable objection to major civil defense programs on the same ground as the opposition to some of the strategic nuclear views discussed earlier. Those who advocate an extreme form of minimum deterrence seek to make the consequences of nuclear warfare so unacceptable that it "could not" occur. To them, civil defense measures tend to mitigate the consequences of nuclear war and thus make it more likely. This view is contrary to the best strategic thought.

Except in this extreme view that populations should consciously be made as vulnerable as possible (as hostages to the peaceful behavior of their governments), it makes no sense to refrain deliberately from measures that could save millions of lives in the event of a nuclear war. This had been the position of the Kennedy administration, which transferred civil defense responsibilities to the Department of Defense and initiated a nation-wide shelter program. It should be clear that at least a major fallout protection program is the logical counterpart of the attempt to restrain and control the consequences of nuclear war. The emerging doctrine of controlled and limited response is based in part upon the possibility that nuclear weapons will be used against military targets rather than cities. Then—assuming the Soviets were constrained to follow the same rules, notwithstanding their present contrary strategy—civilian casualties would not result so much from blast as from fallout; and protective measures could mean the difference between 100 million casualties and several million.

Secretary McNamara has called civil defense an integral part of our over-all defense posture, and pointed out that the "effectiveness of an active ballistic missile defense system in saving lives depends in large part upon the availability of adequate fallout shelter for the population."[38] The basic passive defense requirements would appear to be:

> 1) maximum possible fallout protection for populations;
> 2) organization, equipment (such as communications and radiation monitoring devices) and a stockpile of food and other supplies to permit survival during a period of two to three weeks of intense radioactivity;
> 3) some hardening for blast protection of key governmental facilities and storage sites and provision for continuity of government;
> 4) insofar as possible, the removal of major counterforce targets from population centers; and
> 5) planning for contingencies in which strategic evacuation might be desirable.

The last point requires a brief comment. The advent of missiles and the resulting reduction in warning time have rendered impossible the tactical evacuation of large cities. But in a situation of great international tension, threatening the initiation of nuclear warfare, the option of at least partial evacuation of certain major urban areas might be desirable. The Russians are believed to have made a good start in this direction, by preparing evacuation plans for their large cities. It is argued that such evacuation is extremely provocative, that the enemy might interpret it as preparation for actual attack and therefore be tempted to pre-empt. There are some risks in this direction; but suppose the Soviet Union proceeded to evacuate its cities and threatened those of Europe and the United States? It would be too late then to improvise for the movement and care of large masses of people. As a minimum, therefore, more thought needs to be devoted to this problem. In-

[38] Same, p. 125.

dications that the United States was at least preparing to keep this option open over the uncertain course of the future would help support the credibility of the strategic deterrent.

Mobilization and Recovery Bases

Finally, there is the question of the mobilization base. For years, American military and civil planners have been divided between two concepts of nuclear war: a spasm-like 24-hour exchange of nuclear weapons in which any mobilization would be out of the question; and a highly unrealistic assumption of a World War II type of build-up and movement of troops and supplies overseas, notwithstanding the effect of enemy nuclear attacks. This has been sardonically described as "shipment of unavailable goods, supplied and loaded by people who have been killed, from ports that have been destroyed"—an unrealistic "broken back" war, in which each side would continue such military operations as it could mount while trying to recover from nuclear strikes. Apart from major thermonuclear war, many other circumstances might require a major increment in Western strength, such as the Berlin crisis of 1960-61. Particularly there is a need for local war mobilization capacity.

Stockpiles of some essential tools and supplies are also required, to try to keep the country alive after a nuclear attack and begin reconstruction. This enormous subject raises many problems of organization as well as stockpiling and mobilization policies. For example, a good case could be made for regrouping the reserve component structure of the armed forces into two categories. One would be called up for partial mobilization, as during the Berlin or Cuba incident, serving the traditional function of a "reserve." The other would have primarily a home guard mission, providing, in effect, the martial law which would almost certainly be required after a nuclear attack. We cannot categorically exclude certain requirements by assuming the nature of a possible nuclear war. At the same time, the United States cannot afford to cover all conceivable contingencies. We need a mobilization-base policy which covers the most likely requirements, especially for local war, provides some insurance for post-attack recuperation, and hedges, to the extent possible, against the military requirements for supplementing the forces in being, the forces which will inevitably be the decisive factor in a nuclear war.

Much remains to be done for realistic planning in this whole area of passive defense. Nowhere is this more true than with respect to NATO as a whole. If U.S. policies have been unclear, and in some cases even self-contradictory, those of Europe have been even more so. Under the premise of strategic indivisibility, it makes little sense for the United States to follow one set of policies and Europe another. There is always an enormous gap between what is practical in political and economic terms and what is theoretically desirable. Nevertheless, both for reducing the effects of a nuclear catastrophe and making it less likely to occur, a substantial reinvigoration of NATO's entire planning and operational structure for mobilization and passive defense is in order.

A final note on chemical and biological warfare is called for. From all public indications, protective measures in the West may lag behind those undertaken in the Soviet Union. The Soviets do not apparently share our "psychological blindness caused by the brilliant glare of publicity surrounding nuclear fission"; and they have an active interest in offensive usage of chemical and biological agents as well.[39] The potentialities of nonlethal incapacitating agents are far-reaching indeed. A surprise attack on a Western capital followed up by specially inoculated or protected troops could produce a *fait accompli* far more easily than conventional forces. The West cannot allow the Soviets to develop a lead in this area any more than in nuclear weapons. There are possibilities of self-administered immunity shots against biological agents, for example, which have not been fully explored. Yet a curious public apathy

[39] Cecil H. Coggins, "Is Russia Outstripping Us in Weapons of Mass Destruction?"; Speech before the Commonwealth Club of California, San Francisco, December 7, 1962. *Vital Speeches*, February 15, 1963, p. 263. The speaker, an M.D. as well as a retired Admiral and an official of the California State Disaster Office, has sounded an authoritative and timely warning.

and official silence have enveloped this whole area. Surely nothing is gained by ducking unpleasant realities in this field any more than with regard to nuclear weapons. Chemical and biological weapons are far more than a civil defense problem. Even their retaliatory use requires planning and readily available means of delivery. And if a nuclear stalemate should develop, these may be the strategic weapons of the future! As in many other areas, Europe's scientific and technical resources could usefully be co-opted into a realistic NATO focus on chemical and biological warfare.

* * *

In summary, what can be said about the West's strategic position? Although there are gaps in some of the supporting areas enumerated above, especially in the non-nuclear forces of the alliance, the United States, and hence NATO, has an incredibly powerful, well-protected, nuclear striking force. This force has the flexibility to carry out a counterforce type of strike intended to partially disarm an enemy, while retaining a secure reserve to deter retaliatory attacks on cities. Even in a second strike, these forces would still be superior to those of the Communist bloc striking first!

But because of the awesome consequences of any nuclear exchange, which will continue to worsen over time, the West's strategic superiority cannot, by itself, solve NATO's security problems, even though it remains the *sine qua non* of their solution. The paradox of our era is that nuclear warfare is too destructive and unpredictable to be an instrument of national policy, even though nuclear armaments and nuclear threats remain such instruments. The availability of force, in short, is a vital means of influencing an opponent, even if never employed in combat. It therefore becomes important to look at the future as Soviet military planners may see it.

Through the Soviet Looking Glass

Although Soviet society and Communist ideology exert a pervasive influence on military thought, they are not, by themselves, controlling. Evolution in strategic thinking occurs in the Soviet Union much as it does in other countries, reflecting national objectives and generally following rather than leading technology.

The Soviet Union has lagged behind the United States by several years in many aspects of military technology, and there has been an equivalent doctrinal lag in some areas. But there have been some Soviet innovations in strategic thinking, and Soviet strategy is sufficiently flexible and pragmatic that continual adjustments can be expected. The doctrinal lag seems to relate to the extent of practical experience as a nuclear power, as well as to the long lead-time involved in modern weapons. It exists in similar form in Europe. Britain's nuclear concepts have sometimes seemed to parallel those of the United States as of three years ago; and French military thought, in turn, is now about at the point Britain reached some years in the past.

In addition national strategy is naturally shaped by such factors as geography, traditions, alliances, and available resources. The Soviet Union, primarily concerned with consolidating its political control of the Eurasian land mass, has therefore stressed land armies and medium-range air power. By contrast the United States, which has had to contend with global responsibilities as the leader of a maritime coalition, has concentrated on strategic air and sea power. It is not surprising, then, that the advent of atomic weapons produced somewhat different strategies in the two countries at the outset. Stalinist Russia's initial reaction to atomic weapons was, in the words of one expert, "marked by the ostensible rejection of any belief in their exceptional importance. Since 1953, however, the Soviet Union has come to grips with the problems posed by the existence of these weapons."[40] The revision followed to some extent the cycle of Western attitudes discussed earlier in this chapter. After a period of emphasis on tactical atomic

[40] Herbert Dinerstein, "The Revolution in Soviet Strategic Thinking," *Foreign Affairs*, January 1958, p. 241, reprinted in *The Soviet Union, 1922-1962*, edited by Philip E. Mosely and Hamilton Fish Armstrong (New York: Praeger, for the Council on Foreign Relations, 1963), pp. 361-372.

weapons (the increased firepower viewpoint), the Malenkov faction proceeded "from the assumption that the destructiveness of nuclear weapons had created a real opportunity for reliance on a policy of deterring the United States." Conflict promptly ensued with both political and military leaders who believed that the Soviet armed forces had to be strengthened and that only capitalism would be destroyed in a nuclear war.

Ups and downs of this debate continued for the next several years. In Premier Khrushchev's January 1960 speech he explained the Soviet version of massive retaliation and emphasized nuclear warheads and rockets while proposing a cut in obsolescent conventional forces. This statement appeared to trigger anew the opposition of the military traditionalists (and budget claimants) who echoed some of the same thoughts about the inapplicability of nuclear weapons to all situations which had been heard in the West.

It is hard to assess the role which doctrinal disputes may have played in the subsequent cancellation of the planned force reduction, for this took place in the context of the U-2 incident and the Berlin crisis, which gave added weight to the arguments of the Russian military. However, the traditional sources of information upon which Western specialists on Soviet military thinking relied were supplemented in mid-1962 by a remarkable volume produced by a group of Soviet military experts and published by the Soviet Ministry of Defense. *Voennaya Strategiya* [Military Strategy][41] is, as its introduction indicates, the first work published since 1926

[41] Marshal V. D. Sokolovsky, ed., *Voennaya Strategiya* (Moscow: Soviet Ministry of Defense, May 1962). Since no English translation was available at the time of first writing this chapter, I am particularly indebted to my research assistant, Mrs. Carole W. Parsons, for her hard work in summarizing and translating from the Russian original. Her ability to deal with difficult technical passages was invaluable. I am also grateful to Col. Thomas W. Wolfe (USAF, Ret.) of the RAND Corporation for sharing with me some of his thoughts on the implications of this book. There are now several translations with commentary available; and although some of the interpretations of various passages differ from those herein, the differences do not, in the main, affect the over-all evaluation. The two leading English versions are: Herbert S. Dinerstein, Léon Gouré, and Thomas W. Wolfe, *Soviet Military Strategy*, The RAND Corporation (Englewood: Prentice-

which deals with Soviet military strategy as a whole. Intended as a textbook for the theoretical training of Russian officers as well as for general circulation in the Soviet Union, it is unusually frank in its approach. Most Western experts regard it as a revealing insight into Soviet thinking, notwithstanding the self-serving nature of some of the argumentation. Factional disagreement on the extent to which nuclear weapons can be decisive is evident between the lines of *Voennaya Strategiya*, although it is deliberately played down in the text.

One of the few public Soviet reviews of this book[42] praises its emphasis upon thermonuclear warfare but condemns its neglect of land forces, mobilization capacity and related aspects. The one viewpoint which appears quite categorically in the book is the traditional one that any major conflict involving the nuclear powers will automatically escalate into general nuclear warfare. (However, this can be interpreted as a deterrence-contributing policy position or as a prediction rather than as a determination to make it so.) More recent writings have stressed probability rather than "inevitability" of escalation in discussing local war. Given this assumption, *Voennaya Strategiya* asks and answers some key questions about the objectives in nuclear war.

> Should the objective be the defeat of the enemy's armed forces, as in the past, or the annihilation and devastation of objectives in the rear of the country and its disorganization? The answer which Soviet military strategy gives to this question is that both of these goals

---

Hall, 1963), and Raymond L. Garthoff, *Military Strategy* (New York: Praeger, 1963).

[42] P. Kurotchkin, *Red Star*, September 22, 1962. Several speeches by Marshal Malinovsky neatly avoid taking sides by stressing *both* "decisive thermonuclear rocket warfare" and victory by the "combined efforts of all arms and services." See, e.g., the July 1962 statement in *Kommunist*, and the February 22, 1963 speech on the 45th anniversary of Soviet armed forces reported in *The New York Times* (International Edition), February 23, 1963.

> should be attained simultaneously. The annihilation of the enemy's armed forces, the destruction of objectives in the rear and its disorganization are part of a single indissoluble military process. Two conditions are basic to the solution of this problem: first, the necessity of decisively destroying the aggressor in a minimal period of time for which it is necessary to simultaneously drain his military, political and economic capability to conduct war; second a real possibility of achieving these goals simultaneously with the aid of the existing means of military struggle.[43]

In explaining their version of the "optimum mix," the Soviets apparently assume a comparable Western strategy; but it should be noted that the first edition of this book appeared in print before any publicity had been given to the emerging doctrine of controlled response. By the end of 1963, a second edition had been issued by the Soviets with a number of changes designed to strip the enemy "of any illusions that they are unprepared to rebuff him."[44] While answering the proponents of city-sparing strategies (controlled nuclear war is an illusory hope of capitalists to save their system) the authors reassert, partly no doubt for propaganda reasons, the thesis of the first edition that the imperialists "will try to liquidate the social system of the members of the socialist camp, right up to the complete annihilation of whole states in the socialist fraternity."[45] But, as Colonel Wolfe points out, their rather detailed analysis "indicates that the authors have at least done their homework on the subject." The second edition therefore reveals some interest in, but nevertheless confirms the initial Russian rejection of, Secretary McNamara's concept that principal

[43] *Voennaya Strategiya,* cited, p. 229.

[44] The second edition (Moscow, 1963) was also published by the Defense Ministry. The shifts in emphasis in Soviet thinking which it reveals have been thoroughly analyzed by Thomas W. Wolfe in "Shifts in Soviet Strategic Thought," *Foreign Affairs,* April 1964, p. 475. Col. Wolfe's forthcoming book (*Soviet Strategy at the Crossroads*) will analyze these trends in greater detail.

[45] First edition, p. 337.

military objectives should be the destruction of the enemy's military force, not of his civilian population.[46]

One vital question that cannot therefore be answered is whether in an actual conflict, as distinguished from anticipatory propaganda, the Soviets would in fact follow city-sparing rules. All that can be said from *Voennaya Strategiya* is that there is enough flexibility in the military thinking of the Soviets to accommodate such a doctrine if they found it in their interest. A basis for a selective counterforce emphasis can be found in such statements as: "The basic goal of . . . undermining the military power of the imperialist coalition . . . might be achieved by inflicting upon selected targets, rockets and airborne nuclear blows."[47]

At the same time, however, the counterforce targets are mentioned side-by-side with the "economic base of the imperialists' warmaking capability" and their system of governmental and military control. We can probably conclude (and prudence counsels us to so assume) that at present Soviet doctrine actually does envision attack on Western cities as well as military forces, and an early employment of tactical nuclear weapons in any major conflict.

With respect to the distinction between first strike and second strike, the book emphasizes the decisive initial phases of a nuclear war and refers to "the first massive rocket strike with which our armed forces would respond to the unleashing of nuclear war by the imperialist aggressors." At the same time there are references to the possibility of surprise nuclear attack prepared by the imperialists and the need for "repelling" it. Repelling such an attack implicitly recognizes the value of pre-emption, i.e., destroying as much as possible of the enemy's striking power before he can launch it. In short, there is nothing in Soviet doctrine which

[46] In the July 1962 issue of *Kommunist*, Defense Minister Malinovsky reacts to President Kennedy's "we might have to take the initiative" statement by citing the CPSU dictum that the "main thing is to prevent war" and at the same time stressing Soviet readiness for a "massive nuclear-missile strike" —presumably pre-emptive, should an aggressor "rush to war."

[47] *Voennaya Strategiya,* cited, p. 339; see also p. 441.

would preclude an evolution toward the kind of thinking about thermonuclear war which is now emerging in the West, although it should be noted that the Soviets are also placing considerable emphasis on active defenses against missiles.[48]

The Soviet Union has long been much more civil defense conscious than the United States and has had a shelter and evacuation program for several years. The Russian strategists have pointed out that defensive measures against the "nuclear blows of the enemy pursue, at the same time the other, more important goal, not to permit massive losses among the civilian population."[49] There is also an interesting discussion of the relative vulnerabilities of the Soviet and Western economies to nuclear attack in which the Soviet survival and recuperative potential is held by the book's authors to be greater because of greater dispersal of targets and a lesser dependence on imports.

One of the most interesting features of both editions of *Voennaya Strategiya,* in addition to the extensive quotations from Western military writers, is the detailed discussion of U.S. and allied military strength, drawing in part on the pamphlets of the Institute for Strategic Studies, cited earlier in this chapter. The figures used are comparable with and in some cases larger than those given in Table 6. No equivalent statistics are given for the Soviet Union. Nevertheless this may be the first time that a fairly wide group of Soviet readers has been exposed to actual numbers of Western aircraft and missiles. While the Soviet reader cannot make the kind of comparative analysis presented in this chapter, there is enough material on the effect of nuclear weapons so that he can draw his own conclusions about the devastation which the West could deliver on the Soviet Union. He might conclude that

[48] See *Soviet Military Strategy* (RAND edition, cited), p. 315. In the *Foreign Affairs* article, cited, Colonel Wolfe comments on the fine line between "the Soviet conception of a pre-emptive and a retaliatory strike." (p. 483).

[49] *Voennaya Strategiya,* cited, first edition; see also Léon Gouré, *Civil Defenses in the Soviet Union,* The RAND Corporation (Englewood: Prentice-Hall, 1962).

the Soviet peaceful coexistence doctrine is essential, for there would be no victor in a nuclear war. Possibly the encouragement of such a conclusion was one of the reasons the book was published. We might therefore hope that it will soon be translated into Chinese!

The Soviets have claimed a superiority over the West in nuclear weapons because of the size of their hydrogen bombs.[50] In part, their emphasis on large yields (a 58-megaton bomb has reportedly been tested) is a result of the accidents of research and development which led Russia down the path of very high-thrust rockets. By following up on the work of captured German scientists the Soviets were able to startle the world with Sputnik and develop a commanding lead in rocket boosters. But since they did not need to miniaturize guidance components and warheads they fell behind in some aspects of nuclear weapons technology. Similarly their successes with liquid-fueled rockets inhibited development of solid fuels. They did not, moreover, exercise their capacity to turn out liquid-fueled rockets "like sausages," as Khrushchev once boasted. Having achieved the rocket capacity to boost enormous weights, the planners responsible for Soviet warhead development followed the same "bigger bang for a buck" line which was current in the United States in the 1950s. The Russian "roar for a ruble" version has been geared to minimum or finite deterrence as far as strategic nuclear weapons are concerned, with a deliberate political emphasis on the blackmail, intimidation, and terror aspects of weapons effects. The Soviets claim to have used their "nuclear might to shield Socialist Cuba, avert aggression against the Chinese Peoples Republic, and to safeguard the independence of Egypt, Syria and Iraq."[51]

What the West might call deterrence (and the Soviets call support of Socialist objectives) at lesser levels of violence is to be provided by the massive strength and quality of the Soviet armed

[50] *Voennaya Strategiya*, cited, p. 219. See also the February 22, 1963 speech by Defense Minister Malinovsky, cited in note 42 .

[51] See Wolfe, cited, p. 479.

forces which are armed with tactical nuclear weapons as well. Since, as we have noted, emphasis on counterforce is the preferred strategy of the stronger power, deterrence by massive threats to cities is the preferred strategy of the weaker one. This is in fact the present situation as between the United States and the U.S.S.R. But it is important to distinguish a declared policy of total devastation from realistic options in the event the moment of truth arrives. For the Russians to act in accordance with their doctrine if the Soviet form of deterrence failed would be suicidal (as well as homicidal) for the reasons already outlined. Faced with such a choice, the Soviets might well wish they had bought an intercontinental counterforce option in addition to the partial one they already have for the targets within range of their MRBMs.

In their current emphasis on "wars of liberation" it is obvious that the Communists hope to deter the West from interfering with the forces of socialism. But Cuba showed that this deterrence is not credible to the West unless vital Soviet interests are at stake. Thus the Soviets today find themselves in somewhat the same situation that critics of American policies once postulated for the West in the belief that a missile gap favored the Soviets and that the West was over-relying on massive "deterrence."

In sum, the combination of doctrine, weapons development, and economic pressures has now confronted the Soviets with a missile gap of both numerical and qualitative proportions. Their current minimum deterrence orientation is both a rationalization of this situation and a contributing cause. The key question, therefore, is what will the Soviet Union do in the immediate future.

Voennaya Strategiya devotes relatively little attention to the important distinction between a first and second strike, although other Soviet writings do show awareness of the value of initiative. Nor, for obvious reasons, does the book stress the vulnerability of Soviet rockets and air bases to Western attack. But the second edition reacts strongly to Western statements about Soviet vulnerability and indicates that the Russians are taking measures to rectify at least their major vulnerability deficiencies. They are apparently expediting their nuclear submarine program with Polaris-type missiles for this purpose. They were shaken earlier by the revelation that the U-2 was able to take excellent photographs of missile installations, thus partially removing the curtain of secrecy which had compensated for the softness of construction. It seems reasonable to assume, therefore, that the Soviets will accelerate the protection of these bases as soon as feasible. But complete hardening and concealment is costly and extremely difficult for the large, liquid-fueled rockets which now form the bulk of Soviet missilery. It seems probable that the Soviet Union will take partial "quick fix" measures but defer any massive effort to put striking forces underground until Russian solid propellent technology has produced the equivalent of the Minuteman. Khrushchev's reference to evading the West's detection net by firing missiles around the world over Antarctica suggests an attempt to capitalize on the Soviet lead in rocket thrust. But such a trajectory cuts down on accuracy to an important degree.

Bearing in mind the average three-year doctrinal lag, the Russians could theoretically try to catch up in counterforce terms. But as Secretary McNamara has said:

> The Soviets could, over the next few years, build a large force of hardened second generation ICBM's; they could . . . expand and improve their MRBM/IRBM systems . . . improve their active defenses . . . maintain a large and modernly equipped army . . . develop . . . some sort of . . . defense against ballistic missile attack; they could modernize and improve their large fleet of submarines including ballistic missile-firing types; they could continue the space race . . . expand both military and economic aid to the non-aligned nations . . . create an efficient agricultural economy . . . push the development of heavy industry; or they could increase the standard of living of the Soviet people—but they cannot do them all at the same time.[52]

[52] February 6, 1963, Congressional statement, cited, p. 22.

The Soviet budget presented in December 1962 showed the effects of this severe competition for resources. Although the published defense total was up 500 million rubles to about 14 billion rubles, this is about a 3 per cent increase. The Finance Minister referred merely to "maintenance of Soviet armed forces on a proper level." The actual 1963 budget (excluding research and space projects) is estimated to have been slightly over $15 billion, an increase of 4 per cent over 1962. The 1964 and 1965 budgets are expected to increase even less, although no major reductions are likely in the near future in the light of expanded missile protection and nuclear submarine programs.[53] But with defense already claiming between 12 and 18 per cent of the over-all GNP, something else will have to give way. With a GNP less than half that of the United States the Russians are spending almost two-thirds as much on defense. The oficial Soviet figures show 9 per cent; the Institute for Strategic Studies estimates that 18 per cent is more realistic; while a $34 billion expenditure against a GNP of $260 billion gives 13 per cent. One student of Soviet strategy sees signs of a "give" in the reduced claims of superiority which is now expressed merely as "sufficient means to restrain any aggressor."[54] This possible rationalization of a second-best posture further underscores the competition for resources—which may well have been a factor in Khrushchev's ouster.

In any case, there is the all-important factor of lead time. By the time the Soviets have put into effect whatever corrective measures they contemplate, several years may have passed. And by then Western technology may have developed antisubmarine and antimissile techniques which could produce another gap in favor of the West. Even without such a breakthrough, the strategy for the West outlined in this chapter offers reasonable promise of strategic

[53] *The Washington Post*, December 11, 1962, p. 10; *ISS, The Military Balance, 1963-1964*, cited, p. 3; *The New York Times*, January 6, 7, and 8, 1964. The dollar equivalent of the ruble figure is very difficult to estimate correctly. For discussion, see Hitch and McKean, cited, Ch. 6. The ISS converts it at a realistic rate of exchange to roughly $34 billion.

[54] Wolfe, cited, p. 485.

superiority for at least several more years. This raises the all-important question: what advantages can be taken of this superiority while it lasts? Some possible alternatives are suggested in the concluding section.

Conclusions: Objectives, Disarmament, and the Future

Power and policy interact as means and ends. A program objective such as strategic superiority can also be a means to other policy objectives. Part I spelled out the broad tasks for America and Europe in the evolving world of the 1960s. In this chapter we have suggested a strategy for the West but without reference to the uses of military power in pursuance of a stable world order. Again it should be stressed that I am discussing the availability of power as a means of influence on the Communists rather than as the means of inflicting military defeat. For as we have seen, a nuclear war with millions of casualties would be a Pyrrhic victory at best, and a mutual disaster at worst.

As a minimum, Western strategic power must provide deterrence at all levels as a shield behind which the West can tackle its many vital political and economic challenges. The original concept of "containing" the Soviet Union was based upon the premise that if external expansion was prevented the forces of internal evolution would eventually bring about useful changes in Soviet conduct. This, with some variations, is still the hope—and the basic policy—of the West. But it may not be inappropriate to ask whether NATO cannot take advantage of such strategic military superiority as it has to hasten the processes of change. In the longer term, the combined industrial, economic, and population resources of Europe and the United States, rather than military power as such, may provide the decisive elements of superiority.

There appear to be three broad alternatives. One possibility would be a more aggressive, forward policy based on an expanded Western force posture designed to bring maximum pressures to bear on the Soviet Union. It would use military power as an operative force in the chessboard sense, though it would not necessarily resort to armed violence. At the other extreme would be a policy of gradual relaxation, with the West reducing its strategic edge and decreasing its defense budgets in the hope an easing of pressures would accelerate the "embourgeoisement" of the Soviet Union. A third possibility would be to seek a satisfactory *modus vivendi,* if not actual solutions on major East-West issues by maintaining and negotiating from the substantial margin of Western military and economic strength.

With regard to the strategic nuclear component in the over-all Western power position, there were some indications during the Kennedy administration of a backing away from the implications of the limited and controlled or "damage limiting" counterforce option. For example, Secretary McNamara's testimony to Congress in February 1963 was widely interpreted as playing down a counterforce strategy because it stressed "striking back after absorbing a first blow" and forecast the likelihood of a declining Soviet vulnerability. But by the 1964 Congressional briefings, the emphasis had been clarified.[55] It is one thing to recognize and adjust to the fact that a disarming first strike so effective that the United States would escape all retaliation is unattainable. But it is quite another deliberately to abandon the West's option of striking only military targets and leaving the enemy the desperate choice of yielding or initiating suicide. The well-known "two scorpions in a bottle" analogy is not yet entirely accurate. The situation rather resembles two men covering each other with pistols while dueling with swords. The one with the bigger and more accurate gun may not want to shoot, but he can afford to be more daring in the sword play, as long as he does not mortally threaten his opponent.

This chapter has attempted to demonstrate that relative nuclear strength can make a difference in political terms. At the very least the West can deter the Soviet Union from resort to nuclear

[55] See Kaufmann, cited, pp. 93-98.

weapons in any case other than actual invasion of her territory and perhaps even then. Traditionally the West has looked at deterrence from the defensive side only. This is understandable, for NATO exists only as a defensive alliance. But in some respects, the shoe is now on the other foot, and the West's superiority could furnish an umbrella for a more aggressive conventional strategy. If (as seems remote in the extreme) NATO mobilized its full manpower and economic potential, it could very possibly roll back some Communist power from at least the periphery of Eurasia. Albania, for example, is an isolated Communist appendage; and even if the Soviets desired to defend it (which is almost as doubtful as anyone else wanting it) a "liberation" policy backed by the West might succeed. North Viet-Nam and North Korea are possibilities on the other flank. In America"s own back yard a cautious employment of maximum military power should be able gradually to eliminate communism's bastion in Cuba without undue risks of general war.

The total Communist bloc active military forces are estimated by the Institute for Strategic Studies at about seven and one-half million—including Red China. NATO alone has almost six million, and if other regional pacts and U.S. allies are included, the total *exceeds* the Communist bloc by almost half a million men. NATO's combined GNP is now two and one-half times that of the Communist bloc—a ratio which should last through the 1960s at least. Finally, there is no comparison between Western and Communist technological and mobilization potential, notwithstanding Red China's enormous population. It is important to understand that if the West wanted to double or triple its defense spending on non-nuclear forces while retaining the umbrella of its strategic nuclear superiority, and seeking the maximum feasible active and passive defense systems, it could seek to force the Soviets out of Eastern Europe and terminate the cold war on very favorable terms, though probably short of "victory" in the traditional sense.

There are many pros and cons here, of course, and account would have to be taken of the domestic economic, political, and social implications of such a spartan posture. I, for one, would not advocate such a course of action; but the point is that this option is open in theory, even though it is highly unrealistic in practice. For one thing, there would be substantial risks, and most people in the West appear unconvinced that it is necessary to take them. The "time is on our side" theme which is implicit in Western containment policies suggests that the requisite sense of urgency for such a crusade is lacking. Then too, as noted earlier, the implications of interdependence call for a common NATO policy both in Europe and in major confrontations outside it. If Europe is finding it difficult enough to meet even the minimum defense goals, it would hardly double its conventional effort in order to take the offensive! In any case, NATO is by definition a defensive alliance whose members are bound by the United Nations Charter. Finally, even the United States was unwilling to take on the challenge of "liberation" during the earlier period when its potential military superiority also might have made it possible. The economic sacrifices might be less now than in the disarmed days before Korea, but the potential risks are far greater. So as a concession to political reality the first alternative can be put aside, although some theoretical possibilities will be present for at least a few more years should NATO feel compelled to press strongly against the Communist bloc.

The second alternative would stress a deliberate and unilateral deceleration of the arms race. This, it can be argued, could release Soviet resources for consumer spending, hasten the liberalizing tendencies within the system, and eventually bring about a true East-West *détente*. It is conceivable that this might be the result, for the growing Russian middle class can exert some restraining influences over the government's reversion to heavy arms expenditures which would reduce their standard of living. If from the Russian standpoint the calculated risk of lowering their guard led to no capitalistic provocations, the habit of trust might grow. This course is particularly attractive to those who hold that fear and suspicion of the "imperialists" is the main motivation in Soviet conduct. These fears are present, and they do influence Soviet behavior; but to credit them as dominant factors simply ignores the revolutionary nature of the Communist system and almost half a century of its doctrine and practice. Expert Kremlinologists can and do debate these matters continually. My own feeling (admittedly as a non-expert) is that we simply do not know enough about the dynamics of Communist society to influence it from the outside. If the forces for mature and responsible behavior are present, they will probably follow their own path, regardless of what the West does or doesn't do—short, of course, of extreme provocations, and given continued containment by a unified Western world. This "given," as noted elsewhere, will require hard work on both sides of the Atlantic. But that is why it is so important. We cannot be sure that by giving up such existing leverage as the West has we would not merely make it easier for Soviet leadership to redress the military balance. Having done so, they might emerge more determined than ever to bury the West. On balance, the evidence that making life easier for a sworn revolutionary will corrupt him to the point of reciprocating does not seem compelling enough to justify the risks.

It is important to distinguish the military and foreign policy alternatives which I am discussing here from the practical decisions about the programs which support them. There will be areas in which increased defense spending produces diminishing and incommensurate returns. For example, once the West has enough missiles to attack all of the enemy striking forces which can be targeted and its major population and industrial centers as well, with something extra for insurance and psychological effect, further increases add very little to our posture. A leveling-off can be predicted, therefore, in American strategic retaliatory forces, as they are called; but the relative emphasis should shift to missile defense, and particularly research and development, so as to maintain the strategic edge insofar as possible.

If we reject the alternatives of major policy-oriented increases and decreases in Western strategic forces (i.e., beyond those program adjustments that technology and changes in Soviet forces require), only the third possibility remains. This alternative would stress making maximum use of Western power during the relatively few years in which we can maintain meaningful strategic superiority. The focus would be on negotiation of critical political issues and, where possible, on arms control measures. There is a difference between what might be called arms restraint in military decisions and negotiated agreements. The former category includes precautionary measures to prevent accidental or unauthorized use of a nuclear weapon; flexibility in doctrine, forces, and controls to reduce the need for a hasty and perhaps miscalculated decision; steps to minimize the catastrophe if war should occur; maintenance of communications with the other side in a crisis; and avoidance of unintended provocations. All of these are sensible and prudent objectives which can be pursued without formal agreements and should be an integral part of Western military planning.[56] Both sides have in fact reacted prudently to moves by the other.

We must also recognize the political and psychological importance of the long-range goal of general and complete disarmament, unattainable though we may think it. Whatever the prospects for a major success, the West must continue to participate vigorously in the disarmament arena in order to build sympathy and understanding for its positions. No one can quarrel with any measures designed to reduce the dangers of the twentieth-century world to the lowest levels consistent with the underlying political conflicts. For although arms may aggravate tensions, they do not create them. In the last analysis, no over-all East-West disarmament arrangements will be possible until the free world's conflict with world communism has been settled or at least allowed to lapse into the realm of theory, like the Christian-Moslem divisions of the

[56] An excellent summary of the concept of arms restraint is contained in a speech by John T. McNaughton, as General Counsel of the Defense Department, at the International Arms Control Symposium, University of Michigan, December 19, 1962.

Middle Ages. This dilemma brings us to the problem of realistic negotiation.

There seems to be a tolerably widespread delusion in the West that formal disarmament or disengagement proposals can be developed which we can persuade the Soviets to accept out of self-interest—that is, what Westerners would conceive the Soviet interest to be if they were sitting in the Kremlin. But in attempting to change seats intellectually the Westerner inevitably carries with him such concepts as that of the "reasonable man" created by the Anglo-Saxon common law. This mythical but useful person reflects the standards of his community. He is willing to compromise, he has due regard for the rights of others, and he exercises normal caution with respect to the effect of his actions on these rights. The trouble is that a Communist, even by his own definition, is not a "reasonable" man. What would be in the interest of a "reasonable Russian" from the standpoint of lowering the risks of war, reducing tension, and safeguarding vital security considerations may not be in the interest of the Communist activist. For he must first of all maintain internal security and controls—which may require some degree of international tensions; and second he wants to promote, not retard, the chances of world communism. He wants security at home both for its own sake and the better to pursue aggressive tactics elsewhere. He will engage in tactical maneuvers in the disarmament field, but he does not really want disarmament unless it paves the way for the "triumph of socialism." On these terms the West does not want it either. As the Director of the U.S. Arms Control and Disarmament Agency said in a recent annual report, the Russians are interested only in the expansion of Communist influence by gaining military advantage. President Johnson started 1964 by reminding the Soviets—as his three immediate predecessors also found it necessary to do—that it was time for deeds instead of words.

This is not to say that the Communist bloc wants war, or even situations containing fairly high risks of conflict. Evidently the Russians do not (although the Communist Chinese may be another matter); but they also know that the West does not want these things either. Since they, as the offensive, revolutionary elements, can control their own actions and gauge their moves according to the expected Western response, they do not seem to lie awake nights worrying about the risks. When the Soviets complained about provocative flights of SAC under the "fail-safe" procedures, the United States responded with President Eisenhower's proposals for safeguards against surprise attack. But Soviet conduct at the Geneva Conference, called to consider that topic, belied their avowed concern with the problem. When the Russians miscalculate, as in Cuba, and the stakes get too high, they merely follow Lenin's advice and take one step backward. Consequently it is prudent to ask why the Communists should want real and mutual disarmament measures as distinguished from unilateral or propagandistic ones.

Unless the West seriously begins to threaten action which could lead to war, there are only two possible reasons for such interest at the present time. First, the Russians are certainly aware that the Chinese might be able to embroil them against their will in a conflict which could get out of control. But it would be most difficult for the Russians to deal overtly with the imperialists against their Chinese "brothers," despite the ideological differences between them. Peking's anger at the test-ban pact led to much speculation about an end to the alliance. Khrushchev responded by proclaiming that there was still "a single Sino-Soviet strategy for the victory of communism." Two front-page stories in *The New York Times* shortly after proclaimed: "Khrushchev Bars Accord with West Against China." That this predictable viewpoint should be "news" shows how quickly wishful thinking can outrun realities. Despite the leadership changes in the Kremlin and the Chinese atomic test, Sino-Soviet relations appear to be getting no better, and it may be that a long-term rapprochement between the West and Russia might eventually isolate Communist China. But the more the West talks about it the less likely it is to happen. The factors that may eventually cause a permanent rupture are inherent in the relationship. The extent to which these factors can be exploited through public arms control and disarmament negotiations with the West is limited, although a nondissemination pact might exacerbate the Sino-Soviet rift much as the test ban did.

The other possible motive is economic. As noted in the preceding section, the Soviets simply cannot do everything: compete for space, harden and expand their missile force, solve the agricultural problem, expand heavy industry, and keep up present levels of consumption. The present Soviet military program is encountering the ever-increasing complexity and cost of modern weapons, and the arms race is clearly beginning to hurt.[57] Agricultural failures required wheat purchases in the West; over-all Russian growth appears to have dropped from the annual 6 per cent or more in recent years. Many Western economists dispute the CIA's downgrading of Soviet growth to less than 3 per cent in 1963 and 1964;[58] but the available public evidence does support a downward trend.

The Soviet Union's economic troubles, coupled with Western superiority, should provide the West with some leverage in negotiations, but the areas of enforceable agreement on military forces and deployments are few. It is not likely that in exchange for U.S. cancellation of, say, two or three of the planned Polaris submarines the Soviets would agree not to build an equal number of their own. And the West would have difficulty in confirming that the Russians had in fact kept such an agreement. But if the arms race cannot be negotiated, it can be made painfully expensive for the Soviet Union. Suppose NATO were subtly to convey the following message to the Soviet Union:

> We are not going to yield our military advantage so as to enable you better to pursue the goal of world

[57] This conclusion is supported by the Joint Economic Committee's collected hearings and studies, "Dimensions of Soviet Economic Power," 87th Cong., 2nd sess. See especially Martin J. Kohn, "The Soviet Economy in 1961," p. 232.

[58] See the CIA estimates reported in *The New York Times,* January 8, 1964, p. 1.

> communism. On the contrary we are going to apply all the pressure we can and make you compete in every possible field. Our combined GNP is almost three times yours, we have a higher technological base, and more slack in our belts. We therefore make you the following proposition: for each concrete step you take *away* from your military preparations and your aggressive policy toward the non-Communist world, we will unilaterally exercise restraint in our military measures, which will ease your economic pressures.

This is not so much a fantasy in political communication as one might think. Something like this is implicit in the behavior of both sides since the Cuban missile crisis. But it should not be assumed that the process is irreversible. The concept of getting a clear message through is a valid one. And the essence of that message should be that the West has the power and the determination, the will and the weapons to block forever the Communist goal of a revolutionary Socialist camp leading to a Communist world order. If the Soviet leadership does not or cannot bring themselves to accept this conclusion, then there is no choice but to continue the risks and costs of the arms race. The Soviet Union might then be forced to abandon all of its domestic goals in order to maintain its myth of world revolution.[59]

If on the other hand the Soviets choose to rejoin the world community, they can be assured of enhancing their net security from outside military threats and at the same time devote their resources to building their own society. Admittedly this is asking the leopard to change his spots, and as with a leopard it may be beyond his ability. But only by such a change, voluntary or not, can "peace" become a meaningful word. The odds for a gradual Soviet

[59] Moreover, the arms race has political risks for the Soviet Union, as well as economic consequences. As *Survey* pointed out, Khrushchev's dilemma was "how to preserve revolutionary dynamics despite the danger of world war." Hopefully, they will find that, given continued Western strength, they cannot preserve it. See "Thermonuclear Co-existence," *Survey*, December 1961, reprinted in *Survival*, January-February 1962, p. 37.

acceptance of the fact that they cannot eat their domestic cake and have their world revolution too, seem far better in 1964 than they did in 1961. Thus the West might as well play its military cards for their full political value and seek the only kind of concession that makes sense in this "through the looking glass" world.

4

Managing the Nuclear Power of the Alliance

One cannot conceive of a national role without disposing independently of modern military power.

DE GAULLE

NATO's nuclear problem is one of the most discussed, but least understood, issues confronting the alliance. The proposal for a multilateral NATO missile force, for example, has agitated politicians, journalists, and strategists—if not yet public opinion—to an unusual degree on both sides of the Atlantic. To understand this furor over what is in actuality a rather modest proposal for a future force which might eventually constitute less than 10 per cent of NATO's strategic power, one must examine the roots of the alliance's nuclear problem. Actually it is not one but many problems, representing the political, economic, and military cross-currents of fifteen sovereign nations. It has been written and argued about at length. Indeed, the literature on this subject seems to be expanding almost at the speed (though not necessarily with the illumination) of light.[1]

[1] Albert Wohlstetter's "Nuclear Sharing: NATO and the N + 1 Country," *Foreign Affairs,* April 1961, was one of the seminal articles. Robert E. Osgood's *NATO: The Entangling Alliance* (University of Chicago Press, 1962), and Henry A. Kissinger's *The Necessity for Choice* (New York: Harper & Row, 1961), are among the leading U.S. books of recent vintage. In Europe, Alastair Buchan's *NATO in the 1960's* (New York: Praeger, for the Institute of Strategic Studies, 1960), plus his article in the January 1962

In this chapter we are primarily concerned about the *management* of the West's strategic nuclear power, which has been reviewed in Chapter 3. The role of tactical nuclear weapons and their somewhat different control aspects are discussed in Chapter 5. This distinction between tactical and strategic is necessarily somewhat arbitrary, for the intention of the user is as relevant as the size and range of the weapon used. A rock thrown at a Kremlin leader by the U.S. Ambassador standing in Red Square could even be considered a strategic weapon. Nevertheless, some distinction is needed for discussion purposes. Recognizing that there is a continuum from the pistol up through the ICBM, we might consider the upper part of the spectrum strategic for what it can do to cities or enemy strategic weapons systems, affecting the enemy's ability and will to wage war. Tactical weapons, by contrast, are involved in attacking or defending forces, territory, installations, or interests which do not jeopardize a nation's heartland. "Strategic" in this sense connotes major, if not total war, although it does not necessarily involve total destruction or unconditional surrender; and it envisages the use of nuclear weapons. "Tactical"

Foreign Affairs ("The Reform of NATO"), are supplemented by Raymond Aron's articles in *Figaro* (especially those of May 1962) and his "de Gaulle and Kennedy, the Nuclear Debate" in the August 1962 *Atlantic*. Other European views are found in books by Helmut Schmidt, *Defense or Retaliation: A German View* (Edinburgh: Oliver and Boyd, 1962), Pierre Gallois, *The Balance of Terror* (Boston: Houghton Mifflin, 1961), and F. W. Mulley, *The Politics of Western Defense* (New York: Praeger, 1962). Virtually every recent issue of the major periodicals has had at least one article on this subject. Especially noteworthy are Malcolm W. Hoag's "Nuclear Policy and French Intransigence" in the January 1963 *Foreign Affairs*, William R. Kintner and Stefan T. Possony's "NATO's Nuclear Crisis," and James E. Dougherty's "European Deterrence and Atlantic Unity" in the Summer and Fall 1962 issues, respectively, of *Orbis*. My own "NATO's Nuclear Debate: Washington's View," in *The Reporter* of July 5, 1962, gave a contemporary account of U.S. thinking. Virtually all the leading U.S. and European columnists have written at length about the nuclear problem in NATO. The reports of the Defence Committee of the Assembly of Western European Union, (e.g. Document 251, October 1962, and Document 290, October 1963) are especially valuable sources of factual data. The most significant statements of leading officials are usually reprinted in *Survival*, published by the Institute for Strategic Studies, and in the *Atlantic Community Quarterly*.

refers to a conflict of lesser magnitude and objectives, which might or might not involve nuclear weapons.

The Roots of the Problem

The merging of three principal streams has created the present difficulties regarding strategic nuclear power, which must be counted among the most serious confronting NATO. First, a "crisis of confidence" in the American guarantee of Europe's defenses developed as the Soviet Union acquired the ability to devastate North America. Next, there has been a growing awareness of Europe's potential unity and power with overtones of "defensive sovereignty"—to which nuclear armament is believed by some to be central. Finally, the direct military threat of Soviet medium-range missiles to Western Europe has rendered some of NATO's present forces in Europe increasingly obsolescent. The problems these streams have caused for different countries are described briefly in this chapter and the feasibility of various deterrent forces is then analyzed in the light of cost, technical and control problems. Finally, the major alternatives and conclusions for the alliance will be examined.

The Crisis of Confidence

Not long ago a European told the author, "American intellectuals started a chain reaction by pointing out that Europe might not be satisfied with the American guarantee of its defense, once the Soviet Union had attained the ability to destroy American cities. This made us wonder whether the Russians might think the possible loss of New York would be too much for the Americans to risk in defense of Paris. So finally we did come to be worried over what the Russians would believe the Americans thought the Europeans should think!"

To leave aside these multiple mirrors of national attitudes, the acquisition by the Soviet Union of significant numbers of nuclear weapons and the means to deliver them did raise questions about the credibility of the American deterrent for Europe. One answer might be to reassure the Europeans about the determination of the United States to defend them, whatever the risks.[2] Another, quite widely suggested in the early 1960s, was that "Europe" should acquire its own nuclear deterrent. A now familiar further variation was evolved by the French government under President de Gaulle, who has stated quite frankly that in the nuclear age no country can afford to rely upon another for its defense. This most serious conclusion undercut the entire philosophy of collective security which had characterized U.S. policy since World War II. Finally, some actions could be taken to strengthen U.S. power and make it more credible. These included: The Kennedy administration's initial priority on attaining an invulnerable retaliatory force; a conventional build-up in Europe; the evolution of the restrained counterforce strategy; and the effort still underway to bring the Europeans abreast of the facts of life in the nuclear age and, by increasing allied participation, to raise their confidence in the applicability of America's strategic power to their defense.

Defensive Sovereignty

The so-called crisis of confidence of European members of NATO with respect to the American guarantee coincided with the European political renaissance which appears sometimes as nationalism and sometimes in the unification movement. It often produced the argument that, since defense is the very essence of sovereignty, the new Europe needed a much greater degree of control over its own defense for domestic political purposes. If Europe should evolve into a single political unit, then must not a European Defense Ministry control the means of its own defense? And in the nuclear age these means would inevitably involve ownership of nuclear weapons. The emphasis here is not so much on the dependability of the American deterrent. Rather, it is claimed that a

[2] The NATO Heads of Government Meeting in December 1957 was aimed particularly at this goal. See *NATO—Facts About the North Atlantic Treaty Organization* (Paris: NATO Information Service, 1962), pp. 33-34 and Appendix 12.

Europe equal in population to either America or Russia, and between the two in economic strength, cannot continue to be a "military satellite" of the United States. A European "great power" should control its own destiny on the great issues of war and peace. Moreover, it has been argued that nuclear weapons and technology are synonymous with scientific leadership and prestige, as well as with military power. Just as a lack of nuclear weapons allegedly condemns Europeans to the role of foot soldiers and spear carriers, in contrast to the American "atomic cavalry," the lack of a major nuclear establishment denies them the side benefits of technical and industrial advances. To holders of this view, peaceful uses of atomic energy do not provide the same technological thrust as a military program. Moreover, the need for political control of nuclear armaments could add momentum to the advancement of a united Europe.

The Military Threat

In NATO's original defense concept the shield consisted of ground, air, and naval power backed with U.S. tactical nuclear weapons; and the sword was nuclear retaliatory power, provided mainly by the American and British strategic air commands, and supplemented by other U.S. and allied naval and land-based aircraft. The purpose of the shield was to defeat, or at least delay, small-scale hostile actions of a local character, and thus force an aggressor to make a conscious decision to go to war.[3] The shield would provide a forward defense which, in turn, would allow the sword to be effective in deterrence or, if necessary, in retaliation. This concept was appropriate as long as the Soviet threat was limited in practical terms to a massive ground assault with tactical air support. Even the improvement in Soviet manned bomber capabilities changed the picture only in degree, for there was still time to activate air defenses and get the retaliatory forces into action.

As the Soviets built up an arsenal of medium-range ballistic

[3] See the NATO fact book, cited, p. 83.

missiles (MRBMs) in Eastern Europe and expanded their stockpile of nuclear weapons, the threat took on a new dimension. These missiles are now estimated to total over 700, although some are sited in the Far East rather than Europe. They are capable of striking NATO air bases with at most a few minutes warning. Except for Polaris, the European-based retaliatory forces depend for the most part upon fighter-bombers, since the obsolescent Thor and Jupiter missiles are being phased out. In effect, the Soviets have acquired an ability to leap over NATO's shield in a surprise attack and severely blunt, if not shatter, the European-based elements of the sword. Even if they failed to achieve surprise, their tactical missiles are sufficiently mobile to make them difficult targets. And, in any case, the NATO fighter-bomber aircraft are growing less effective in terms of ability to penetrate Communist air defenses.

All of this adds up to a threat which gives credence to Khrushchev's claim that his MRBMs made Western Europe his "hostage." The result was that General Norstad and the International Staff planners at SHAPE developed a requirement for several hundred MRBM missiles. According to one authoritative account,[4] "Norstad's MRBM concept calls for a rocket having a range of about 1,000 miles—therefore not a strategic weapon to be used against bases inside Russia," which could "strike fast at Soviet airfields, troop concentrations and logistical complexes in the rearward sectors of the main battle areas for Germany."

Viewed from the standpoint of Europe alone, there can be no doubt that this requirement is valid. But this was just where it was challenged. For the concept of NATO is that Europe is not an autonomous theater of operations, but the forward area of a continuous defensive zone from East Germany across the Atlantic and the United States to the Pacific. In the nuclear era this global approach to deterrence is essential. The position reached by the

[4] Charles J. V. Murphy, "NATO at a Nuclear Crossroads," *Fortune*, December 1962, p. 85. Mr. Murphy is a close personal friend of General Norstad and the article presumably reflects at least some of the latter's views.

Kennedy administration after lengthy interdepartmental discussions in Washington was described by Charles Murphy as follows: "The U.S. representative, Thomas K. Finletter, startled the Allies (and dumbfounded Norstad when the word was flashed to SHAPE) with the forthright declaration that the United States had concluded there was no valid requirement for the MRBM. SAC and the Polaris fleet, in the American view, could execute the near-in tactical job for the SHAPE forces."[5] This dispute was not only between Washington and General Norstad as the Commander of U.S. forces in the European theater. Norstad's unusual success as the Supreme Allied Commander, Europe (SACEUR) reflected his ability to represent *European* views as well as American and to retain allied confidence; and many Europeans were firmly behind the MRBM proposal. Initially, an effort was made to treat MRBMs on the narrowest possible basis, as a prudent modernization of tactical European-based strike forces, to avoid the political pitfalls of strategic debate. Technical, cost, and various political arguments delayed action under the Eisenhower administration until after the 1960 elections. Then, as noted above, the new administration's concepts challenged the underlying rationale of the military need. The matter inevitably became part of the overall strategic debate which continues between America and Europe.

Conflicting Views, Facts and Fictions

On matters this complex, no large political entity commands a unanimous viewpoint. Many shades of opinion within the U.S. government cut across political, departmental, and professional lines. American officials in Washington sometimes differ with their colleagues stationed in Europe, and one part of the Pentagon may disagree with another.

Extended to the European continent as a whole, generalizations become even more suspect. "European" attitudes are best discussed

[5] Same, p. 222.

at the national level, where the nuclear problem has produced its most acute political effects.

Great Britain

Britain started the atomic era as a partner of the United States, following the so-called "Tube Alloys" agreement between Roosevelt and Churchill in 1943. As the cooperation took organizational form, Canada came to participate in the work of the Manhattan District as did many individual European scientists. This endeavor led to the successful nuclear detonation at Alamogordo, New Mexico, in 1945 and the subsequent bombing of Japan. Cooperation was terminated, however, under the strict antidisclosure provisions of the MacMahon Act (The Atomic Energy Act of 1946) and was only restored gradually in the succeeding years under liberalizing amendments of 1951, 1954, 1956, and 1958.[6] The British proceeded independently to develop an atomic bomb, exploding a fission weapon in 1952 and a thermonuclear device in 1957. This achievement played an important part in the British "New Look," set forth in a 1957 White Paper prepared by Defense Minister Sandys which outlined a five-year plan for defense.

Like the American counterpart some three years previously, the British "New Look" placed primary reliance upon nuclear weapons. Britain had already achieved substantial progress toward what the Joint Committee on Atomic Energy called "a capability on its own of fabricating a variety of weapons." Since this standard had been designed to effectively limit cooperation to Britain, that country became eligible to receive U.S. weapons design information, nuclear materials and the non-nuclear components of weapons.

Under agreements pursuant to the new legislation, the British again became nuclear partners of the United States. This relationship encouraged British efforts to reduce defense costs by reliance on nuclear weapons for all types of major conflicts.

[6] A concise summary of these developments is contained in the English-Speaking Union's *Fact Sheet* No. 6 of April 1959 by Aley Allan.

In addition to this scientific cooperation, the British and American bomber commands had long enjoyed an intimate operational association stemming from wartime strategic bombing under the U.S.-U.K. Combined Chiefs of Staff. Thus, until the so-called "fourth country" problem arose, and while manned bombers were the principal means of delivery, the U.S.-U.K. nuclear partnership appeared to satisfy the needs of both countries. The United States received valuable base rights in Britain; Bomber Command's target list was closely coordinated with that of SAC; and Britain was an "independent" nuclear power, a status which partly compensated for other developments that have eroded her position as a world power since the war.

As the missile era progressed, however, Britain encountered difficulties. The attempt to develop its own intermediate-range ballistic missile was cut short in 1960, after enormous expenditures when the Blue Streak project was cancelled. It had become apparent that actual costs would far exceed early estimates and that the missile might be obsolescent, or worse, before it could become operational. Something has been salvaged from the Blue Streak. Its booster should be an important element of the European space program under the seven-nation launcher development organization (ELDO) by 1965.[7] But for a weapons system, Britain has had to rely upon its force of about 180 V-bombers. Standing for the Vulcan, Victor and Valiant aircraft, they can carry medium-to-large-yield weapons as well as the Blue Steel stand-off missile, which was to have been replaced by the American Skybolt. The power and effectiveness of what has been called "SAC's Kissing Cousins" should not, however, be underestimated.[8] Following the 1957 NATO Heads of Government decision to place intermediate-range missiles in Europe, sixty American

[7] ELDO is associated with the European Space Research Organization (ESRO) which, however, has a slightly different membership and has reserved the right to use either ELDO rockets or those offered by America's NASA. See *The Washington Post*, April 30, 1964, p. A5.

[8] This is the title of an informative article on the RAF by Richard Peet which appeared in the January 1964 *Air Force Digest*.

missiles were operated from British bases by the Royal Air Force. However, the warheads for these missiles, which are now being phased out, were retained in U.S. custody under a dual control system whereby both U.S. and British officers must participate in a launching.

In discussing the 1962 British White Paper on defense, one commentator noted that the five years since the 1957 "New Look" have "revealed a good deal about the costs, the disappointments and the embarrassments of trying to be an 'nth country' in a period of big power nuclear plenty . . . . It led Professor Norman Gibbs, a British military historian, to write: 'The experience of Britain during the past five or six years suggests that in the West, no single nation other than the United States can continue to afford to create and maintain an effective deterrent of its own.' "[9] Not only was Blue Streak a costly failure, but the short-range Blue Water missile, a competitor of the U.S. Sergeant, was cancelled two years later, much to the dismay of British industry. These expensive and unsuccessful development efforts led to major political difficulties for the Conservative government.

The announcement, just prior to the December 1962 NATO meeting, that the United States might not continue the Skybolt, made Britain's nuclear dilemma even more acute. The timing (probably a result of the U.S. budget cycle and the imminence of the NATO meeting) was in many respects unforunate, although it had been foreshadowed by earlier U.S. doubts as to the cost and technical feasibility of the Skybolt system. From the beginning, the United States had refused to allow itself to be maneuvered into a commitment to produce the weapon, and agreed only that when and if produced, it would be designed for compatibility with British aircraft and that it would be made available to Britain. Because its potential availability was a crutch upon which the government relied at the time that Blue Streak was eliminated, the British government and press tended to play down the conditional nature of the undertaking.

[9] H. A. DeWeerd, "A British White Paper on the Thin Red Line," *The Reporter,* May 24, 1962, p. 27.

Obviously Britain could not afford to carry on the Skybolt program—which had already cost about $500 million, of which Britain contributed about $25 million. It might require a billion dollars altogether just to complete development, leaving aside the $1.5 billion still needed for procurement. Therefore it is not surprising that the British press called for an "agonizing reappraisal" after the cancellation.[10]

The Skybolt issue dominated the December 1962 meeting at Nassau between Prime Minister Macmillan and President Kennedy. The timing of this first meeting between the two leaders since the Cuban crisis made the question of national deterrents doubly relevant, since the Europeans had been reminded by Cuba that action by the U.S. to preserve its own interests could have led to a war in which they might have been unwillingly involved. The Nassau communiqué of December 21 indicated that the Prime Minister declined the U.S. offer to continue Skybolt by equally sharing future costs, but agreed to accept U.S. Polaris missiles (minus warheads) for British submarines. This was placed in the context of the multilateral offer to NATO (in which the French were sincerely—although perhaps optimistically—invited to share), the indivisibility of strategic defense, and the importance of non-nuclear forces—all important defense concepts of the Kennedy administration. In particular, there was a cautiously worded reference to making a start "by subscribing to NATO some part of the forces already in existence which could include allocations from U.S. strategic forces, from the United Kingdom bomber command, and from tactical nuclear weapons now held in Europe. Such forces would be assigned as part of a NATO nuclear force and targeted in accordance with NATO plans." But as we shall see in discussing other European attitudes and problems, this suggestion by no means solved the problem.

It is worthy of note that the communiqué also specified that

[10] *The Washington Post*, December 12, 1962, p. 1, carried a revealing analysis of the reaction. See also the selections from Secretary McNamara's Congressional testimony on Skybolt contained in William W. Kaufmann, *The McNamara Strategy* (New York: Harper & Row, 1964), pp. 124-125.

these forces would be used for international defense "except where Her Majesty's Government may decide that supreme national interests are at stake"—a concession to the independent deterrent theme which made the Skybolt cancellation so traumatic in the first place.

Quite apart from the Blue Streak and Skybolt difficulties, the entire question of Britain's independent deterrent has been subject to considerable political fire at home. The Labor Party and its several knowledgeable defense experts have pointed out with embarrassing frankness that Britain's force is really neither independent nor a deterrent. The Conservative government nevertheless steadfastly maintained the worth of its "independent contribution" to the deterrent,[11] despite its failures to meet the technological demands of modern nuclear armament, its high costs, and the political agitation from the left (which has on occasion advocated that Britain lead the way in forming a non-nuclear club).

Secretary McNamara's June 1962 speech at Ann Arbor appeared to support Labor's arguments against independent nuclear forces. But, undoubtedly prodded by the British government, McNamara added the clarification that he had not been talking about Britain whose bomber command and nuclear weapons "have long been organized as part of a thoroughly coordinated Anglo-American striking force and targeted as such." The Prime Minister subsequently made the distinction between the "constitutional" independence of British forces and their dependence in practice.[12] That the political difficulties were not imaginary was shown by the blasts from his own party which greeted Macmillan upon his

[11] A subsequent official phrasing was that while the British effort is comparatively much smaller, its "contribution to the Western deterrent remains significant. It is by itself enough to make a potential aggressor fear that our retaliation would inflict destruction beyond any level which he would be prepared to tolerate. Moreover, it adds considerably to the flexibility and dispersal of the total nuclear forces availability to the West and thus to their retaliatory power." See the February 1962 White Paper on Defense excerpted in the May-June 1962 issue of ISS' *Survival.*

[12] See *The New York Times,* June 24, 1962, and the London *Times,* June 27, 1962.

return from the December 1962 Nassau talks. Against a background of press headlines proclaiming the Polaris for Skybolt substitution as a "sell out," a "Munich," and "the culminating humiliation for the British people," dissident Tories were alternatively complaining about the high costs of building nuclear submarines, the delays involved, and the prospect of further restricting Britain's own deterrent. The announcement in February 1964 that modifications to the V-bomber and Blue Steel combination now had extended its range at the critical lower altitudes illustrates the continued concern with the longevity of the British deterrent.

Intimately involved in the rationale of the British is their sense of special relationship with the United States, which they ascribe (probably incorrectly), to their nuclear status and U.S. reliance on British bases (now reduced) and Polaris berthing facilities. The changes which times, trends, and two world wars have brought to Britain's role as a major world power, have left major psychological scars.[13] The maintenance of Britain's nuclear capability reflects an understandable reluctance to give up this status symbol of a "big power" in world politiics. The primary role of Britain's nuclear forces is to act in conjunction with U.S. strategic forces, but there is the subordinate role of supporting Britain's ground and naval forces with nuclear weapons, should this become necessary, in peripheral conflicts. However, a number of influential Britons have recognized that their nuclear capability is a dwindling asset with a growing price tag, and that its main utility may be that of a bargaining counter vis-à-vis the continent, and especially France.

The entire question of Britain's defense posture was a vital

[13] When former Secretary of State Dean Acheson told a West Point student conference that Great Britain has lost an empire and not yet found a role, but that the attempt to play a separate power role is about played out, the angry reaction in Britain appeared to be unusually strong. In part, it may have seemed that the comment was a calculated move by the administration. Also, the statement added insult to the Skybolt injury at a time when the Common Market negotiations were going badly for Britain, giving the British the impression of being beset on all sides. See *The New York Times,* December 6, 1962.

issue in the 1964 U.K. general elections. Labor spokesmen have stated that: "we wish to cease attempting to maintain our independent British nuclear deterrent for both economic and political reasons."[14] With Labor in power, however, the economic (i.e., defense industry) and political reasons may be felt to bear down more heavily on the other side of the question. In any case, an orientation period of several months—and perhaps some trial and error—must be expected before the Labor government can chart its politico-military course with any accuracy.

Meanwhile, Britain is being hard pressed to maintain its non-strategic forces. The British Army of the Rhine (BAOR) has been described as "one of the worst equipped in the world" by none other than Britain's director of munitions and stores. These forces still depend upon American warheads, suggesting that Britain's development of tactical nuclear weapons may not have kept pace with its strategic weaponry.[15] The elimination of conscription has caused a manpower bottleneck, so that Britain's forces East of Suez have, like the BAOR, suffered from the government's inability to pay the nuclear piper while holding defense expenditures at a stable level. The dilemma therefore persists, although there are signs of a growing British willingness to merge their national nuclear power into a larger European or NATO entity.

France

Whatever Britain's independent contribution to the deterrent may have provided in the way of an international status symbol, it has exacerbated relations within the alliance and particularly with France. London tends to be a stop of convenience between Washington and Paris. American official visitors have frequently encountered problems in toning down communiqués stemming from Anglo-American talks so that they would not offend the French.

[14] Denis Healey made this statement in an interview published in the June-July 1964 issue of *NATO's Fifteen Nations,* p. 31. He also referred to Labor's opposition to the multilateral force and to its thinking on Europe being closer to that in Bonn than to that in Paris.

[15] See DeWeerd, cited, p. 28.

Their British counterparts, on the other hand, have sometimes found it in their interest to play up the special relationship. Whatever form the communiqué took, it was sure to be followed by a rash of interpretative articles in the British press to the effect that the Anglo-American discussion had, in effect, decided on matters of allied strategy, which were then presented to the continental powers.

Many commentators treat France and De Gaulle as synonymous with respect to the *force de frappe*. It is true that the General's personal pique at Anglo-Saxon intimacy, which he regards as an affront to French dignity and prestige, goes back to World War II and is evident in his memoirs of that period. Actually, however, the first French decision to acquire a national atomic capability was made by the Socialist Guy Mollet in 1956. De Gaulle's accession reinforced and expanded the program, but the motivations of the several leaders involved are a mixture of many factors.

First, there is the matter of national prestige—the feeling that the "grandeur and destiny" of France can only be satisfied by nuclear power status and rights of admission or refusal of participation in nuclear test-ban talks and similar negotiations among the nuclear elite.

The French strategist, F. O. Miksche, wrote some time ago: "We must not expect others to risk nuclear retaliation in defense of the interests of another nation. . . . A country without nuclear weapons loses its freedom of action and puts itself into the unpredictable hands of the atomic powers."[16] He had in mind not so much the possibility of an attack upon France, but rather the failure to support such French "interests" as led to the invasion of Suez. However, the failure of the United States to support that ill-fated venture was not altogether unpredictable; otherwise the French and the British presumably would have felt free to share their plans with the United States instead of concealing them.

[16] *Aussenpolitik* (No. 5, 1960), quoted in Helmut Schmidt, *Defense or Retaliation*, cited, p. 81. General de Gaulle has said much the same thing himself in several of his press conferences; see e.g., *The New York Times*, July 24, 1964, p. 2.

Suez crops up so frequently in connection with French attitudes that it may be worth repeating a key fact bearing on the Soviet involvement. Notwithstanding the announced U.S. hostility to the invasion and the complete lack of U.S. support for its allies vis-à-vis Egypt, when the *Russians* threatened retaliation against Paris and London, the United States assured both capitals that our NATO guarantee against such attacks stood firm and promptly put SAC on a precautionary alert, a fact which was not lost on Russian intelligence. It is sometimes argued that such firmness about a controversial issue would be less certain if Suez had occurred in the late 1960s instead of the 1950s. But notwithstanding the growth in Russian nuclear power, the West's relative position in counterforce terms should be at least as favorable then as it was in 1956, when U.S. strategic forces were quite vulnerable.

The failure of De Gaulle's efforts in 1958 to establish common U.S.-British-French global policies (and to obtain thereby a veto for France on worldwide military actions, especially over the employment of nuclear weapons) confirmed his determination to make France at all costs a nuclear power able to be independent in what he calls the "completely new era" which followed Hiroshima.[17] General de Gaulle re-emphasized the basic tenet of French policy in his first address to the new Gaullist-dominated Assembly in December 1962: "Within the Atlantic Alliance, at present indispensable for the defense of the Free World, one cannot conceive a role for France unless she disposes independently of modern military power," i.e., nuclear weapons. French Minister of Defense Messmer has written: "an alliance . . . can never dispense with the need for a national effort, be it only to affirm a legitimate national point of view."[18]

Here, then, are three pragmatic aspects of nuclear prestige: free-

[17] James Reston has given a complete and apparently authoritative analysis of De Gaulle's 1958 proposals (and lays to rest the popular misconception that they were never answered by the U.S.) and of the intermittent dialogue which followed. See *The New York Times*, May 1 and May 3, 1964.

[18] Pierre Messmer "The French Military Establishment of Tomorrow," *Orbis*, Summer 1962, p. 206. A somewhat similar article appeared in the May 1963 *Revue de Défense Nationale*.

dom of action, a role for France, and the ability to back up national positions in dealings with one's allies.

Second, there is the element described earlier as a reluctance to rely exclusively upon collective security in a nuclear age, an attitude made explicit by many French spokesmen. Moreover, General Pierre Gallois and others have claimed that for effective deterrence, one need only be able to "tear an arm off" an aggressor, not destroy him. Most U.S. experts regard this argument as an unpersuasive attempt to provide military rationalization for a political objective. Indeed, Gallois has made such vitriolic attacks upon American policy that the good faith of his arguments is open to question.[19] There is a story about a man who justified his own determination to take a mistress by proclaiming the self-fulfilling prophecy that his wife was going to be unfaithful! Proceeding from an *a priori* conviction that France must be a nuclear power, French apologists have likewise moved on to the allegation that its chief nuclear ally must therefore be unreliable.

Third, a feeling exists among many high-ranking French officials that giving French forces a modern nuclear role is the only way to revive the morale which had been drastically set back by the series of defeats in World War II, Indo-China, and North Africa. The threat which the OAS and other dissident elements posed to the French nation was a real one, and it came close to unleashing civil war. The loyalty of the career officers, who are the backbone of the French Army, was very much at stake. It has therefore been argued that the national identity of the French forces must be enhanced, rather than merged into a European or NATO context. This goes far to explain the withdrawal of the French fleet from its NATO assignment and the ambiguous status in NATO of some of the French forces withdrawn from Algeria. By stressing that French arms are an instrument of French destiny, and by involving the military in the national nuclear effort, President de

[19] See for example, Gallois' "The Trap Offered de Gaulle" in the October 1963 *Bulletin of the Atomic Scientists*, and my reply, "The Gall of Monsieur Gallois" in the same issue, or his similar piece in the December 1963 issue of *NATO's Fifteen Nations*.

Gaulle hopes to recapture the political loyalty of the military which has, at times, come dangerously near the vanishing point.

Fourth, there is an element of intra-European bargaining. French pre-eminence on the Continent in the nuclear field adds to their pile of chips in bidding for leadership, an activity which sometimes takes on the complexion of a poker game. The inability of the United States to provide nuclear assistance to France under the applicable laws, and America's unwillingness to modify or interpret them liberally, has been taken as confirmation of the French need to go it alone. Moreover, France has refused to grant the United States nuclear stockpile rights at French bases, necessitating the removal of several U.S. tactical fighter squadrons. Officially the issue was lack of French control over the employment of U.S. nuclear weapons, but in large part it was a pressure device in the over-all nuclear controversy. (At the same time, however, French forces in Germany are backed up by U.S. warheads.)

The Gaullist vision of a regalvanized France at the head of a dynamic Europe of the future requires a measure of independence from the United States, which only the possession of nuclear weapons can bestow. By the 1970s, France apparently aspires to a position of nuclear pre-eminence within Europe, analogous to that which the United States has had in the West as a whole. In scientific research, atomic energy for peaceful uses and military technology, Europe will have to look to France. Also, from its future "clients" France might be able to recoup a substantial part of the large investment which the attainment of such a predominant role will inevitably require. Given this view, France is finding some consolation in the American refusal to share its know-how and weapons, for only by having to do the entire job alone can France acquire the scientific and industrial manpower, atomic energy facilities and general technological resources necessary to become the "Manhattan District" of Europe.[20]

Critics of De Gaulle's policies are in the uncomfortable position

[20] Minister of Defense Messmer, cited in footnote 18, states: "For our country, the French military programs are an irreplaceable factor of scientific, technological and industrial progress."

of applauding his undeniable achievements in restoring political stability, reviving the French economy, and cutting out the Algerian cancer, at the same time that they are disclaiming the means he has chosen to accomplish these near-miracles. Foreign observers too often lose sight of the close link between French means and ends. For the De Gaulle mystique and the revival of national pride are the very instruments of his successes. It is not inconceivable that just as his endorsement of "*Algérie Française*" was dropped once his power was consolidated, some of the extreme forms of nationalism may give way once they have served their short-term purpose. Those who do not subscribe to this evaluation have expressed the hope that progress can be resumed when De Gaulle passes from the scene. But the *force de frappe* may then have become so much of a national endeavor that any successor government would feel bound to carry on the program. More than one Frenchman has suggested to the author that even a Communist government would do so! In any case, both the underlying and ensuing problems are sure to survive De Gaulle.

Thus the fact of a national French nuclear program must be accepted, whether the United States approves or not. It remains to examine some facts and fictions about the *force de frappe* and its effectiveness.

The French have formed a "strategic nuclear force" as one of the three major components of its armed forces. (The others are "the forces of intervention"—the bulk of the army, navy and tactical air forces—and the "operational Defense of the Territory (DOT)" which are cadres dispersed throughout the country and trained for para-military home defense.)[21] The Strategic Air Command is initially equipped with forty Vautour aircraft, which may be capable of carrying the few nuclear devices that France has produced, although one of its commanders has been heard to say: "At present, *I* am the *force de frappe*." By the end of 1965 it is

[21] The series of articles by Messmer, cited, and others in the *Revue de Défense Nationale* are now definitively supplemented in the national defense section of *The First Five Years of the Fifth Republic of France*, published by the French Embassy's Information Division (New York) in mid-1964.

planned that this Command will have 50 Mirage IV light bombers able to deliver the atomic bombs of 20-60 kilotons then available, supported by the 12 KC 135 aerial tankers which the United States surprisingly agreed to sell France. Skeptics have pointed out that since many more tests would be necessary to refine the weight-yield ratio of French weapons, the ability of the Mirage to carry an effective nuclear payload over long ranges is somewhat in doubt. Moreover, even if the problems related to weight-yield ratios are solved, manned aircraft, however valuable a part of a large strike force which includes missiles, have a decreasing probability of penetrating enemy air defenses. Lacking air defense suppression missiles, the French Strategic Air Command could deliver only a relatively small payload to Soviet targets, even in a first strike. In a second strike, after a Soviet pre-emptive attack, these aircraft would suffer from the same vulnerability discussed earlier in connection with the NATO MRBM proposal. However steps are being taken to provide dispersal and at least some protection.[22]

It can be argued that even a low probability of delivering one Hiroshima-size weapon on Moscow's Red Square could deter the Soviet Union from attacking Paris; but that possibility must be contrasted with the near certainty that France would disappear from the map if it was unprotected by other forces during such a conflict. The analysis in Chapter 3 suggests that such a minimal deterrent may be ineffective in deterring anything less than an attack directed at the jugular—such as an aggression against French forces in Berlin or elsewhere. In the short run, the French *force de frappe* would appear to suffer from the boxing axiom that a good big man will beat a good little man every time. In the longer term, however, the French are planning their own strategic missile system, along the lines of Polaris. The submarine com-

[22] Robert Kleiman has published a good nontechnical summary of the French nuclear program, "What France is Out to Get," in the January 1964 Readers Digest, p. 100, drawn in part from his book *Atlantic Crisis* (New York: Norton, 1964).

ponent, as distinguished from the missile itself, is reportedly fairly well advanced.[23]

As the level of strategic sophistication grows among French leaders, they are increasingly aware that "a rose does not a summer make," and a few nuclear weapons do not make an effective deterrent force. But, as Raymond Aron put it, "to acquire such a force in ten or fifteen years, one must begin now."[24] The point was made earlier that technology rarely stands still; it is a constant struggle for qualitative and quantitative superiority, of offensive versus defensive weapons and countermeasures versus counter-countermeasures. Whether either France or Europe can catch up from a fifteen-year lag to compete equally in this race—which, however, may be slowing down—remains to be seen.

What are the prospects for the next stage of the *force de frappe* with regard to missiles? By 1970 warheads should have been refined to an appropriate weight-yield ratio. The French have made progress in the technology of solid fuel development and could probably achieve a Polaris or Minuteman-type vehicle before the end of the decade. The most probable stumbling block will be guidance systems—a complex of problems which the United States was able to solve only after five years of constant test firings. Radio guidance (the easiest) may be subject to jamming; inertial systems require a high degree of accuracy and reliability in all components of the missiles; and star-tracking systems are still only in the development stage. Still, there is no reason why, given a big enough investment, the French should not solve the guidance and control problem satisfactorily (particularly if the British entered into a partnership with them), although the 1970 estimate for an operational system may be optimistic.

More is involved than strategic nuclear weapons. Pierre Messmer points out that "with respect to each of the services, the two successive five-year plans are characterized by the appearance of nuclear explosives of French origin which, consequently, are ex-

[23] *The First Five Years of the Fifth Republic of France,* cited, p. 29.
[24] *The Atlantic,* August 1962, p. 37.

empt from the political and military limitations that weigh on explosives of American origin." These are to include "atomic weapons of kiloton or subkiloton yield with ranges from twenty-five to ninety miles,"[25] that is to say, tactical nuclear weapons presumably of the same types developed by the United States and Britain.

We shall examine the utility and risks of such weapons for the tactical defense of Europe in Chapter 5, but they do serve a quasi-political function. Here are the "toys" for all three services which, it is hoped, will accomplish the third French objective of modernizing the armed forces and restoring their pride in and identity with the nation. Then too, as in the case of Britain, such weapons might be used to back up conventional operations in peripheral areas, although from the standpoint of French interests there are far fewer such areas now than was the case ten years ago. French forces in Germany, unlike those in France, presumably have arrangements for wartime supply of U.S. weapons on the same basis as the other allies. Within the French Community, there would appear to be few, if any, places and circumstances where tactical nuclear weapons might be usefully employed—or where they would even have significant deterrence value. The military problems there are more of a gendarmerie, or counterguerrilla nature.

One might therefore conclude that the enthusiasm for nuclear armament in the abstract is a French version of a phase which the United States went through in the early 1950s. Indeed, the cycles of attitudes about nuclear armaments have followed a roughly parallel course within each of the nuclear powers. The experience of others seems of little use; only the discovery through experience that the possession of nuclear weapons can bring less, rather than more, flexibility to foreign policy suffices to advance the cycle.

Experience with costs, for example, tends to dispel the theory that nuclear explosives permit a reduction in other categories, such as manpower and conventional armaments, with a consequent

[25] Cited, pp. 210, 213.

over-all reduction in the defense budget. The French are not going quite so far in this direction as the United States did under the so-called "New Look," or as Britain did a few years later. On the basis of a projected 4 per cent annual rise in gross national product, France increased its defense spending from $3.5 billion in 1962 to more than $4 billion in 1964, and, it may reach nearly $6 billion by 1970. The available estimates of how much France is actually spending each year on the nuclear components of her military establishment vary widely. But a conservative guess would place the figure at over $1 billion if the isotope separation plants are included. The Minister of Defense has argued that a uranium isotope separation plant ($708 million) costs less than the equipment for two armored divisions (about $400 million each). While he recognizes that a nation cannot rely on nuclear weapons alone, he implies that modernization will effect a substantial reduction in numbers of troops and combat units to offset the high cost of new matériel, so that the percentage of GNP spent on defense will stabilize.[26]

Experience in the United States and Britain, and in France—which has already found it necessary to request substantial supplementary funds for the Pierrelotte isotope plant—suggests that spending estimates must be continually revised upwards. If so, tighter management can save only so much; the defense budget must rise in relation to GNP, or the latter must grow at a faster rate or else major cuts must be taken, either in conventional forces or in nuclear armaments. Once committed to the capital costs of a nuclear program, planners tend to sacrifice conventional forces and general combat support. This is what critics say the

[26] Messmer, cited. French defense budget figures include some costs accruing from past wars such as veterans' pensions and the like, which inflate the actual amount spent on current forces. The official figures for the *force de frappe* do not take into account plutonium production and other supplementary appropriations, adding at least one billion francs to the 2,400 million cited by Messmer in May 1963. See article No. 3 of the "Club Jean Moulin" series cited in footnote 65 below. The relatively few public references to nuclear costs of French forces are invariably larger than the official figures, suggesting that the latter are deliberately understated.

United States did under Eisenhower and Britain was doing until recently.[27] If a parallel course is followed in France, there will inevitably be a diminution in the quality and quantity of the French contribution to NATO—a diversion of alliance resources about which the other members, and especially the United States, may properly complain. Not only does this diversion fail to buy anything useful from the NATO (as distinguished from the French) standpoint, but it helps creat additional problems.

The problem of nuclear diffusion, whether applied to France or to a hypothetical "nth country," will be discussed later in this chapter. From a purely military standpoint, however, the nuclear strategy outlined in Chapter 3 must be based upon global rather than regional concepts. This requires the closest control and coordination of planning, targeting and operations. Unity, rather than division, of command and control is needed if the asset of a restrained counterforce capability is to have political significance. Moreover, even in the worst case of an actual conflict, it would be important to avoid spasm-type responses and an orgy of uncontrolled destruction of population centers on both sides. Obviously, the chances of mutual restraint are greatly reduced if one element of the Western striking force attacks Moscow while the other elements limit themselves to military targets.

[27] See the preceding discussion on Britain. In the United States, Generals Taylor, Ridgway, Gavin and others made similar criticisms of the Eisenhower administration's defense policy. U.S. major national security expenditures declined from $50.4 billion in 1953 to $46.9 billion in 1954 and $40.6 billion in 1955 and 1956. Despite increases in Air Force budgets, these over-all reductions were made possible by large cuts in the army—declined from $16.2 billion in 1953 to $12.9 billion in 1954, $8.9 billion in 1955 and $8.7 billion in 1956. See Appendix D of House Document No. 100, 85th Cong., 1st sess., 1957, "United States Defense Policies Since World War II." It must be recalled, however, that the "New Look" was also based upon the termination of the Korean War, which had caused U.S. defense expenditures to rise from $12.9 billion in 1949 to the $50 billion-plus level of 1953. Nevertheless, the official policy was one of "increasing reliance upon atomic weapons of all types—including as a principal deterrent and retaliatory force, massive atomic and hydrogen attack upon cities," in order to obtain "national security at acceptable cost." Hanson Baldwin's column in *The New York Times* of December 13, 1953, gives a good summary of the "New Look."

Circumstances in which the French *force de frappe* might actually be used in an attack on Soviet cities are hard to imagine, so that the problem is one of France claiming to have an "independent" trigger to the *U.S.* strategic forces. Since it might be difficult to distinguish between a French attack, limited though it would be because of the small capability, and the beginnings of an all-out Western strike, the Soviet Union might feel it could not afford to wait for clarification before responding, especially since so much of its strategic force is vulnerable. This could make the *force de frappe* a potential "detonator" for the over-all strike forces of the alliance. And it, in turn, is connected to the trigger of French tactical nuclear weapons. Indeed, it is this blackmail potential against the United States which the French tacitly rely upon to compensate for the unilateral ineffectiveness of their national forces in relation to a major nuclear power like the Soviet Union. French strategic doctrine, as announced by General Ailleret and others, appears to be making a virtue of necessity by insisting that the alliance stick to the "massive retaliation" type of posture which, as we have seen, the United States has long since abandoned.[28]

But if the French feel that decisions involving the life and death of their country cannot be left to the President of the United States, it is even more certain that decisions involving a sizable part of the world's population cannot be left to the chief executive of France. There is little doubt that in a tense situation in which France threatened to employ its strategic nuclear forces independently, the United States would be compelled to disassociate itself—publicly and perhaps dramatically—even from such a close ally as France. Thus a vicious cycle could start in which the fact of national nuclear forces in Europe would lead the United States to reconsider the automaticity of its commitment to European defense. In practical terms, this could mean a phase-out of American power from the continent and a withdrawal not only of nuclear forces, but of the six divisions which we now maintain

[28] See *Revue de Défense Nationale,* August 1964.

there. That this would be disastrous for Europe as a whole is clear. The result would be a Europe inadequately defended by its own forces, unprotected by the United States, and subject to easy neutralization by the Soviet Union. The key objective of Soviet policy since the war—to drive a wedge between America and Europe—would thus have been achieved in spite of, not because of, its aggressive nature! To avoid this cycle, other solutions must be found which can give France and Europe a reasonable sense of participation in decisions affecting the common destiny of the West. Whatever the solutions, they should minimize the chances of small national forces bringing on a thermonuclear war under the worst possible conditions, whereby a single element arouses the Soviet hornets' nest without drawing any of its stings!

There seems to be no immediate solution to the dilemma posed by France, although there are ways of mitigating risks and promoting evolution in a more sensible direction. Since France evidently cannot be induced to abandon its national nuclear effort, we shall have to agree to disagree. Meanwhile we must keep trying to blunt such sharp edges of disagreement as the distinction made by the United States between France and Britain. As Raymond Aron expresses it, the unofficial reason for this distinction is that "in Great Britain, the generals are obedient and the Prime Minister believes in Atlantic cooperation, which raises the vital question, are these two conditions realized in the Fifth Republic?"[29] Indeed, the situation does seem to involve a vicious circle: the United States will not share nuclear weapons with France because it does not cooperate on an Atlantic basis, and France does not cooperate because the United States does not share its weapons. As the preceding discussion illustrates, however, this is an oversimplification.

While it might be possible to treat France as having independently made "substantial progress" so as to qualify for nuclear sharing on the same basis as Britain, this would not produce a change in basic French political attitudes. And on the negative side, it would surely encourage the aspirations of other countries for

[29] *The Atlantic,* cited, p. 36.

nuclear status. Worst of all, it might tend to confirm the De Gaulle thesis that in the nuclear age, the only safe motto is *sauve qui peut*, instead of collective security. Even without any change in American nuclear assistance policies, it may be possible to develop practical cooperation at the military level which will help insure the coordination so vital to nuclear operations.

But whatever the United States does or does not do, the effects of practical experience as an "nth country" may well make the French more cooperative, especially after critical decisions about the future shape of Europe have been settled. Cost and technical difficulties, similar to those encountered by Britain, may engender a less nationalistic approach to what is, after all, a problem for the alliance as a whole.

In the more immediate future, it will be particularly interesting to see how France approaches its obligation as a signatory of the Brussels Treaty that the level of its operational nuclear stocks "shall be decided by a majority vote of the Council of Western European Union."[30] For by announcing that its *force de frappe* is "operational," France must either comply with this commitment, or renounce the very instrument which contains the limitations on German nuclear armament!

There are already signs that many top French officials understand, and to a limited degree accept, the reasoning behind the American concern over their nuclear program. As one of them said to the author: "If I worked for the American President, I would advocate precisely the policy which he has in this respect. But I do not. Since I work for General de Gaulle, I must pursue the course dictated by *his* logic." That logic, as we have seen, has many

[30] Article 3 of the Arms Control Protocol to the Brussels Treaty provides that "When the development of atomic, biological and chemical weapons in the territory on the mainland of Europe (i.e., excluding Britain) of the High Contracting Parties, who have not given up the right to produce them, has passed the experimental stage and effective production of them has started there, the level of stocks that the High Contracting Parties concerned will be allowed to hold on the mainland of Europe shall be decided by a majority vote of the Council of Western European Union." See p. 243 of the NATO fact book, cited.

elements, not the least of which is political and psychological. The satisfactions derived from being a nuclear "power" may reach its maximum returns within another few years and permit French policy to take new directions, depending perhaps on what may have happened elsewhere in Europe in the meantime. Although the timing was questionable and the details vague, French officials have suggested on several occasions that cooperation with Britain, or even a "European" atomic force was a future possibility. But the key word seems to be "future." Americans must recognize, however, that there is an inchoate resentment against Europe's continued military dependence on the United States. France will doubtless continue to play on such sentiments wherever possible. De Gaulle may, therefore, have some success, even though there appear to be no sound ways of lessening the basic dependence on the United States—and few Europeans want to substitute for it a nuclear dependence on France.[31]

Germany

The so-called "German problem" is in the background of much of the thinking about nuclear weapons and Europe. This is more than a matter of attitudes toward Germany, for the Germans themselves are acutely aware of their position in the front lines of NATO—in effect, the potential battleground of any war fought in Central Europe. Their plea to the alliance might be phrased: "If *you* hesitate, *we* are lost." Yet the Germans, by virtue of their wartime legacies, are in a special position. Many of them prefer not to be reminded that "thanks to Hitler, it will probably be a

[31] Secretary of State for Foreign Affairs Habib-Deloncle repeated in the French Senate the European force suggestion which he had made to the European Assembly at Strasbourg. Minister of Defense Messmer followed this up ten days later with similar remarks at the press conference. See *The Washington Post*, October 16 and 25, 1963, p. A24. More recently, Franco-German differences on a variety of fronts have led France to play down this theme. See for example Drew Middleton's dispatch in *The New York Times*, Sunday, August 9, 1964, Section IV.

long time before countries abroad are able to look on the Germans as a normal people once again."[32]

Chapter 2 reviewed briefly the agonizing steps through which Europe—and France in particular—came to accept the necessity of German rearmament. After the "European Army" concept of the European Defense Community failed to obtain French ratification in 1954, the Brussels Treaty Organization was revived and given an arms control mission. Its guarantees against a new German militarism were combined with British assurances to maintain forces on the Continent, and Germany was then admitted to NATO as a sovereign state.

As part of this process, Germany undertook unilateral declarations "not to manufacture in its territory" any atomic, chemical or biological weapons, and to observe limitations and restrictions on other categories of armaments. For the latter, however, the Treaty provides procedures for modification.[33] In short, the manufacture of nuclear weapons on German territory is prohibited, but the manufacture elsewhere—for example, in France, Spain, or the United States—or the possession by Germany of nuclear warheads manufactured by someone else is not. Even the basic prohibition on manufacture could be changed if the other members of the Brussels Pact agreed to revise the applicable protocol—which, however, is unlikely.

The 1957 Heads of Government Meeting decided *inter alia* to maintain U.S. nuclear stockpiles in Europe for the wartime use of allied forces. Under the 1958 amendments to the Atomic Energy Act, which permitted more liberal sharing of information and matériel, a number of bilateral agreements were negotiated with NATO allies. They provided for weapons systems to be made compatible with U.S. warheads, and for allied forces to be trained

[32] Helmut Schmidt, cited, p. 170.

[33] Long-range and guided missiles, major warships and strategic bombers are also not to be manufactured. However, these prohibitions can be (and in some cases have been) modified pursuant to requests by the Federal Republic and SACEUR, with the approval of a two-thirds majority of the Brussels Treaty Council of Ministers.

in their employment. Since most of the aircraft, artillery, and tactical missiles were furnished to NATO under the U.S. Military Assistance Program, compatibility was not a significant problem. What has proved to be difficult is negotiating the international agreements and undertakings required by U.S. laws. A host of politico-legal problems has delayed several of them for long periods. They are in effect in Germany, however.

Under the Military Assistance Sales Program, the German army has purchased eight-inch howitzers, Corporal and Sergeant missiles and the longer-range Pershing. The air force has aircraft, including the F-104G, being produced by a European consortium, which can carry nuclear warheads. As far as tactical delivery systems are concerned, German units are in exactly the same position as U.S. forces and those of other allies.[34] They would be provided with nuclear warheads from stockpiles maintained for the purpose in the event that the president ordered their release. But the basis of Germany's concern is the possibility that a presidential release might not be obtained before much of Germany had been overrun by the enemy. The complex politico-military issues affecting the role of, and decisions to use, tactical nuclear weapons in the defense of Europe are discussed in Chapter 5.

Public discussion in Germany has often blurred the distinction between warheads and delivery systems. References to equipping German forces with the very latest weapons and the demand in the "Generals' Memorandum" of 1960 that the Bundeswehr should have the same weapons as the forces of its allies, have added to the confusion. Helmut Schmidt has strongly criticized former Defense Minister Strauss for publishing the memorandum and the Adenauer government for "constant public advocacy of nuclear weapons for the Bundeswehr," but he also fails to clarify the question of wartime access to (and decisions on the use of) nuclear weapons as compared to their peacetime possession.[35]

[34] For details, see the Institute for Strategic Studies, *The Military Balance 1963-64* (London: 1964) and the WEU Assembly documents cited in footnote 1.

[35] Helmut Schmidt, cited, pp. 104, 171, 186.

For the present, any prospect of nuclear weapons under the *national* control of the Federal Republic would raise the deeply felt fears of German resurgence which lie just beneath the surface in many European countries, particularly those which endured Nazi occupation. In addition to the deeply unsettling effect such developments could have on intra-European relationships, the Soviet Union might consider the nuclear armament of Germany an extremely provocative action. The Russians would find themselves under considerable pressure to counter such a development, either by provoking major tensions in Central Europe or even by some equivalent sharing with other members of the Communist bloc though this would not appear to be in Moscow's own interests. One U.S. expert has even suggested that transfer of control to Germany would be interpreted as a move so hostile that it could risk a pre-emptive Soviet strike.[36]

Apart from the political and emotional reactions outside Germany, there is a risk that the possession of a national nuclear capability might encourage elements within Germany to press for a stronger independent line, particularly in regard to unification, which could have unpredictable and perhaps dangerous consequences. The Germans themselves are well aware of these dangers. Helmut Schmidt, for one, makes a number of persuasive arguments against a German nuclear capability from the standpoint of purely German interests.[37] During the 1957 controversy which followed Adenauer's decision to seek tactical nuclear delivery systems for Germany, eighteen German physicists led the protests. Others of their countrymen appeared to share the European view that the atomic armament of Germany could increase the otherwise small risks that undesirable elements might some day again emerge in a dominant position.[38]

At the same time, the Germans have a special and justifiable sense of vulnerability, the front-line complex referred to earlier.

[36] Klaus Knorr, *Bulletin of the Atomic Scientists,* September 1960, p. 276.
[37] Cited. See Chs. 6 and 10.
[38] See *The New York Times,* April 13 and April 15, 1957, *Le Monde,* April 17, 1957, and the London *Times,* April 15, 1957.

They are likewise sensitive to alliance arrangements which emphasize discrimination against Germany. These two factors have led to strong German support for various proposals to create a European or a NATO nuclear deterrent, such as the proposed multilateral force, which would enable Germany to participate on a basis of equality, but without raising the aforementioned specter of a national nuclear force.

Thus the Germans have been staunch backers of General Norstad's MRBM requirement, and they were the only European member of NATO to respond promptly with specific initiatives to various U.S. suggestions about an international force. At the December 1961 NATO meeting, the Germans reportedly urged that the decision to use nuclear weapons be decided by General Norstad jointly with the country under attack; and they raised "as a matter of urgency the question of creating a nuclear force controlled by NATO itself . . . following the lines of the year-old American proposal."[39]

For the next several years, German interest in nuclear weapons seems likely to remain within the NATO context. But the longer-range likelihood is that if Britain and France both continue to pursue the goal of national nuclear power, the pressures within Germany to follow suit may be irresistible. The issue reverted to the shadows during the early months of Chancellor Erhard's regime; but ex-Minister Strauss, among others, can be counted upon to raise it in the future.

To say the least, it would severely strain Germany's alliance with the West, if the more reasonable demands were not accommodated to some degree. On the other hand, meeting them in full could provoke even greater stresses within NATO, among the neutrals in Europe, and especially within the Communist bloc. Hence comes the feeling that the West can avoid being impaled on the horns of this dilemma only by progress toward international nuclear co-operation, such as the multilateral force, in which Germany can participate.

[39] Louis Rukeyser in *The Baltimore Sun,* December 15, 1961; see also Flora Lewis' article in *The Washington* Post of the same date.

On one hand, it is French determination to join the nuclear ranks which raises the problem most painfully for Germany. On the other, France has so much at stake in the success of the Franco-German rapprochement that cooperation with Germany in nuclear matters is always a distinct possibility. At the same time, official French opinion does not seem unduly alarmed about the "German problem." This appearance lends support to rumors that such cooperation already exists; that the Germans are secretly subsidizing the French nuclear efforts in return for a share in the knowledge or even the weapons; or that the Germans are actively participating with scientists and technical personnel. I have been unable to find any hard evidence to support these rumors, while some evidence tends to refute them. Indeed one journalist has suggested that the primary sources of the rumors were high officials in both the German and French Ministries of Defense, implying that the "cooperation" may represent more of a bargaining or tactical aim than a present reality. From their own standpoint, the French may see their head start of several years in building the *force de frappe* as their real trump card against any future German resurgence with nuclear ambitions.

The Germans find themselves caught between their fundamental postwar ties with France and a fear of being left to the mercy of De Gaulle, with no retreat available. They are thus trying to balance their politico-military dependence on the United States (involving Berlin, unification, and the U.S. deterrent and forces stationed in Europe) with their politico-economic dependence on France. When the two pull in opposite directions, the balancing act calls for a high degree of skill. But given a choice between a junior nuclear partnership with France (unlikely, at best) and participation in a broader arrangement–European or NATO–the Germans seem certain to opt for the latter. This makes it all the more important to find a solution to the problem of managing the nuclear power of the alliance.

Other Countries

If the United States and, to a lesser extent, Britain are NATO's present nuclear powers, France the declared nuclear status seeker, and Germany the potential problem, what of the others? Italy might conceivably be next in line, although the traditional Socialist opposition to nuclear armament makes this seem unlikely during the Center-Left experiment.

However, Italy has a "quintipartite" complex in highly developed form. The Italians are informed about, but do not take part in, bilateral U.S.-U.K. discussions, tripartite negotiations with France, and quadripartite activities with Germany on Berlin and related matters. It is therefore quite understandable that the Italians feel unjustly excluded from the activities of the other four and resent being treated as another one of the smaller NATO members, who are expected to rely upon North Atlantic Council meetings for their chance to participate. The United States has gone out of its way to accommodate this Italian sensitivity, but finds itself frequently inhibited by the exclusive tendencies of the other large powers, or the competitive jealousies of the smaller ones. From a long-range standpoint, these frustrations could create a seed-bed in which nuclear acquisitiveness could grow. Some years hence, a rebirth of rightist nationalism might produce an Italian De Gaulle who would see in nuclear weapons the best route to gaining acceptance of Italy's claims for a greater status. It is a healthy sign, therefore, that the Center-Left government and Foreign Minister Saragat have stressed the Atlantic and European framework and a multilateral, rather than unilateral approach to the nuclear problem.

The Benelux countries, Portugal (and, of course, Iceland) have thus far displayed no interest in becoming individual nuclear powers. Norway and Denmark are opposed even to the locating of nuclear weapons on their territory, and so seem unlikely even to consider national production. Their attitude reflects a strong tradition against the stationing of foreign forces in their countries in peacetime (which rules out the necessary custodial detachments for U.S. weapons) as well as opposition in principle to atomic weapons.

Canada is a special case. Despite its early participation in the Manhattan Project and its substantial profits from the export of uranium, a minority intellectual-pacificist school prevented until very recently not only the acquisition of nuclear weapons but the stationing of U.S. warheads in Canada. This had presented a serious problem for North American air defenses, since the more advanced defense missiles must employ nuclear warheads for maximum effectiveness.[40] Lester Pearson's government came to power in 1963 with a pledge to fulfill Canada's nuclear commitments, including accepting U.S. stockpiles for Canadian forces stationed in Europe. But he has maintained Canada's traditional insistence upon maximum consultation and control. It seems highly unlikely that Canada, having eschewed national production of nuclear weapons for the decade that its theoretical capacity to make them has existed, will seek to join the ranks of the nuclear powers.

Greece and Turkey have neither the ability nor, thus far at least, any interest in developing national nuclear establishments, particularly inasmuch as U.S. weapons are available for their defense if needed. Turkey, however, was sensitive to the withdrawal (uncomfortably soon after the Cuban missile crisis of 1962) of the squadron of Jupiter missiles which it, like Italy, had accepted at NATO request. Such acceptance was an act of considerable courage in the face of Khrushchev's counter-threats of 1957-58. Although obsolescent and extremely vulnerable from a military standpoint, the missiles were, for Turkey at least, an important psychological reassurance as to the U.S. commitment to its defense, for which some substitute must be found.

With respect to the general problem of nuclear diffusion, the pessimistic estimates of several years ago that by now over a dozen nations could—and many would—be producing nuclear weapons, have not been borne out. The pioneer National Planning Association study was reinforced in its somber tone by F. W. Mulley's conclusion that any country with a decent-sized reactor running could produce one or two bombs within three years of decision at a capital cost of about $31 million.[41]

[40] A good analysis is contained in Ch. V of Melvin Conant's *The Long Polar Watch* (New York: Harper & Row, for the Council on Foreign Relations, 1962).

[41] *The Politics of Western Defense*, cited, p. 257. Mulley's appendix on

It is true that of the five stages in bomb production (procurement and refining of uranium ore, operation of a reactor to produce plutonium, the extraction of weapons-grade plutonium, and actual fabrication) only the two plutonium stages involve major difficulties. Belgium, Canada, Czechoslovakia, East and West Germany, India, Italy, Japan, and Sweden all have one or more sizable power reactors operating or under construction, and others could easily join the list. The capital costs of $50 million or less are minuscule in today's multibillion dollar defense environment, so that there is relatively little doubt about capacity; and advancing technology makes the task even easier.

More recently, however, it has come to be recognized that the problem is as much political as economic and technical. Except for France and China, no other potential "nth" country has exercised its option in the past fifteen years. In an excellent and thorough analysis, the military and scientific correspondents of the *Manchester Guardian* point to the more optimistic factors.[42] There are political repercussions at home and abroad to be considered in a decision to produce a nuclear bomb. Moreover, the realization is growing that a few weapons are militarily meaningless without sophisticated and costly delivery vehicles—in short, that a "bomb" is not a weapons system. And not to be discounted is the expressed opposition of the present major nuclear powers to further proliferation, as well as the example of self-restraint given by several smaller but technologically advanced countries. Sweden has decided against the recommendations of its military advisers and postponed a decision until 1965.[43] Switzer-

---

potential weapons production draws upon his experience as rapporteur of the Defense Committee of the Western European Union Assembly as well as upon the prior NPA technical report (Davidson, Kalkstein and Hohenemser, *The Nth Country Problem and Arms Control,* January 1960).

[42] Leonard Beaton and John Maddox, *The Spread of Nuclear Weapons* (New York: Praeger, for the Institute for Strategic Studies, 1962).

[43] Mulley, cited, p. 262, attributes this choice to the fact that by 1965 Sweden will have accumulated enough plutonium for weapons purposes, while Schmidt, cited, p. 174, credits Sweden's desire to support efforts to close the nuclear club.

land, which once decided in principle to seek nuclear armaments, has apparently left the matter in abeyance. One cannot completely discount, however, the possibility that "De Gaullian" frustrations might one day take the dangerous route of offering nuclear assistance—for example, to Israel—to further French political influence. Within NATO, the political pressures for national nuclear establishments seem likely to be confined to France and Germany for several years at least, and then perhaps only Italy will be added to the problem. But the over-all European interest in having a greater say in alliance nuclear policies remains strong.

U.S. Attitudes and Policies

The preceding discussion dealt with possible specific additions to the nuclear club. While unofficial assessments may rank countries in terms of relative desirability as members, to do so officially within an alliance creates difficult diplomatic problems. Britain's preferred position is only partly due to its early start. Britain's record of domestic stability and responsibility in world affairs compares very favorably with that of any of the continental powers. The first four French Republics, for example, were hardly models of internal order, and the fifth came into being under the threat of civil war. German and Italian history in the twentieth century also speaks for itself. Nonetheless, the U.S. atomic energy legislation goes to great lengths not to specify that Britain is preferred; the criteria were designed to permit this result, while appearing to apply equally to all countries. However, there are strong American objections in principle to any nuclear proliferation, regardless of the countries involved.

The earliest postwar concepts in this respect were based on the twin illusions that secrecy could preserve the American monopoly (*effective* security might have at least prolonged it), and that international control of atomic energy was possible. The second assumption was shattered by the failure of the Baruch Plan in 1946-47, and the Soviet detonation of 1949 dispelled the first. Yet American policy remained firm against any further spread of nuclear weapons. The legal requirement for "substantial progress" as a condition for sharing cut in both directions, however. It may have served as an incentive to the French, who were more than a little shocked when they learned in 1960 that their two explosions were not considered sufficient to qualify.

As the cold war grew in area and intensity, the earlier restrictions on nuclear sharing were modified somewhat, particularly to permit cooperation with Britain. Then, in 1957, one year after the Hungarian and Suez crises and a few months after Sputnik heralded Soviet missile progress, NATO met at the Heads of Government level. Against a background of heightened tension, decisions were taken to deploy U.S. IRBMs in Europe and maintain American nuclear stockpiles on the Continent for the use of allied forces in the event of armed aggression.[44]

The United States also undertook to liberalize the sharing of information about nuclear weapons with its allies. Accordingly, the 1958 amendments to the Atomic Energy Act were approved by the Joint Committee, but with some reservations. Its chairman referred to the new authority as virtually a "do-it-yourself" kit, since, at least as far as Britain was concerned, nuclear materials, design information and non-nuclear weapons components could be transferred. For allies who did not qualify as having made substantial progress on their own, there was still equipment for weapons and reactors and information for planning and training and for weapons systems development. The rationale of the administration was that by deploying nuclear weapons for common defensive use and sharing knowledge "which will make our allies partners in this endeavor, resistance to the international control needed to prevent . . . the promiscuous spreading and possible irresponsible use of nuclear weapons" would be avoided.[45] In short, it was hoped that uncontrolled spread could be prevented by limited and restricted sharing. As already noted, this arrangement

[44] See the NATO fact book, cited, p. 34.

[45] Data from the hearings and committee reports are contained in House Report No. 1849, 85th Cong., 2nd sess., 1958, "Amendment to the Atomic Energy Act of 1954."

set the pattern for NATO, whereby the United States has developed nuclear stockpiles under U.S. custody in countries where the necessary agreements have been negotiated, and is training the allied (including French) forces in their use. In everything therefore except legal ownership, custody, and the decision to release the weapons, the allies are generally on a common nuclear footing, contrary to some popular impressions.

But at the same time the Eisenhower administration participated in nuclear test suspension negotiations, partly in hopes that this would discourage other candidates for the nuclear club, and the Kennedy administration followed through by achieving a partial test-ban treaty. His successor has expressed interest in continuing the search for an enforceable total ban. President Kennedy's speech to the U.N. General Assembly in September 1961 accepted the goal of general and complete disarmament and included measures to prevent "the transfer of control over nuclear weapons to states which do not now own them." President Johnson has reiterated this objective with respect to the Eighteen Nation Disarmament Conference at Geneva, and early in 1964 he proposed a freeze on nuclear weapons systems.

Notwithstanding occasional dissenting voices within its own ranks the U.S. administration also continues to put the antidiffusion principle into practice with respect to France. Persuasive arguments have been made that, since De Gaulle is going ahead with the *force de frappe* anyway, the United States might as well assist him and thereby save time, earn goodwill (or at least curtail resentment), and liberate resources that France could better devote to other military tasks. Nonetheless, it has apparently been decided that to make another exception for France would open Pandora's box still wider, stimulate the desire of others to join the club, and cloud the consistency of U.S. opposition to nuclear diffusion.

In the course of implementing any major policy, some apparent inconsistencies are bound to appear, as they have in this area—for example, the continuing special treatment of Britain and the sale of jet tankers to France. Nevertheless, for almost twenty years the United States has followed a relatively straight and unwavering path. It is therefore appropriate to examine the reasoning behind this policy and determine to what extent it can and should apply in the future.

The "No-sharing" Rationale

One major element is the belief that while restrictions on sharing are themselves an arms control objective, they are also a means to more comprehensive measures. The greater the number of countries involved, the fewer the chances of effective arms control or disarmament agreements. Years of patient negotiation—even when limited to the United States, Russia, and Britain—have thus far produced in concrete results only the limited test-ban treaty, on which the signatures of France and Communist China are conspicuously absent. Such hopes as there may be for the future tend to be diminished by further multiplication of the number of nuclear powers concerned. Also, a shift in U.S. opposition to diffusion might weaken the Soviet hand in resisting pressures for nuclear assistance to Communist China or to members of the Warsaw Pact.

Aside from the arms control aspects, nuclear diffusion could appreciably increase the risk of war by accident or miscalculation. Not only might a small-scale nuclear conflict between smaller states, say Israel and Egypt, quickly draw in the major nuclear powers, but the difficulties of identifying the origin of a particular nuclear attack would be multiplied.[46] At present, any nuclear attack upon the United States can be conclusively presumed to have come from Russia. It is significant that during the Cuban crisis President Kennedy specifically warned that any attack emanating from Cuba would be treated as if it had originated in Russia. Press

[46] America's tracking and warning nets cover only a part of its total frontiers, and even in the areas covered it is not easy to pinpoint the origin of an incoming missile. The Ballistic Missile Early Warning System (BMEWS), may be refined to the point that it can track a trajectory to its origin, perhaps after several fixes, and satellite infrared detection systems will be even more accurate for this purpose. But suppose the launch is made from the sea? Only limited time may be available for critical decisions involving retaliation, and positive identification might be lacking.

reports that Castro "contemplated" a nuclear attack on New York (that is, if he had possessed the means) can be put down to the bombast of a frustrated and immature Cuban leadership. But neither Moscow nor Washington could rest comfortably if a Castro-type regime had the nuclear means to blackmail its protector. As another example, Communist China may seek to force Soviet backing for a seizure of Formosa when its bomb becomes operational. Then, too, there are dangerous instabilities that might be created in the Middle East or Asia, should any of the traditional adversaries gain control of even one or two nuclear weapons. The new nationalism of many former colonies has far from run its course. Sukarno's Indonesia and Nasser's Egypt are but two states in which chauvinistic concern for power and prestige might lead toward the nuclear rainbow. Nasser has already demonstrated and boasted of his rockets, and Indonesia reportedly has ambitious plans involving a space launching with Soviet assistance.

Even among the larger and presumably more responsible powers, there is always a possibility of accident. This danger is frequently exaggerated in the press—at least as far as U.S. weapons are concerned—because of the multiple safety systems employed. In several airplane crashes or explosions involving atomic weapons, a very localized contamination from radioactive materials was the only nuclear complication. All U.S. weapons designs are carefully tested for their safety features. Efforts are made to detonate them under a variety of conditions which might arise in the event of an accident, and any that do not actually test "safe" are modified until they do. Twenty years of handling large numbers of weapons has yet to produce an unintentional detonation. But this is not to say one could not occur; and under the wrong circumstances it could prove disastrous.

Inevitably, the more weapons that are produced and handled, the greater the risks. It is most improbable that either of the two major nuclear powers would launch a retaliatory attack based upon one unexplained explosion in its territory because they have too many other means for evaluating whether they are being attacked. But the same would not be true for an accidental atomic explosion involving two smaller rivals who would almost of necessity start out with a hair trigger. Also, their nuclear devices and control systems would most likely be far cruder, intensifying the risk of accidental or unauthorized detonation.

There are important military arguments against national nuclear forces, which Albert Wohlstetter's classic article on the subject explains in great detail.[47] In brief, such forces are costly; they may be divisive; and they add little or nothing to the existing umbrella provided by a major nuclear power. In fact, their vulnerability to pre-emptive attack may cause them to be more of a liability than an asset. In some circumstances, they could be sufficiently provocative to risk bringing on the very attack they are supposed to to deter. It is, however, just the theoretical possibility of triggering a thermonuclear war which makes national nuclear forces seem desirable to their proponents and condemns nuclear sharing in the eyes of the others concerned. It may appear to some that the United States' opposition to nuclear proliferation is merely a cloak for its own selfish national interest in maintaining a virtual monopoly of strategic weapons within NATO; but an objective look at the future world which might result from a reversal of that policy suggests that other countries too have a vested interest in the United States continuing its opposition.

The United States and NATO's Nuclear Problem

Because the United States' historical opposition to transferring control of nuclear weapons to additional countries is well founded and likely to be continued, the various European attitudes outlined in this chapter have brought grave concern to the last three administrations. President Eisenhower found it necessary to relax some of the restraints in 1957-58, in the hope of perpetuating exclusive U.S. control of nuclear warheads until such time as they might have to be released to the allies concerned, that is in the event

[47] Albert Wohlstetter, "Nuclear Sharing: NATO and the N + 1 Country," *Foreign Affairs*, April 1961.

of armed aggression. But this did not go far enough to satisfy European concerns in general or head off the French nuclear program. Several years ago, General Norstad proposed to make NATO itself the "fourth nuclear power," in the form of a multilateral atomic authority which would give the alliance control of the nuclear components now held in exclusive U.S. custody.[48]

All kinds of propositions were batted back and forth among allies during the period from 1958 to 1961. Excellent and well-documented accounts are available,[49] so that a blow-by-blow recapitulation would serve no useful purpose here. All the conflicting national attitudes discussed in this chapter came to the fore. The United States was torn between its no-diffusion principle and the need to satisfy the legitimate interest of the Europeans in a greater degree of participation. The Pentagon reflected a variety of viewpoints, often oriented around preferences in each service for a particular weapons system. The State Department found itself divided between advocates and opponents of a multilateral strategic nuclear force. The Atomic Energy Commission and the Joint Committee on Atomic Energy were involved in the complexities of U.S. cooperation with the IAEA and the nascent EURATOM, particularly in regard to preventing the diversion of

[48] Norstad made it clear, however, that he was talking about forces and weapons systems with NATO missions, i.e., those falling within his sphere of responsibility as SACEUR, and *not* about a NATO strategic force—which "has not been suggested by me, or my headquarters." One of the best statements of General Norstad's views is contained in his address to the NATO Parliamentarians Conference in Paris, November 1960, which is extracted in the January-February 1961 issue of *Survival*, and in Mulley, cited, pp. 93-95. The "fourth nuclear power" argument should be distinguished from the *modernization* of NATO strike forces discussed previously in terms of the MRBM proposal. In discussing the latter, General Norstad spoke of "extremely mobile units, some of which may operate at sea, and some of which may operate from land," for the prospect of Polaris missiles seemed to offer the kind of invulnerability needed in any NATO MRBM force. After his retirement General Norstad proposed a three power (U.S., U.K. and France) executive committee empowered to act by majority vote. *The New York Times*, May 9, 1963.

[49] See Footnote 1, especially Osgood (Ch. 8), Mulley (Ch. 6), Kintner, and Dougherty.

plutonium to military uses. All of the various proposals, including General Norstad's MRBM requirement, were caught up in this bureaucratic Sargasso Sea. Since the maximum nuclear sharing that one group of U.S. leaders was prepared to accept fell short of the minimum which another group felt was required, little progress was possible.

In the last days of the Eisenhower administration, Secretary Herter put forth a compromise position at the December 1960 NATO Ministerial Meeting. The communiqué noted that the United States "had suggested the concept of an MRBM multilateral force for consideration by the alliance," of which the Council "took note . . . with great interest and instructed the permanent representatives to study the suggestion and related matters in detail." The U.S. offer of five Polaris missile submarines was subject to agreement on multilateral political control. It was also tied to the purchase by the European allies of one hundred additional Polaris-type missiles.[50] Instead of acting on this proposal of a "lame duck" government, the Europeans understandably preferred to await the views of the incoming administration.

One of the first tasks which the Kennedy administration addressed was an intensive inter-agency review of NATO problems, in which former Secretary of State Dean Acheson played a leading role. This study strongly confirmed that NATO was the keystone of American security. At the Oslo Ministerial Meeting in May 1961, Secretary Rusk confirmed the offer of Polaris submarines, but the communiqué merely spoke of "continuing . . . studies of all aspects of the military posture of the alliance." One week later, however, President Kennedy told the Canadian Parliament at Ottawa that:

> The United States will commit to the NATO command area five–and subsequently still more–*Polaris* atomic missile submarines, subject to any agreed NATO guidelines on their control and use, and responsive to the needs of all members, but still credible in an emer-

[50] Osgood, cited, p. 233.

> gency. Beyond this we look forward to the possibility of eventually establishing a NATO sea-borne force, which would be truly multilateral in ownership and control, if this should be desired and found feasible by our allies once NATO's non-nuclear goals have been achieved.[51]

This carefully worded declaration reflected the Pentagon's concern that the nuclear issue should not paralyze the alliance to the detriment of the conventional build-up, and left the ball pretty much on Europe's side of the court. But Europe's interest in the matter turned out to be nowhere near as coherent or united as had been thought. Efforts by the American Ambassador to engender constructive discussion in the regular meetings of the North Atlantic Council failed to bring forth a meaningful European response. Secretary Rusk explained in a press conference in the fall of 1961, that "the problem of nuclear control is quite literally of the utmost complexity . . . going to the very life and death of nations and the heart of the responsibilities of government. . . . It is not something we can decide for the Europeans."

For the time being the Kennedy administration let the matter lie, to focus instead on the conventional build-up in Europe and the pressures of the Berlin crisis. During the December 1961 and May 1962 NATO meetings in Paris and Athens, respectively, Secretaries Rusk and McNamara concentrated upon educating the statesmen of the alliance about the East-West strategic balance and argued that there was an excess—certainly not a shortage—of nuclear power within the alliance as a whole. This conviction lay behind Ambassador Finletter's statement to the North Atlantic Council that there was no military need to station more missiles in Europe, including General Norstad's MRBM, since SAC and Polaris could adequately cover the targets of concern to SACEUR.[52] It also reflected the administration's belief that nuclear warfare has made any concept of "theaters" obsolete except for

[51] See *The New York Times,* May 18, 1961.
[52] Murphy, cited, and p. 163, above.

administrative purposes. The speed and destructiveness of modern weapons argue for basing the strategic (as distinguished from tactical) defense of a given area outside that area. While hardly a politically salable proposition, such an arrangement would afford more warning time and less vulnerability to surprise attack. A large missile force based in Europe could guarantee that an enemy strike against it would cause enormous civil destruction and casualties. In short, it was argued, command and control of nuclear war is not only indivisible but must operate on a global rather than a regional basis.

At Athens, the United States made a political and psychological gesture to Europe by "assigning" the five promised Polaris submarines to NATO. In reality, however, they remained under the American Commander of the U.S. Atlantic Fleet to whom they were transferred in his alliance capacity as SACLANT. The U.S. delegation went to the conference with the decision neither to press actively for a multilateral NATO missile force, nor to weaken the U.S. stand against national nuclear armaments. But they stressed the irreversible character of our commitment to Europe's defense and the importance of greater interdependence within the alliance. McNamara apparently set forth for the first time the full range of our calculations about nuclear war, stressing the substantial preponderance of U.S. power—and the size of our stockpiles available in Europe for the use of European forces if required.

Evidently the shock of confronting the alliance with the facts of life had good results. One diplomat was quoted as saying, "For the first time in ten years I know where America wants to go, and I am content to follow." Arrangements were made to continue the sharing of information and to develop procedures, hitherto lacking, for allied consultation on the location and deployment of U.S. nuclear forces in the common defense—the so-called "Athens formula."[53]

[53] A further elaboration of the American viewpoint at the time is contained in my "NATO's Nuclear Debate: Washington's View," *The Reporter*, July

Athens laid the groundwork for some of the subsequent actions, which were, however, taken in the NATO Council and military structure rather than in the formal ministerial sessions. The annual Paris meetings in December of both 1962 and 1963, and the spring sessions at Ottawa in 1963 and the Hague in 1964 were relatively quiet, at least as far as the nuclear deterrent issue was concerned. As so often happens, it was a political controversy over a collateral matter which gave it a new momentum.

As we have seen, the Skybolt cancellation proved to be a traumatic event for the Macmillan government; the hastily called (and even more hastily staffed) meeting at Nassau followed hard on the heels of the December 1962 NATO Ministerial Meeting. And, in the words of the communiqué, it "created an opportunity for the development of new and closer arrangements for the organization and control of strategic Western defense . . . such arrangements in turn could make a major contribution to political cohesion among the nations of the alliance."[54]

More specifically, Kennedy and Macmillan agreed to assign some of the forces already in existence to a NATO nuclear force —the so-called interallied nuclear force—and that "the purpose of their two governments with respect to the provision of the Polaris missiles [to Britain] must be the development of a multilateral NATO nuclear force in the closest consultation with other NATO allies."[55]

It should be recalled that the latter concept was directly descended from the Herter offer of December 1960 and President Kennedy's statement the following spring at Ottawa. A small but influential group within the U.S. government, especially the State Department, had long advocated a multilaterally owned and

---

5, 1962, p. 21, from which some of the foregoing has been reprinted with permission.

[54] Joint Communiqué by President Kennedy and Prime Minister Macmillan following discussions held in Nassau, Bahamas, December 18-21, 1962. *The New York Times,* December 22, 1963.

[55] The interallied proposal was also known as the "paragraph 6" forces (from the communiqué) in contrast to the "multilateral" or "paragraph 5" concept.

manned force as the only realistic step forward which could be taken; and discussions had already been held with several governments.

With the mandate of Nassau, these efforts were intensified, giving rise to an extended series of briefings and exploratory discussions with European leaders during 1963. France summarily rejected a U.S. offer to discuss an arrangement similar to that reached at Nassau with Britain.[56] The Germans, however, were interested, as were the Greeks and the Turks. The British, despite their intimate involvement in the genesis of the whole matter, grew first noncommittal, then increasingly opposed, especially as the focus of the proposed multilateral force shifted from submarines to surface ships. Rome found itself embroiled in a major ideological issue over the matter, which complicated the Christian Democrats' negotiations for a coalition with the Socialists.

The end result was two sets of talks which got underway late in 1963. In Paris, a working group (Belgium, Germany, Great Britain, Greece, Italy, the Netherlands, Turkey, and the United States) concerned themselves with the political, legal, and economic problems of a multilateral missile force. A subcommittee met simultaneously in Washington to focus on the military and technical aspects. Apparently, the concept was found completely feasible from the military, legal and administrative stand-points, although the basic political decision to proceed remained open.

The inevitable publicity over these activities during 1963-1964 created more than a little confusion as to what U.S. policy really is. On the one hand, American officials have been accused of a "hard sell," if not actual arm-twisting of the "reluctant" Europeans. On the other, there have been official pronouncements to the effect that the United States is merely trying to accommodate European desires in the matter and is indifferent as to the

[56] In President de Gaulle's January 14, 1963 press conference he commented: "France has taken note of the Anglo-American Nassau agreement. As it was conceived, undoubtedly no one will be surprised that we cannot subscribe to it. . . . In sum, we will adhere to the decision we have made: to construct and, if necessary, to employ our atomic force ourselves."

outcome. The truth is probably that some individuals are in fact indifferent, if not opposed, while others feel that the project, or something like it, is essential to the whole alliance and that only strong American leadership can get it moving. But at least, even among opponents of the MLF, there has been an encouraging receptivity in Washington to the aspirations and interests of the Europeans. We shall return to the substance of the concept later on.[57]

Meanwhile, the interallied nuclear force proposed at Nassau had been established in May 1963. Far less controversy and publicity was involved, inasmuch as its operative units (Britain's "V" bombers and three U.S. Polaris submarines) were already committed to NATO. For this very reason, however, the political effect was far less significant. This tended to confirm the illusory nature of international control of *national* forces, as opposed to those with actual international or "multilateral" ownership. The Allied Tactical Air Forces (British, Dutch, Belgian, and German) in Central Europe are closely coordinated with, but not a part of, the force, although they too are supported by U.S. tactical nuclear weapons. During the summer of 1963, a Belgian general was appointed as Deputy to SACEUR for nuclear planning, and liaison has been worked out with the American strategic targeting headquarters at Omaha, in which European staff officers take part.

Other consultation and nuclear data-sharing programs have also been going forward, so that by 1964 some practical progress was noticeable, even though no solutions to the more basic problems have yet been found.

Some Practical Problems: Costs and Controls

Before we examine the alternatives for the future and practical possibilities for solving NATO's nuclear problem, a few more facts

[57] *The Washington Post*, July 19, 1964 (p. E1) contained an informative feature article of the MLF. More recently, the press and periodical coverage of MLF has "proliferated" geometrically.

need to be developed. Critical issues are the probable cost of various hypothetical forces which might be created, and the problem of political and military controls.

The organization of the nuclear power of the alliance has many aspects, but the jugular question is that of command and control. (Pentagon jargon adds to this phrase "communication," and then shortens the whole complex to "C cubed" or C^3.) Too often the problem is treated merely in terms of a weapon itself. Alternatively, the political levels of a governmental hierarchy are overemphasized. But in fact, there is a continuum which runs from planning to final execution.

The infinitely complex weapons of modern warfare break down into a few major elements. In a missile, this includes the warhead, the guidance system, and the vehicle itself. A manned aircraft likewise has its warheads or bombs, a crew to provide continuous guidance, and a delivery vehicle, which might be the aircraft itself or a stand-off rocket. Then, there is the launching platform for the system, a pad, airfield (or in the case of a stand-off device, an aircraft), a submarine, a barge or ship, a railroad car, a truck, etc. The personnel who operate and man the weapon are an integral part of the control system and must be treated as such. The basic ingredient of a military force is discipline, as indispensable today as in the time of Alexander the Great. Without discipline, and the organization and training which produce it, a military force is merely a conglomeration of individuals and hardware. Discipline itself is an important instrument of command and control. No organizational diagrams, or communications and electronic devices, can substitute for the loyalty, obedience, and judgment created by the discipline and traditions of a military service.

Working upwards from the weapons themselves, there are the command channels through which instructions reach the weapons, including control and safety devices, and all the information-gathering and decision-making mechanisms of the government concerned. At the apex must be an ultimate organ of political decision which can give the command "execute!" on matters affecting the nation's life or death. In America, of course, this institution is the presidency, including the duly constituted successor to presidential power.

The order of succession specified by Congress under its constitutional mandate has been much in the public eye since the assassination of President Kennedy. But there are also very real (if less publicized) problems in ensuring that, in times of tension, some one who can exercise presidential power is located in an invulnerable spot in case the president should be killed or cut off. This might have to be a flying aircraft, a railroad car, or a command ship at sea, in view of the ability of enemy missiles to destroy Washington and likely alternate presidential locations. This matter is receiving priority attention as part of the command and control problem. The White House has a special signal unit with hundreds of communications specialists and the most modern equipment, whose sole responsibility is to ensure that the president can be reached at all times, under all conditions, no matter where he may be.

Anterior to all of these are the politico-military policy-making processes to produce the broad stategy which the weapons systems are intended to carry out. From this strategy and various implementing decisions flow the detailed planning for the use of the weapons and the selection of targets. These targeting decisions must be translated into guidance, in the form of information coded on cards or tapes for use in missile computers or strike plans and operational orders for aircraft.

Other distinctions occur among techniques of control: there is ownership and custody in the traditional legal meaning of these terms; manning of the weapons and operation of the launching platform; and custody (in the physical sense) of the warheads or other essential parts including communications. Finally there is participation in the whole range of planning and perhaps a veto on decisions.

Suppose that three states wish to participate in a hypothetical nuclear deterrent force. There would be many ways for insuring that no one can operate the system without the consent of the others. For example, the over-all manning and operation could be divided up among teams, each composed of nationals of all participants. Or, each state could man and operate a one-system element, such as the launch platform, firing mechanism, guidance, or warhead. In the absence of an over-all command channel in which all participants had confidence, each national element might require some special communications authorizing it to perform its function. But this is not necessarily as cumbersome as it sounds, for modern technology has developed what is called a "permissive link"– in effect, a lock which must be released by an external electronic signal in code before the function which is blocked can proceed. As this is a fairly new development, there are still some problem areas; but the technical feasibility has been proven and the devices exist.

There are additional system elements of decision, targeting, and planning in which various degrees of participation or veto rights could be worked out. Limitations on the weapon could be imposed by built-in guidance with respect to targeting. If the targets selected for a particular group of missiles were commonly agreed upon, that guidance could be given to the missile computers in such a way that it could not be changed by the weapons crew, or without an external permissive signal. State A, for example, could thus ensure that its interests with respect to targeting could be enforced, even without further participation in the weapons system itself.

Let us imagine that the hypothetical nuclear force has built-in targeting guidance pursuant to an agreed strategy. The chain of command terminates in three "foolproof" buttons located around a table where authorized representatives of the three states are located at all times. As we have seen, it is technically feasible to set up the control system so that any one or all of the buttons must be activated before the missiles can be fired. Each of the three therefore could have negative control, inasmuch as his button represents a "safety catch." But then no one has positive control, since his "trigger" is dependent on the release of the other two safety catches. Conversely, the system could permit any one button to activate the force, but then none of the others would have negative control. This may seem to belabor the obvious, but it is surprising how many discussions of the problem ignore the physical impossibility of combining both trigger and safety catch within a single system comprising two or more equal decision-making entities.

This is why Alastair Buchan rendered singular service to the discussions of control by directing attention away from the button-pushing aspect. He proposed instead to talk about "contrôle" in the French sense of "examination, verification, the right to criticize," instead of in the English context of physical power over something. "The basic European desire," he states, "is not so much for operational control of bombers and missiles as *pour controller* American strategic policy, to gain some measure of control over the context of peace and war."[58] In short, he is talking about the upper levels of the control continuum, i.e., participation in strategic planning and policy making. If States A and B were satisfied that C would act pursuant to their common policy, each might give up having a "control," as distinguished from a "contrôle." The only other way to get around the dilemma of triggers and safety catches would be to eliminate any human participation and have the retaliatory force automatically fired by a bomb detector system. Thus, if *X* number of detonations of *Y* magnitude were recorded, the missiles would be activated. But it is almost inconceivable that any nation would so surrender its destiny to such a *deus ex machina*. Furthermore, if there were more than one possible source of an attack sufficient to trigger this system, the wrong country might be attacked. One state could neatly eliminate two rivals by a few well-placed detonations! Automaticity of this type is thus a negation of, rather than a solution to, control. A prearranged firing (either automatic, or via delegation to a military commander) which is subject to being "over-ridden" by political authority would make the system "fail enabled"—as opposed to "fail safe";

[58] Alastair Buchan, "The Reform of NATO," *Foreign Affairs*, January 1962, p. 180. This article is a shorter version of a monograph in the Adelphi Papers series of the Institute for Strategic Studies, of which Mr. Buchan is Director.

but this would also be hazard-prone, and thus almost equally undesirable.

Costs

The United States has invested well over $100 billion in strategic deterrence since the end of World War II. This includes research and development and procurement, as well as operation and maintenance of all U.S. strategic systems—aircraft, missiles, and carriers. A similarly all-inclusive slice of the defense budget for the last few years would indicate that the United States has been spending nearly $13 billion a year just to maintain and improve this capital investment.[59] This is approximately two-thirds of what the European members of NATO combined now spend on all aspects of their defenses. For "Europe" or any single nation to stand completely on its own in deterring the Soviet Union on a global basis would probably require something approaching this order of magnitude in resources. This, of course, raises several key questions:

1) Would the proposed force be designed to deter without any reliance upon U.S. strategic forces?

2) Is it to have a second-strike capability (invulnerability), or is it to be limited to a first strike?

3) Would it require a damage-limiting or counter-

[59] According to the McNamara House Appropriations Committee statement, cited, p. 16, $15 billion is the annual cost of U.S. nuclear programs. The 1963-64 "strategic retaliatory forces" budgets average $8.3 billion per year (pp. 42, 153), to which must be added $1 billion from general R&D and some $3.5 billion for elements of the "general purpose forces" with nuclear capabilities. This $12.8 billion total does *not* include any overhead furnished under the "general support" category, which would raise the total to over $15 billion a year. The $8.3 billion in the actual strategic "program package" breaks down as follows: Personnel: $1.2 billion; procurement: $4.6 billion, including some for the Navy; Operation Maintenance and Construction: $1.5 billion; and R&D: $1 billion (See pp. 157-158). The FY 1964 budget includes $7.3 billion for strategic retaliatory forces, while the FY 1965 figure drops to $5.3 billion, reflecting the fact that the bulk of the capital and R&D expenditures have already been made. See Secretary of Defense Statement to the House Armed Services Committee, January 27, 1964, Table 1.

force capability, or would it be only a countercity retaliatory system—with lower accuracy requirements?

4) To what extent would the United States assist by making available warheads, missile technology and matériel through either grant or sale?

The size, cost and feasibility of various hypothetical forces turn so much on these and many other questions, that only very rough estimates can be made.[60] A minimal force built without U.S. technical assistance and serving primarily political purposes, like the French *force de frappe*, might cost close to $1 billion per year by the time it was operational. The five-year cost, including nuclear weapons development, of a 50-bomber force might therefore be in the range of $3 billion to $5 billion. (The French are also spend-

[60] These rough cost estimates are based upon unclassified sources: Messmer, cited, pp. 208-209; "Minuteman Now Part of Bomb Force," an Associated Press dispatch appearing in *The Washington Post* of December 12, 1962, p. A9; a speech by Deputy Secretary of Defense Roswell Gilpatric to the Treasury Department Conference, January 19, 1962 (Dept. of Defense Press Release of that date); the National Planning Association's *1970 Without Arms Control*, Planning Pamphlet No. 104 (Washington, D.C., 1958), p. 21, and various documents on the federal budget, especially McNamara's House Appropriation Committee statement, cited. Actual cost figures are classified in some cases, so that these estimates may not be entirely correct, but approximations at least reflect the relative magnitudes involved. I am indebted to John Maddox, formerly associated with the Institute for Strategic Studies, for sharing with me some preliminary calculations which he had made.

The foregoing sources indicate that a supersonic bomber costs about $5 million (for a Mirage IV) to $7 million (for a B-52); missiles vary widely, from over $30 million each for the liquid-fueled *Atlas* to just over $3 million for a *Minuteman* and silo (including some R&D charges). A single *Polaris* missile without launching equipment costs only about $1.5 million; but a sixteen missile *Polaris* submarine comes to over $120 million or nearly $8 million per delivery unit. Hence the range of hardware costs. The R&D and weapons development estimates reflect French and British experience and are very rough approximations. Operating and maintenance costs are figured on the assumption that a mixed force of 1,000 bombers and 500 missiles currently costs the U.S. Air Force over $2.5 billion per year for personnel pay, O&M and construction. Costs would of course vary according to the actual weapons "mix" and the number of operating bases.

ing funds to develop missiles and submarines; hence the lower estimate for the bomber force alone.)

For a larger force composed of missiles, the goal might be a countercity, retaliatory type deterrent which could assume that 50 to 75 warheads would be delivered on target even *after an all-out enemy attack*. As a rule of thumb (taking into account survivability, reliability, accuracy, and penetration factors) from five to ten times this number, let us say, or 500 missiles might have to be deployed, depending on the assurance desired.[61]

By far the lion's share of the cost goes into research and development. A country starting from scratch, with no outside aid, would have to build reactors, plutonium extraction plants, nuclear test facilities and missile test ranges, and so on—a large and costly infrastructure. The first few missiles are enormously expensive; but the cost curve drops sharply with mass production. A force of 100 missiles may therefore be only about 30 per cent less expensive than one of 500 missiles. Taking the larger figure, and assuming an advanced industrial-technological base, but no direct outside aid, the five-year cost might be a range of $11 billion to $16 billion, divided about equally between: research and development; hardware; and operation, maintenance and supporting costs. Extensive technical and nuclear help from the United States and utilization of established U.S. missile production lines could, of course, reduce this range by one-third to one-half. But, as we have seen, it is unlikely that such American help would be forthcoming for an "independent" venture.

Moreover, it must be recalled that the completed force would at best be a minimum deterrent if considered alone. If we assume that our hypothetical force is to operate completely independently, with no sharing of the American strategic umbrella, it would be

[61] This rule of thumb differs somewhat from the assumptions discussed in Ch. 3; but it takes into account much the same factors. For example, to deliver 50 missiles, precisely on target, from 75 to 125 would have to survive an enemy strike. Unless the entire force were at sea, up to four times that number (300-500) might be needed, even with some degree of hardening and/or mobility to survive against massive attack by hundreds of enemy missiles.

manifestly inadequate against a major power like the Soviet Union. It could not even target, let alone destroy, the 700-plus Soviet medium-range missiles now aimed at Europe. Hence, to add any kind of a damage-limiting or counterforce capability would require tripling or even quadrupling its size. Here the hypothetical ratios discussed in Chapter 3 would be relevant, so that the optimum size to counter the Soviet Union would be around 1,500-2,000 delivery units—probably a mix of missiles and bombers. To increase our basic 500 missile force to, say, 1,500 units, we must add to its \$11-16 billion cost (including the overhead and development) about \$6-9 billion more for additional hardware, including warheads, plus something for expanded research and development. Added operating costs would come to at least \$1.5 billion per year. Thus the capital outlay plus the five-year operating costs would be in the \$27 billion to \$36 billion range. And we should recall that the United States found that the development of an adequate global deterrent required three or four times that amount over the past fifteen years. The current USAF (i.e., excluding Polaris) outlay to maintain and improve a strategic force of about that size is over \$6 billion a year, or roughly \$30 billion for five years. U.S. forces are more diversified and sophisticated than the hypothetical force discussed above; but at the same time much of the basic research and overhead has already been paid for.

The three hypothetical forces discussed above are compared in Table 7. Taking the middle (500 missile) case as the most reasonable one for a "European" deterrent, linked to that of the United States, we can see that its cost would require a sizable increase in European defense spending. Even if U.S. assistance were made available, the five-year cost might be in the \$7 billion to \$10 billion range (roughly twice what France is now spending)—which represents a great deal of money in anyone's defense budget!

Alternatives for the Future

The last four NATO meetings and the interallied dialogue which surrounded them appear to have brought a growing acceptance of the U.S. contention that there is no over-all shortage of nuclear

TABLE 7
Possible Cost Ranges for Hypothetical Strategic Nuclear Forces
($ billions)

Force number	I	II	III
Type and size	50 supersonic bombers	500 missiles	1,500 mix of aircraft/missiles
Main criteria	Political influence (psychological deterrence)	Assure delivery 50 warheads in second strike (minimum retaliation)	Good deterrence plus damage-limiting
Cost:			
Basic initial research and development (nuclear and aircraft or missiles) and infrastructure	2.5 - 3.5	3.5 - 5.5	5 - 7
Capital investment in hardware (including warheads)	.3 - .5	3.5 - 5.5	10 - 15
Five-year operating costs of full force (personnel, construction, operation, and maintenance)	.5 - 1.0	4.0 - 5.0	12 - 14
Total	3.3 - 5.0	11.0 - 16.0	27 - 36

striking power within the alliance. The problem is how it is divided and managed. As a basis for discussion, therefore, we shall accept the basic proposition explained in the preceding chapter. This is that the strategic power projected for American forces over the next five years will be fully adequate to handle all targets in the Soviet bloc which conceivably might have to be attacked and which can be targeted. It follows then that there is no *military* need for additional strategic forces on the continent of Europe. But the Europeans are increasingly resistant to the political implications if they mean that Europe should continue to rely exclusively upon American strategic power and the will of the U.S. government to employ it in their defense. This, say the Europeans, leaves them in the status of American military satellites, which is not a sound basis for the future of NATO. Indeed, NATO's nuclear dilemma represents a clash between immovable military logic and irresistible political forces. In such a confrontation, both must yield in some measure.

There would appear to be five broad alternatives for managing the nuclear power of the alliance in the future:[62]

First, there might be a strategic divorce, a non-Atlantic pattern of Western political organization. Europe would then have to look to its own defenses, strategic as well as tactical, and create such deterrent forces as it could quite independently of the United States.

Second, the *status quo* of a dominant U.S. monopoly of atomic warheads within NATO could be maintained, with bilateral

[62] Each analyst seems to have his own system of classification, but the alternatives coincide to a remarkable degree. In addition to his *NATO: The Entangling Alliance*, Robert Osgood has published a number of thoughtful monographs on the subject for the Washington Center of Foreign Policy Research. Alastair Buchan and Philip Windsor's *Arms and Stability in Europe* (New York: Praeger, for the Institute of Strategic Studies, 1963), reflects the ideas of a joint British-French-German study group. The book includes the Institute for Strategic Studies' Adelphi Paper No. 3, April 1, 1963 ("The Control of Western Strategy") which contains a very realistic discussion of the various possibilities. William Kintner has rendered a valuable service by collecting and analyzing over a dozen specific solutions proposed by various individuals in "Political Command and Control of NATO Forces," Foreign Policy Research Institute, University of Pennsylvania, November 1963. Likewise, John Newhouse has brought together the whole range of NATO issues in two admirable staff studies for the Senate Foreign Relations Committee: "Problems and Trends in Atlantic Partnership" I and II. I am indebted to all of the above authors for the stimulation of comparing notes during the past two years.

arrangements to cover allied weapons systems. European dissatisfaction could then take the form of whatever additional national nuclear forces the countries concerned were willing and able to create; or, there might be a renewed enthusiasm in some countries for the non-nuclear club idea, which the British Labor Party put forward while out of power and which enjoys considerable support among European Socialists.

Third, the whole nuclear problem could be made less troublesome if the alliance shifted to a non-nuclear policy and relied upon U.S. atomic weapons solely to deter the other side from using them. Since the nuclear-conventional balance and the economic capabilities of the alliance are discussed in subsequent chapters, this alternative will not be discussed in detail here. It would not, to be sure, solve the nuclear problem politically; but it might make it less militarily relevant. If NATO Europe could maintain, say, 60 to 80 first-line divisions in central Europe, nuclear weapons would no longer dominate the political-military scene.

Fourth, there might be an independent European contribution to the deterrent, which would have to be provided initially by Britain and France, but subsequently could be expanded on a multinational basis. In the longer run it might become an integrated force, responsive to a single European political entity, should one be created. Like Britain's Bomber Command, it could be constitutionally independent in the sense of being free of a U.S. veto; but in practice, it would be closely integrated with U.S. forces.

Fifth, a NATO deterrent might be created, in which the United States would participate actively, possibly along the lines of the multilateral force now under discussion. The majority of U.S. strategic forces would, however, remain under national control. Concurrently, ways might be found to improve NATO's functioning and decision-making. One approach would increase European participation in the planning and targeting of U.S. strategic forces so that they would take on more of an Atlantic character. Another would create a nuclear executive committee of the three nations with atomic forces. A third variant would seek a highly centralized political-military structure in NATO, to which the members might increasingly delegate authority. Finally, it might prove desirable to re-examine General Norstad's ideas for greater NATO control of *tactical* nuclear weapons, which are discussed in Chapter 5.

Strategic Divorce

A strategic divorce would represent a conscious intention on both sides of the Atlantic to make Europe completely independent of the United States in defense matters as quickly as possible. The United States might, for example, undertake to sell to the European nations all of the nuclear warheads and delivery systems which could be produced over and above U.S. requirements. It could also furnish training and technical assistance for the development of a major strategic nuclear force in Europe. This would require further changes in the Atomic Energy Act, and although these might be obtained, if backed strongly enough by the administration, the United States would be revising its entire policy against nuclear diffusion—which is unlikely as well as undesirable. Under such a plan, the United States would phase out its forces in Europe and adjust its own strategic posture. As quickly as the new forces were capable of the missions involved, the United States could turn over to them the responsibility for targeting areas of particular concern to Europe. Presumably, the United States would also withdraw its ground and tactical air forces in Europe, leaving the Europeans with the task of filling this gap. The considerable U.S. savings, both in balance of payments and in actual costs might, in part, be applied to the nuclear weapons which would be furnished.

Although Europe could spend in the United States most of the $10 billion to $30 billion which would be required for a worthwhile force, a European nationalism sufficient to support this kind of independent venture would almost certainly include an autarchic insistence that as much production and procurement as possible be done in Europe. The favorable impact on the U.S. balance of payments would be less under these circumstances. Moreover, the establishment of new production lines could delay the creation of the European force by an additional two or three years.

This book has developed the thesis that the world power structure of the late 1960s will require the United States and Europe to work in harness rather than at cross-purposes. Obviously, the strategic-divorce alternative contradicts this assumption. Also, it seems doubtful that the European elements favorable to such a program could carry sufficient weight with national parliaments to obtain the substantial sums involved. The lower (and more manageable) the costs, the less effective would be the force involved. As we have seen, a force which could hold its own against the U.S.S.R. without reliance on the United States is a $30 billion-plus proposition. The smaller "minimum" deterrent would leave Europe more or less at the mercy of Soviet "salami" tactics, except for the U.S. interest in European security—which would have been adversely affected by the withdrawal of American forces. And apart from the marginal utility of a small nuclear force, even a lower price tag of $10 billion to $15 billion would raise problems of feasibility. General de Gaulle himself has encountered parliamentary difficulties in getting much smaller sums appropriated for his own nuclear program.

Finally, the control problem would merely shift from its present trans-Atlantic focus to become an intra-European issue. The Germans, the Turks, and to some extent the French, want a trigger, while the other European countries are more worried about the safety catch. In the absence of a supranational European government, the result of a U.S. withdrawal could be a *sauve qui peut* scramble for national nuclear forces. It is true that, as Jean Monnet and others have argued, the need for military unification to provide nuclear control in Europe could give a boost to the drive for political unity. But De Gaulle's veto of Britain's Common Market application, which sidetracked that drive, was a political act. It is by no means clear that the route of military functionalism could succeed where economic functionalism failed in overcoming French political objections. But for the purposes of this strategic-divorce alternative, it is not really relevant whether Europe exists as a political entity or remains a geographical grouping of sovereign states. For the crucial issue here is the relationship between America and Europe, however the latter is constituted.

After such a divorce, the United States and Europe would become so mutually independent that either could presumably become involved in conflicts up to and including nuclear war without involving the other. If Communist China should have a moderate-sized nuclear force of its own by the late 1970s, basic divergencies in interests and in willingness to run risks might make concerted action by the United States and Europe impossible. Faced with such a situation, the United States could deal with the menace of Communist China unrestrained by a Europe which could claim the option of sitting out the conflict. It is not inconceivable that Russia might make a similar choice. However, such freedom of action would be a two-edged sword. Russia might equally neutralize Europe in the sense of forcing it to stay out of a conflict with Communist interests in Africa or the Middle East, especially if the United States should be unwilling or unable to meet the challenge alone. In this case, the advantages accruing from America's and Europe's independence of each other would be overshadowed by great risks for the West.

In any event, the strategic divorce alternative would be fundamentally opposed to the antidiffusion policy as well as to the underlying assumptions about European-American ties. It would deny NATO any future at all, and it would rob the United States of any voice in European security, which is still essential to its own. This is the basic point that Ronald Steel and others who write about "the end of alliance"[63] overlook. For the realities of power and interest in the 1970s—political and economic as well as military—are likely to be different only in degree from those of a decade or more ago. The Soviet threat may or may not recede still further; but the stable world order which might, some day, permit an end to alliances in general can be structured only by Europe and the United State acting in harmony.

[63] Ronald Steel, *The End of Alliance: America and the Future of Europe* (New York: Viking, 1964).

The Status Quo

If no affirmative decisions can be made, the present situation will continue as a matter of course. At the same time, there could be a conscious recognition that the *status quo* is preferable to any attainable alternative. We should recall that U.S. forces are not the only ones with nuclear capable weapons. On the contrary, allied units are armed with modern short-range tactical missiles and aircraft, for which the warheads are kept in U.S. custody. Conceivably these could be adapted to medium-range missiles similarly deployed, although their location might cause some political difficulties. But the rub, as many Europeans see it, is that the warheads depend on a political decision made exclusively by the U.S. No one, excepting perhaps Barry Goldwater, seriously challenges the necessity for political control. It is the exclusively U.S. nature of the decision-making system that is politically nettlesome, however necessary it may be at present. One long-term consequence of the situation would probably be an intensification of the French nuclear effort and a parallel rise in German ambitions and frustrations. Moreover, whether or not Britain's strategic forces were eventually brought into a common framework with the Continent, other European nations might be encouraged in time to follow the French lead in developing nuclear arsenals subject only to their own control.

The bill for four or five separate deterrent forces at $5 billion to $10 billion each, adds up to a formidable diversion of Europe's resources; and they would be of marginal military effectiveness because of their mutual independence. Moreover, this situation would produce the very proliferation on a worldwide basis which U.S. policy is designed to discourage.

Over a period of five to eight years, a continuation of the *status quo* might eventually develop into the strategic divorce alternative, although in the short term the effects would be less serious. It already seems likely that the French will encounter increasing difficulties in going it alone in the nuclear field. As we have seen, the so-called German problem, and that of the "nth" country in general, are unlikely to become acute in practical terms within two or three years.

Although the NATO treaty does *not* terminate in 1969 as some press stories have implied, the twenty year anniversary—after which any party may withdraw on one year's notice—does fall in that year. Therefore the alliance cannot afford to allow these questions to drift much beyond 1966 or 1967. The effects of U.S.-French differences have already hampered NATO. If similar corrosion develops with other allies, a running exchange of polemics across the Atlantic might develop, which, in turn, could stir up American congressional and public emotions to the point of rash reprisals. If U.S. disengagements resulted, Europe would be left inadequately defended and with merely the illusion of independence, a consequence that could benefit only the Communists.

In summary, the *status quo* does not appear sufficiently dangerous in the short run to warrant a change for its own sake, or the hasty adoption of unwise alternatives. On the other hand, the longer-term dangers are too great to ignore.

The third possibility—making nuclear forces less relevant by developing a primarily conventional defense posture—might be achieved within the nuclear *status quo*. This deserves more serious evaluation than it has had. But unless Socialist-oriented governments with a strong bias against nuclear armaments come to power in several of the major European countries, it is unlikely to attract much interest. We can therefore discount it for purposes of this discussion.

A European "Contribution"

The fourth possibility would be an independent European contribution to the over-all deterrent. It would differ from the first alternative in that Europe's efforts would be part of the over-all strategic forces of the West, and from the second alternative's encouragement of "national" forces, in that the efforts could be multinational.

A "European" force could result from an arrangement between the British and the French for bilateral coordination, similar to that which SAC now has with Bomber Command, or it could involve a mutual two-key system, analogous to that which governed the RAF's Thor or the German army's Pershing missiles. Such a force could conceivably be broadened in the future to include German, and perhaps Italian, participation. Moreover, it could evolve naturally out of existing arrangements, and be fitted into over-all allied targeting plans.[64] Another possible framework might be created by disinterring the European Defense Community (EDC) and reconstituting it along lines suitable for providing a central European defense organization, with a single defense budget and command structure.

The difficulty is that the abortive EDC was to be the third leg of a triangular basis for European union, which involved not only the Coal and Steel Community on the economic side, but a European political community as well. Since common defense policy can be made only in the light of common political decisions, a revived EDC would have to be made responsive to the Common Market's Council of Ministers, if that group's political functions could be broadened sufficiently to cover major defense issues. However, while any number of such theoretical frameworks can be imagined, few bear much relationship to present political realities in Europe. Nevertheless, it may not be premature to look ahead several years on the assumption that Europe can resume its progress toward political unity. There are relatively few detailed French studies of strategic problems which are not propagandistic apologies for the *force de frappe*. One of them, prepared by "Le Club Jean Moulin," a French study group, has not had the attention it deserves outside France, and its conclusion is worth quoting:

> Europe must do nothing which diminishes the American guarantee of its security. That would be strategic and political folly. On the other hand, Europe cannot accept a denuclearization which would be a

[64] This has already had some discussion in the press. See, e.g., the London *Times*, June 24, 1962, *The Economist*, May 5 and May 12, 1962, *The Washington Post*, October 25, 1963. Henry Kissinger, "NATO's Nuclear Dilemma," *The Reporter*, March 28, 1963, and Hanson Baldwin, "Europe's Nuclear Defenses," *The Reporter*, April 25, 1963, have both advocated that

> default and would withdraw from it all possibility of action for the control of nuclear armaments. . . . The road, though narrow and strewn with difficulties, leads to a bipolar nuclear force, to the equal association of the United States and a European federation in a reorganized Atlantic alliance. . . . In the face of the French choice and the division of Europe, the Americans believe it impossible for them to share major responsibilities. The Europeans believe such sharing necessary. That impossibility and that necessity can only be reconciled in the construction of a United Europe with a common policy and a common defense.[65]

The logic may be sound. But logic is one thing and political will another. A common European defense can come about only when Europe has answered by its own political action the question once posed by Secretary Rusk: "What is Europe and who speaks for it?"

If a United Europe now seems unlikely to evolve out of the Common Market, in the near future, especially as long as it is without Britain, what other possibilities exist?

The Brussels Treaty's Western European Union (WEU) organization would be one of the better ones, since it bridges the membership gap between the EEC on one hand and Britain on the other. The recent intensification of the nuclear debate has reopened the possibility, argued as early as 1958 in an American book on NATO, that WEU should become Europe's defense organization.[66] In 1959, F. W. Mulley, a British M.P. who was then rapporteur for WEU's Defense Committee, proposed a "joint European strategic nuclear force within WEU." However, his more recent book, noting the unsympathetic attitudes of the governments involved, particularly

---

the United States should encourage this process by rendering advice and assistance.

[65] The study appeared as a series of five articles in *Le Monde*, December 17 to 24, 1963. The quotation is from Number 5 of the series, December 24, p. 3.

[66] Ben T. Moore, *NATO and The Future of Europe* (New York: Harper & Row, for the Council on Foreign Relations, 1958).

his own, places greater emphasis on a NATO framework.[67] In October 1963 the WEU Assembly's Defense Committee (which in the past has argued for a European deterrent based on WEU) recommended a multilateral force under NATO. The proposal was, however, defeated in the full Assembly.[68]

Some of the more cogent arguments for utilizing WEU as a military nexus are those advanced by James E. Dougherty.[69] After a comprehensive analysis of the literature on the subject, he recommends that the United States "offer to make the Western European Union an independent nuclear power, provided that Britain and France will subject their nuclear capabilities to joint control within the WEU framework." Since WEU has been in existence for some time and has a treaty life of fifty years, it would offer a vehicle for the transfer of French and British national nuclear forces to joint control. At the same time it would provide for a close relationship with the United States through NATO, of which WEU has been a more or less a silent subsidiary since its embryonic command structure was integrated into NATO following the Korean War.

WEU once provided the framework for German rearmament after EDC failed. It might now be the means of salvaging the failure of Britain's attempt to enter the Common Market. Moreover, so runs the argument, if Britain does join the EEC later on, WEU would be the ideal defense counterpart for that organization, for the membership of the two would then coincide. With established economic and military legs, the political hypotenuse of the European triangle would be easier to build.

Compared with national efforts, a multilateral grouping of this kind would have geostrategic space advantages and a superior combination of economic and technological resources. Dr. Dougherty

[67] Mulley, cited, especially pp. 86-91. His later views are explained in an article in the Spring 1963 issue of *Orbis*.

[68] The rapporteur's draft recommendation is available as a WEU document and is reprinted in part in Kintner, "Political Command and Control of NATO Forces," cited, p. 43-44.

[69] James E. Dougherty, "European Deterrence and Atlantic Unity," *Orbis*, Fall 1962, p. 371.

also suggests that WEU's practical experience in arms control arrangements could provide a basis for mixed military teams to control the nuclear weapons deployed in any one country. But that advantage is more apparent than real. As noted earlier, the WEU may not be able even to compel France to live up to its existing treaty obligations with respect to the size of her nuclear stockpile. And for military functions other than arms control WEU's international experience and standing do not begin to compare to those of NATO.

In any event, the rock upon which any proposal of this type seems bound to come to grief is the control problem. Given seven sovereign members of WEU, effective political decision-making and control would require an extraordinary degree of harmony and trust, and this goes back to the root of NATO's problem. In part, as we have seen, the control question reflects a European concern that under some circumstances the United States might not use its nuclear weapons in Europe's defense—or conversely, that it might do so prematurely or unwisely. Whether any European country would trust its WEU colleagues in this respect more than it would the United States is also rather doubtful.

An opinion survey several years ago found that European leaders believe the enthusiasm for pooling armaments in "Little Europe" to be fully compatible with a strong endorsement of NATO. They also thought that the Atlantic alliance would remain essential in a continuing cold war struggle. Several surveys of French opinion between 1952 and 1957 reveal that, except for the period immediately after Suez, the United States was considered by far the most reliable ally in the event of war. Even the unfavorable attitudes generated by the 1960 summit failure did not seriously affect confidence in NATO or the presence of American forces in Europe.[70]

[70] See Daniel Lerner and Morton Gordon, *European Leaders Look at World Security* (Cambridge: Center for International Studies, MIT, 1960), p. 46. "Revue Française de l'opinion publique," *Sondages*, Nos. 1-2, 1958, pp. 45-54, especially pp. 48-49; and the USIA's report of post summit trends in British and French opinion reprinted in *The New York Times*, October 27, 1960. However, Lloyd A. Free's *Six Allies and a Neutral* (Glencoe: The

French attitudes since De Gaulle have reflected more of his belief that a unified Western Europe could have its own policies, independent of the United States, and constitute a "third force." But the same surveys also revealed considerable ambiguity in French policies and attitudes toward Britain and other European powers.[71] Even General de Gaulle gives lip service to the concept that under present conditions, the Atlantic alliance and the American power which it provides are necessary for France.

Elsewhere in Europe—particularly among the smaller countries, but also in Germany—there is no doubt that confidence in the United States, especially on defense matters, is considerably higher than for any other ally.[72] In any case, it is difficult to imagine that those political objectives of Germany or Britain or indeed of France which cannot be satisfied by reliance on the United States would be met by relying instead upon a European consortium, let alone another single ally. It is hard to find a knowledgeable German, for example, who believes that the *force de frappe* in any way reinforces Germany's vital interests.

It has been suggested that this point could be met by a special U.S.-WEU relationship providing for "two fingers on the trigger, one American and one European." In point of fact, however, the European finger would be hooked up to seven separate nervous systems, which could create the dilemma that either everyone has a trigger or everyone has a safety catch. No one can have both. The only solution therefore is that advocated by the French study cited earlier—a very real degree of European unification which

---

Free Press, 1959), points up some of the long-term French hostility to American leadership which was intensified by Suez. See pp. 95-109.

[71] Mimeographed summary, Institut Français de l'Opinion Publique, June 8, 1962.

[72] A recent French book throws some interesting light on the essential role the United States has had to play in any successful European enterprise. Bernard Baudry, *Euro-America* (Paris: Plon, 1962), especially pp. 41-49, 70-90. John Pinder, *Europe Against de Gaulle*, (New York: Praeger, 1964), and U. W. Kitzinger, *The Politics and Economics of European Integration* (New York: Praeger, 1964), provide additional evidence that the Gaullist concept is not accepted by many Europeans.

would evolve into a single political authority with one nervous system, instead of seven. Such a development is, at best, a considerable distance in the future. At heart, it is something the Europeans must do by themselves, and will do if the reasons are sufficiently compelling in their eyes.

The remaining question is whether the United States could and should assist by holding out the prospect of nuclear assistance as an incentive to unification, much as economic aid under the Marshall Plan inspired European economic cooperation. However, this would put the United States in the somewhat awkward position of pushing the Europeans to create an institutional receptacle for assistance which, unlike the Marshall Plan, the United States does not really want to give—at least to any organization in which it is not an active participant. The counter argument is that "it is in the logic of the present historical situation that Europe will sooner or later develop an indigenous deterrent. The crucial issue is whether it will be built with U.S. assistance and in such a way as will reinforce the trend toward a genuine NATO confederation, or whether it will be built in defiance of the United States, in which case, it will not augur well for the future of the alliance."[73]

Perhaps at the most, the United States should expand its previous indications of potential cooperation. America might say, in effect: When, as, and if the Europeans agree that an indigenous deterrent is needed to the point that they create an organization capable of managing and controlling it, the United States will then assist such an entity. President Johnson struck this note as Vice President (with reference to the multilateral force) by stating in Brussels that "evolution of this fleet toward European control as Europe marches toward unity is by no means excluded." It does not seem desirable, however, for the United States to use the nuclear tantalus to entice the Europeans in this direction faster than they would otherwise go. There are a number of good reasons for restraint.

A "European" force would add relatively little from the military standpoint. It might duplicate strategic forces which the United

[73] Dougherty, cited, p. 421.

States would feel obliged to maintain in any case, especially if the United States did not have confidence in the political decision-making mechanism which controlled its use. If close coordination permitted some reduction in the American effort, there would be a net addition of several billion dollars to NATO's combined defense expenditures, even with American help. A sizable amount of European scientific and technical manpower, as well as economic and industrial resources, might be tied up without adding much to the West's over-all technological base. There are probably higher priority areas where Europe could make a greater scientific contribution to the future security of the alliance.

A reasonable figure for a small European force of several hundred missiles built with American technical but not financial help might be $7 billion. This sum would buy the equipment for about eighteen European armored divisions. Alternatively, it could equip, man and operate ten infantry divisions for about five years—bringing the central front up to thirty divisions and adding three or four on NATO's flanks for good measure. Europe's security would obviously be enhanced by such an addition, while the nuclear investment would yield a questionable increment from a purely military standpoint.

Finally comes the question of the U.S. interest in, and degree of control over, such a force. If the United States held a veto through any of the types of negative controls discussed previously (e.g., custody of the warheads), this would largely counteract the political rationale of a "European" force. But if the United States had no control, two sets of risks would accrue. On one hand is the possibility of a paralysis in multilateral European decision-making which could vitiate the credibility of the force in time of crisis; on the other, there is the theoretical risk that the force could be used in circumstances contrary to American interests.

The "stuck safety catch" risk might persuade the United States that it could not rely on the European contribution, necessitating contingency plans and forces to duplicate the target coverage. The "hair trigger" risk could have the consequence of American disassociation from Europe in a crisis if the use of the force to initiate nuclear warfare independently were threatened.

However, there are ways of minimizing both dangers. The targeting guidance for the European missiles could be locked into the system in such a way that it could not be changed without U.S. participation. This would guarantee that if the force were used at all, it could only attack targets that were on the U.S. mandatory counterforce list and not on the list of optional or proscribed targets, such as major population centers. As Malcom Hoag has pointed out, "we give nothing away if the nature of the response fits our global operation. This vital proviso can be simply met, for example, by keeping the missiles of the European force aimed at key vulnerable Soviet missile installations."[74] An alternative approach would have the European force designed as part of the alliance reserve to be withheld during the early stages of a conflict. It would be employed as a last resort, and only if the enemy had attacked European cities. As a countercity retaliatory force, the control problem would be less acute, since the missiles would be fired only in the worst case of general nuclear war. We shall return to this possibility again.

Another important American interest in the control problem reflects the arms control and disarmament dialogue with the Soviet Union. As one European study has noted, "there is an inescapable dualism in American policy which makes it essential for her to reassure her fellow superpower, the Soviet Union, at the same time as she helps to build up the strength of her allies."[75] This dualism can also become a dilemma, as shown by the repeated American efforts to assure the Soviets that the proposed multilateral force would not involve German nuclear armament and would help to contain, rather than encourage, proliferation. Presumably, any European force in which the United States had sufficient confidence to give

[74] "Missiles for France?," RAND Paper No. P.2594-1, June 1962, p. 18. Mr. Hoag has elaborated his views along lines similar to those contained in this chapter, in "Nuclear Policy and French Intransigence," *Foreign Affairs*, January 1963, p. 286.

[75] ISS (Adelphi Paper No. 3) cited, p. 4.

up a significant measure of control would not be judged dangerously provocative by the Russians. But they could be counted upon to oppose it and to obstruct it wherever possible.

Because of these problems, other alternatives ought to be explored before the United States takes a final stand with respect to any prospective European deterrent. Action now—either to foreclose or guarantee nuclear assistance—would be based on the predictions of relatively few leaders speaking either for themselves or, at most, for a single country. There is, to be sure, a ground swell of public opinion which has seized upon the nuclear control issue to vent a vague desire for enhanced status as compared to the United States. These sentiments might become dominant in a European political organization; but it is also possible that the mere act of creation of such a unified body politic would have satisfied the underlying urge for equality. Or the issue might have shifted from nuclear strategy to other considerations entirely. In sum, when there is an authorized spokesman for "Europe," the United States will perforce have to listen carefully. And if the political desires for an independent nuclear component are still present, America would be well advised to respond. But it can then do so in the light of the reality of the organization which is to exercise control, rather than its hypothetical complexion.

This indeed seems to be the view of several American spokesmen, if not of the government as such. In a speech in Copenhagen, McGeorge Bundy commented that "it would be wrong to suppose that the reluctance we feel with respect to individual, ineffective and unintegrated forces would be extended automatically to a European force, genuinely unified and multilateral, and effectively integrated with our own." Others have pointed out that it is not the United States which stands in the way of any desires of Europeans to unify their defense policies.

In conclusion, therefore, the alternative of an independent "European" contribution to the nuclear deterrent must be set down as a possibility for the future, but not as a very good immediate prospect, for Europe's "march" toward unity has slowed to a crawl. We have rejected the strategic divorce possibility as undesirable and the *status quo* as untenable over a long period. A non-nuclear strategy seems unattainable, and an independent European deterrent is, to say the least, premature. What then remains? Before reaching our answer through this process of elimination, we must clear away some confusion regarding a "NATO" alternative.

A NATO Deterrent

Nowhere can language be more treacherous than in discussions of this topic, for in point of fact NATO has several nuclear deterrent forces. The United States, after all, is a member of NATO and has provided the bulk of its strategic power for the past fifteen years. Elaborate stockpile arrangements exist with many of the other members, including West Germany, from which American warheads would be released in time of war for use with the artillery, missiles, and aircraft now in the hands of allied forces.

The Allied Tactical Air Forces in Central Europe are, in a sense, nuclear deterrent forces through the availability of these weapons. Moreover, as noted earlier, the entire British "V" Bomber Force, plus several American Polaris submarines have been assigned to NATO and operate under SACEUR's deputy for nuclear planning. They are a part of the interallied nuclear force mentioned in the Nasau communiqué. And soon there will be the French *force de frappe,* which though proudly proclaimed as an independent national force, will serve at least one member of the alliance, if not NATO itself. It is necessary, therefore, to define with some precision *what* forces one is talking about, under what command arrangements, and subject to what political control.

When General Norstad several years ago suggested making NATO the fourth nuclear power, he was talking mainly about tactical and medium-range systems based in Europe, for which the warheads were American, but which could be given up to international control, although presumably still subject to U.S. custody and a veto. There have also been occasional suggestions that the U.S. Strategic Air Command be "assigned" to NATO. Here too, it is necessary to clarify slippery language. In one sense SAC could be considered a part of NATO—by virtue of close coordination with other NATO forces on targeting. Certainly, it provides the cutting edge of NATO's "sword," although SAC is a purely national command. If "assignment" envisaged merely the adding of other allied vetoes, the prospect of paralysis in time of crisis might tempt the Soviet Union into dangerous initiatives. And neither Congress nor American public opinion in general could be expected to tolerate such a move at the present time.

A purely nominal assignment of SAC to NATO—perhaps like the Athens arrangement whereby five Polaris submarines were transferred to SACLANT (an American officer)—would have no real substance. For the concept of a NATO deterrent to be meaningful, it must change the *status quo* by giving the European members something which they do not now have, e.g., an enhanced degree of strategic participation, even if not actual control of American nuclear weapons.

From time to time, there have been proposals which would, in effect, divide American strategic power between national and NATO commands.[76] Mulley, for example, after pointing out that it is too much to ask the United States at this stage to place all its nuclear weapons, including those based in the United States, under joint NATO control, suggests that all American nuclear weapons in Europe, plus British and French nuclear forces, be placed under a new NATO "Supreme Commander, Nuclear Weapons (SACNUC)."[77] Alastair Buchan suggested a similar arrangement with a "Supreme Commander Deterrent (SACDET)."[78] Robert Osgood, being less optimistic about a NATO nuclear force, has not added to the potential alphabet soup, but does agree that the

[76] This was reportedly considered in the so-called Bowie Study done in 1960. With subsequent modifications, it became an element in the proposal made at the December 1960 NATO Meeting by Secretary Herter and in the current multilateral force concept. See Osgood, cited, Chs. 8 and 9.

[77] Mulley, cited, p. 103.

[78] Buchan, *NATO in the 1960's*, cited, pp. 70-76. SACEUR's existing Nuclear Deputy—a Belgian general—could conceivably evolve into a nuclear commander, although he has a purely advisory role. See the June 1964 *NATO Letter*, p. 9.

diffusion of nuclear capabilities under joint control is preferable to diffusion under independent controls.[79]

But even if the United States found it politically feasible to transfer a significant part of its own strategic forces to the alliance, this would contradict the basic premise of unity of command, centralized control, and global targeting. A division of the American nuclear striking power into two autonomous parts would merely truncate its political effectiveness against the Soviet Union. However, a smaller part might be so assigned to the alliance; or additional forces could be created which would serve in lieu of some which the United States might otherwise have provided—in effect an adjustment within the over-all "mix" of strategic forces. This was the thrust of the original American proposal in 1960 and of the proposed multilateral force now under discussion. The latter would involve some 25 merchant ships, each armed with 8 Polaris missiles—a formidable force of 200 delivery units. But if it actually comes into being, the United States would presumably feel free to adjust its strategic nuclear program to an appropriate degree.

Turning now to the familiar problem of control, we find a cornucopia of suggestions for reorganizing NATO's machinery. From various individual experts have come proposals for an executive committee composed of the heads of the three nuclear powers—a middle ground, as General Norstad put it, between control by all fifteen members and control solely by the U.S. President.[80] While this is a reasonable enough suggestion in theory, there would be three obstacles in practice. First, as among the executive committee members, the control problem would remain. Second, it seems certain that few, if any, of the other powers—and certainly not Germany or Italy—would acquiesce in being left out. They would probably prefer to continue to rely on the United States alone rather than have that control watered down to include Britain and France but not themselves. Finally, by making a directorate of the

[79] Osgood, cited, Ch. 9.

[80] See General Norstad's speech to the Academy of Political Science, *The New York Times,* May 9, 1963.

atomic powers, the plan would add to the incentives for additional countries to follow suit.

Other commentators have explored voting formulas which would allow all members to participate but still give due weight to the nuclear powers;[81] or, the smaller powers could rotate membership in an executive body, as in the United Nations Security Council. But no matter how ingenious the formula, the fact is that NATO's nuclear problem stems from fundamental considerations of national power and interests, as well as political and psychological factors. If, nevertheless, a voting formula to cover basic issues of war and peace could be agreed upon, one would not have had the problem to begin with.

Klaus Knorr has grasped this nettle with respect to control of a NATO MRBM force. He proposes a complicated division of NATO membership whereby, under certain conditions, participants could at any time withdraw (but not use) their weapons, and declare their neutrality—without thereby blocking the others from acting.[82] This brings out the unpleasant reality of the NATO control problem. The dilemma is between such independent action —which would tear the alliance apart in a real crisis, and the possibility of paralysis through a multiple veto. However, the foregoing suggestion would seem merely to sharpen one of the horns, rather than solve the dilemma.

A somewhat different approach might be to recognize the impossibility of any all-pervasive answer and try to reduce the areas of major difficulty. If, for example, the alliance were to treat nuclear weapons according to the category of their intended use, rather than as a monolithic whole, the problem takes on a different perspective.

We saw in Chapter 3 that the controlled counterforce option really involves two forces: one designed to attack enemy military

[81] See Henry Kissinger, *The Necessity for Choice,* cited, p. 167 and *The Reporter,* March 28, 1963. See also a WEU proposal in *Deutsch Korrespondent,* June 4, 1963, cited in Kintner (note 62).

[82] Klaus Knorr, "A NATO Nuclear Force: The Problem of Management," monograph, Princeton Center of International Studies, 1963.

targets and thus reduce the damage they can do; and one to be held in reserve—even during a conflict—to deter enemy attacks on Western cities. For the former, there seems little choice but continued American control. But for the latter, intended to be used only in the final stages of a war when all restraints had failed, the control problem is less relevant. Here such a formula as any country whose cities were attacked, plus one other nuclear power, might provide at least a theoretical solution. And hopefully, since there would be no need for an early, hair-trigger, response, it would never be tested in practice.

Needless to say the "reserve" component would have to be highly survivable, with provision for authorized representatives of the states involved to reach an emergency command center. This arrangement could also be adjusted to give members some assurance against Soviet nuclear blackmail by providing for a limited "tit-for-tat" retaliation without a multiple veto. Like other suggestions, this one has its drawbacks; but the concept of a decentralization limited to the *in extremis* category may have some merit if all else fails.[83]

Still another way of tackling the problem is to try to build NATO into an effective supranational decision-making body. At present, political realities in Europe are hardly favorable. While De Gaulle is in power, France, for one, would react with strong opposition; nor for that matter, is it clear that the United States is prepared to see NATO evolve into a sort of international Ministry of Defense.

Over the long term, however, this approach may be the soundest solution to both the nuclear control problem and the over-all defenses of the free world. We shall examine some of the specific possibilities in Part III. For the present, it should suffice to note that a number of thoughtful suggestions have been made for a gradual transition to a single politico-military entity responsible for the planning, control, and execution of nuclear strategy for the

[83] This concept is spelled out in greater detail in my "Decentralizing Nuclear Control in NATO," *Orbis*, Spring 1963, p. 41.

alliance as a whole.[84] In the meantime there are a number of other steps which could be taken which are worthwhile in themselves, regardless of whether full-scale reform of NATO ever becomes feasible.

The Multilateral Force Proposal

Perhaps the most far-reaching is the multilateral force, which is currently at the center of the stage. Widely attacked, much misunderstood, and often controversial, the MLF concept is not—nor was it intended as—a complete solution to the nuclear control problem. What it does offer is a full-fledged partnership—with considerable growth potential—in a specific force between the United States and those European nations which are interested.[85]

The proposed force would operate under an international governing board. The participants, as a collective entity, would be in effect the sixteenth member of the alliance. Militarily, the MLF would presumably be assigned to SACEUR much as are the forces of any single nation. But by virtue of its international ownership, operation, and manning, it would be something new under the sun —a major step forward in multinational political and military cooperation.

If the concept of mixed-manning—not with several sets of national teams each checking on the other, but as a homogeneous crew with international loyalties—is a politician's dream, it also seems in some ways to be a commander's nightmare. But the more the concept has been examined by naval experts within the alliance,

[84] See the ISS, Adelphi Paper No. 3; Alastair Buchan "The Reform of NATO"; *Foreign Affairs*, January 1962; Mulley, cited, Ch. 7.

[85] Presently participating in explanatory talks in Paris and Washington are Belgium, Britain, Germany, Greece, Italy, Netherlands, Turkey and the United States. *The Washington Post*, Sunday, July 19, 1964, p. E1. Additional background on the concept is contained in articles by Robert Bowie *(International Organization*, September 1963), Captain John Cotton *(Die Werkunde*, March 1964) and Alastair Buchan *(The New Republic*, August 1964). Ambassador Gerard Smith's commencement address at Annapolis in June 1964 contained the full rationale for and explanation of the MLF. (Department of State Press Release). General Gallois has made a typically distorted attack upon the MLF concept in the December 1963 issue of *NATO's Fifteen Nations.*

the more such obstacles as language, food, discipline, and loyalties have appeared manageable. In earlier days both the British and the American navies were "mixed manned"—as are many of the world's present merchant ships. The twenty-five surface ships will present less difficulties in this respect than would the submarines originally contemplated.[86] By way of demonstrating the mixed-manning concept, seven of the potential participants are conducting an experiment utilizing an American guided missile destroyer, the Ricketts (formerly the Biddle, renamed in honor of the late Vice Admiral Ricketts, who had been instrumental in laying the groundwork for the MLF).[87]

There are, to be sure, some complex problems of international law. But the law is a living thing, which becomes what its subjects agree to make it. A truly international force of this type could become a precedent with interesting possibilities for international peace-keeping operations—now done by the United Nations with national contingents—as well as for other forces of the alliance, such as SACEUR's mobile fire-brigade force. If most of the nations now taking part in preliminary discussions should agree to establish the MLF, it would comprise all of the larger NATO powers except France. And even France may find it in its own economic and political interests to take part, once its national nuclear status has been achieved.

In June 1964, Britain proposed including aircraft (the U.K.'s TSR-2 or the U.S.'s TFX) and land-based missiles (Pershings) in the MLF concept, thus providing a "mix" of weapons. The matter has been studied by the international military sub-group which had earlier considered the merchant ship proposal. The conservative government's motivations were unclear, and may have involved a combination of delaying tactics, maximizing Britain's role

[86] The cost and construction period, as well as training time, would be considerably less for a surface ship. And contrary to some reports, its vulnerability is not significantly less than that of a submarine, because of its ability to merge with other shipping and to utilize shallows and coastal areas. See, Cotton, cited. The ships will not, however, contrary to some misimpressions, be disguised as merchant ships. They will be legally and in fact warships, recognizable as such from close range.

[87] *U.S. News and World Report*, August 3, 1964, p. 48.

at minimum cost, or marketing the TSR-2. And while there are some conceptual problems to including tactical systems, this initiative does at least show the growing interest in "multilateralizing" some of NATO's nuclear forces. The pre-election statements of Britain's Labor Party leaders showed little interest in either the sea-based MLF or the Conservative's government's proposed modifications. Since coming to power, Harold Wilson and Denis Healey appear to be seeking means of phasing out Britain's deterrent—the existing V-Bombers and future Polaris submarines—by contributing them to an Atlantic force of some kind. The precise outcome of the various discussions scheduled for the winter of 1964-65 cannot be predicted, of course; but it seems likely that some sort of international force will result.[88]

The United States has indicated a willingness to at least reconsider the MLF decision-making arrangements when and if Europe creates a political unity able to control a European force. Even though American missiles and warheads would be transferred or sold to the international MLF—requiring Congressional action—the United States would retain a veto, as presumably would certain other participants. Various voting formulas, as among the European participants, are reportedly being explored. The theoretical prospect of an eventual withdrawal of the American veto has been much belabored. Actually more Europeans would probably oppose such a development than would favor it. And in any case, the concept of an evolutionary force requires that all of the major participants, including the U.S. (and its Congress), would have to agree to any such far-reaching change in the light of the then existing situation.

Again, it must be recognized that the MLF does not "solve" the control problem of a U.S. or multiple veto. But by the same token, it does not increase the number of national nuclear powers. In fact, it may remove some of the incentives for additional proliferation by giving countries like Germany a greater degree of par-

[88] See footnote 14, and Buchan, *New Republic*, cited. His article is reprinted in *The Congressional Record,* August 4, 1964, p. 17351.

ticipation in a joint nuclear deterrent, thus paving the way for broader non-dissemination agreements. In a very real sense, then, the multilateral force concept is designed to meet a political objective. But it uses a military means which will add significantly to the variety and dispersal of the striking power available to NATO—in partial fulfillment of the MRBM requirement outlined earlier. Military instruments, it should be recalled, are without meaning unless they can serve political purposes. Surely the advancement of NATO solidarity through a practical joint venture is a worthwhile objective. The economic costs (estimated to be about $2.5 billion), while substantial, would be less than under any comparable way of giving Europe a share in the strategic deterrence. In addition, by utilizing the international medium of the sea, the naval MLF would avoid the political and military problems inherent in land-based MRBMs. Thus the force appears to offer an opening through which the alliance can move forward from dead center, since the MLF, while open to all, is not subject to obstruction by France.

Even if the force is not created at all, the thorough exploration has constituted an unparalleled education for all of the participants—the United States included—in the complexities of managing the alliance's nuclear power. The exhaustive studies by international groups have showed the feasibility of joint ownership and manning, which might be applied to other weapons systems, tactical as well as strategic, in the event that the original MLF proposal is not adopted. And if a sea-based MLF does come into being, it should advance mutual understanding even more by providing a concrete focus for consultation, and a basis for further evolution.

The multilateral force is therefore one step toward the development of what might be called an "Atlantic" deterrent. But it is not the only one. A greater European participation in the management of the U.S. deterrent would help give it more of an Atlantic character. By concentrating on the earlier stages of the control process, politico-military planning, the development of strategy and the deployment and targeting of weapons, one emphasizes the concept of *contrôle* in the French sense of verification and examination, rather than physical *control*.

For the major striking forces of the alliance, there would seem to be no available substitute which would work better than American leadership and responsibility. But the president could add to his constitutional duty as commander-in-chief, the informal role of manager of the nuclear power of the alliance. In this capacity, he could presumably seek and act upon the guidance of his NATO advisory board. If the ultimate decision to fire nuclear weapons has to be made by the President of the United States, the Europeans deserve at least the assurance of participation in the planning process. Some general guidelines or understandings should be feasible on the following points: what targets would be attacked under various contingencies; the circumstances under which the president would direct the launching of U.S. strategic forces (e.g., a Soviet nuclear attack on Europe or an all-out conventional assault); cases where the force would clearly not be used (minor incursions and the like); ambiguous contingencies where the fullest possible consultation would be undertaken in the light of the existing circumstances; and the weapons and forces which the United States would maintain in Europe.

Past NATO efforts to agree on guidelines of this type have not been entirely successful, perhaps partly from the lack of understanding of the nuclear problem by the Europeans and partly from insufficient consultation procedures to enable those governments to avoid charges of abdicating responsibility. A good start has been made on sharing information; although, from what can be learned, the nuclear information committee, established after the Athens NATO meeting, still tends toward a one-way operation in which the United States informs rather than consults the Europeans. However, Europe must learn to walk in the nuclear field before it can run—a process that the MLF should help considerably. And perhaps most important of all, the MLF, by providing a jointly owned nuclear force which will be an international responsibility, can serve as an operative focus for consultation and cooperative planning—activities which otherwise tend to become highly theoretical.

Further developments of the NATO liaison at the Omaha strategic targeting center, joint seminars, and political-military war-game sessions can contribute to the development of a true strategic dialogue. Other institutional mechanisms can be devised once a good beginning has been made. It may not be too farfetched to suggest giving the Europeans a sense of responsibility for *American* security. Could not some European crews, for example, man U.S.-based missiles; or share in the operations of the North American Air defense system—including the seaborne warning stations? The conceptual point is that in strategic terms there is no such thing as American security or European security. There is only Atlantic security—or perhaps, *in*security if NATO cannot satisfactorily come to grips with the challenge of managing its nuclear power.

As the leader by necessity, if not by choice, the United States must show the way by considering European political sensibilities, even when these conflict with purely military logic. America must be able to imagine what it would be like if the shoe were on the other foot—if Europe alone possessed the nuclear arsenal and the United States faced a powerful foe in the Pacific. Any indications that Europe, an ocean away, might withdraw or withhold some of its nuclear forces from the West coast would be greeted with the same consternation here that the analogous impression, however erroneous, has in fact caused in Europe. American arguments for a non-nuclear build-up, the reluctance to share nuclear weapons, the dismantling of the Thor and Jupiter IRBMs, opposition to SACEUR's MRBM proposals, whatever the actual merits of each, have all contributed to European misunderstanding. And conflicting views and statements from Washington have not helped. Verbal reassurances are simply not enough. Europe must feel that NATO as an institution, not just the Pentagon, helps determine the deployment of weapons and forces for the common defense. Consultation arrangements will help; so will the MLF partnership if it comes into being; but equally important will be American willingness to listen, as well as to speak. None of these, nor all of them, can completely resolve the insoluble problems discussed in this chapter. But they can, with patience and a moderate amount of luck, assist NATO's nuclear crisis to pass quietly into history as the Soviet challenge becomes less menacing.

5

The Nuclear-Conventional Balance: Europe's Defenses

It makes no sense that the NATO countries should continue to live in mortal fear of a nation inferior in population and material resources, and remain impaled on the horns of a defeat or suicide dilemma.

B. H. Liddell Hart

The preceding two chapters have dealt with the problems of strategic nuclear warfare. Here we must examine the nonstrategic components of European, and Atlantic, defense. Of course, strategic and tactical defenses, like weapons so categorized, do not divide neatly into compartments. They are interrelated in fact and theory. Many of the forces of the alliance are dual purpose, having both limited and general war missions and nuclear and conventional capabilities. It is not even entirely accurate to distinguish sharply between deterrence and defense, equating the former with strategic aspects and the latter with tactical in the event that deterrence fails. Although the strategic nuclear deterrent is an umbrella over tactical operations and may inhibit escalation, the myriad uncertainties simultaneously create a potential continuum of violence.

Even nuclear and conventional are not always helpful labels to apply to forces and concepts, for this terminology begs too many important questions. Although the original NATO concept of the sword and the shield has been partially outmoded, that image perhaps best describes the focus of this chapter in relation to the two preceding ones. Here we shall discuss the shield, that is, the defense of the European area of NATO, rather than strikes by the sword against enemy targets beyond the area of conflict. One cannot talk intelligently about European defense without specifying where the defense is to occur, against what attack, and with what weapons.

The Defense Zone

For convenience, we may define NATO Europe's defensive front as the eastern boundary of the members' territory. This forms a line running roughly 1,900 miles south from the North Cape to Trieste, then southeast for over 600 miles along the Adriatic to Greece, eastward for 1,300 miles across Macedonia and Turkey's Black Sea Coast, and finally south again for 400 miles to the Iraq-Iran border. The total NATO land frontier increases from 4,300 crow-flight miles to some 5,300 in terms of actual terrain. The land area west and south of this line, excepting Britain and Portugal, comprises Allied Command Europe (ACE) under the Supreme Allied Commander, Europe (SACEUR). Allied ground, sea, and air forces are divided into four subordinate commands: Northern Europe (Norway, Denmark, Schleswig-Holstein and the Baltic approaches), Central Europe (roughly from Hamburg south along the East German, Czech, and Austrian frontiers of Germany), Southern Europe (Italy, Greece, and Turkey), and Mediterranean.

Austria's neutrality is a two-edged sword: a Soviet occupation could seriously threaten Northern Italy and cut communications between the Central and Southern European areas; for, except by skirting Lake Geneva into France, the Alpine passes cross either Austria or neutral Switzerland. On the other hand, withdrawal of Soviet forces from Austria has reduced the threat in this area; and a violation of its neutrality would presumably call for appropriate countermeasures. Further east, Yugoslavia's relative independence from the Communist bloc also provides a buffer for NATO's Adriatic flank.

On the central front, SACEUR must defend a zone shaped roughly like a right triangle varying in depth from the slim 75 miles from Lübeck to the North Sea at the apex to the 700 mile base from Passau at the Austrian border to the Bay of Biscay. The length of this front is over 700 miles, and the Soviets are only 50 miles from the Rhine at one point. The area south of this salient, the so-called Fulda gap, is geographically favorable for the defense, for natural chains of river valleys and rolling hills afford good protection and control of access routes. To the north, on the other hand, the flat plains of Hanover are ideal for armored penetrations and constitute a traditional invasion route.

Subsequently in this chapter we shall examine some of the special political and military problems of defending NATO's northern and southern flanks, the special case of Berlin, and the role of the naval forces. The main Soviet military capability against Western Europe is aimed at NATO's vitals, along the central front, although this is not necessarily the most likely Soviet choice for an attack. But if NATO is equipped to handle this most serious case, it should be able to cope with the lesser contingencies. These may arise without deliberate intent by either side, for example, in a conflict growing out of satellite uprisings or Communist probes or pressures tactics in Berlin. But before focusing on this range of contingencies, it is appropriate to address the larger problem of calculated attack—not because the probabilities are greater, for they clearly are not—but because the ability to handle them is a measure of NATO's over-all defense posture and its political stance with reference to the Communist bloc.

Many critics of NATO are troubled by inconsistencies between strategy and force structure. Henry Kissinger, for example, points out that "had NATO carried out the implications of the prevalent strategic doctrine, the sole function of the shield forces . . . would have been to determine that a general Soviet advance had in fact begun"—that is, to serve as a trip-wire for the Strategic Air Command. Noting that these forces are much larger than required for such a mission, yet too small for effective defense, Kissinger urges the "necessity for choice" between conventional and nuclear options. He then redeems his argument, but undercuts his own criticism by noting that the choice is not entirely the West's to make.[1]

It is appropriate, and necessary, to think about the unthinkable; but it is quite another proposition to base plans on trying to know the unknowable. Policy makers, comptrollers, and academic analysts are strongly tempted to seize upon a single "most likely" form of attack and compress defensive preparations accordingly. But most of the disastrous military mistakes in history have resulted from trying to make the choice of terrain, tactics, timing, and weapons for the enemy. One has to assume not one or two possibilities but the full range of actions of which the enemy is capable. NATO's task is to confront the Communist bloc with the prospect of failure throughout this entire range. And this requires not a choice between two alternative strategies, but an optimum strategy for each contingency within the available resources. Thus it may be wise to avoid self-limiting choices, to maintain as many options as possible, and to retain some ambiguity as to the precise response an enemy will meet. But within such a general posture, priority should, of course, be given to meeting the more likely challenges.

In the timing of a deliberate attack, the Communists have two basic choices: to launch a surprise attack with their ready forces deployed in Eastern Europe, or to maximize their strength through mobilization or redeployment, which would put NATO on notice and give the West time to mobilize as well. Within each of these categories, the Soviets can limit their attack to non-nuclear weapons, use some tactical nuclear weapons in a limited fashion, or engage in large-scale nuclear support, which would certainly lead to general intercontinental war.

As to location, the basic choices involve the northern or southern flank or the central front. There is also Berlin, where Western determination could be put to a test on home grounds, so to speak; and there are always possibilities of out-flanking NATO via Iran,

[1] Henry A. Kissinger, "The Unsolved Problems of European Defense," *Foreign Affairs*, July 1962, pp. 519-539. The same theme is elaborated in his other articles and books.

or elsewhere in the Middle East, or by penetration of North Africa. Finally, in objectives, Communist bloc action could range from the politico-military pressures of a build-up of forces, to an attempt to disrupt the alliance by a military probe, to an attack with limited geographical objectives—perhaps a *fait accompli* seizure of territory —up to a military conquest of Western Europe. We shall consider each of the most likely combinations and examine the defensive preparations which each suggests for NATO.

The Forward Forces of the Communist Bloc

The Group of Soviet Forces in East Germany consists of 10 tank divisions and 10 of motorized infantry in a fair state of combat readiness, plus support elements. East Germany adds about 6 divisions (plus large paramilitary and police units); Czechoslovakia and Poland each have about 14 divisions, and Hungary 4. The Soviet Union also has 4 divisions in Hungary and 2 in Poland. This potential forward force of 65 divisions[2] must be adjusted downward because of the lower battle-worthiness of the Satellite divisions and their potential political unreliability. Western analysts have always had to hedge on the question of whether to count the Satellite forces as an asset or a liability to the Soviet Union. At the very least, and quite apart from the logistic difficulties of employing all available combat units, the Soviet Union

[2] These rough estimates are based upon data in the Institute for Strategic Studies' *The Military Balance 1963-64* (London: 1963), and its "Disarmament and European Security" study of August 1963 (especially the detailed tables in Volume II); F. W. Mulley, *The Politics of Western Defense* (New York: Praeger, 1962), see especially p. 45; B. H. Liddell Hart, *Deterrent or Defense* (New York: Praeger, 1960), Ch. 9; Helmut Schmidt, *Defense or Retaliation* (London: Oliver & Boyd, 1962), p. 63. A slightly lower estimate of Communist forces was given by Assistant Secretary of Defense Nitze in a speech to the Cleveland Council on World Affairs, March 2, 1963, (Dept. of Defense Press Release, March 2, 1962). He credited the bloc with 22 Soviet divisions in East Germany and Poland and 35 satellite divisions in lesser states of readiness—presumably again excluding Hungary as not being directly in the central front area. Secretary McNamara's November 18, 1963 speech to the Economic Club of New York also emphasized Soviet weakness relative to NATO.

would almost certainly have to maintain a reserve to insure rear-area security and guard against the possibility of obstruction or even defection by Satellite units. A reasonable adjustment therefore might permit 16 to 18 Soviet divisions (out of the 26 deployed in Eastern Europe) plus another 16 to 18 Satellite divisions to be employed in offensive operations. Then, under the guise of maneuvers or rotation, or via infiltration, another 8 to 10 Soviet divisions might be brought forward from European Russia without giving NATO clear tactical warning, producing a total surprise attack force of about 40 to 45 divisions.

These units could of course be reinforced and almost doubled within a month by overt mobilization. But in that case, NATO would have notice and time for its own preparatory measures. There is considerable disagreement among Western experts as to how many combat divisions the Soviet Union could support in sustained offensive operations, taking into account existing transportation nets, and the Communist logistic tail, which is considerably thinner than that of most Western armies. There is also the fact that Communist divisions are smaller and have less firepower and mobility than their NATO counterpart.

Leaving the post-mobilization case for the moment, the potential force of 40 to 45 divisions is the primary D-Day threat on the central front. This force could be supported by a Soviet tactical air force of some 3,000 planes and many short-range missiles. Most of the latter are believed to have a tactical nuclear capability since they are assigned to the Missile and Artillery Command, in which control of Soviet tactical nuclear weapons appears to be centralized.[8] With respect to the non-use, limited use, or general use of nuclear weapons, the last contingency is perhaps least likely, as it would involve general war.

The General War Context

If all-out war should nevertheless occur, and especially if some preparatory mobilization had been in effect, Communist armies might

[8] See *The Military Balance, 1963-64,* cited, and a speech by Secretary of

attempt a lightning sweep across Western Europe in conjunction with nuclear strikes against NATO airfields, communication and logistic centers, and key defense positions. Their objective would be to occupy large areas as a basis for negotiating a favorable conclusion to the war and hampering allied counterattacks.

Presumably, the Soviets would hope to achieve a tactical victory before NATO could make the agonizing political decisions that would be required to initiate intercontinental nuclear exchanges. Or they might hope to hold Western cities hostage (either by occupying them or threatening them with nuclear destruction) to deter retaliatory strikes.

In September 1962 NATO conducted a command post exercise, "Fallex 62," which went somewhat along these lines, with nuclear weapons being used freely by both sides against military targets. The German magazine *Der Spiegel* published a detailed critique of this exercise which led to the arrest of the editors for publishing official data and precipitated the government crisis in which Defense Minister Strauss was replaced.

According to the article's description of the hypothetical results, millions of dead were assumed, "the chaos was unimaginable . . . and impeded the advance of the Communist divisions which had also been severely hit. Nevertheless, they attained major territorial gains in the Northwestern part of the Federal Republic . . . Hamburg was not defended . . . the medical setup was the first to break down . . . food supplies and the preservation of vital industries and traffic routes did not fare any better. Air defense proved to be completely inadequate. It was impossible to keep the refugee flow under control. . . ."[4]

The possibility of this type of war, however remote, suggests a number of areas in which improvements in NATO defenses may be needed. But an essential prior question is how to balance the

---

the Army Cyrus Vance to the Southern Governors' Conference, White Sulphur Springs, West Virgina, 1963, Dept. of Defense Press Release.

[4] "Conditionally Fit for Defense," *Der Spiegel*, October 10, 1962. An official reference to the exercise is contained in the November 1962 *NATO Letter* (NATO Information Service, Paris).

enormous cost of making maximum preparations for defense in such a war with the competitive needs of other and far more likely types of conflict. Yet the degree of precautions taken will presumably affect Soviet calculations and may therefore influence the likelihood of the event itself. In brief, NATO's best guarantee against nuclear war in Europe is to be prepared for it.

There are two basic questions involved in balancing costs and risks, to which we now turn. The first is one that goes to the heart of Atlantic defense: Are there any circumstances under which a major nuclear war might be limited to the European area and not involve forces external to the theater? Differing assumptions on this point have contributed to the controversy over additional medium-range missiles deployed in Europe, and to the nuclear control dilemma. As we have seen, military logic suggests a negative answer, at least as far as Western policy is concerned. And politically, a war in which the United States and the Soviet Union remained sanctuaries would be a negation of NATO's underlying purpose. Any prospect of Europe being a nuclear battleground for the superpowers must be anathema to its inhabitants. Yet, European concern over the continued validity of the American guarantee has sometimes led to the paradoxical conclusion that preparations must be made for just such an event. America has therefore been hard put to respond to all reasonable European concerns on this point without thereby tending to confirm those very fears.

The answer is certainly not to duplicate in Europe the forces which are already available outside it. For, as we have seen, American strategic power is essential to, as well as adequate for, the conduct of damage-limiting operations against enemy nuclear forces. The European "theater" cannot therefore be made self-sufficient. The time-worn axiom that the senior commander in a given area must control all of the forces necessary for his mission hardly applies to a potential nuclear conflict of global proportions. But what then is the answer?

Increased European sharing in the management of the nuclear power of the alliance, along the lines suggested in the previous chapter and through a multilateral missile force in the European area, is one important ingredient. The political environment of strategic indivisibility must also be maintained. Additionally, the continued deployment in Europe of large numbers of American troops and their families helps to ensure the automatic involvement of the United States in any conflict. And the third essential is that NATO have enough defensive potential on the ground to preclude an unimpeded Soviet sweep through Western Europe during a general war.

This is, of course, the basic function of the NATO shield. But it brings us back to the classic question of how much is "enough"? Thus it in turn raises the second issue of cost-effectiveness: what types of defense can have a dual utility, that is, makes some contribution in both nuclear and non-nuclear contingencies without excessive costs? Let us take a look at a few basic areas.

Emergency Planning and Civil Defense

One of the lessons from Fallex 62 was the importance of stand-by emergency legislation and at least rudimentary civil defense measures, especially fallout protection, throughout NATO generally, but particularly in the forward combat area in Germany. There can be no real protection from a massive nuclear attack; but since the extent of a hypothetical nuclear disaster cannot be foreseen, it is cheap insurance indeed to take rudimentary survival measures and make emergency plans for continuity of government. Public apathy, if not actual opposition, would probably preclude more comprehensive measures involving large-scale preparation or participation by the public. But this does not mean that quiet precautionary measures cannot be taken now with a good deal more effectiveness than has been the case. For by the time a real crisis had aroused public concern, it could be too late to improvise.

NATO has an elaborate civil emergency planning structure involving innumerable committees, generally organized along functional lines for petroleum, communications, surface transport, medical support, refugees and the like. But as a general matter, the work of these committees has been completely divorced from the higher politico-military echelons of the alliance, and have worked in a bureaucratic and highly unrealistic world of their own. Perhaps the time has come to realize, as the United States has done, that civil defense is an integral part of the over-all defenses. A much closer practical coordination is called for between active and passive defenses.[5]

Although the NATO fact book notes that "the greatest emphasis is placed on saving human lives and on making the provisions required to enable the population to carry on,"[6] the actual work in this area has been supported at a very marginal level because of the widespread assumption that there will either be no war at all or a thermonuclear war in which Europe would be destroyed. On the assumption that there are many contingencies, what may appear to be nearly hopeless in the worst case may be manageable for a good many others, especially those which seem much more likely to occur. A conflict in Europe could take many forms. There are a vast number of practical measures—ranging from preparatory emergency legislation and refugee control to stockpiling and other passive defense measures—which could be initiated or accelerated at very low cost. And most would meet our "multiple purpose" test, since they would also be useful in almost any conflict in Central Europe larger than a skirmish, and would have peace-time utility for disaster relief.

European Air Defense

The problem here has been one of finding a defense which would be reasonably effective in a non-nuclear tactical environment and yet not be completely vulnerable to a few attacks on its vital components. Despite countless hours of meetings, discussions, negotiations, plans, and technical explorations, the alliance has been unable

[5] The NATO Parliamentarians Conference Eighth Annual Session passed a resolution recommending that "the Civil Defense Adviser be made directly responsible to the Secretary General of NATO." See the *NATO Letter*, cited, December 1962, p. 23.

[6] *NATO—Facts About the North Atlantic Treaty Organization* (Paris: NATO Information Service, 1962), p. 152.

to come up with a truly workable solution. SHAPE's Air Defense Technical Center has made progress in bringing together many experts from different countries. But the separation of political, economic and military planning which is inherent in NATO's organizational structure has supplemented national differences in preventing a realistic balancing of the military, technological, political, and economic elements.

Any air defense system is inherently and incredibly complex. The speed of modern aircraft, to say nothing of missiles, makes defense on a purely national basis an anachronism in a limited geographic area like Western Europe. Fortunately, this is widely recognized. Progress has been made in organizing according to sectors, irrespective of national boundaries. But even if the problems of warning and radar coverage are solved, there remain the challenges of ground-to-air and air-to-air defenses. These problems not only present the utmost technical difficulty, but involve expenditures measured in billions of dollars. Inevitably the members of the alliance have engaged in a fierce competition, and have often tried to design the specifications for equipment, so that home industries would get the benefits of contracts.

After years of study NATO was on the point of agreeing to a "ground environment" of the same general type as the U.S. "SAGE." But it was argued that this system might be virtually obsolescent before it could be installed because of technical advances and the vulnerability of its key elements to enemy attack. Although the experts divide ranks on the feasibility of various concepts, it should be possible to establish quite an effective defense against non-nuclear air attacks, which would involve aircraft rather than missiles, since the latter cannot carry a worthwhile payload unless it is a nuclear weapon. That much at least makes sense—politically, economically, and militarily. And with some hardening of key sites, it would also have utility in a conflict where the use of nuclear weapons was limited. Progress is being made, according to the few items that have appeared in the press, so that a start may have been made in the NATO Air Defense Ground

Environment (NADGE) system by the time this appears in print.[7] But the harder question, and the one which concerns us here, is whether it is worthwhile building a defense against missiles.

This is, of course, related to the over-all anti-ICBM problem, on which promising research work is being done, but a really effective defense lies in the more distant future. There are some experts who believe that improvements in Hawk and in Nike-Zeus could produce a reasonably workable defense for Europe, inasmuch as the medium-range problem may be technically easier to meet than the long-range one. It can be argued that NATO need not admit that London, Paris, Rome, and other cities are and must forever remain completely at the mercy of Soviet MRBMs. A defense system with only a 25 per cent or 30 per cent kill rate might not be economical in terms of the cost for each missile destroyed, but it could more than make up the difference in terms of allied confidence. For this would reduce the gap between the high European vulnerability to Soviet missile attack and the somewhat lower American vulnerability. Moreover, the uncertainty as to which missiles would be intercepted greatly complicates an enemy's targeting plans.

On the other hand, a cost in the tens of billions would be unjustified unless it offered a much higher assurance of protection than that. And the enemy can always improve his offensive weapons systems through multiple warheads and decoys at least as fast as the defense can catch up.

My own view is that a useful antimissile defense in Europe is highly suspect as to feasibility, would absorb resources better used elsewhere, and in any case fails to meet the test of applicability to contingencies other than general nuclear war. Since we are assuming that Europe need not prepare for a nuclear war on a "theater" basis, and can count on external strategic forces, the best defense against *long-range* nuclear missile attacks may be a good offense—that is, a damage-limiting counterforce capability. Resources available for air defense therefore seem best applied to nonnuclear conflict but perhaps with some low-cost insurance against

[7] Details of NATO activities in the air defense field can be found in the NATO fact book, cited, Ch. 12.

very limited nuclear attacks. This is true both for area defense of Europe as a whole, and for defense of troops in the field against low-flying air attacks. Here technology seems to be on the verge of producing some effective new types of ground-to-air weapons which would have a big payoff in less than general war situations.

Europe and the Missile Balance

One of the military facts of life confronting NATO is the formidable array of medium-range missiles which the Soviet Union has aimed at Western Europe. Their short time of flight and high effectiveness against present air defenses means that a surprise attack could destroy a significant part of the alliance retaliatory power which is based in Europe. It was in recognition of this situation that General Norstad campaigned for "a peculiarly European land-based medium-range missile system"[8] to be assigned to his command.

In previous chapters we have seen that strategic, political, and cost considerations all argue against trying to make Europe independent of externally based forces—at least as far as counterforce attacks on enemy striking elements are concerned. There are nevertheless some technical reasons why any of the various MRBM systems which could be developed could have a greater accuracy and "kill" probability than either ICBMs launched from the United States or sea-based systems like Polaris. On the other hand, even to approach the same degree of invulnerability, a land-based MRBM would either have to be hardened or mobile. There seems to be little enthusiasm in Europe for large numbers of missiles touring the roads on trucks or the placing of hardened silos so as to draw fire in an area of such high population density.[9] The net conclusion of those who have examined the problem most carefully seems to be that the over-all strategic arsenal of the alliance is needed in any

[8] Charles J. V. Murphy, "NATO at a Nuclear Crossroads," *Fortune*, December 1962, p. 220.

[9] For an interesting discussion from the European standpoint, see Institute for Strategic Studies, Adelphi Paper No. 3, "The Control of Western Strategy," April 1963, p. 13.

case to make a significant dent in Soviet capabilities; and that once it goes into action, added MRBMs in Europe make a difference which varies with the assumptions, but is marginal for most cases.

There is yet another function which medium-range missiles might perform for NATO in a general war context. It is obviously important to prevent the Soviet Union from reinforcing its forward forces with replacement troops and supplies. Attacks on rail junctions, bridges, road nets, and the like are known in the trade as "interdiction." But because of their rear area location and proximity to population centers, it is hard to envisage nuclear weapons being used against them except as part of a concerted strategic attack pattern. And in this case, SAC and other Allied forces would also be hitting counterforce targets in the Soviet Union. As the United States is said to have pointed out in the North Atlantic Council, it is this attack which counts, so that additional MRBMs appear marginal.[10] Must one conclude then that no missiles are needed in Europe?

On the contrary, some missiles located there can add uncertainties for the Soviet planner. Where legitimate and nonduplicatory roles can be found for them, they may be worth something in terms of psychological reassurance for Europe.[11] One such role is against those tactical targets for which it is hard to assign long-range missiles in advance. Moreover, information as to which of the targets most vital to a field commander had escaped the over-all attack is more apt to be available at the front than thousands of miles away. The so-called "fog of war," familiar enough to World War II commanders, would be multiplied a hundredfold in a nuclear engagement. Therefore in a possible "broken-backed" war of uncertain duration, some decentralization appears prudent as a hedge against breakdowns in communications. And shorter-range tactical systems might also be relevant to a nuclear conflict of more limited scope or even to an all-out conventional attack.

Here, then, is one contingency requirement that can be met

[10] Murphy, cited, and Ch. 5 above.

[11] A good analysis of the problem can be found in Adelphi Paper No. 4, "The Defense of Western Europe," May 1963, p. 15.

through a mix of such missiles as Sergeant, Pershing, and Mace, strike aircraft, and last but not least, carrier-based aviation. And such an array, if not yet fully in being, appears to be very close to achievement. SACEUR, it should be recalled, also disposes of Britain's V-bombers, a number of U.S. Polaris submarines with sixteen missiles each, and many strike aircraft. If an effective VTOL (vertical take-off and landing) plane can be developed which could be scattered at isolated locations, the utility of manned aircraft would be greatly enhanced, for the invulnerability to an attack on a few airfields would be cut enormously. If the 200-missile multilateral force, or MLF, comes into being, SACEUR will also have a say in the targeting of this highly invulnerable strategic system. Moreover, as we saw in the preceding chapter, the problem of organizing and managing strategic nuclear power is as much political and psychological as military; and the MLF should be particularly useful in that context. On balance, therefore, once the damage-limiting and interdiction functions are recognized as general-war strategic missions, sufficient missiles for insurance and to help in the land battle seem likely to be available. In due time, some adjustments in the over-all "mix" might be desirable as between aircraft and missiles, in long-range versus short-range, sea-based versus land-based, and mobile versus hardened versions of the available weapons systems. But such adjustments need not involve any *major* changes in the resources NATO devotes to the unlikely case of general nuclear war.

Ground Forces

So far we have ignored a fundamental element of defense—the ability to hold the terrain. Some forces are clearly necessary on the ground to delay, harass, and counterattack the enemy. But it is difficult to envisage coordinated operations by large bodies of troops in the environment of major nuclear war. Supply would be disrupted or nonexistent, with communications unreliable; and fallout would be spreading rapidly over large areas. Casualties, both civil and military, would be enormous, transportation would be destroyed, and confusion the order of the day.

Preparations to operate effectively in such circumstances could add tens of billions to NATO's defense budget. Communications would have to be duplicated; key installations hardened; and troop areas protected, at least against fallout. And because whole units could be wiped out, many more forces would be needed. But for the most part, the arguments that have been made for sizable increases—or cuts—in NATO's ready forces have not been aimed at this case, but rather at less cataclysmic circumstances. No one can foresee the nuclear war environment with enough clarity to be very precise about force-level requirements for ground defense.

Assuming that NATO has at least the minimum number of divisions needed to cover the major routes of attack, whatever force-levels NATO feels is justified for other cases should represent an acceptable risk for the general nuclear war contingency. For enemy forces will also be badly hurt; and they will have to advance through the same confusion and nuclear chaos that impede the defense.

Nevertheless, according to one well informed source: "the main emphasis of [Soviet Army] training continues to be the advance of tank and APC-borne infantry formations across radiation contaminated ground at an average rate of 60 miles a day."[12] This makes it worthwhile to look at means of conducting a better general-war ground defense without adding significantly to costs—especially if they also improve NATO's ability to meet other types of attacks. The key is decentralization—supplementing the regular forces (which would be primary nuclear targets and whose mobility would be in doubt) with paramilitary local defenses, including various types of barriers and defended strong points.

Local Defense

Such concepts have been repeatedly urged by such military experts as Liddell Hart, F. O. Miksche, and Sir John Slessor, to name but a few.[13] But the concept has apparently fallen on deaf ears at

[12] ISS, *The Military Balance 1963-64*, cited, p. 5.

[13] Hart, cited, pp. 65, 172; Miksche, "The European Shield," *NATO's Fifteen Nations*, August-September 1962, p. 22; Slessor, *Strategy for the*

SHAPE and elsewhere. Within Germany itself, a plan for a zonal defense based in part on this concept was considered in the early debates on German rearmament and the subsequent controversy over the so-called Bonin Plan.[14]

The current West German defense establishment includes "territorial defense units" as part of the reserve structure. But if the *Der Spiegel* account of Fallex 62 is correct, it is little more than a nominal force.[15] The cost of training and equipping effective home guard units to furnish a local supplement to regular military forces would certainly be small, especially in Germany. In fact, as compared to adding regular divisions, their cost in relationship to their potential contribution is minuscule. For by the careful use of demolitions, antitank weapons, and guerrilla tactics, such forces could significantly impede a Soviet advance, gain valuable time for the defensive forces, and force the enemy to concentrate his forces so as to present worthwhile targets. Prepared barriers with defended strong points to provide covering fire could add to the effectiveness of such forces.

Composed of local men, the territorial units would have the

West (New York: Morrow & Co., 1959), pp. 85-87. See also Malcolm Hoag, "Rationalizing NATO Strategy" (RAND Paper P-2940, 1964), and James E. King, Jr., "Toward Stability in Central Europe" in Arnold Wolfers, ed., *Changing East-West Relations and the Unity of the West* (Baltimore: The Johns Hopkins Press, 1964), pp. 162-165.

[14] See Gordon Craig, "NATO and the New German Army," Ch. 7 of *Military Policy and National Security*, William W. Kaufmann, ed. (Princeton University Press, 1956). Interest in some of Colonel von Benin's concept appears to be reviving in Germany. Adelbert Weinstein has written two useful analyses in the *Frankfurter-Allgemeine Zeitung* of September 18 and 25, 1963.

[15] *Der Spiegel* commented that "for the hundreds of thousands of Bundeswehr reservists who had completed their tours and who were assumed for game purposes to have reported to military assembly points, there were no commissioned or noncommissioned officer cadres, and certainly no weapons. The territorial defense units with their few heavy engineer units were hardly up to their assignments. For action against tanks which had broken through, no territorial defense units were available at all." Since then, however, German Defense Minister Von Hassel has spoken of his intention to fill out these forces.

advantage of familiarity with the terrain and the incentive of defending home ground. There are, of course, potential political sensitivities affecting Germany and its NATO partners, as well as the Soviet Union, which would require delicate handling. But if German militia units were integrated into the over-all central front defense plans, and provided with essential munitions and cadres from regular allied forces, these objections could be overcome; for they would be NATO rather than national forces. And in view of their relative lack of armor and mobility, the necessarily defensive mission of such specially tailored "forward defense" divisions, as they might be called, would be apparent enough to avoid provoking hostile bloc reaction.

In the same context, the role of demolitions is important. Although portable, low-yield atomic demolitions are reported to be available, there are some added risks of unintended escalation, and the nuclear control problem would be more difficult. But where their use was necessary, such devices could be handled by special units and put in place only in time of extreme danger. For most missions, the improved traditional demolitions and techniques should permit blocking of narrow village streets with rubble, mining by-pass routes, felling trees across forest roads, and the like. (It is not inconceivable that had the French used these tactics against German armor in the Ardennes in May 1940, instead of assuming the terrain to be unsuitable for tanks and attempting to keep access routes open for their own forces, the fall of France might have been avoided. For the Meuse crossing might have been delayed until Allied reinforcements could have been switched from the left flank.[16]

Logistics

Another remediable defect in NATO's overcentralized posture for coping with the nuclear war contingency is the vulnerability of logistic centers. The supply structure has evolved from occupation

[16] See Winston S. Churchill, *The Second World War* (Boston: Houghton Mifflin, 1949), Volume II, pp. 37-45, and Liddell Hart, cited, p. 104.

days into a serious of supply depots, each organized on a vast scale and containing many days' supply of key items. But this system presupposes an ability to operate supply convoys and rail movements over long distances and refugee-clogged roads, which is highly questionable in a nuclear war of any size; moreover, the depots themselves, whose locations are quite well known, could be destroyed by a few accurate MRBMs.

It should be possible to lease or build storage facilities near the bases of the combat units to be supplied which could contain all classes of supply, reducing the present tendency to concentrate quartermaster items at one point, ordnance at another, and signal stores at still another. Guarding such decentralized small depots could be a problem, but if the local defense-militia concept were also implemented, a ready resource of manpower would be available for such security missions. The relevance of dispersed VTOL aircraft to this concept is also worth noting.

It makes little sense for U. S. units to have sixty- to ninety-day supply goals, while allied forces on the same front have only thirty days or less. A rationalization of the present logistic system, which is purely national rather than a NATO responsibility, would appear to be in order. Sales of any U. S. stocks in excess of the agreed level to the Allies could generate the extra matériel needed for the militia and decentralized depot concepts.

Surprise Attack with Tactical Atomic Support

A determined Soviet attack supported by a limited use of tactical nuclear weapons is a slightly more likely contingency. The most probable case would be a *coup de main* aimed at limited gains in West Germany. Once such a risky commitment had been made, the Soviet Union might conceivably use a few tactical nuclear weapons to clear a way through a major blocking force and achieve their objective before NATO regained its balance. Unlike the preceding case, which presumed a willingness to fight a general war if necessary, the Soviets would probably not attempt major nuclear strikes or interdiction because of the danger of escalation.

A decision by the Soviets to risk a limited offensive use of nuclear weapons would come about either if they miscalculated Western determination to resist, or if NATO had denuded itself of the tactical nuclear capability to counter the Soviet initiative. Included in limited use is what could be termed a nuclear demonstration of "will." Here the objective is not so much one of destroying or immobilizing a military target as of conveying to an enemy the dangers of escalation and a determination to raise the ante if he persists in his hostile actions. Such a limited nuclear reprisal could become a tit-for-tat exchange, with considerable dangers of escalation. But it could also produce a settlement at the lowest possible level of nuclear violence if one side called the other's bluff successfully. Whatever the pros and cons of such a strategy, which has been discussed by a number of other writers,[17] the West will always have this capability available to counter enemy demonstrations or threats.

Some battlefield nuclear weapons must be retained in Europe to ensure that the spectrum of allied capabilities matches that of the Soviet Union. There are probably sufficient nuclear-capable systems now on the Continent or included in NATO programs to meet this need. Secretary McNamara has pointed out that the number of U.S. weapons on the Continent has increased 60 per cent between 1961 and 1963,[18] so that the problem is not one of adding more weapons but one of doctrine, organization, and control. Also, the pitfalls of several much-talked-about denuclearization plans must be avoided. Even an agreed and inspected nuclear-free zone in Central Europe could leave the West at a significant logistic disadvantage in the event of Soviet reintroduction of nuclear systems —which could be done relatively quickly. This would create a gap

[17] See Glenn H. Snyder, *Deterrence and Defense* (Princeton University Press, 1961), pp. 198-225; Robert Osgood, *NATO, The Entangling Alliance* (University of Chicago Press, 1962), pp. 155-57; Thomas C. Schelling, "Nuclear Strategy in Europe," *World Politics*, April 1962; Klaus Knorr and Thornton Read, ed., *Limited Strategic War* (Princeton, Center for International Studies, 1962).

[18] Speech to the Economic Club of New York, cited.

between conventional operations and strategic warfare which the Soviets could exploit by forcing on NATO the difficult choice between acquiescence and escalation to general war. The requirement for denying this option to the Communist bloc will remain no matter what level of conventional deployment NATO obtains.

The Non-nuclear Surprise Attack

We come to the third option in the attack-with-ready-forces category: the non-nuclear surprise attack. This possibility has brought on much controversy and confusion over NATO's nuclear-conventional balance. It is important to bear in mind that weapons are means and not ends. NATO's objective is not solely a matter of whether to use particular weapons systems; rather it is to defend every foot of NATO territory as effectively as possible, taking into account the full range of possible consequences.

In the earlier years of NATO, when the West had a virtual monopoly of nuclear weapons and massive retaliation was the American strategic concept, NATO's underlying political directives were shaped accordingly. They also reflected the politico-economic fact that war-ravaged Europe, then just starting on the road to recovery, simply did not have the resources to make any other strategy effective. Hence, the two assumptions incorporated into SHAPE planning under the Eisenhower administration were that "nuclear weapons would be used, if necessary, from the onset" and that "under no circumstances was a war in the NATO area ever to be treated as a limited war."[19]

In its reassessment of NATO strategy, the Kennedy administration drew upon the many criticisms from both Europeans and Americans such as General Maxwell Taylor. His *The Uncertain Trumpet* reflected the army's fear that over-reliance on strategic retaliation guaranteed NATO's inability to respond to a conventional attack by other than nuclear weapons. Since a two-sided nuclear war in Europe promised more destruction than defense, the Soviet Union might count on deterring a Western nuclear response

[19] Murphy, cited, p. 214; See also Osgood, cited, Ch. 5.

by its own atomic capability and thus open the way to a successful conventional attack.

The logic was clear: if NATO in fact was "impaled on the horns of a defeat or suicide dilemma" as Liddell Hart had argued well before the Kennedy administration assumed offiice, then the remedy was to expand the conventional means to avoid defeat.[20] According to one account, Dean Acheson's influential study of NATO at the beginning of the Kennedy administration endorsed the goals of thirty active and thirty reserve divisions. In elaborating General Norstad's concept of a "pause," Acheson's purpose was to "buy time to enable statesmen to consider the use of force without having always to look immediately into the nuclear abyss."[21] The pause was therefore designed to avoid automatic employment of nuclear weapons against any Soviet thrust larger than an incursion, and thus permit an evaluation of enemy intentions before reaching irrevocable political decisions.

To many Europeans, however, especially the Germans, the pause had the distasteful connotation of allowing the Soviets to negotiate from the *de facto* control of NATO territory. Consequently, the emphasis was shifted to raising the threshold at which nuclear weapons might have to be employed. More recently, talk about a threshold (which was never satisfactorily defined) has given way to more generalized expressions of the need for more conventional strength in Europe.

In retrospect, insufficient account was taken of a fairly widespread European wish to deter the Russians if possible but to avoid being defended at all. Having seen conventional war in much closer perspective than most Americans, they tacitly preferred defeat to eventual liberation for the survivors amidst smoking ruins. One has only to read a good account of World War I trench warfare to understand one reviewer's conclusion that it is permissible to prefer "that the world end with a brief atomic bang, not a long

[20] Cited, p. 90.
[21] William Kaufmann, *The McNamara Strategy* (New York: Harper & Row, 1964), Ch. III.

drawn out whimper as at Verdun."[22] Because man is emotional as well as logical, more than a few Europeans espoused a policy of speaking loudly but carrying no stick at all. If deterrence failed, that was just too bad. There might then be a rush for what has appropriately been called "pre-emptive surrender."

A number of experts on both sides of the Atlantic have expressed the fear that emphasizing conventional defenses merely serves to weaken the nuclear deterrent. Since the immediate consequences of an attack would be less, it can be argued that an aggressor would be less inhibited. But by the same token some defense, rather than accommodation, is much more certain. With the certainty that aggression would be met with substantial force and perhaps defeated, plus the further possibility of escalation, the net effect on the deterrent should be greater, provided, of course, that a theoretical defense strategy does not outrun the actual capabilities on the ground.

The debate over NATO strategy has been so widely reported in the press and in recent books that elaborate reconstruction here seems unnecessary.[23] As one writer concluded:

> The Europeans, by and large, would have none of the new doctrine. It was not that they were themselves at ease with the Eisenhower strategy, or that they were indifferent to the unprecedented dangers that go with a nuclear strategy. It was simply a case of deciding on practical considerations that the new American doctrine,

[22] See, for example, Alistair Horne, *The Price of Glory: Verdun, 1916* (London: St. Martin's Press, 1963). (Reviewed by Robert Doty in *The New York Times,* International Edition, February 23, 1963).

[23] The best historical summary is contained in Robert Osgood's *NATO, The Entangling Alliance,* cited, Ch. 6. Henry Kissinger has provided useful analyses in *Nuclear Weapons and Foreign Policy* (New York: Harper & Row, for the Council on Foreign Relations, 1957), *The Necessity for Choice* (New York: Harper & Row, 1960), and more recently in "The Unsolved Problems of European Defense," *Foreign Affairs,* July 1962, pp. 515-541. *Building the Atlantic World,* by Robert Strauz-Hupé, James E. Dougherty, and William Kintner (New York: Harper & Row, for the Foreign Policy Research Institute, 1963) includes an up-to-date analysis of the debates on conventional forces.

> however well intentioned, would not substantially increase the deterrent to aggression and, even less, save Europe in the event of war.[24]

In fairness to the Europeans, it must be admitted that Washington rarely spoke with a unified voice as to what the new American doctrine really meant. Some people who simply disagreed with it deliberately distorted its implications.[25] Secretary McNamara himself admitted "that we have failed to convey the basic fundamentals of the strategic problems confronting our nation in this nuclear age."[26] Attempts to get the Europeans to take off the strategic blinders (which the Eisenhower administration had fastened on them) served merely to sharpen their suspicions. Thus the lower estimates of Soviet military power given in several speeches by Defense Department officials were greeted in Europe less by substantive disagreement than by concern that the administration was paving the way for force withdrawals.[27]

One useful lesson can be drawn from NATO's recent nuclear debates: American lectures delivered in public, no matter how brilliant, are no substitute for a dialogue within the alliance in hammering out realistic defense concepts. A number of U.S. studies made on a purely unilateral and classified basis apparently led the administration to conclude that a two-sided nuclear war in Europe did not come out well for NATO, no matter how much damage was done to the Communist bloc. A knowledgeable British official reports that in one of these games:

> . . . involving just three NATO Corps, nuclear weapons were "used" against military targets only, in an area of 10,000 square miles which contained no large towns or

[24] Murphy, cited, p. 219.

[25] See for example Bernard Brodie's attack on the advocates of what he called "CWE"—for conventional war in Europe—in the May 1963 issue of *The Reporter.*

[26] Testimony before the House Armed Services Committee, January 27, 1964; *The New York Times,* January 28, 1964, p. 1.

[27] For example, Secretary McNamara's speech to the Economic Club of New York, November 18, 1963 and Assistant Secretary Paul Nitze's remarks

> cities. In this "battle" lasting only a few days, it was assumed that the two sides together used a total of between 20 and 25 megatons in not fewer than 500 and not more than 1,000 strikes. It turned out that 3½ million people would have had their homes destroyed if the weapons were air burst and 1½ million if ground burst. In the former case, at least half the people concerned would have been fatally or seriously injured. In the case of ground burst weapons, all 1½ million would have been exposed to a lethal radiological hazard and a further 5 million to serious danger from radiation.[28]

For a war conducted along the entire central front, the casualties could be five to ten times higher.

The case for the conventional build-up, which this type of analysis provides, might have been much more persuasive to the European foreign and defense ministers and their staffs if they had helped to frame the assumptions for such studies and shared in drawing the conclusions. Unfortunately, although SHAPE and the Military Committee also wrestle diligently with these same issues, the staff planning procedures and NATO's structural separation between political and military components are not suited to consensus-building before policies are molded by the rigidities of national positions.

It is understandable that a new government such as the incoming Kennedy administration should have wanted to take its own look at the problem *in camera* prior to engaging in interallied negotiations. But once the broad outlines of national policy are clarified, a two-way exchange is a much more effective process of persuasion than the hard sell of a predetermined package.

A measure of progress is already noticeable in sharing basic data, and in communications on the Minister of Defense level. NATO exercises are beginning to involve political-level officials

---

to the Cleveland Council on World Affairs, March 2, 1963 were followed by suspicious or critical comment in most major European papers.

[28] Sir Solly Zuckerman, "Judgment and Control in Modern Warfare," *Foreign Affairs*, January 1962, p. 201.

of the governments and to apply realistic rather than arbitrary politico-military assumptions. They mark a considerable improvement over the 1955 "Carte Blanche" exercise which managed to frighten the Germans and confound, rather than advance, NATO planning.[29]

A number of European writers, if not their governments, are coming around to the support of the maximum possible non-nuclear defense. Interestingly enough, two of the best European books on NATO have been produced by a German SPD Bundestag member and a British Labor MP.[30] Some advocates of a conventional build-up may, however, be right for the wrong reasons, insofar as their reasoning is based upon a premise of nuclear disengagement or a phase-out of American nuclear power from the Continent.

Leading U.S. officials have become somewhat less categorical. General Taylor, recalled from retirement to serve as President Kennedy's Chairman of the Joint Chiefs, modified his published views and stressed the need for atomic weapons in defense of Europe during the hearings on his confirmation. Secretary McNamara's 1963 testimony to Congress included statements that at present NATO forces "would not be able to contain an all-out conventional attack without invoking the use of nuclear weapons." After noting the improved ability to "deal with a much greater range of Soviet actions" on a non-nuclear basis, the Secretary added that "we must continue to do everything in our power to persuade our allies to meet their NATO force goals so that we will possess alternative capabilities for dealing with even larger Soviet attacks." His 1964 statement, however, placed less emphasis on persuasion, merely noting that "the forces envisioned in NATO plans for the end of 1966 . . . could hold an

[29] William W. Kaufmann, ed., *Military Policy and National Security* (Princeton University Press, 1956), pp. 225-226, and Klaus Knorr, *NATO and American Security* (Princeton University Press, 1960), p. 240.

[30] Mulley and Schmidt previously cited. Eugene Hinterhoff has written persuasively on the subject in a series of articles in *The Tablet* (London) May 25 and June 1, 1963, as has Alastair Buchan in several of the works cited.

initial Soviet attack on the Central Front using non-nuclear means alone . . . although . . . we are still some distance from achieving them."[31]

Prospects for Defense

Assuming the requisite improvements in NATO policy-making and a greater American sensitivity to European attitudes, what are the prospects for defending without nuclear weapons against a conventional surprise attack? The Communist force, as we have seen, would probably involve a maximum of 40 to 45 divisions on the central front. Taking into account the smaller size and fire power of these units, the equivalent in NATO's standard divisions would be about 30. There would be intensive air action, and high explosive bombs would be dropped on key NATO targets, at least in the front lines. There might also be diversionary attacks by Soviet forces in the north, especially against the North Cape area of Norway, or perhaps in Macedonia. Also, the Soviets might attempt long-range air drops to secure key river crossings and mountain gaps, and to harass rear areas. According to one account, the Soviet Union now has as many as 27 airborne regiments and the lift to carry two 20,000-man airborne divisions in a single operation. Most of the Soviet air transports have the range to reach the Rhine from Soviet territory and return to bases behind the iron curtain.[32]

The classic assumption that the attacker needs three-to-one superiority has many exceptions and qualifications. But it is necessary to distinguish tactical superiority at the points of attack which are the aggressor's choice, from the strategic ratio along the front as a whole. The approved NATO force goal on the central front is 30 divisions, of which some 25 are currently avail-

[31] Statement Before the House Subcommittee on Department of Defense Appropriations on the Fiscal Year 1964-1968 House Defense Program, February 6, 1963, p. 55, and Statement Before the House Armed Services Committee, January 27, 1964, pp. 58-59.

[32] Bruno Maurach, "Die sowjetischen Luftlandetruppen," *Revue Militaire Générale,* October 1962, p. 373.

able. This includes the 6 American divisions (5 plus 3 armored cavalry regiments), the British Army of the Rhine (BAOR), and the Canadian brigade totalling about 3 divisions, 10 German divisions, and 2 each from France, Belgium, and the Netherlands.

Improvements in firepower, mobility, and communications have allowed the ratio of space to force to increase repeatedly from the one-mile-per-division equivalent in several nineteenth-century campaigns, to 4 or 5 miles in World War I, 8 to 10 miles in World War II, and finally to a 25-mile estimate at the present time.[33]

NATO's total West German frontier from the Baltic to Austria is almost 800 miles long—which would average 33 miles for each of 24 divisions if all were on line. In the 350 miles of relatively open terrain in North Germany, there are only about 14 divisions, an average of about 25 miles to the division. The actual defense lines, which follow geographic profiles rather than the ins and outs of political boundaries, might be reduced to 250 miles. But at least 4 divisions would be needed for a mobile reserve, so that there is still a 25-mile average division sector. In the south, 10 divisions must cover about 400 miles, or 40 miles each, although the terrain is more defensible.

The situation is complicated by maldeployments resulting from political and administrative considerations. Forces of the former occupying powers are generally located within their old occupation zones, and France has most of its forces in the home country. Dutch and Belgian divisions are stationed behind their own frontiers. Available caserns tend to be removed some distance from defense positions, requiring a major forward displacement in the event of war. Lateral mobility is limited by road nets, logistic considerations, and the like. All in all, it appears extremely unlikely that present NATO strength could cope satisfactorily with even the surprise 45-division assault without early resort to nuclear weapons. For the enemy can mass his forces at one of the

[33] Some interesting historical perspectives on the ratio of force to space are contained in Liddell Hart, cited, Chs. 10 and 16.

several natural invasion channels and at the same time maintain some pressure along almost the entire front. He could easily achieve at least a five-to-one superiority at the point selected for a breakthrough and, by exploiting it, compel the NATO forces to withdraw toward the Rhine. But as the attacker's lines of supply lengthened, it is doubtful whether he could control more than a portion of West Germany before he would need major reinforcements—which brings mobilization factors into play on both sides and changes the nature of the case. Nevertheless it is just this ability to attain a partial success by a *fait accompli* which is at issue. NATO can hardly retain the confidence of its members if even the most heavily defended sector is vulnerable to such a *coup de main*. This is why General Norstad and the Germans have insisted upon a "forward" defense capable of defending NATO at, or close to, the frontiers.

It is easy to emphasize such negative factors at the expense of NATO's unprecedented accomplishments as a peacetime coalition. A multinational alliance has forged a defensive structure which has increased its combined strength tenfold since its inception. Habits of cooperation and collaboration have been developed step by step within international staffs and chains of command. The field commanders themselves are confident that they can perform their missions. Deficiencies there are; but NATO is no paper tiger. The American Seventh Army, for example, has been called the most combat-ready peacetime force ever assembled. Morale is high—and most important, the sense of confusion or defeatism which one might expect to find by listening to the pundits in various capitals is totally lacking in NATO's military structure, where the professionals have developed strong rapport. Thus, by contrast, at the field level there is the quiet confidence of men who know what they have to do and how to go about it.

Some fifteen years ago the author served as an officer of a Seventh Army unit. Even in those days, when plans called for a rapid retrograde movement toward the Rhine, constant emphasis on readiness and innumerable rehearsals produced a surprising level of competence and confidence. More recently, talks with several division commanders produced the following assessment: "If the bell rings, we hit the ground running—not backwards but forward to our main defense lines. When the first wave hits us they get a bloody nose. The second wave gets another one. By the third wave, if we don't use nuclears, we are beginning to be hurt. If the enemy can produce a fourth wave, he'll get through; but we'll still be in there fighting."

A firm foundation therefore already exists. Only an incremental improvement is necessary. Even five more divisions properly deployed would change the picture considerably, for they could provide the mobile reserves to redress tactical superiority at the point of attack, and contain a breakthrough, especially on the North German plain. They should not be impossible to obtain. Germany's approved force goals already call for two more divisions; if France earmarked two more from the forces formerly tied down in Algeria, the remaining one could be created by some restructuring of British, Canadian, and Benelux forces in the North.

A central front goal of thirty active divisions has survived from the pre-New Look goals decided upon at Lisbon. If NATO met that level, or even just took some of the remedial measures outlined above (e.g., making an effective local anti-tank and paramilitary defense, decentralizing supply storage and distribution, improving lateral mobility of the shield forces), the chances of a successful surprise conventional attack could be made very small indeed. The relative value of such "trade-offs" for extra divisions as a greater number of smaller-sized less mobile units, militia-defended strong points, and the like, need not be explored in detail here. The point is that the problem could be solved without a substantial increase in costs. And the West would then not be tied to a nuclear defense, although that option would always remain open should things go badly.

Crisis and Mobilization

Whether the foregoing measures to handle the surprise attack are worthwhile will depend on the second category of possibilities: a thrust by all available Communist bloc forces, following mobilization and forward deployments. Here the number of potential forces is much larger, for the Soviet Union maintains from 120 to 150 active line divisions (Western estimates vary considerably), which could be brought up to full strength on fairly short notice, although equipment and support might be lacking for some. We must assume that two-thirds of the 75 to 80 divisions now maintained in European Russia would be available to reinforce the surprise attack spearhead of 40-plus divisions described above. The Communist bloc could therefore mount a formidable offensive of 80 to 90 divisions in Central Europe, and at the same time make limited secondary thrusts at both NATO flanks.[34] There are, of course, practical limitations in terms of geography, logistics, and transportation on the size of attacking force which the Soviets could support in sustained offensive operations. But Western experts are not in agreement on the effects of these limiting factors. There are too many unknowns to permit a high degree of confidence in whatever detailed estimates are made, although the general order of magnitude is probably correct.

It can be assumed that NATO defenses would be considerably augmented during the period between the first signs of Soviet

[34] These estimates of Soviet forces are drawn from the ISS *Military Balance,* and its disarmament study cited in footnote 2. Soviet divisions are not, of course, on a par with Western types in terms of strength, firepower or staying ability, and must be adjusted with perhaps 1.5 or 1.3 Soviet divisions to one U.S.-European-type division. This division slice (the strength of a force divided by the number of divisions) is about 60,000 for the United States (960,000 men for a 16 division force) compared with only 15,000 for the Soviet Union (2.2 million men for 150 divisions). Either the Soviets do not have anything like those figures, or their divisions must be virtually without combat support. Some of the difference, to be sure, is "fat"—a reflection of the higher standard of living of the Western soldier. But some of it must be in firepower, mobility, communications, and engineer and medical support for which it is hard to assign a numerical value, but which surely increases the effectiveness of the U.S. division. Thus the 1.5 to 1 ratio favoring the U.S. division is probably on the conservative side. (See "The Division Slice" by Colonel Irving Heymont, USA, in the October 1962 *Military Review*). See also McNamara's January 27, 1964 statement, cited, p. 58.

mobilization and an actual attack. Yet as "Operation Stairstep" showed during the 1961 Berlin build-up, the United States as well as European NATO members have serious defects in their mobilization machinery. A major effort has been made to correct American deficiencies through revision in the reserve component structure, pre-positioning of stocks, improved air and sea transportation, and the like. Operation "Big Lift" in the fall of 1963 was in part a test of the revised procedures; and although some Europeans feared that the exercise was a preliminary step toward American redeployments, it did demonstrate that the U.S. ability to move large numbers of troops to Europe for a heightening crisis had been much improved since 1961.

There is reason to think that the European allies are increasingly aware of their own deficiencies. Yet unless there is a major effort to overhaul the second and third echelon forces of the alliance, the number of effective reserves that could be brought to bear within two weeks of mobilization is quite small. During a period in which strategic thinking is dominated by nuclear concepts, the post-"M-day" reserve forces have a relatively low priority. While procedures are in effect for bringing understrength units up to wartime levels through reserve manpower, a number of second and third echelon units exist mainly on paper. Equipment is often lacking, obsolete, or not readily available. The slow pace of NATO standardization restricts the operational flexibility of the defensive forces, for each national army must be supplied with spare parts from its own depots. Italian divisions, for example, might have great difficulty in operating on the central front because the stocks maintained there for U.S. or French forces may not be of the right type.

NATO as a whole has not yet recognized the vital distinction between force *augmentation* for deterrence, and mobilization for war. The nuclear emphasis has created a dangerous paralysis in which it has been assumed that there will be either no war or total war, and that in the latter case, mobilization would be irrelevant. This polarization does not even reflect present-day realities, let alone those of the future. Suppose the Soviet Union were to undertake a significant force build-up, to put pressure on the West. If NATO could not muster a credible defense posture to cope with it, there would be little choice but accommodation or to hope that the Soviets would not call the West's bluff with respect to thermonuclear war. Or, the West might find it necessary to signal its determination and improve its readiness should there be another test of wills over Berlin.

It is probably unrealistic to expect the NATO countries to maintain large reserve forces in a high state of readiness and with a full complement of modern equipment. But the concept of augmentation of regular forces by periodic active-duty training of selected reserve units may furnish a practical alternative. The history of the cold war suggests a cycle of tensions, relaxations, and crises; and there is no indication that it will not continue this way. The ability to produce some supplementary personnel and units on location *quickly* may be far more important both for deterrence and for defense than doubling the number three months later. Instead of periodic "crash" build-ups followed by reductions, NATO should be able to schedule reserve training programs so that several regiments from various countries are always on duty—thus increasing the active shield forces—and at the same time providing a pool of ready units from which augmentation could be accomplished in time of crisis. The manpower, personnel, fiscal, and support problems would not be easy ones to solve. Yet for most European countries, this alternative would probably be more acceptable than lengthening the period of conscription and far less costly than the pay and allowances for an equal number of active duty personnel.

NATO's 1950-51 planning envisaged a covering force of 34 divisions (18 active and 16 ready reserve); but at the Lisbon meeting of the NATO Council in February 1952, NATO undertook to raise a total of 50 active divisions, 34 of them on the central front, and to double the reserve troops, looking to a grand total of 96 divisions by 1954.[35] For a variety of political and economic

[35] See, generally, Liddell Hart, cited, p. 89; Osgood, cited, Chs. 2 and 4; NATO Information Service, NATO, *Facts About the North Atlantic*

reasons these goals were never met; and as already noted, NATO has only attained 80 per cent of even the revised 30-division goal for the central front. Even with an augmentation-rapid-mobilization scheme such as that suggested above, NATO would do well to have 45 divisions deployed within the few weeks in which the Soviets could poise nearly twice that number. True, not all of the Communist forces could be transported, deployed, and supplied simultaneously. But the cumulative weight of an attack of this size would probably have the defenders in retreat and desperately throwing in reserves which were poorly trained, organized, and equipped. Unless the conflict had escalated so as to permit interdiction of enemy movements, the attacker would have a steady flow of reinforcements with which to exploit salients, despite over-lengthened lines of communication. The result would very likely be Soviet capture of politically significant areas and the prospect of an eventual setback for NATO, or resort to general nuclear war. Because of the West's over-all strategic superiority, NATO could conceivably "win" such a nuclear conflict in a meaningful way. But if things went badly, it could also develop into a Pyrrhic victory in which most of Europe would be destroyed, along with much of the United States and Russia.

The Role of Tactical Airpower

Thus the real problem for NATO centers on the massive conventional assault in which the Soviets counted on deterring a nuclear response. Of critical importance here is air superiority. In a conventional war, the Soviets might have an initial quantitative advantages in tactical airpower in Europe. (The reinforcement of American tactical air was one of the major undertakings during the 1961 Berlin build-up.) Reliable figures are hard to come by on

---

Treaty Organization, Paris, 1962, Part I; and Lord Ismay, *NATO—The First Five Years* (Paris: NATO Information Service, 1955), p. 47. Since, with the exception of the Lisbon figures (50 divisions, 4,000 aircraft, and 704 major combatant vessels for 1952), NATO force goals have not been announced, there are some inconsistencies in the published estimates.

an unclassified basis. The Institute for Strategic Studies reports as of 1964 that the earlier estimate of 4,000 operational aircraft in Soviet tactical forces is now too high by at least a quarter because of transition to more modern versions.[36] But taking into account the 1,000-plus jets in the satellite air forces should bring the grand total to nearly 4,000. According to the same source, NATO tactical air forces in Europe include some 3,500 aircraft; but they could be rapidly augmented from the United States to approach parity in quantity, and Western quality is undoubtedly higher. As the F-104G now being produced by a European consortium replaces older aircraft in European inventories, and the expanded U.S. Tactical Air Command acquires the new F4C (the air force version of the navy's F4H) and eventually the still more advanced F-111 (TFX), NATO air strength will show considerable qualitative improvement. The extent of the numerical balance favoring NATO will depend upon how fast the Communist bloc moves in its own modernization program.

A few years ago the prospect of major air and ground combat in Europe with conventional ordnance seemed preposterous to many professionals, and it still seems so to quite a few. But those who studied the situation most closely were surprised to discover that "iron bombs" can still cause heavy damage to enemy airfields and ground installations. They also found that the vulnerability of NATO fighters to a similar attack can be cut down inexpensively by the use of tactical air shelter protection,[37] and that modern fire control and air-to-air missiles, plus Western pilot skills and tactics, can compensate for some quantitative inferiority. Of particular importance would be short and vertical take-off-and-landing (STOL and VTOL) aircraft which can be easily concealed and protected and do not need large, expensive, and vulnerable air-

[36] Cited; see page 4 and 7-9, and the "national forces" enumerated for NATO on pp. 15-24.

[37] Secretary McNamara has noted that "in a non-nuclear war situation, this measure would contribute much more to our combat power per dollar invested than additional aircraft or more modern aircraft." February 6, 1963 statement, cited, p. 81.

fields from which to operate. NATO appears to be making some research progress in VTOL aircraft, but the full development potential has certainly not been realized.[38]

Western tactical air defenses, including Hawk which, like the F-104G, is being produced in Europe, are reasonably effective against most Soviet aircraft. On the other hand, Soviet surface-to-air missiles (known as SAMs in professional jargon) have also been much improved in recent years.

On balance, it is by no means certain that NATO would lose control of the air within a short time in a conventional war in Europe. But it could not, with present forces, attain a decisive enough margin to compensate for the Soviet edge in ground forces. Equally important, after a week or two of air combat, the factors of attrition and combat fatigue on men and machines could seriously degrade NATO's nuclear ability. And, as we have seen, maintaining the option of nuclear defense is essential to denying it to the enemy. On the other hand, taking into account America's ability to reinforce rapidly, the attrition would work both ways and would ultimately favor the side with the greatest over-all strength in tactical air power.

The West's Options

What can NATO do to meet the challenge of a massive conventional attack *without* having to resort to general war within a very short period? Several complementary options are open in theory: First, the alliance could allocate the economic resources necessary to match Soviet strength; second, it could reorganize its forces so as to get greater defensive potential from the present level of effort; third, NATO could supplement defensive forces with an offensive capability aimed, for example, at satellite instabilities in the event of conflict; fourth, NATO could seek a strategy of controlled nuclear defense which would reduce the risks of escalation to all-out war. Finally, there might be possibili-

[38] See John W. R. Taylor, "VTOL—The Key to NATO Air Power," *NATO's Fifteen Nations*, December 1962-January 1963, p. 90.

ties in arms control which could ease NATO's defense burden.

In practice, however, NATO's civilian and military leadership have all too often been unwilling even to consider any such possibilities. The underlying assumption is that nothing can be done which would make a significant difference. Therefore, so runs the argument, the alliance must depend for the preservation of its interests upon nuclear deterrence—and, if that fails, upon prompt initiation of all-out nuclear war. And as long as such circular reasoning dominates, its conclusion will inevitably be right. For nothing will be done by political leaders as long as the professionals concerned adhere in the 1960s to patterns of thought formed in the early 1950s. The military, in short, say they "cannot" because the politicians will not; and the latter certainly will not as long as the former say they cannot. It may be worthwhile therefore to consider the more promising possibilities in greater detail. They are not by any means mutually exclusive; on the contrary, they tend to be complementary; and taken together, they may well constitute a realistic alternative to NATO's present posture and strategy.

An Expanded Non-Nuclear Posture

As we will see in looking at the political-economics of defense, there are no economic or manpower factors which would make it impossible to match or even top Soviet strength in land forces and tactical airpower. The concept of Soviet hordes sweeping over Europe is a widely held myth. From the standpoint of the U.S.S.R., however, as one U.S. official noted, it may appear that *NATO* has the hordes.[39] But there are practical obstacles which make it highly unlikely that NATO will produce them. First, there is geographic space. Billeting and maneuver facilities are already extremely scarce in the critical forward areas. Even if the forces could be raised, manned, and equipped, it is not clear where

[39] Assistant Defense Secretary Paul H. Nitze, Cleveland speech (cited, footnote 2). He supports this point by noting that NATO has 5.8 million men under arms compared to 4.3 million for the Warsaw Pact, and 2.2 million men in allied ground forces in Europe compared with 2 million for the Soviet Union (without, however, counting the satellites).

they could be stationed in crowded Western Europe on a peacetime basis. And it is true that the chances of European parliaments voting the necessary conscription and financing are not good under any circumstances. The case for matching the Soviet Union in conventional standing forces simply does not emerge as compelling in the absence of an offensive-oriented strategy. To some degree, however, NATO's ability to defend forward requires an ability to counterattack the enemy's flanks and threaten his rear—which, in turn, argues for a greater number of mobile armored divisions. But there are potential dangers in urging such an expansion in conventional strength on the ground that the West wishes to avoid nuclear conflict (perhaps encouraging the Soviets to act on the assumption that they would not meet a nuclear response), and then failing to provide the requisite non-nuclear forces. If the lead time between a change of strategy and the creation of the means to implement it is too long, a dangerous gap could develop. Nevertheless, it may be worth taking a closer look at the relationship between forces and costs.

The full equipment for an infantry division runs to about $300 million for the United States and perhaps $250 million in Europe. For a modern armored division the price tag may exceed $400 million. The annual manpower cost also varies from about $25 million to over $100 million.[40] And to keep one division in the front lines requires an administrative and logistic slice of at least twice its size.

To defend NATO's central front adequately without nuclear weapons against a post-mobilization conventional attack, at least 60 divisions might be needed within a month. This figure takes

[40] These estimates are based upon data in: Pierre Messmer (French Minister of Defense), "The French Military Establishment of Tomorrow," *Orbis*, Summer 1962, pp. 207-209; Col. F. O. Miksche, "Economic, Technical and Political Aspects of the European Shield," *NATO's Fifteen Nations*, December 1962-January 1963, pp. 38-43; and Secretary McNamara's February 6, 1963 statement, cited, p. 56 and Table 6. An FY 1963 appropriation of $2.6 billion for army military personnel in the General Purpose Forces category is needed to maintain sixteen active divisions—an average of over $150 million each (which includes a part of the "division slice").

into account the attacker's need for superiority, and the fact that 90 Soviet divisions may be the equivalent of only 60 to 70 Western-type division.[41] If this minimum of 60 NATO units were divided evenly between active and truly "ready" reserves, full stocks of new equipment might be required for some 20 to 25 divisions. To this one-time expenditure of $8 billion to $10 billion must be added the annual manpower costs for the increase of 5 divisions over present active forces, perhaps $0.5 billion. Supporting administrative and logistic forces would have to be increased proportionally; and new bases, infrastructure, and additional tactical airpower would be needed. The annual cost of the increase might be doubled to perhaps $1 billion. Thus the five-year cost for NATO to expand its forces to this size could total about $15 billion—over and above the sums needed to maintain and improve the existing forces. Even this amount would only cover the central front to a minimum degree, leaving major deficiencies in conventional capability on the flanks. For maximum insurance, a force structure of 40 active and 40 first-line reserve divisions might be involved. This would raise the additional five-year costs to $25 billion or $30 billion.

To put it mildly, the availability of such a sum is open to question. Aside from the pressures that exist in Europe to reduce existing military budgets, it is by no means clear that the United States will maintain indefinitely the level of defense spending attained by the Kennedy administration. The determination to avoid an arbitrary ceiling on the American defense budget may be eroded by balance-of-payments considerations or by political factors; and successors to Secretary McNamara may lack his ability to budget according to priorities without the discipline of a fixed limit.

The difference between the level of about 30 active divisions and a posture of 40 to 45 divisions represents some additional risk, to be sure; but to adopt the higher one might simply repeat the experience after the Lisbon meeting of 1952, when none of the

[41] See footnote 34, above.

members came close to fulfilling the approved force goals. Moreover, it is reasonable to inquire about the costs and effectiveness of alternative forms of insurance to cover the risk, and whether the standard NATO-type division is really needed for a purely defensive mission. A reorientation of defensive concepts for the central front could perhaps make better use of the available resources.

Maximizing the Defensive Potential

One variable is the balance between active and first-line reserve divisions. Greater emphasis on the latter would save on mobilized manpower and the high costs of paying personnel on active service. Equipment costs would nevertheless be the same; and, assuming a larger total number of divisions, it would be substantially larger; additional storage areas and depots would be needed; and reserve training would have to be vastly expanded. Experience suggests that even the best reserve units require fairly long periods of active duty before they are combat-ready. The compulsory reserve service obligations to support such a program would run head-on into the political obstacles which affect conscription in almost every NATO country.

Nevertheless, on a five-year basis, NATO could probably get two or more first-line reserve divisions out of the money saved by deactivating one—which would appear to be a worthwhile swap within certain limits. The gamble would be that NATO would have sufficient warning to get these units activated and back in place before an attack. Arms control measures, such as observation posts, roving inspectors, overlapping radars, could greatly increase the assurance on this point. And it might be that some such shift in NATO's active and reserve balance could be traded for valuable inspection rights; for the Soviet Union might feel that its security would be enhanced by a reduction in NATO's active duty forces with their offensive potential.

A second possibility would involve some sacrifice in the mobility of NATO divisions, which is an asset of questionable value anyway in a defensive war in a limited area. Instead, some of the units could be broken up into smaller, static, "forward defense" divisions and used in conjunction with defended strong points, conventional and nuclear demolitions, and the territorial militia combination suggested earlier. This concept, it should be recalled, meets the "multiple-contingency" test.[42] On the other hand, any extensive system of fortifications suggests to the Germans a permanence of the present border between East and West and carries a politically unpopular implication. But here, too, the added assurance to the Russians that NATO's forces were in fact capable of only defensive missions might be traded for favorable arms control or political concessions which would offset some of the scheme's disadvantages.

Alternatively, if the arms control route remains blocked, NATO might wish to expand the offensive mission and potential of its forces. Particularly, in view of instabilities in the satellites, guerrilla-type units could be trained for air drops into Eastern Europe in the event of war. There, they could form the nucleus of resistance forces which, if adequately supplied by air, could tie down large numbers of Soviet troops. This scheme appears to have considerable merit as a supplementary deterrent, for the Soviets are psychologically sensitive to possible revolts in Eastern Europe. By itself, however, such an approach would hardly redress the conventional military balance.

A final possibility, which would add to NATO's flexibility and further strengthen other measures, would be to develop a doctrine for the employment and control of tactical nuclear weapons. To be credible in its application and thus serve as a deterrent, and also to be effective for defense, such an option must not provide built-in escalation or have severe civil damage as its automatic by-product.

A Nuclear Option for European Defense

The challenge is to find a tactical doctrine which permits but does not require NATO to initiate the use of nuclear weapons. Secretary McNamara has pointed out that "while it does not neces-

[42] For some interesting comments on this point, see Adelbert Weinstein's

sarily follow that the use of tactical nuclear weapons must inevitably escalate into global nuclear war, it does present a very definite threshold beyond which we enter a vast unknown."[43] Many theorists have speculated about this unknown and evolved a number of possible concepts. Thomas Schelling, for example, suggests a deliberate raising of the ante by a demonstrative use of nuclear weapons to persuade the Soviets that a conflict was "getting out of hand but is not yet beyond the point of no return;" but he warns, "danger is the central feature of the use of nuclear weapons."[44]

Moving upwards in the scale, it might be possible to have an atomic trip-wire so linked to a nuclear escalator, that hopefully no one would trip it in the first place. But this must operate automatically (or under the sole control of front-line commanders) or it must depend on the vagaries of multinational decision-making in a crisis. The first would be an irrational abdication of political responsibility. And the second would face NATO with such unpalatable defeat or suicide alternatives, if deterrence failed, that an enemy might be tempted to gamble that the alliance would choose the former.

Other advocates have sought a complete nuclearization of NATO's shield forces.[45] This proposition may have had some validity when the Soviet stockpile was so small that the threat to Europe was almost completely conventional; but today the fact that a two-sided nuclear engagement would be virtually certain invalidates the notion that tactical atomic weapons can compensate for deficiencies in other forces. Any broad-scale use of nuclear weapons in Europe, especially if interdiction of rear-area targets

---

articles in the *Frankfurter Allgemeine Zeitung* for September 18 and 25, 1963.

[43] February 6, 1963 statement, cited, p. 18.

[44] *World Politics*, cited.

[45] Strausz-Hupé and colleagues, *Building the Atlantic World*, cited, is one of the best available analyses on this subject. Although I am not in agreement with their view that this is the only choice, or that tactical nuclear defense is workable except as a last resort, I am indebted to them for many valuable discussions on this subject. See also my article, "Decentralizing Nuclear Control in NATO," *Orbis*, Spring 1963.

were attempted, would almost certainly escalate to general war and the use of strategic forces from the United States and the U.S.S.R. But if it did not, NATO Europe would be just as badly if not worse off for the reasons explained earlier. Even if NATO were able to hold some kind of defensive line militarily, the casualties and civil damage could be enormous.[46]

There appear to be a number of pitfalls in the notion of "dual capable" forces. If they are designed primarily for nuclear war, they will lack ability to fight well on a non-nuclear basis. If designed for the latter type of conflict, but with organic nuclear support, these weapons may have to be used anyway to avoid destruction and capture early in the conflict.

A better solution is to abandon the myth that concentration on nuclear defense can solve NATO's military problems. Instead it should be regarded as an option needed for deterrence purposes and for insurance. This suggests that the atomic support should be organized into special units with their own delivery systems, much as the army's heavy artillery now is organized into separate battalions and groups assigned to corps and armies. The armament of such units could range from the Pershing and Honest John missiles, which are already in separate units, down to the Davy Crockett type of "bazooka." Their responsibility might include providing atomic warheads for the organic artillery of other units, in the event a conflict became nuclear, to facilitate security and control. Such a separation of the nuclear components from the conventional forces could provide one "fire-break" in the escalation chain, but still insure that atomic weapons were available if needed.

It is clear that NATO must maintain sufficient nuclear potential to counter effectively the initiation of nuclear warfare at any level by the Soviet Union. Equally, NATO should avoid guaranteeing that a potential aggressor need not concern himself with encountering a nuclear defense, for this would enable him to mass his forces with relative impunity. What appears necessary, there-

[46] See footnote 28 above.

fore, is a degree of deliberate ambiguity about NATO's response. Ambiguity of doctrine must be coupled with the flexibility to fight effectively with whatever weapons seem best suited to the alliance's interest—in the light of the circumstances prevailing at the time. Escalation to the use of tactical nuclear weapons and eventually, if necessary, to strategic counterforce attacks must not be ruled out. But the agonizing choices involved should be forced upon the enemy at each stage rather than self-imposed upon NATO through rigidity of doctrine or force structure.

A second "fire-break" behind that of the conventional-nuclear distinction might be a geographical limitation on the use of atomic weapons. NATO might, for example, adopt the policy that in the event of Communist aggression which cannot be repelled by conventional means, tactical nuclear weapons would be used against enemy forces but initially only within the territory being attacked. Thus the onus of first use could be countered to some degree; for, however expert the Communists may be at confusing the issue of who crossed whose border first, they cannot evade the fact that their forces were counterattacked with a nuclear weapon while penetrating NATO territory. This would leave the next move up to the aggressor. He could withdraw; he could continue the battle (and allow the use of tactical nuclear weapons against his forces); he could threaten or carry out retaliation in kind; or he could escalate the conflict. But unless the enemy was prepared for general war *ab initio*, a face-saving nuclear demonstration (or threat) and a cease-fire or withdrawal would be the most likely course. When the Soviets underestimate an opponent's determination, as they did in placing missiles in Cuba, Leninist tactics permit them to back off and ease the risks, while claiming credit for saving the peace.

It is clear that NATO could not afford to observe the "own territory only" constraint if the enemy chose to employ his nuclear weapons, for this would give his own rear areas an unwarranted immunity. NATO's next response might be to extend the range of its nuclear strikes as far on the Communist side of the border as the invading forces had penetrated NATO territory.

This would create a nuclear combat zone which would offer a transitory stability, since extensive military operations within it would be difficult to mount. Probably the enemy would have disengaged before this stage had been reached, for the prospects of rapid escalation would be high—by accident, design, or misinterpretation on the part of either side. But NATO would have preserved maximum flexibility and at the same time provided the enemy a chance to correct his miscalculation at each of the three separate fire-breaks—the initial conventional resistance, the nuclear attack on invading forces, and the nuclear strikes within a fairly narrow zone—before resort to extended nuclear operations would be required.

The primary difficulty in this concept is that of determining when the conventional defense is no longer effective and who is to make the determination—our familiar political control problem revisited. The country actually under attack might have one set of interests, perhaps calling for the use of nuclear weapons, while other members of the alliance, especially if the conflict were localized, could have an opposing interest in restraining escalation in location and levels of violence.

Indeed, it is only in the least likely case of a massive Soviet attack on the entire alliance that NATO is apt to be forced by events into the unanimous response on which planning is based under the present system. In any less clear-cut case, a failure of some collective response to "an attack on one" might well tear the alliance apart at its most critical juncture. Even this hypothetical possibility, as we have seen, is at the root of many of NATO's problems.

A procedure such as the following, agreed to in advance and possibly made public for the benefit of the Soviet Union, might solve this dilemma. Any country being attacked by Communist forces would have the right to request tactical nuclear strikes against those forces through the military chain of command. If SACEUR agreed with the request, it would immediately be placed before the North Atlantic Council. If an impasse resulted there, under whatever procedures were in effect, the Council would delegate the political decision back to the government of the country or countries under attack. Then, upon its decision, nuclear warheads would be released to commanders of NATO forces engaged in combat—but only for low-yield, short-range weapons capable of being used in this defensive context. Atomic demolitions, for example, could be placed ahead of the enemy forces and detonated by remote control. The fact that the weapons were being employed within the country authorizing this action should prevent their use except as a last resort. Both the blast effects from NATO weapons and the immediate consequences of Soviet retaliation, if any, would be borne by the country concerned, whose government is better able to balance the risks than anyone else.

No NATO country would be able to involve the alliance in nuclear support for an incident of its own making, because its request would require the concurrence of NATO's highest military authorities. In effect, SACEUR would be confirming both the fact of Communist aggression and the military need for nuclear defense in the light of the current situation as reported through his command channels. Political control of any initial nuclear military operation would thus be in the hands of the authorities most immediately concerned. Any subsequent authorizations for nuclear strikes outside that member's boundaries, or other measures which would increase the danger of rapid escalation, would be decided by the alliance as a whole through direct governmental consultation, the North Atlantic Council, and SACEUR, as under the present system.

This concept, it should be noted, is not the same thing as an advance delegation to any country attacked; for it is important that NATO consultation procedures be followed. Only where they result in an impasse would the alliance authorize one country to act for it; and initially only within that country's own territory.[47] This, in effect, is a very limited trigger given by the

[47] This concept offers some additional incentives for developing the so-called "neutron" type weapon, of which the primary effect is in lethal radiation of short duration, rather than in the nuclear blast. Such weapons would

alliance to a member in time of severe crisis. It is therefore less dangerous than a group of national nuclear deterrents would be, for the authority delegated is to raise the level of violence by one degree rather than several.

Since deliberate ambiguity of response is a central feature of this concept and the decision to employ nuclear weapons would be taken only in the light of actual events, NATO's military commanders might be concerned by the lack of planning criteria. A further variant on the scheme could be adopted to meet this need. NATO could pick either geographic or size-of-attack criteria: any penetration of over, say, 20 or 30 miles, might be assumed to require a nuclear response. Or, any attack involving as much as a Soviet field army (about 3 divisions plus supporting units) might be similarly treated in NATO's plans. But because the first criterion touches on the sensitivity of several countries as to a possible loss of their territory before the alliance responded, the second one might be more acceptable. At the least, it might help to mute the interminable arguments between the "all-nuclear" and "non-nuclear" extremists.

A decision-delegating procedure of this type should go far to assuage the German and Turkish fears that the United States might not release the weapons which it alone controls under the present system in time to avoid major losses of their territory. It would appear to provide a better balance between deterrence and defense than either the present system or a complete non-nuclear strategy. It also should take maximum advantage of Soviet fears of escalation, while minimizing the risks. For if the West followed a policy of maintaining a full spectrum of capabilities, the enemy's options of retaliation or escalation would not appear very attrac-

---

be ideal for defensive use, inasmuch as destruction would be limited, and employment against a concentration of enemy troops would cause high combatant casualties, but without residual effects to friendly forces entering the area or to civilians outside the zone of immediate impact. According to press reports, the technical feasibility of such weapons has been established; but their production would presumably require continued testing—at least underground, if not in the atmosphere.

tive. In particular, if NATO had enhanced its conventional posture through the remedial measures advocated in this chapter, the threshold at which nuclear weapons might have to be employed would be much higher. More time would be available for political decisions, and they could be made in the light of more flexible alternatives for subsequent stages in the conflict.

Nuclear Control Requirements

A number of implications for organization and control flow from such a nuclear doctrine. We have seen that strategic forces targeted on a restrained counterforce or damage-limiting basis must operate globally under centralized control. But for those forces held in reserve as a countercity deterrent and used only as a last resort, control might be decentralized to some degree. An analogy to the limited delegation of authority to the country attacked might be worked out for an international strategic force to insure against blackmail. Thus, should Khrushchev's successors revert to his tactic of threatening the nuclear destruction of the Acropolis, the Greek government could then be given exclusive authority to direct the firing of a single missile which would be enough to ensure the destruction of a comparable Russian target. In the event, the Greeks might or might not actually direct such a reprisal to be carried out; but the mere possibility should dissuade an enemy from rash threats, or counter them once they were made.

Turning from strategic conflict to the middle case of medium-range weapons, we have already seen that nuclear interdiction is too closely intertwined with strategic operations to permit a separate command and control system. While some of the suggestions advanced in the last chapter for enhancing European participation in nuclear planning may be applicable here, it seems inescapable that the final release authority must remain in the hands of the President of the United States. This is the present situation, since American stocks of warheads for the longer-range missiles and aircraft in Europe are kept in American custody and further protected by electronic locks. The system reportedly works well technically, and it would be hard to improve upon it under any realistic alternative. The political pressures in Europe for sharing this control should be very largely satisfied by the limited delegation concept advanced above. For it is the initial use of battlefield nuclears which most concerns the European members of NATO who are in the front lines.

But these battlefield and demolition nuclear weapons must also be controlled so as to prevent unauthorized release, and yet be responsive to the political decision of the country attacked, under the concept explained above. Initially, American custodial detachments might retain possession of the warheads, with U.S. permissive links providing additional insurance. But the United States would have to agree in advance—perhaps at the time a crisis arose—to act as agent for the North Atlantic Council under the procedures outlined. SACEUR, if an American, would then be acting only in his capacity as military commander of the alliance and not as a U.S. officer. This would require a high degree of European confidence in SACEUR's ability to "take off" his U.S. uniform; but for the most part, the distinguished American soldiers who have served as SACEUR have had this confidence to a surprising extent. Difficult legal problems would be involved for the United States. Even if formal amendment of the Atomic Energy Act should be found unnecessary, concurrence of the Joint Committee would be essential. Yet these problems could be overcome, if the alliance and the U.S. administration agreed that this was the best solution to NATO's tactical nuclear problem.

In the longer term, it would appear desirable to create special tactical nuclear support units along the lines discussed earlier. Such a special force could be multilateral in nature, and responsive to a NATO chain of command—which in turn would need secure communications links with the various governments to whom the political decision to use nuclear weapons might be delegated. This command would man stockpile sites in key areas—perhaps co-located with U.S. warhead storage facilities; and it might be backed up by air-mobile detachments. If the permissive link were used, separate release procedures would have to be developed for the various storage areas, so that unlocking the weapons designed to support, say Turkey, would not simultaneously release those in other areas. The technical problems are difficult, but no more nearly insuperable than under present arrangements.

If a tactical nuclear doctrine such as this were incorporated into NATO's planning, its defensive potential would be enhanced, and the sometimes conflicting interests of the United States on one hand and the Europeans on the other would both be served. Before reviewing our analysis of the central front, we have one additional approach to explore.

Arms Control and European Security

It is only in recent years that arms control measures have been recognized as having the potential to *increase* security even when comprehensive disarmament is out of the question. But the strategic situation in Europe is basically asymmetrical in many respects, so that the theory is far easier than the application. The Soviets are presumed to be the aggressor and thus to have the initiative; the territory of the Warsaw Pact, including all of the U.S.S.R., is far greater than that of European NATO. Thus proposals for withdrawals from Central Europe tend to create far more problems for the West than for the East. There is little available real estate in Western Europe on which to deploy the forces now in the forward areas of West Germany. And if any sizable part of the U.S. contribution were returned to the United States, the Russians could return their units withdrawn from East Germany much more quickly. The same factor of easier redeployment would apply to nuclear weapons, making the nuclear-free-zone type of proposition more advantageous to the Soviet Union.

With respect to broader measures, the various U.S. and Russian proposals are too complicated for any specific treatment here. In April 1962 the United States submitted a draft disarmament treaty outline to the Seventeen Nation Committee on Disarmament meeting in Geneva. On a few points it paralleled the Soviet proposal which had been put forward a few weeks earlier; but the over-all thrust was considerably different. If the first stage of the

American plan—certainly the most feasible of the two from the standpoint of Western interests—were actually put into effect, all types of armaments would be reduced by almost one-third. In addition, there would be ceilings on the size of armed forces. Leaving aside the formidable problems of verification and enforcement, the net effect, according to one analysis, would be to weaken further the inferior side—NATO in conventional forces, and the U.S.S.R. in nuclear arms.[48] This would compel NATO to rely more heavily on a nuclear strategy, which, as we have seen, can be disadvantageous as well as unnecessary.

The consensus of most Europeans (excluding the doctrinaire Socialists) who have studied the impact of arms reductions or withdrawals from the standpoint of Western interests is that most of the advantages accrue to the Soviet Union. Only a settlement of such major political issues as Berlin and the division of Germany could make possible a mutual East-West security arrangement which would not tend to consolidate the *status quo*. And while arms control measures could appropriately be included in a political package, they cannot bridge the gap alone.[49]

This is not to say, however, that there are no useful arms-control possibilities. We have already noted that the risks of greater NATO emphasis on reserve divisions (i.e., reliance on time to mobilize them) could be reduced by overlapping radars, inspection posts, and the like. Similarly, smaller and more static forward defense divisions, supplementing defended strong points, would cut into NATO's potential for a counterattack into East Germany. This might make possible some reduction in the Soviet forces there. Thus there could be some limited areas for profitable exploration within the alliance and with the U.S.S.R.; but there do not seem to be any panaceas available in the context of arms control.

[48] Institute for Strategic Studies, *Disarmament and European Security, The Effect of Implementing the First Stage of the Soviet Draft Treaty and the United States Proposals* (London: 1963).

[49] This was particularly the thrust of the thinking of the ISS conference at Bad Godesberg, Germany, in the summer of 1962. Some of the work of

A Perspective on the Central Front

Let us whimsically suppose that the NATO countries had created a single defense minister, with unlimited authority to reorganize and redeploy forces, irrespective of national policies. And, since we are being fanciful, let us further assume that they told this imaginary defense czar: "You can take all of NATO's present military assets and use them as you will; your job is get a workable defense covering all of the possible contingencies but *without* spending any more money than the present budgets provide for NATO committed forces."

We have seen that NATO has an effective deterrent against a Soviet nuclear attack; the higher the level of violence, the more the West can match and outmatch the Communist bloc, even though the aftermath of such a war is not pleasant to contemplate. If it agreed with the approach outlined in this chapter, the new defense ministry would presumably put into effect those relatively inexpensive measures which met the test of applicability to both the unlikely nuclear attack and the more likely non-nuclear contingencies. Thus NATO would revitalize its civil emergency planning and preparations; it would acquire a good air defense against conventional attack; and it would decentralize at least some of its vulnerable logistic centers. It would continue to program tactical nuclear weapons systems, but would not invest major funds in more land-based MRBMs. It would increase its tactical air power, and accelerate VSTOL aircraft development. On the ground, NATO would redeploy some of its divisions so as to be in better position to cover the main invasion routes. It might swap several active divisions for a truly ready reserve structure, reorganized in conjunction with militia so as to make a network of defended strong points, backed by highly mobile reinforcements. It would shift its mobilization focus from a maximum but slow-paced build-up to rapid augmentation for crises; and the

the joint British-French-German study group on arms control has been published by the ISS in Alastair Buchan and Philip Windsor's *Arms and Stability in Europe,* cited.

alliance would seek to reduce the risks of undetected Soviet preparations by bargaining for mutual warning facilities. Finally, as additional insurance, NATO would establish a doctrine for a defensive use of nuclear weapons designed to minimize escalation risks and thus permit some decentralization of the decision to employ them, but with the weapons still under secure control.

Before we complete our imaginary journey, let us adopt for a moment the role of the Soviet Union's chief military planner. As he confronts NATO's new posture, he finds that a surprise attack shows little promise of a successful *fait accompli.* He sees that he cannot count on paralysis to prevent NATO from using nuclear weapons if necessary. He then considers the possibility of intimidating the alliance by a build-up; but he finds they can mobilize almost as fast as the Warsaw Pact countries—ending up with more than 60 well-trained and equipped divisions geared to a forward defense. Moreover, he knows that the West is prepared to exploit any disaffection that develops behind the iron curtain during a conflict. Finally, he weighs the probable outcome of a nuclear exchange—and quickly puts those papers back in the safe. His report to the Kremlin may be filled with impressive statistics about "the military supremacy of the Socialist Camp"; but its between-the-lines message will be: don't count on military support for any adventures you may be planning in Western Europe.

As we return to the real world from this flight of fancy, we are quickly made aware that NATO has no single defense ministry; that its members are at odds about strategy; that its available resources are misplaced and overlap or duplicate. Nevertheless, we may ask whether, in view of NATO's impressive past achievements in overcoming the inevitable limitations of alliances, it could not go much further toward a comprehensive and effective defense. And the answer, at least for the crucial central region, is unquestionably affirmative. All that is required is the casting-off of outworn cliches and inhibitions and the instituting of a realistic search for the most viable trade-offs. Among the inhibitions, however, are European fears that any changes could pave the way for U.S. withdrawals, or for a weakening of the American guarantees with respect to nuclear weapons. This means that the joint approach to problem-solving, including detailed interallied collaboration at all levels, is a prerequisite to overcoming these fears and suspicions.

NATO's Flanks

The vital central front guards the heartland of Western Europe around which NATO is built. But the alliance's understandable preoccupation with the defense of this area has resulted in some neglect of the northern and southern flanks, where an attack with limited objectives, or even just the exploitation of border incidents, seems much more likely. The very fact that an attack on the central front would bring Soviet forces in direct contact with those of the United States generates risks of a very high order. But in northern Norway, Macedonia, and the area of Turkey bordering Armenia, a limited thrust designed to isolate a single member of the alliance and destroy NATO's cohesiveness seems much more in keeping with Soviet tactics.

Norway, with a tiny population of 3.6 million, a long and vulnerable coastline, and a land frontier with both Russia and Finland, is extremely difficult to defend. However, it presents some imponderables for Soviet planners. If Communist forces avoided Finland, they would have to pass through a narrow mountainous and fjord-studded region unsuited for land warfare. If they approached from the south through Finland, even the neutral Swedes might be moved to take a defensive stand along with Norway. Sweden's armed forces, by far the strongest in Northern Europe, are a force to be reckoned with. The spy trial of the Swedish Colonel Stig Wennerstrom revealed to some degree the extent of Soviet "reckoning." At the same time, it would be relatively easy for Soviet forces operating by sea or with airborne units to seize a number of key areas. Much of northern Norway is so sparsely populated that gradual infiltration could result in a *fait accompli* to support trumped-up Soviet territorial claims.

It may be beyond the capability of the alliance to defend all of Norway's territory physically; but it is not impossible to assure that any Soviet action will be discovered promptly and counter-attacked. The attendant possibility of a conflict backed fully by NATO forces should involve sufficient imponderables about escalation to deter Soviet action in the first place.

With total armed forces of only about 35,000 and a defense budget of less than $200 million, Norway has tried to make the best use of its scarce manpower through a number of reserve regiments and home guard forces. Norway's geography places a high premium upon air and naval forces, and both are being modernized. The air force is currently planning to obtain modern fighters, while the vital reconnaissance mission reportedly will be augmented by the addition of specially equipped aircraft.[50]

It is essential to assure that any conflict involving Norway equally involves the rest of the alliance, and particularly the United States. This is the responsibility of allied forces in Northern Europe with headquarters in Norway. Danish and German, as well as Norwegian, forces are assigned to it. Norway's tradition has prevented the stationing of allied forces on its soil in peacetime, which would have prohibited the deployment of custodial detachments for atomic weapons even if Norway desired them. But like other Scandinavian nations, Norway has maintained a non-nuclear policy.

Because it is politically essential that the forces of other allies be involved at the outset of any conflict in this region, some adjustment in NATO's command arrangements might be necessary, particularly to provide for the participation of American naval and air forces. A NATO mobile "fire brigade" with its own atomic support and transport could also make a significant political-military contribution to the defense of the northern flank, although logistic difficulties might require some prepositioning of supplies, and Norway's own infrastructure and planning would have to be more closely coordinated with NATO.

The northern flank's importance is enhanced by the fact that the Baltic exits should be closed in the event of war. Organization

[50] See "Watchbird in the North" by Erik Lunde in *NATO's Fifteen Nations*, December 1962-January 1963, p. 66.

has been improved through the new Baltic sub-area command, which brings to bear German naval strength as well as that of Norway and Denmark. With modern mining and antisubmarine techniques it should be possible to deny Soviet passage from the Baltic submarine bases into the Atlantic. Parallel measures in the North Atlantic between Norway and Iceland could further limit Soviet submarine potential. The major polar routes to North America pass over Norway, making this area of potential significance from the standpoint of aircraft and missile warning.

The Southern Flank

The two main areas of vulnerability in the South appear to be the eastern edge of Macedonia and Thrace (at one point Communist Bulgaria is only about 25 miles from the Aegean Sea) and Turkey's eastern frontier bordering the Soviet Union and Northern Iran. Although the long Turkish coast facing the Black Sea is theoretically subject to amphibious attack, the Soviet Black Sea navy is not believed to be suited for this purpose. As with the Baltic exits, however, wartime control of the Bosphorus and Dardanelles exits from the Black Sea is vital. Here the responsibility is that of Allied Forces Mediterranean with its headquarters at Malta. The navies and maritime air forces of Italy, Greece, and Turkey, plus the British Mediterranean fleet, are assigned or earmarked to this command. The Turkish navy has only about 50 ships, most of them small. The Greek navy is somewhat larger, but neither would be a match for Communist naval forces in the area, which fact emphasizes the role of the Sixth Fleet. In particular, its airpower offers valuable support to both ground and naval forces in the southeast Mediterranean. Many of the carrier-based attack aircraft are capable of carrying nuclear weapons.

Allied Forces Southern Europe, with headquarters in Naples, are responsible for the defense of Italy, Greece, and Turkey. The American Sixth Fleet is earmarked for assignment to this command in wartime, when it becomes Striking Force South, a part of the NATO sword. The air forces of these countries include over 1,000 aircraft, although many are in the obsolescent F-80 series. In land forces, Greece has 10 divisions and Turkey 16. The renowned fighting ability of the Turk is somewhat offset by his country's relatively low technological and economic levels, which create problems in operating and maintaining sophisticated equipment and necessitate assistance from other allies.

If they cooperated effectively, present Greek and Turkish forces appear capable of coping with any attack which could be mounted with the Bulgarian-Rumanian divisions now available. However, if these satellite troops were spearheaded by Soviet divisions introduced into the Balkans, the available NATO forces might have difficulty in holding Thrace and Macedonia. The military problems are complicated by centuries-old political animosities, illustrated by the dangerous Cyprus dispute. This type of internal feud not only offers the Soviets a chance to fish in troubled waters but greatly handicaps the military collaboration, which a glance at the map shows to be the *sine qua non* of defending Thrace.

Although Eastern Turkey is mountainous and boasts few good roads, Soviet forces operating through the Caucasus could probably make a penetration against available Turkish forces. Thus, even more than on the central front, a defensive use of tactical nuclear weapons might be applicable. One method would be air strikes delivered from the carriers of the Sixth Fleet. But because of the psychological sense of isolation of the peoples of the area, especially in Turkey (akin to Germany's "Hamburg syndrome"), the NATO mobile task force has a particular applicability to this area. General Norstad deserves great credit for the creation of this embryo force, to which some seven NATO members have already contributed battalion-sized units.[51] Its first maneuver in Macedonia in the fall of 1962 is reported to have been very successful. Held in reserve, this highly mobile fire brigade can serve a number of vital purposes: it has the capability of quick response;

[51] See, *The Military Balance 1962-63,* and *1963-64,* cited, and the *NATO Letter,* NATO Information Service, Paris, January 1963, p. 25. Subsequent maneuvers of the force, such as *Northern Express,* are discussed in the September 1964 *NATO Letter,* pp. 11-19.

its multinational character is a practical demonstration of NATO solidarity; it provides a source of important training in joint operations; and its exercises can provide the incentive for closer NATO coordination with local forces on the flanks.

This force should rapidly move from its present transitional nature to become a permanent and enlarged NATO mobile force, commonly funded by the alliance, and possessing a permanent headquarters and assigned organic transportation. (This conclusion, incidentally, was endorsed at a recent meeting of the Assembly of the Western European Union.)[52] By rotating national contingents, a pool of men trained in multinational NATO operations could be created. Their experience and alliance orientation could be put to good use in other assignments.

The mobile NATO force could also serve as the primary vehicle for implementing the nuclear defense concept spelled out earlier with respect to either or both flanks. The present plan reportedly calls for tactical nuclear warheads to be supplied by the United States. But if a NATO Tactical Nuclear Support Command were created, it could take over this role as a further strengthening of the alliance.

Whether nuclear weapons were needed or not, a Soviet incursion on either flank would be met initially by the local forces employed there, followed up almost immediately by elements of the mobile force. Its availability holds out to the Soviets the prospect that, by attacking anywhere, they would in effect be shooting at every national flag in the alliance. The political advantages of an alliance force may be greater than the military advantage of a force several times its size drawn from only one member.

The Military Problem of Berlin

The problems of Berlin and German unification are among the most fundamental facing the future of the alliance. From a political standpoint, the defense of West Berlin is a *sine qua non* of the security of the West as a whole. The loss of that city, whether by outright attack or by gradual erosion of Western access rights to

[52] *NATO Letter*, January 1963, p. 25.

the point that the city was forced into submission, would be a blow from which allied solidarity might never recover.

West Berlin's 2,200,000 population is larger than some NATO nations. It is a key industrial center of the West. Even more important, the Allies are committed to maintain Berlin's freedom. Public statements to this effect have been constantly repeated throughout years of Soviet pressure against the city; and they have been endorsed by NATO on a number of occasions. Failure to keep these commitments could undermine collective security and confidence in the West throughout the entire world.

But it is one thing to proclaim a mandatory political requirement for defense of the city and another to provide a military capability for doing so. To begin with, the allied presence in the city is based upon occupation rights. The United States, France, and Britain therefore have special responsibilities unlike those of the other NATO countries. West Germany, of course, has a special concern. Yet it is almost inconceivable that a major conflict involving access to Berlin could arise which would not, *ipso facto*, involve most, if not all, of the other members of NATO. Despite the politico-legal necessity of maintaining the special tripartite and quadripartite responsibility, the Berlin question is as much an alliance problem as defense of the central front or the flanks.[53]

Berlin is an enclave, more than a hundred miles inside Communist East Germany. Access is via autobahn, rail and air corridors (plus certain waterways), which could be easily cut by Communist forces. Here, for obvious reasons, the West is at a severe tactical disadvantage. Within the city itself, the few thousand men of the allied garrison could at best provide a delaying action for a day or two. NATO's 26 central front divisions are probably insufficient to force a way through to Berlin in the face of major Communist resistance without completely denuding the rest of the front. But the situation is not impossible from the

[53] For a well-documented account of the Berlin problem in all its phases, see Jean Edward Smith, *The Defense of Berlin* (Baltimore: Johns Hopkins Press), 1963.

military standpoint. Despite Communist tactical advantages, the West has two strategic trump cards. One is its over-all superiority outlined previously—the ability to use nuclear weapons selectively and maintain superiority no matter to what level the other side raises the conflict. The other is that while Communist forces could probably surround and eventually defeat an allied force attempting to reach Berlin along a single ground corridor, there is no assurance that the conflict would remain so limited. The West could retaliate by seizing East German territory, expanding the area of engagement, and enhancing the possibility of satellite defections and uprisings which the West could exploit. This is a possibility which the Soviets must take seriously, for the consequences could be quite unpredictable and lead to a chain reaction throughout all of Eastern Europe. There are still other measures through which Western superiority could be exploited, for example, in sea power. And in a prolonged Berlin crisis, NATO could build up its forces (as it started to do in 1961) to the point of having a useful capability for military actions involving the beleaguered city. Intercontinental mobility and rapid augmentation capacity are obviously important here.

In the special case of Berlin, the West might have to make an exception from the proposed doctrine of initiating the use of tactical nuclear weapons only in defense. But this would not necessarily be the case if NATO had reached its 30-division goal on the central front and also had the capability for quickly augmenting these forces with another 6 to 8 divisions. Because of the legal and political commitments involving Berlin and the inherently limited objective of forcing access, the allied forces would have a good justification for using tactical nuclear support if it were needed. Nevertheless, it would greatly facilitate governmental decisions to initiate any limited action in defense of Berlin on a purely conventional basis. Thus the special case of Berlin offers added incentive for a modest improvement in NATO's non-nuclear posture. These added capabilities could furnish the essential ingredient for making the West's declared determination to defend the city credible to the Russians. And the extra flexibility could also be useful in numerous other contingencies that might confront NATO in various areas on the periphery.

Naval Power and NATO Strategy

"Atlantic" is the key word in "NATO." It is the geographic embodiment of the link between America and Europe and the lifeline over which communications must be maintained. The Supreme Allied Commander, Atlantic, has a coordinate position in relation to SACEUR; but he is not generally regarded as a coequal. The author once overheard a NATO official, observing SACEUR and SACLANT emerge together from a briefing, ask: "Who is that naval chap with *the* Supreme Commander?"

SACLANT's responsibilities are to protect sea communications and maritime areas, such as Portugal, from air or sea attack, and participate as required in strategic strikes as the NATO sword. For this is the main mission of "Striking Force Atlantic," one of the three main subordinate commands. The others are geographical rather than functional. In discussions of strategic striking power, this force is usually described as a valuable "auxiliary" but not counted as part of the primary strike forces. Some of the attacks against medium-range targets discussed earlier could presumably be conducted by the nuclear-capable carrier aircraft of the United States Second Fleet, which in wartime becomes the Atlantic Striking Force, just as the Sixth Fleet becomes Striking Force South.

The vital role of naval power in defending Northern Europe (especially the Norwegian coastline), the Baltic exits between Denmark and Norway, and the Black Sea exits, has been noted above. But it is sometimes thought that protecting lines of communication between North America and Europe in wartime is unrealistic, since in a general war the outcome would be decided by forces in being; and in any event, ports and the supplies to be transported might well have been destroyed. However, it is quite conceivable that in a very tense situation in which the United States was augmenting its forces in Europe, a limited "undersea" war could take place in which vital shipping was attacked by submarines, much as the Germans attempted to cut the allied lifeline in World Wars I and II.

Naval power is one of the areas in which the West has a decided superiority over the Soviet Union; but the Soviets are concentrating on their potentially strongest asset, namely, submarines. In addition to the threat to communications, these submarines may soon be a formidable component of Soviet strategic power. Too many Europeans have regarded the problem of defense against missile-launching submarines as an American problem. But it may not be long before the ability of such submarines to attack European cities will make this an alliance problem of the gravest concern. Antisubmarine warfare therefore rates the highest priority in research and development. Defense against submarine-launched missiles falls into the category of ballistic missile defense—perhaps the only research and development area meriting an even higher priority. As for the submarine itself, most naval men feel that a reasonably adequate detection and defense is not beyond the bounds of technical feasibility—for example, the technology of "lasers," which is still in its infancy, may have undersea applications. NATO maintains an antisubmarine research center at La Spezia, Italy, which has done some good work. But the technological problems involved are so complex that they could benefit from a major effort involving the combined scientific resources of Europe and America.

This chapter has argued that the central front can be made reasonably secure against all categories of Soviet threat with a relatively modest effort imaginatively applied. Similarly the weaknesses on the flanks are susceptible to at least partial correction. The more the alliance is successful in closing off NATO Europe to Soviet troublemaking, the more will Communist strategy shift to other areas—as it may already be doing. Africa and the Middle East exhibit numerous potential targets of opportunity. There will thus be many instances where the forces of the alliance—whether or not they are operating in its name, might have to be deployed outside the territories or waters of the members. This places an additional premium on mobility and flexibility and thus adds to the utility of naval power.[54]

Conclusion

One cannot discuss military strategy in the nuclear age in other than somber tones. Yet the adequacy of preparation for the employment of military force seems to bear an inverse relationship to the actual need to use it.

The three chapters of this Part II comprise the heart of this book. They have examined the state of NATO's preparations to defend the Atlantic area, and on the whole have found it good. The main problems affecting the strategic elements are not military; rather they concern the political aspects of managing nuclear power. While there does not appear to be any all-purpose solution, a great deal can be done to reduce the consequences of its unavailability. And with respect to Europe, the non-nuclear challenge is susceptible to imaginative and inexpensive responses. A variety of remedial measures could permit the allies to meet the contingency of a surprise attack (or unexpected incident) while also improving their defenses against the unlikely but more serious case of an all-out invasion.

In sum, Part II has attempted to show that NATO has *almost* met the first of its two postulated tasks: to maintain the security of the Atlantic alliance. And it has within its grasp the means of filling in the gaps that remain. Whether it will in fact do so and then go on to address its second task, that of establishing a stable world order for the future, will depend on the political, economic, and structural matters to which we now turn in Part III.

[54] Lord Kennet's WEU report on "Navies in the Nuclear Age" is a useful source of data and appears serially in the *NATO Letter* (Feb, March, and April, 1964.)

PART III

The Evolution of NATO

6

NATO'S Political Environment

Nationalism is not unchanging, eternal, but merely extraordinarily persistent and slow to change.

CRANE BRINTON

Recent developments within the Atlantic alliance suggest that its members have been slow in adapting to the key historical trend in today's world—that the nation-state is becoming too small to accomplish its traditional purposes of military security and economic prosperity. Accordingly, they have engaged in a halting search for a successor. And the logical progression—short of a visionary world government—might be termed a region-state.[1]

Regionalism is a significant political force even in areas removed from the West by thousands of miles and separated from it by centuries of progress. Paradoxically, it may be easier for states in which a national identification has been recently overlaid on a colonial or tribal base to adopt a regional approach than it is for older political entities.

Nationalism is not only "persistent and slow to change" but it is also capable of renaissance. For example, nationalism is both an end and a means of General de Gaulle's efforts to restore French "independence." Its reassertion came at a time in Europe when the regional-community idea was bidding fair to replace it. The tragedy is not so much the resurrection of French nationalism as it is the contagious effect on Europe, and the potential reaction in

[1] An incisive commentary on this search is contained in Leslie Lipson's "Independent or Interdependent," *The Spectator* (London), October 5, 1962.

America. As Raymond Aron expressed it, "If France herself shares today certain symptoms of the infantile sickness that is nationalism, what country tomorrow will escape contagion?"

Internal Politics

Statesmanship has been described as the art of changing what is into what ought to be. Not a few statesmen, experiencing the cumulative frustrations of seeing one country after another immobilized politically by an election just completed or imminent, must have felt that the prospects for any true international consensus were dim unless and until the national election cycles were made to coincide. This is particularly true for 1964-1965 when Britain, the United States, Belgium, Germany, and perhaps France and Italy all will have faced national elections in fairly rapid succession.

Thus, of the three-dimensional political environment within which NATO's future must be assessed, the internal politics of the alliance may be dominant. But the first dimension is clearly linked to the other two: NATO's interaction with the non-Communist world, and its relationships with the Communist bloc, each of which will be examined in turn.

North America and Britain

In the United States, a remarkable domestic consensus has supported, at least passively, America's postwar foreign and defense policies toward Europe.[2] And on the whole, Americans have chalked up a good postwar record in meeting their global respon-

[2] For a more detailed analysis, see the pamphlet edited by Joseph Barber, *Atlantic Unity and the American Interest—A Report on the Views of Leading Citizens in Thirty-Two Cities* (New York: Council on Foreign Relations, 1963). Nearly two-thirds of the respondents in the survey were in favor of having the United States seek to bring into being an Atlantic nuclear deterrent force. Somewhat similar views were found to exist on the part of the "man in the street" in "American Public Opinion and the Atlantic Community," mimeographed paper, University of Pennsylvania, Foreign Policy Research Institute, 1962.

sibilities. But the very size and dominance of this consensus has intensified the isolation—and hence the bitterness—of the dissenters. Whatever else may have been involved domestically in the selection of Senator Barry Goldwater as the 1964 Republican Presidential nominee, his candidacy was supported by more than a few of what might be termed the "ignorant, irresponsible and impatient" elements of the electorate—at least in the area of foreign affairs. While his defeat has greatly reassured the world of continuity in American foreign policy, there is nevertheless a large and respectable segment of the American public which has grown increasingly frustrated with the nation's disproportionate burden of common defense and foreign aid. Even President Johnson's decisive victory has left a politically significant frustration potential, which could generate domestic pressures for a pullback from U.S. commitments and deployments to Europe. That is why the Gaullists and other Europeans who proclaim their independence of the United States may prove self-fulfilling prophets. By helping to produce the very reaction in the United States which they profess to fear, they prove the politico-military truth that independence is a two-sided coin: European independence from the U.S. may equally mean American independence from Europe.

This kind of a quarrel could become disastrous for all concerned. Europe simply cannot provide for its own security except by taking such large risks that America might be forced logically and emotionally to disengage. It would be ironic if after failing with their postwar "ami go home" campaign, the Communists were handed a similar result by interallied political differences. One must not exaggerate such possibilities; but it is well to recognize the latent dangers in American political attitudes. The trade competition symbolized by the "chicken war," disproportionate sharing of assistance to developing countries, and the uncertainties of shifting relationships within and with the Communist bloc, are illustrative of the many issues which could shatter the basic solidarity of the alliance.[3] In addition, of course, there are the

[3] See, for example, three specific cases of Congressional ire regarding

defense and nuclear issues discussed in Part II.

Given reasonably good sense on both sides of the Atlantic, these problems can be handled. But the obstacles are numerous; and they tended to come to a sharper political focus in both the United States and Europe during the various 1964 elections.

Geographically North American, and linked organically to the United States through NORAD for continental defense purposes, Canada is nevertheless a part of the British Commonwealth and a member of both NATO and OECD. Economic geography has dictated close links with the United States, although Canada's trade policy has in theory evolved within the system of Commonwealth preferences. Canadian efforts to resist the natural pull to the South by stressing westward expansion has been as much a part of its history as its delayed struggle for national independence from Great Britain, or the political perils of "bi-culturalism" and the large French-Canadian minority.

The sensitivity to American predominance was particularly evidenced in the long-standing controversy over nuclear weapons for Canadian forces (especially warheads for air defense systems). This was an important factor in Canada's 1963 elections which returned Lester Pearson's Liberal Party to power on a platform which endorsed Canada's previous commitments.[4] Britain's projected entry into the Common Market stirred considerable anxiety in Canada during 1961 and 1962, even reviving talk of a North American Customs Union. While this interest has now slackened, it symbolizes Canada's intimate concern with European development. Canada can be expected to continue as a strong supporter of NATO and the OECD, and to maintain her valuable leadership

---

Europe, which are analyzed in *The Washington Post,* May 27, 1963, p. A1.

[4] There is a series of excellent studies issued by the Canadian-American Committee (sponsored by the National Planning Associations of the two countries). See especially "The Growth and Changing Composition of Trade Between Canada and the United States"; "The Perspective of Canadian Relations," (1962) and "Canada and the Organization of American States" (1963). Melvin Conant's *The Long Polar Watch* (New York: Harper & Row, for the Council on Foreign Relations, 1962) is one of the best works on U.S.-Canadian relations in the defense field.

in United Nations peace-keeping operations. But much will depend upon U.S. wisdom in respecting Canada's greatest sensitivity—being taken for granted in foreign policy and defense decisions.

In Great Britain, the 1960s have already brought a number of domestic political traumas, despite economic recovery from war-caused dislocations and growing industrial modernization. The abortive 1960 Paris Summit meeting cost Macmillan a year of effort. The Nassau Agreement only partially relieved the Conservatives' embarrassment over the cancellation of the Skybolt missile. Britain's own mismanagement contributed to the French veto which, temporarily at least, terminated its Common Market candidacy. Finally, the lurid sex and security scandals of 1963 led many pundits to conclude erroneously that a Labor government would win by a landslide.

During much of 1964, moreover, Britain's external policies seemed caught in an "immobilism" created by the prospect of a national election. Labor's narrow margin of victory, the near crisis over sterling, and on-going economic balance-of-payments difficulties make it unlikely that Harold Wilson can initiate major new departures. In any case, he is likely to find that on such matters as phasing out Britain's independent nuclear deterrent, the realities of political power will provide considerable constraints on his freedom of maneuver. Differences continue within as well as between both parties over nuclear weapons,[5] disarmament, and summitry, as well as on trade and other relationships with the Communist bloc. These issues and the more important ones bearing on Britain's future role in Europe and the Common Market seem likely to be determined less by partisan political considerations than by gradual evolution of national attitudes. The problem is to find a proper balance between Britain's imperial traditions and its reduced power status. Its role seems destined by

[5] Labor's former Secretary of War, John Strachey, found it necessary to fill his excellent book *On the Prevention of War* (New York: St. Martin's Press, 1963) with apologies and explanations for the necessity of discussing such unpalatable topics as nuclear strategy.

the latter factor to be played in a primarily European setting; but nevertheless it should remain within the broader traditional Atlantic and Commonwealth context. A global role for Europe, in partnership with the United States, is Britain's best possible bridge between the past and the future. Labor's fresh approach should at least facilitate the search for a constructive balance.

France

Throughout the unhappy Fourth Republic's endemic domestic crises and external indecisiveness, the friends and allies of France wished for nothing more than a strong, unified, and popular government for that country. De Gaulle's Fifth Republic has certainly fulfilled this wish; but in so doing it has left many other problems in its wake.

"To be great," wrote General de Gaulle as a junior officer before World War II, "one must conduct a great quarrel." If grandeur can in fact be measured by the size and number of disputes engendered, the General must be very close to his goal. Yet neither America nor any other ally can properly object to the internal manifestations of the De Gaulle regime, which has almost literally saved France from itself. The tragedy is that external relationships have had to be distorted to provide the balm for domestic sores. By re-introducing a nineteenth-century nationalism in the midst of twentieth-century interdependence, France has undercut the legitimate interests of its allies in the security of Western Europe.

France removed first its Mediterranean, then its Atlantic fleet from NATO assignment.[6] It withdrew and then failed to return to NATO several divisions engaged in Algeria. It refused atomic storage sites to American fighter bombers, compelling their re-

[6] According to press reports, De Gaulle received a courtesy call by a NATO naval commander who expressed his pleasure at having had French navy ships serving in his command. The general is said to have called an aide and exclaimed: "What was he talking about? I thought all our ships had been withdrawn!" On learning that part of the French fleet was still earmarked for NATO, he promptly ordered them withdrawn too!

deployment; it has obstructed measures to integrate air defenses, vetoed NATO strategy papers, declined to participate in certain NATO planning exercises as well as several maneuvers, and has spurned and then strongly challenged the multilateral force proposal. In sum, France has generally managed to delay, disrupt or sidetrack virtually every forward step the alliance has tried to take since De Gaulle came to power.

While he has explicitly reaffirmed the need for alliance and friendship with the United States and deplored the "journalistic malevolence" which placed them in doubt, his actions have left little room for the give and take which are the essence of a peacetime coalition.[7] French support has been relatively firm in moments of crisis, such as Cuba and Berlin, only to revert subsequently to intransigence. De Gaulle has generally held to a "hard" line in East-West relations, with an obvious eye on Bonn's sympathies where German interests were engaged; and he has refused to take part in disarmament or nuclear test-ban activities. This performance is of course consistent with, and probably necessary to France's determination to become a nuclear power.

In De Gaulle's concept of national sovereignty there is little, if any, room for supranationalism of any sort, whether it concerns NATO, or the United Nations, or the Commission of the European Economic Community. In such a view, NATO itself can have no corporate responsibility for matters of war and peace or East-West relations—an attitude which contradicts the philosophical evolution, though not the legal facts, of the organization's fifteen-year history. Although it is quite possible to misinterpret General de Gaulle's future intentions, which are often expressed with deliberate vagueness, the theme of *national* interests first, last and always runs so consistently through his pronouncements and actions over a forty-year span that any change would seem almost miraculous.

This makes De Gaulle's prospective tenure of considerable

[7] Press Conference of July 31, 1963, reported in *The New York Times*, August 1, 1963.

relevance to the future political environment of NATO. The French government's present term lasts through 1965, but an election might be called sooner, should conditions seem propitious.[8] It is unclear whether the General himself would be a candidate. But it would be strange if a movement founded on the mystique of a single man could continue to dominate French politics without him. As a minimum therefore, De Gaulle must remain the effective leader of the Union for the New Republic (UNR), even if he should retire from active politics to play a behind-the-scenes role.

Among the Fifth Republic's most spectacular achievements must be counted the fracturing of the traditional pattern of French politics and the construction of the first parliamentary majority in the country's modern history. The Gaullist minority owes its firm control first to popular acquiescence, and second to a badly divided opposition. On pocketbook issues of wages, prices, inflation and housing, the Frenchman is his usual articulate and critical self, although the political effects of such economic issues are somewhat offset by the contradictory interests of the various groups. As Julius Caesar put it some two thousand years ago: "In every Gallic tribe . . . and almost in every household there are rival factions . . . the same principle holds good for Gaul as a whole."[9]

On matters of ideology and international politics, however, the Frenchman has tended to abstain since De Gaulle's accession. The exceptions, including the committee *Contre la Force de Frappe*, Jean Monnet's Action Committee, and a few articulate individuals like Raymond Aron who are concerned about France's growing isolation from its traditional allies, are a minority. The main organized opposition comes from the Communists on the left and the remnants of the OAS and other far-right elements. Catholic and Republican center groups, and Socialists on the left, have as

[8] Several articles in *Combat,* August 1963, speculated about this possibility for 1964, and comment to the same effect has continued, looking to early 1965.

[9] *Caesar's War Commentaries,* John Warrington, ed. (London: Dent and Sons, 1933), Everyman's Edition, p. 47.

yet been unable to find a solid issue either of domestic or foreign policy on which to mount a serious challenge to the government.

Barring a major domestic economic crisis, it thus seems unlikely that an opposition candidate could defeat De Gaulle. The normal odds favoring the incumbent are lengthened in France by the state-controlled radio and television which, under De Gaulle, are not noted for granting "equal time" to his opponents. Moreover, President de Gaulle appears to be in the best of health for a man in his seventies. Consequently, the net prospect appears to be another term for the General or a hand-picked stand-in and a continuation of present French policies.

The rest of the NATO alliance therefore faces an uncertain period of attempting to "coexist" with De Gaulle's France. Hopefully, they can do so without sacrificing the principles of collective security, non-proliferation of nuclear weapons, and gradual strengthening of the Atlantic and intra-European ties. The United States and its NATO allies can hardly help De Gaulle to make France a "great power" on the very issues which challenge the validity of these principles. But where these values are not at stake, it is probably in the interest of the alliance to help France to overcome its legacy from the past and regain that sense of "greatness" which is a prerequisite to the acceptance of true international responsibility. Then, perhaps, by the time De Gaulle passes from the scene, he will leave behind a stable and self-confident nation which will no longer need to bolster its self-image at the expense of the international community of which it is traditionally an integral part.

Germany

The political renaissance of West Germany after World War II took place slowly and painfully under the dominance of one man. His special position in history is attested by the commonly accepted description of 1963 as the "end of the Adenauer Era." His successor, Ludwig Erhard, is invariably labeled in the Western press as the architect of German's economic miracle. He must be counted as a man of considerable talent who has established his leadership in a surprisingly short time notwithstanding periodic sniping from within his own Christian Democratic Union (CDU) —and more specifically its Bavarian offshoot, the Christian Social Union, led by former Defense Minister Strauss.

The opposition Social Democrats (SPD) have abandoned their orthodox socialism for a more effective posture on domestic and foreign policy issues. Berlin's dynamic mayor, Willy Brandt, has capitalized upon such issues as pass arrangements to East Berlin to become a national figure and a serious contender for the chancellorship. Germany's only other party of any size, the Free Democrats (FDP), has tended toward a more self-assertive nationalistic viewpoint—although its positions seem as much opportunistic as doctrinal. Splinter parties, such as the representatives of refugee and expellee groups, have lost much of their initial postwar influence as their constituents have become integrated into Germany's political and economic life. Over the long term, a CDU-SPD coalition government—or even an SPD majority, is not an impossibility.

The period before the next German national elections in September 1965 seems certain to be characterized by vigor and controversy. Perhaps it will also see a continuance of the trend toward a true two-party system, which has already broken up the traditional pattern of a socialist industrial belt, Catholic conservative business and agricultural groupings, and a Protestant bourgeoisie. Although such perennial issues as wages and inflation are always in the background, the over-riding focus of German politics is in the foreign policy questions: East-West relations, notably reunification; and European and Atlantic relationships, particularly the competing pulls of Paris as against London and Washington. Both of these issues have their major impact in Germany; and yet both are of wider concern to Europe and the Atlantic alliance as a whole. Germany thus remains the focus of both East-West and interallied tensions.

The Franco-German treaty of 1963 must be applauded as the

symbolic ending of an historic enmity.[10] But its special provisions for bilateral collaboration have brought new problems, beginning with France's veto of the prospective British membership in the European Economic Community, which Germany had supported. Franco-German bilateralism also contradicts the spirit, if not the letter, of the Community Treaty; for a requirement to coordinate two national positions undercuts the goal of consultation among the Six as a whole. The United States has faced similar problems in its varying bilateral defense arrangements as against its wider commitments to NATO as a whole. But unlike France, the United States has taken great pains to insure that its bilateral activities are broadly consistent with the NATO framework, and to keep the alliance fully informed about them.

In the military field, French attitudes toward NATO can hardly be reassuring to a Germany vitally interested in "forward defense." De Gaulle has not only pronounced that "la guerre de l'OTAN en Allemagne ne nous intéresse pas," but he has deployed French forces so that they make little or no contribution to Germany; and even when the *force de frappe* becomes fully operational, it will be so small, relative to the power of the Soviet Union, that its credibility as a deterrent must be open to doubt—even for vital French interests, let alone those of an ally.

By the summer of 1964 the periodic consultation meetings between the heads of governments and cabinet members of the two countries appeared to have reached fairly sterile levels of formality. The press statements by Erhard and De Gaulle led to considerable press comment to the effect that Bonn was being asked to choose between Paris and Washington.[11] Were this the case, it would be a Hobson's choice. For Germany's partial regeneration from the

[10] The text of the treaty is contained in *The Atlantic Community Quarterly,* Summer 1963, p. 276 and as Appendix I of The Senate Foreign Relations Committee's *Problems and Trends in Atlantic Partnership II,* S. Doc. 21, 88th Cong., 1st sess., June 17, 1963.

[11] Drew Middleton's dispatches to *The New York Times,* especially Sunday, August 9, 1964, Section IV, have analyzed the Paris-Bonn dispute in detail. See also *Die Zeit,* July 30, 1964.

shadows of its past has depended equally on its Europeanism, its Atlantic orientation, and its acceptance by France as symbolized by the Adenauer-De Gaulle treaty. When these relationships pull in opposite directions, as they have increasingly done in the past several years in matters economic and military as well as political, the internal stresses on German politics can be considerable.

Politically, De Gaulle's proposals for a consultative grouping of the Six—initially at least, without Britain—have not been acceptable to any of the other five and to the vast majority of Germans. De Gaulle then transferred the underlying philosophy of a loose coalition of states to the bilateral treaty with the Federal Republic. Many, if not all, of the problems reviewed in Chapter 2 are involved here: "little" Europe or "big"; the whole question of British participation; and federalism versus national cooperation. Except for a minority to the political right-of-center, Germany's leaders in both the governing coalition and the Socialist opposition have displayed a commendable patience in trying circumstances. Germany may indeed be in the best position to begin the tortuous process of picking up and reassembling the pieces of European movement.

Militarily, America inevitably has a special defense relationship with Germany growing out of its large military establishment there. Cooperative logistics arrangements and German procurement in the United States (to offset local costs of American forces) have been sourly regarded by France, as have been German-American agreements for joint development of tanks and other equipment. In strategy too, as we have seen in Part II, there remain important differences between Paris and Washington.

On the economic side, one of the most significant of Europe's over-all problems is the fact that the agricultural revolution has crossed the Atlantic to Europe. In the long run, the inevitable transformation of peasant farming to an industrial basis will have far-reaching political and social changes. In the meantime, many functional conflicts beset France and Germany—for example, differing wheat prices in the two countries long stymied any agreement on a common European agricultural policy—which in turn was a prerequisite for EEC trade negotiations with the United States.

French industry enjoys a relatively high level of protection, and needs export markets less than Germany does. The Federal Republic, with an inefficient and protected agriculture, must export industrial goods outside of Europe in order to pay for imported foods. Thus, generally, the German and French interests in liberalization or restriction of trade in industrial and agricultural items are in opposition.[12] An adjustment of this classical economic conflict of interest probably can be made if there is a suitable political framework, like the one originally conceived for the Common Market. Although De Gaulle's threats to withdraw from the German market may bring about a unilateral German concession on grain prices, the ironies of history may show that the very French attitudes which disrupted the European unity movement may have fatally weakened the only framework for compromise within which a lasting settlement satisfactory to both France and Germany could have been made. But whatever the immediate tactical purposes of the countries involved, it hardly serves the long-range interests of Paris, Washington, or London to intensify the strains on Bonn to the point of again producing the schizophrenia on the Rhine which has twice produced disastrous consequences for all.

On the other major issue, reunification, there is also a potential conflict of interest between Germany and its allies. The addition of seventeen million people to West Germany, plus an industrial economy of nearly $20 billion in annual product, might appear to threaten the existing balance among the other leading nations of Western Europe. Nevertheless, all of the other Western powers share a common interest in retaining their commitments in support of eventual unification; for going back on them might endanger Germany's alignment with the West.[13] And these commitments

[12] For more detailed comment, see Pierre Uri, *Partnership for Progress* (New York: Harper & Row, for the Atlantic Institute, 1963), Ch. 3.

[13] The problem is discussed in some detail in Henry Kissinger's *The Neces-*

are strong. President Kennedy, for example, stated in Germany on August 1, 1963: "We believe strongly in the unification of Germany as a free democratic country. And that is our policy in the past, our present policy, and our future policy. . . ." Moreover, the "German problem" is so much the keystone of a lasting East-West settlement in central Europe that the self-interest of Germany's allies impels them to search for a stable solution. An arrangement which perpetuates the artificial division from World War II could hardly be considered viable.

Within Germany all major parties have followed a similar line: no official recognition of East Germany; the "Hallstein Doctrine," which calls for severance of relations with any other country (except Russia) which does recognize it; and continuation of the present special status for Berlin pending unification. Interzonal trade (the German euphemism for the necessary economic relations with East Germany) is in a sense a *quid pro quo* for continued civilian access to Berlin; and it is therefore treated as a special case. Since no one envisages either reunification by force (which West Germany has specifically renounced) or the Soviet acceptance of Western terms for unification, this traditional approach seems to offer little prospect for the short run, and only indefinite hopes for the future.

Under the leadership of Erhard and Schroeder, Bonn has begun a "policy of movement." This is not so much a matter of specific tactics or objectives. Rather it signifies a greater flexibility than the unyielding posture of Chancellor Adenauer.

The SPD has concentrated more on exploiting differences within the CDU coalition than on developing a distinctive foreign policy approach. But Berlin's Mayor Brandt did suggest in the summer of 1963 that German interests might be served by helping to raise the standard of living in East Germany, and thus encourage loosening of the Soviet grip. This trial balloon was immediately denounced

---

sity for Choice (New York: Harper & Row, 1960), pp. 138-139, and Helmut Schmidt's *Defense or Retaliation: A German View* (Edinburgh: Oliver and Boyd, 1962).

by a majority of Germany's politicians as bordering on treason, and the SPD disavowed it.[14] Nevertheless, in the inevitable differences among Bonn, Berlin, and the political parties there are signs that alternative approaches to the goal of unification have been tentatively opened for public discussion. Such a development may prove either a first step toward a solution, or a virtual Pandora's box for the West.

Only two or three years ago a number of observers felt that the political demand for reunification might have passed its peak, in view of the materialism resulting from Germany's economic recovery, and the successful absorption of millions of refugees from the East. But by 1963-64 a new cycle of interest and concern appeared to be in the making. In part, this reflects the political transition from Adenauer to Erhard. But it is also symptomatic of the need for a constructive outlet for German political energies, especially among the younger generation. Initially, they were guided into the European movement, as the best alternative to an unacceptable rebirth of nationalism. But as that movement appeared to lose momentum under the impact of De Gaulle's policies and other developments, interest has revived in the ways and means of obtaining unification. The apparent flux in Eastern Europe and the slow, if uncertain, evolution of attitudes within the Soviet Union, may have increased the German expectation that the time is at hand for new initiatives. Thus NATO, and the United States in particular, will be increasingly involved with the Germans in the search for a solution to the major remaining problem between Russia and the West.

Italy

Italy has shared generously in the postwar economic miracle. Its stability has been threatened from the left, but never overturned. Many sticky issues of domestic policies and economics remain. The

[14] The suggestion was actually made through Egon Bahr, Press Chief of the Berlin Senat, in a speech at Tutzing Academy, July 15, 1963, which was widely reported in German news media. According to press reports, Brandt subsequently denied that Bahr was speaking directly for him, but indicated sympathy for the ideas expressed.

downward economic adjustment that was probably inevitable anyway was hastened by the inflationary wage increases and business insecurity resulting from the first center-left government. But the dominant influence in Italy's political future is likely to be the efforts to bridge the left-right split in politics and correct the spotty distribution of Italy's economic gains. The success or failure of the *apertura a sinistra* has a significance quite out of proportion to its immediate practical consequences. To many thoughtful Italians it is the only exit from the "immobilisme" which has characterized postwar Italian politics, other than a return to the Communist-Fascist dialectic of the 1930's. Yet as the 1962-64 experiments showed, fashioning a viable center-left coalition is far from easy. Regarded with hostility by the far right, and with suspicion by a majority of the propertied, aristocratic, and clerical conservatives, the center-left alliance is feared equally by the Communists and opposed by many left-Socialists as "too little, too late."[15]

In actuality, the Parliamentary alliance (Nenni's PSI was never included in the Cabinet) of February 1962 can also be described as an "opening to the right" for the Socialists, who had long maintained a "unity of action" with the Communists, and it afforded them an opportunity to play a constructive role in shaping Italy's future. If the link between the primary parties of the democratic left and the Communists can in fact be broken permanently, Italy's prospects for internal stability and progress would seem to be fairly good—but only if it can ride out the economic rough weather which lies ahead.

[15] Although the Communist party in 1963 had a larger percentage of the vote than in 1948, it received a remarkably constant 22 per cent of the total votes for the lower chamber in 1948 and 1958. Other political parties, and factions within the dominant Christian Democrats have had major ups and downs. The Socialist PSI (Nenni) and PSDI (Saragat Social Democrats) hailed the 1963 election as vindicating the center-left policy. The PLI (liberal in name only) who doubled their percentage of the vote over 1958, asserted that the experiment had been rejected by the people and that it had advanced the Communist cause. The Christian Democrats, however, merely noted the election report and, officially at least, were silent on its meaning. See "Italy's General Elections, 1963, Texts and Documents," (New York: Italian Information Center, 1963).

Italy's allies have a big stake in the experiment too, for the contending political forces have somewhat divergent approaches to the East-West conflict. The Italian government has, for the most part, been a staunch advocate of NATO, European integration, and friendship for the United States. But the Marxist orientation of the Socialists, and the large voting strength of the Communists have caused extreme sensitivity to matters pertaining to nuclear weapons, the missiles formerly deployed in Italy, and U.S. cold war actions as in Cuba. The doctrinaire Socialist views are quite favorable toward the "three Ds" of denuclearization, disengagement, and *détente.* Fortunately the Social Democrats, whose leader Giuseppe Saragat first became Foreign Minister, and then President of the Republic, do not share in these views. They are both supporters of the Atlantic alliance and unsympathetic to De Gaulle. Nevertheless, Italy's continued support of NATO and participation in such ventures as the proposed multilateral force, will inevitably be tempered by the attitudes of the Socialists.

Taking a long view, a good argument can be made that the Italian stability and progress that would result from a successful center-left government would benefit the Atlantic alliance despite any attendant short-term risks or difficulties. Of course there are groupings on the Italian right in which the fires of nationalism could be rekindled by De Gaulle's "independent Europe" sentiments. We have seen that Italy's "quintipartite complex" has led to demands for special recognition in terms of consultation and participation in interallied and international negotiations: In part, the need for external recognition stems from the delicate balance in domestic affairs. Yet ironically, internal politics may inhibit Italy from taking advantage of the usual opportunities for its diplomatic leadership brought about by the intra-European conflicts discussed earlier. Were Italy able to take the lead in negotiations on European unity, or the multilateral force, the recognition it seeks would follow automatically. Assuming that Italy can find a suitable international role—and the recent appointment of an Italian as NATO's Secretary-General should help—there do not seem to be any immediate rallying points for neo-nationalist forces,[16] although the nuclear status question may eventually arise in Italy, especially if no multinational or NATO solution can be found.

The Smaller Alliance Members

While nearly all of the other members of the alliance are also plagued by domestic controversies such as Belgium's Walloon-Flemish dispute, factional splits in Greece, and Turkey's erratic progress toward internal democracy, only one has threatening overtones for the over-all NATO environment. The tinder box which Cyprus has become will continue to be a source of conflict between Greece and Turkey. This makes a long-term solution a matter of vital concern to the alliance as a whole. Besides inviting Russian meddling and upsetting the stability of the Eastern Mediterranean, this dispute can jeopardize the cooperation between the Greeks and the Turks which is essential for defense of their common interests.

Because most of the smaller countries collectively feel that they must put their hopes for the future upon the alliance, they view with concern any evidence of conflict among the United States, Britain, France, and Germany. The Benelux countries have been strong supporters of Britain's entry into the EEC, and of the continued leadership of the United States within NATO. Foreign Ministers Spaak and Luns rank with "Europe's" elder statesmen; and Holland succeeded Belgium in providing a NATO Secretary-General.

There are trends in the smaller alliance countries—as well as in Germany, Italy, and even Britain, which allow De Gaulle to strike

[16] The Italian-Austrian controversy over the Trentino-Alto Adige area and the degree of autonomy to be granted to the quarter of a million German-speaking residents of the Tyrol has led to terrorist bombings and stirred up high feelings between the two countries, notwithstanding the efforts of both governments to hold responsible discussions. Fortunately the issue has not yet been played up as a pan-German (as opposed to a local Austrian) issue. But if it does not remain under control, the matter could prove troublesome.

a responsive cord with his emphasis on European separatism and a reduction in U.S. influence. However, the prevailing majority, which does not wish to be left alone on a continent dominated by French political, economic and military policies, supports European unity within an Atlantic framework. During a recent academic conference, in response to a French Comment that U.S. policies were designed to make Europe a "Monaco" of the United States, a Dutchman retorted: "We would much prefer that to becoming the Luxembourgeoisie of France!"

Norway and Denmark, as the two Nordic members of NATO, share strong ties with neutral Sweden and, to a lesser extent, with Finland. The Scandinavians have always given strong interest and support to the United Nations and its specialized agencies, especially as to international peace-keeping operations. Domestically, the Socialist-Labor political parties in Norway and Denmark contributed to an inherently anti-nuclear orientation. Nevertheless, there seems no prospect of fundamental changes in attitude which would lessen either country's effective participation in the alliance.

Iceland is sometimes a special problem because its fairly influential local Communist party has campaigned against the important bases and facilities which Iceland makes available to the United States as its major contribution to NATO. Iceland's dispute with Britain over fisheries, and a susceptibility to heavy trade reliance on the Soviet Union, are other potential problems. But they seem less troublesome at present than in the recent past.

The Iberian peninsula poses two interrelated political problems concerning the future of the alliance. Portugal is determined to retain full control over its African colonies. As France once did Algeria, it considers them an integral part of the metropole. This is the last of the major colonial disputes which have caused the alliance so much trouble in the postwar period. Portugal's resentment has focused particularly on the United States, producing a potential defense impact in connection with the Azores bases. But however much Portugal may seek to use its NATO membership to induce support for its colonial policies, it seems unlikely that it would leave the alliance. Portugal's African policies may seem obstinate and outdated to the United States, which is embroiled in a worldwide contest for influence—especially in the newer Afro-Asian nations. But to a small maritime nation, the future of its African territories is no minor matter. The possibilities of constructive influence from Portugal's allies may prove larger if they at least listen with sympathy to its views, notwithstanding its authoritarian regime.

Finally, there is the extremely important question of Spain's role in Europe. Membership in NATO is desired by Spain, and probably by a majority of the members. Its adherence would not only be logical, but could also be extremely important from a military and geographic standpoint. The Iberian peninsula is presently split as to defense arrangements, although this inconvenience is ameliorated by special base agreements between the United States and Spain. The geographic contribution which Spain could make is obvious on the map; its substantial armed forces could add a significant conventional reinforcement capability. NATO badly needs the rear-area training and logistic staging facilities which Spain could make available were it a member.

The opposition to Spanish membership, which is purely political, will remain as long as Franco is in power. In the minds of many Britons and Scandinavians, as well as European labor and socialist groups generally, he is linked with the prewar rise of fascism. Nevertheless, a convincing case can be made that continued exclusion of Spain serves no useful purpose whatever and, in fact, denies the alliance a major opportunity of exposing Spain to outside influence which could help the post-Franco transition to a more representative government. There are already signs that greater liberalism and political growth are accompanying the economic revitalization and expansion in trade, cultural, tourist, and military contacts.

Spain is a member of OECD, and a proposed EEC associate. Whether or not it is ready for full membership in the European family, it should logically be in NATO. It is both European and the motherland of much of the new world, where its influence in Latin America could prove useful in many ways. The arguments that any objections in principle to the Franco regime must be sacrificed for the "anti-Communist" cause have proved notably unsuccessful in moving the opponents of membership. Perhaps it is time for the proponents to stress that Spain is historically, culturally, and economically a part of Europe and should have a constructive role to play in the "new" Europe. Preparation for that role, it seems clear, can better be obtained by cooperation and association than in continued isolation. Last but not least, the addition of a major new member at a time of many uncertainties would give the alliance a renewed sense of vigor and growth. This is not an unimportant consideration, especially in the light of current French attitudes.

It should not be beyond the scope of NATO diplomacy quietly to negotiate some sort of understanding with the countries known to oppose Spanish membership. For example, an invitation to join NATO at the end of a specified period might be tied to an announcement of Franco's transition plans in such a way as to avoid injuring Spanish pride.

In summary, NATO's internal politics will tend to be projected in bigger than life-sized images during the sequence of national elections. On the Continent, one can find a number of observers who believe that a common European pattern may be emerging. To the liberals, this would make labor-socialist governments the wave of the future—if not in 1964-65, then in the next round of elections. Although many North Americans regard socialism in the abstract as a bad word—a "kissing cousin" of communism, in the judgment of not a few politicians—it does not necessarily follow that Atlantic cooperation would suffer in such a state of affairs. For one thing, what most non-Marxist European Socialists advocate domestically is not too much different from what Americans have come to accept—indeed to demand—under more acceptable labels. One of Europe's prominent Socialists told me after his first visit to the United States: "You Americans are the most socialistic country in the world. The only trouble is you don't know it—and if you did, you wouldn't dare admit it."

Some traditional Socialist positions on nuclear weapons, on military service, and on disarmament and disengagement have proved unhelpful at best and more often troublesome from the standpoint of defense. But many of these views, while rooted in Socialist orthodoxy, have emerged as natural debating positions of opposition parties, which would not necessarily be carried over into governmental participation. The consequences of a non-nuclear emphasis would be really serious only to the extent that the governments concerned were unwilling to make the corresponding increases in conventional forces, or somehow failed to preserve for Europe the protection of America's nuclear deterrent.

Greater difficulty might be a tendency to overestimate the decline in the Soviet threat by accepting as permanent the Communist protestations about peaceful coexistence. As long as East-West relations continue haltingly in the direction of *détente*, socialist-conservative differences on this point will consist more of emphasis and timing than of real substance. Should the thaw freeze over again, however, and Russia resume a belligerent posture over European issues, there could be some erosion of Western will under a Socialist-oriented Europe. But on the whole, during the more severe periods of the cold war, all but the extreme leftist factions of European socialism proved reasonably stalwart when sharing in the responsibility of power. And as far as Communist internal penetration is concerned, most Socialist parties in Europe have returned in full the animosity that domestic Communist groups have displayed toward them.

On balance therefore, a possible leftist pattern in European politics seems less dangerous than its rightist counterpart feeding on, and in turn helping to nourish, the smouldering fires of nationalism. One De Gaulle, most observers feel, is more than enough. A German or Italian counterpart would not be a pleasant prospect—even apart from the disturbing memories such leadership in those countries would arouse. Perhaps equally dangerous in the long run would be a European-wide neo-nationalism led perhaps by conservative business interests on the Continent. Such a movement could easily capitalize on both general European great-power aspirations and national political and economic frustrations to produce the anti-American, third-force type of European policy which would jeopardize the future of the Atlantic community—and indeed of the world. This possibility amply justifies America's continuing involvement with Europe and equally underscores the need for sensitivity to legitimate European concerns.

NATO and the Non-Communist World

Now that the colonial issues that bedeviled the alliance for so many years are largely in the past, the major problems in this second dimension of NATO's future are more in the economic than in the political or military fields. The U.N.-sponsored 122-nation conference on trade and development dramatizes the problem of the underdeveloped areas. Many of them are squeezed between rising prices for such critical imports as industrial and farm machinery, and the decreasing or fluctuating prices they receive for the raw commodities which must be exported to pay for them. A common "underdeveloped" front against the industrialized West would put Russia in a good propaganda position, but leave it somewhat vulnerable in terms of its own past and prospective actions. Nevertheless, the early 1964 press reaction to the conference occasionally suggested that the world's East-West split might eventually become "North-South" instead.

The European nations are generally more favorable to commodity agreements and tariff preferences (especially for former colonies retaining some form of economic association) than is the United States—which highlights the importance of coordinated trade and aid policies within the alliance. 1964-1965 may mark the beginning of a more concerted effort by the world's poor nations to mobilize political pressures to play the East-East and West-West conflicts as well as that between East and West for as much as possible. The goals will probably be less concerned with direct grant aid than with preferential trade, low interest loans, and various indirect subsidies.

When the bargaining sessions under the General Agreement on Tariffs and Trade (GATT), the so-called "Kennedy Round," get underway, a major feature will be American tariff negotiations with the Common Market. In the "Dillon Round" of GATT negotiations at Geneva from 1960 to 1962, the United States gained at least as much in dollar concessions affecting its exports as it gave up in the way of import concessions. In some cases, because of legal restrictions, the United States was unable to move as far in lowering tariffs as the Common Market proposed. The new authority in the Trade Expansion Act should greatly improve American bargaining leverage. There are some signs, however, that the most liberal trade elements in the Common Market countries may have less influence in the new negotiations, especially while the transition from high-cost producers caused by competition within the EEC is at a painful stage. The preparatory U.S.-EEC discussions in May 1963 very nearly reached an impasse between the American emphasis on broad reciprocal tariff reductions and the European (especially French) insistence upon equalization of existing disparities first. A last minute compromise which combined both approaches allowed the planning to go forward.[17] But the basic issue remains unresolved as far as negotiations are concerned.

Discrimination is implicit in a regional trading bloc such as the Common Market, and it is permissible under GATT and "most-favored-nation" principles only when it supports the political purposes of a customs union. In theory, the short-run displacement of trade from external sources will be balanced by greater prosperity within the trading bloc, and its resultant demand for goods will lead to a long-range increase in world economic efficiency. But in

[17] A good summary discussion is contained in *The New York Times*, May 26, 1963, Section IV, pp. 1-2. See also, "Problems and Trends in Atlantic Partnership II," Staff Study, Senate Foreign Relations Committee, 88th Cong., 1st sess., S. Doc. 21, June 1963, pp. 40-45 and 68.

practice, there is a lead time in which the trade displacement from external to internal sources can be harmful. Moreover, the tendency for capital to seek protected bases within the common tariff wall often contributes to balance-of-payments difficulties.[18] These adverse effects on world trade—and in this case particularly, on the United States—highlight the importance of mutual tariff reduction.

During the next few years, while patterns for the future are being set, a political sense of interdependence, community, and partnership is essential to the harmonious resolution of inevitable economic conflicts. The United States, for example, accepted many forms of discrimination by Europe for the sake of progress toward Europe's recovery from World War II. Some similar rationale for the whole Atlantic world, both internally and externally, is needed to contain domestic pressures for short-term economic advantages which will exist in both Europe and America.

The problem of adjusting to the common external tariff of the EEC is difficult enough in itself. It is vastly complicated by the effects on underdeveolped areas, with their myriad special arrangements and needs. Creating the stable world order, which I have postulated as a major task for America and Europe, will require pressing attention to the challenge of economic development. This is far more than a moral duty for the West; it is a political necessity—as it is also in the long-run economic interest of all countries. Yet trade and aid are so inseparably linked in all their forms that close and continuous coordination is needed between America and Europe. Fortunately, a mechanism exists through the OECD for concerting efforts, equalizing the aid burden, and avoiding duplication. More detailed discussion is beyond the scope of this book. But there is a rather close parallel in OECD's economic field

[18] For a concise and nontechnical discussion of the positive and negative impact of regional trading blocs, see Don D. Humphrey, *The United States and the Common Market* (New York: Praeger, 1962), especially Ch. 1. Another useful survey is contained in the Joint Economic Committee's "The European Economic Community and the United States," Subcommittee on Foreign Economic Policy, Joint Committee Print, 87th Cong., 1st sess., 1961.

to NATO's military need for a common framework of political assumptions governing Atlantic partnership.

Finally, there are many problems which are not primarily economic and which are not directly related to the Communist politico-military challenge, although they may be susceptible to exploitation. Indonesia's threats and actions against Malaysia, Indian-Pakistani hostility, Egyptian-Arab determination to eliminate Israel, and the near-chaotic conditions in parts of Africa are just a few examples which are perennially in the headlines.

One or more major NATO members are involved to one degree or another in all of these disputes. Should France, for example, decide to promote its influence by undertaking to furnish to other countries the nuclear weapons or technology which the United States and Britain have refused to disseminate, the mischief caused could be beyond reckoning. Even without such deliberate recklessness, if the NATO allies act at cross-purposes, or just fail to interest themselves in each other's current problems, they may, in John Donne's words, learn too late "for whom the bell tolls."

NATO has provided a number of multilateral forums in which such problems can be discussed, in addition to the normal bilateral channels of diplomacy. As with OECD in the economic field, machinery exists for political consultation in NATO, a subject to which we will revert in Chapter 8. The critical factor is the will to employ the machinery to good advantage. Here a distinction can be made between a broad framework of common purposes and slavish deference to the more direct involvement of an ally. There were times in the postwar period when the United States was somewhat over-responsive to the colonial sensitivities of its NATO allies. Yet at the other extreme, the harshness of American condemnation of the Suez adventure is hard to justify.

On the European side, current French attitudes toward the Vietnamese conflict strain the bounds of "common purposes." The French experience and contacts could, however, be a reinforcing influence in Indo-China if they were directed at a form of neutralization that was not merely a euphemism for an American withdrawal.

Nearer to home, De Gaulle's visits to Latin America need not be regarded with suspicion and alarm by the United States. The very fact that he is representing neither the Colossus of the North nor a returning colonial power can make his influence there useful to all—including the Alliance for Progress. The days when that continent could be treated in the Monroe Doctrine context as America's "back yard" are gone; and European involvement there is no more harmful to the Atlantic alliance than is the growing U.S. presence in Africa, which traditionally was Europe's preserve. A "spheres of influence" arrangement between America and Europe seems more likely to breed distrust and divisiveness in an age of interdependence than is a philosophy of mutual involvement—provided only that "influence" is sought and exercised responsibly.

Relations with the Communist Bloc

NATO has a better record of consultation on arms control, disarmament, and summitry than is commonly realized. Such consultation does not, of course, eliminate conflicts in national positions and attitudes. But, it does mitigate the suspicions, misunderstandings, and public differences which can complicate negotiations and permit Soviet exploitation. Europe has always been especially sensitive to the possibilities of an American-Soviet settlement reached over their heads. Yet it is inevitable that the two most powerful nuclear powers should maintain an intermittent dialogue in an effort to reduce the risks of conflict. The Truman, Eisenhower, Kennedy, and Johnson administrations have all faced the dilemma between allied sensitivities and the necessity for grasping any opportunity to reduce East-West tensions. For the most part, the United States has diligently sought an allied consensus before undertaking talks with the Soviets in any form. But the dilemma is currently heightened both by the flux within the Communist world and the transition which the alliance itself is undergoing.

Germany remains the central problem of East-West relations. The Federal Republic's domestic politics are intimately concerned with Berlin and unification. Soviet political, economic, and military interests are heavily committed both in East Germany and Poland. This central front area encompasses the greatest military concentrations on both sides of the Iron Curtain; and it is here that the most attention has been focused on nuclear-free zones, disengagement, inspection posts, and the like.

It does not seem beyond the bounds of reasonable optimism that a settlement in Central Europe could be worked out over time. For example, German and Western acceptance of the Oder-Neisse line could be combined with other guarantees and incentives to the Soviet Union which could permit what is now East Germany to become a neutral provisional state under a four-power guarantee, like Austria. If the stationing of military forces in that area—and perhaps also in a zonal belt on the Western side of the border—could be effectively prohibited, provision might be made for the neutral state to associate itself with West Germany after a specified period of years. Greater Berlin would require special treatment, and might have to be given an international status.[19] In view of the Soviet withdrawal from Austria, recurrent rumors of troop reductions elsewhere in Eastern Europe, and the undeniable evidence of strong nationalist stirrings in the other satellites, the Russians might eventually be prepared to settle for a truly neutral buffer zone of states rather than an unstable array of unpopular regimes kept in power by Soviet force.

The endless ramifications of actual negotiating possibilities are less relevant to NATO's political environment than questions of pace and direction. These questions raise the dilemma noted earlier. A good case can be made that maintaining inter-allied confidence over the long term is worth more than quicker progress toward a European "settlement" with the Soviet Union. The forces already at work within the Communist world may create incentives for such a settlement, to come of its own momentum in due course. If not, and the Soviet attitudes underlying the threat to Europe re-

[19] Senator Claiborne Pell has been one of the few outspoken American commentators on the need for flexibility regarding Berlin. See, for example, his article in the *Saturday Evening Post* of February 8, 1964, p. 8.

main, there is little NATO can afford to offer at the bargaining table which would change Russia's orientation. It will, however, be important for the West to remain receptive and avoid returning to the rigidity which necessarily characterized much of the past decade.

Even if a satisfactory long-term solution could be found in Central Europe, the goal of a stable world order would be merely somewhat nearer. Innumerable challenges and problems would remain elsewhere; and it is my view that an underlying unity of purpose between America and NATO Europe would still be very much needed. It should not, therefore, be sacrificed upon the altar of intermediate progress on East-West issues, no matter how important they appear or how great the political temptations.

The coming challenge of Communist China has opened up another area of inter-allied difficulty, for French recognition of Peking in 1964 (following Britain's example of 1950) underscores the fact that many NATO members differ from the United States in their views of the Chinese Communist threat to Asia and how best to cope with it.[20] Such differences reflect divergent interests (e.g., De Gaulle's desire to restore French influence in Indo-China), responsibilities, and power. Some flexibility among the Western powers may be an asset in dealing with Red China. But, as suggested earlier, some understanding of the limits of disagreement is essential, along with clarification of the West's long-term objectives and strategies. Since the Far East is geographically outside of NATO's area, there is a need for special machinery and a basic framework of alliance solidarity in order to meet this potential threat to the peace which Russia can no longer restrain and cannot yet oppose by force.

[20] On January 23, 1964, 33 senators introduced S. Res. 287 (88th Cong., 2nd sess.) which sought to persuade our French allies to reconsider their position (on recognizing Red China) and noted, *inter alia*, "all men who cherish freedom have been gravely disturbed by the growing cleavage between France and America in recent years" and implored the French "not to underestimate or minimize the strength of American conviction on this issue." The resolution cited British experience as showing the lack of benefits from recognition of Red China.

A final aspect of East-West relations deserves special note, for it combines political, economic, and military considerations. This is the thorny problem of East-West trade, particularly in so-called strategic items. Starting with the Korean War, the alliance has maintained a coordinating structure linked to, but not formally under NATO auspices, for developing lists of embargoed items. The difficulty has come not with actual armaments, but in machine tools, oil pipes, electronic equipment, and the like, which have potential for military production or support. Then there are many commodities of little or no strategic importance, which are in short supply in Russia. Their import could permit diversion of Soviet production capacity to military goods. Two different views exist on the problem, one generally supported by the United States, and the other reflected most often by Britain. The United States has applied more stringent controls on its own trade than most of its allies, and pressed for a restrictive NATO policy. It has also made distinctions between Communist China, Russia, and the European satellites. The underlying assumption has been that in a long-term confrontation with the Communist bloc, Western interests are best served by denying the enemy access to as many critical materials as possible, thus complicating Soviet military production and adding to the strain on her resources.

The other view is that maximum trade in nonmilitary goods is highly desirable, since it promotes East-West contacts, improves the over-all international climate, hastens the "embourgeoisement" of Soviet society, and by making Russia more dependent on imports, may inhibit the development of domestic sources. In part, this reflects actual policy judgments on East-West relations as a whole; but it also serves as a convenient rationalization for pursuing parochial economic interests.

From time to time, domestic business interests in all NATO countries have pressed strongly to be allowed to fill particular orders. This has in turn generated competitive pressures between countries and caused not a few major political wrangles—the oil pipe case of 1963 involving Germany, Britain, and Italy being a case in point.

Differences can be expected to continue, although the large grain sale to the Soviet Union by the United States has apparently modified the traditional American position to some extent. At least one Briton replied to U.S. complaints about his country's trade with Cuba with the acid comment that just as the U.S. had a wheat surplus, Britain had a surplus of buses! Even if a more liberal view comes to prevail, it will still be important to maintain the principle of controlling strategic trade with the Communist bloc as well as the legal and administrative machinery for doing so.

More recently, attention has been focused on the Soviet desire for long-term credits to pay for imports, rather than on the goods themselves. Under Secretary of State George Ball journeyed to Paris in the fall of 1963 to plead the case for NATO consultation and agreement on guidelines in order to prevent the Soviets from "shopping" for the most favorable terms and taking advantage of competition between Western countries. Although the allied response has not been particularly encouraging, this approach of common ground rules appears to make good sense.

Just as the trade control field has been hampered by commercial rivalries, NATO's efforts to coordinate policies on cultural and scientific exchanges with the bloc have also encountered divergencies. In theory, culture and science should be above politics, but in practice, the Communists have used them as calculated instruments of foreign policy. On the other hand, the NATO countries, by insisting on reciprocity, have opened the Iron Curtain to an important degree of outside influence. The problem is therefore less one of control—in the negative sense—than of harmonization of travel and exchange policies with the over-all NATO approach to East-West relations.

Notwithstanding the natural divergencies and the difficulties that inhere in an alliance of sovereign nations, NATO's efforts to present a common front to the Communist bloc in cases where this is important have been far more successful than the critics suggest. For it is the occasional glaring failure that makes the headlines—not the quiet and successful day-to-day cooperation of the foreign ministries.

All three dimensions of NATO's political environment—internal, external, and East-West—thus reveal a common element: the need for a framework of coherent purposes and common assumptions within which the inevitable conflicts over details can be submerged.

7

The Political Economics of Defense

Politics and Economics are the seamy sides of one another.

RICHARD MAYNE

Scarcely a generation ago what we now call economics went by the title of political economy, which suggested an interrelationship that today's specialized practitioners tend to ignore. In the current jargon of defense, "requirements" and "capabilities" are too often treated as predetermined quantitative categories. Instead, they should be recognized as interrelated functions of that intangible, political "will." NATO's evolution will depend in good measure therefore on how these political economics affect the common defense.

During the centuries of their rivalry, Sparta and Athens interpreted their respective requirements in accordance with their national aspirations. In terms of the technology and resources of the period, Thucydides found their war potential to be roughly comparable. But first one city-state and then the other achieved temporary superiority, depending on its success with alliances, the mobilization of internal resources, the quality of its leadership, and the degree of external threat perceived. Sparta, in particular, owes the martial implications that have survived in its name to the political assumption of its earlier kings that war was the basic function of the society.

Perhaps the greatest self-imposed myth of today is that Western Europe is incapable of defending itself against the "red hordes" of the Soviet Union. A more realistic assessment of Soviet strength, which takes into account weaknesses as well as assets, will show that the traditional picture of overwhelming Warsaw Pact preponderance simply does not square with the facts. Secretary of Defense McNamara sought a truer perspective, when he counseled that,

> What most needs changing is a picture of ourselves . . . at bay, outmanned and outgunned except for nuclear arms no longer exclusively ours. We should not think of ourselves as forced by limitations of resources to rely upon strategies of desperation . . . with a population of almost 450 million people, an aggregate annual product which is fast approaching a trillion dollars, and a modern and diverse technological base without parallel, facing the Soviet Union and its European satellites with their hundred million fewer people and an aggregate output no more than half that of the West.[1]

NATO's internal debates about forces have centered on a few additional ground divisions for the central front. The basic question is the political-military one of relevance rather than the economic one of available resources. At the peak of World War II, the present members of NATO fielded the equivalent of some two-hundred-odd divisions for the Allies, and nearly as many for the Axis!

A rough analogy can be drawn from an insurance salesman's account of his dealings with two families in identical financial situations. One was firmly convinced that it could afford only an absolute minimum in life and fire insurance. The other, which had experienced unexpected disasters, believed that the minimum it must have was over ten times as much. Yet both were convinced

[1] Remarks to the Economic Club of New York, November 18, 1963, Text, Dept. of Defense Press Release, p. 5.

that the dominant question was *not* the desirability or worth of the insurance, but their own ability to pay the premiums!

It is much easier to assume arbitrary limits on resources for defense than to weigh judgments about the threat against the competing demands for resources which are, in fact, the limitations on programming. Every member of the alliance, including the United States at several different times, has simply subsumed the difficult judgments about these matters under some sort of ceiling on defense expenditures. It would seem preferable to concede that this is the political reality rather than to pretend that a defense effort, set in the last analysis as a matter of political judgment, represents a precise balancing of requirements and capabilities.

In a full-scale war effort, the upper limit is determined not so much by total gross national product (GNP) as by subsistence standards of consumption and the demands of essential economic activity to support the military effort. Even the United States, which did not really attain its mobilization peak in World War II until just before the end of the conflict, exceeded 45 per cent of GNP devoted to defense. Other countries may have been even higher.[2] However, in a period of cold war, defense spending has to be related to other goals such as economic growth, price stability, social and economic programs, levels of consumption, and tax and fiscal policies.

An exhaustive study by the Stanford Research Institute measured increases in annual European levels of defense spending of $5 billion, $10 billion, and $15 billion, and the corresponding increases in military manpower of one-quarter to three-quarters of a million men, against a number of criteria.[3] These included such

[2] Charles J. Hitch and Roland N. McKean, *The Economics of Defense in the Nuclear Age* (Cambridge: Harvard University Press, 1960), p. 39.

[3] Francis P. Hoeber, William B. Dale, and Sperry Lea, *The Economic Potential for NATO Strategies, 1962-1975*, Stanford Research Institute, Menlo Park, California, 1962. This study (SRI Project IMU-2351-101) was done for the Office of the Chief of Research and Development, U.S. Army, and the author is indebted to Mr. Hoeber and to SRI for their cooperation in making available a copy of the unclassified version. It is cited hereafter as the Stanford study.

factors as GNP and growth rates; manpower in numbers, age groups, and unemployment; productive capacity and utilization; and balance of payments. The study concluded that all of these levels, including the annual increase of $15 billion, could be reached within two or three years and maintained by the alliance as a whole or by the non-U.S. members of NATO alone without economic dislocations or excessive inflation.

Of course, individual country capabilities vary. The Stanford study considered various bases for projecting the increases by country: present rate of defense spending; current GNP; and predicted GNP growth (adjusted for slack in the economy as measured by unemployment). With some allowances for special problems, all the projections were found feasible, which suggests that the total cost burden could easily be met out of the total economic resources of the members.

Two points are noteworthy: First, the average annual increase in GNP to be expected exceeds even the largest defense increment postulated. Second, the multiplier effect of the additional governmental expenditures on GNP growth could offset much of the increases. Some economists, for example, will argue that the entire U.S. cost of the Korean War was compensated for by the growth in GNP which the governmental expenditures produced.

Table 8 shows a simplified projection of GNP and defense expenditures for the combined non-U.S. members of NATO.

A 5 per cent annual share of GNP for the five years 1964-1968 would produce total defense expenditures of about $95 billion. Increasing this to 6 per cent, or, alternatively, adding 10 per cent of the annual dollar increment in GNP, would produce about $115 billion, a $20 billion net increase. If the non-U.S. members spend $20 billion in 1964, and spread out a $15 billion increase over the five years, the total would be $136 billion; and assuming the added expenditures took up economic slack, the GNP should grow at a comparably faster rate, totaling $424 billion in 1968 instead of $409 billion and thus offsetting the defense costs.[4]

[4] The multiplier effect (assumed to be a factor of one in the table) would

TABLE 8

Projection of GNP and Defense Expenditures for NATO Members, Excluding the United States

(In billion dollars)

Year	*Approximate $GNP at Factor Cost (1962 prices)*	*Assumed Annual $GNP Growth (at 4 per cent)*	*Absolute Annual 5 per cent Increase in Defense Expenditures*	*Constant 5 per cent of GNP*	*Constant 6 per cent of GNP (actual 1963 average)*	*10 per cent of Annual $ Growth in GNP*	*Assumed Increase of $15 Billion in Defense Expenditures over 5 Years*	
							Annual Amount	*New GNP from Increase (at 4 per cent growth)*
1964	350	14	20	17.5	21	20	20	350
1965	364	14.6	21	18.3	21.9	21.4	23	368
1966	379	15.2	22	19.0	22.8	22.9	27	385
1967	394	15.8	23.1	19.7	23.7	24.5	31	404
1968	409	16.4	24.3	20.5	24.6	26.1	35	424
Total, 5 years 1964-1968	(409)	76	110.4	95.0	114.0	114.9	136	(424)

GNP is such a broad indicator that it takes into account most resource constraints. But in the special category of military manpower, the proposed increases could cause some difficulty in areas of full employment. Nevertheless, the largest proposed increase of 750,000 men (associated with the $15 billion figure in the Stanford study) proved to be less than 30 per cent of the present armed forces of the member countries on the central front.[5] This figure would be the equivalent of about 3 per cent of the males of military age, only 0.75 per cent of the total labor forces, and about 25 per cent of the combined unemployment. According to these various measurements, the increase should be feasible without causing serious dislocation or manpower shortages, except of course for the rare situations of substantial full employment.

Finally, increases in defense spending might well be complicated by problems growing out of balance of payments or other financial difficulties, but these should be manageable within the alliance as a whole. The current U.S. payments problem as it affects NATO is discussed subsequently.

To say that the *political* feasibility of a defense budget increase for Europe is open to doubt puts the matter mildly; but few economists would dispute its economic practicality. In the United States, there appears to be no economic obstacle to a comparable increase. Certainly, as Hitch and McKean point out, there is no magic number like fifty or seventy-five or one hundred billion dollars which fixes the limits of economic tolerance. The only limitations are those of common sense, appreciation of the threat, debt financing, the domestic budget, and national politics. In practice the Treasury sometimes has more to say than the Pentagon about the order of magnitude of the American defense budget—which is not necessarily bad. As Jonathan Swift observed in *Gulliver's Travels*, "The treasurer is allowed to cut a caper on

vary according to the means of financing, the extent of unused capacity and unemployment, and the types of expenditure made. But it might easily be greater for individual countries.

[5] Britain, France, Germany, Italy, Benelux, Denmark and Norway were included for purposes of the study as Landcent countries.

the straight rope at least an inch higher than any other lord in the whole empire,"

For discussion, we can assume that a $10 billion to $15 billion defense increase (a rise in the percentage of GNP from over 10 per cent to 12.5 per cent) would easily be manageable for the United States. Let us suppose that NATO decided to increase its annual defense spending by $25 billion over a five-year period (apportioned at $15 billion in Europe and $10 billion in the United States, to equalize the burden somewhat). Allowing for the build-up time, this might produce $100 billions in *extra* defense funds over the five years. What could the alliance do with an investment of this magnitude? According to the cost figures estimated in Chapter 5, it could equip and operate for five years nearly 60 additional infantry or armored divisions—or provide 75 divisions for almost four years. Or it could buy and operate 50 divisions for five years and have enough left over to assure tactical air superiority, a complete air defense system of the most sophisticated type, and naval modernization. All this, it should be understood, would be a net addition to the ground, air, and naval strength already in being or programmed, and it would be in excess of the present impressive strategic and tactical nuclear capabilities of the alliance. With such a posture, NATO should be able to adopt a true strategy of challenge to the Communist bloc. By forcing the Soviets to face both nuclear and conventional superiority in Central Europe or undertake enormous sacrifices to meet it, NATO, over a period of time, might be able to bargain successfully for a withdrawal of Soviet power from Eastern Europe.

But if, as suggested earlier, the political will in NATO for an offensive policy is lacking, what would be the value of the additional forces? For one thing, they would completely fill in all gaps in the spectrum of deterrence. Every member of the alliance could feel secure from the Communist threat, however constituted, wherever applied. Security, of course, is never absolute; but in relative terms, the alliance would hold out to the Soviets the certainty of failure of any aggressive act, whether aimed at NATO territory or against important interests of the members elsewhere.

The *de facto* acceptance by the Communist bloc of a permanent, stable, non-Communist world order might well be accelerated by such a prospect. In the longer term, realistic political settlements which could permit disarmament might become more likely.

If this course of action is clearly within the bounds of economic possibility, and if it might even be beneficial in growth terms, why is it not adopted? The basic answer seems to be an intuitive feeling on the part of European citizens and their political leaders that the Soviet threat to the Continent is receding. One does not build sea walls against an ebbing tide. And, so runs this premise, even if the tide turns (i.e., to a neo-Stalinism), we can always deter any aggression because of our nuclear power. But suppose the enemy fails to believe that we would employ such a destructive force against salami tactics? What if he attempts to grab Hamburg, seize Northern Norway or cut into Thrace, or block the Western access to Berlin? Suppose that by then the West's "disarming" or damage-limiting counterforce option has lost most of its potential because of Soviet hardening? Would we really want to be forced to the horrors of nuclear war to defend our interests?

At this point in the dialogue, most of the European audience will probably have left in their new cars, with a shrug of impatience, en route to less somber entertainments. Of those remaining, a few will not be susceptible to persuasion, either because they are committed to the *force de frappe* or some other *sui generis* position, or because they cannot revise their image of a Western David and his nuclear slingshot confronting the Communist Goliath. Others, perhaps underestimating the West's long-term economic superiority, will fear stimulating the Soviets to resume the arms race and thus offset NATO's gains. Meanwhile the small residue who concede the validity of the argument will point to the hopelessness of changing majority opinion. In short, the fear that was the initial motivation for building NATO's forces is no longer present. The attention span of the European (and perhaps American) public on defense matters is short. And habits of mind are strong. Also, on the other side of the build-up argument, there are dangers in planning on the basis of the more optimistic views of what *could* be done in the future after a substantial lead-time, and thus discounting too much the present deficiencies in the forces actually on the ground.

If the political will places a ceiling on the defense effort that is far below even the most conservative view of economic capability, what guidelines should we seek? Table 9 lists the total defense expenditures of the NATO countries since the founding of the alliance in 1949. It is encouraging to note the steady increase in absolute amounts for NATO Europe since 1954. Except for Germany, however, the percentage of GNP devoted to defense by most of the larger countries has declined since 1956, as shown in Table 10.

For the period 1964-1968 it seems likely that this trend will continue. Absolute amounts devoted to defense may well decline in some countries, while in others there will be small rises. Of course, some increase—perhaps as much as 3 to 4 per cent annually—is necessary merely to stay abreast of rising costs. Over-all, for NATO Europe, defense expenditures increased 4 per cent from 1958 to 1959, 7 per cent in 1960 and 1961, 13 per cent in 1962, and about 8 per cent in 1963. Table 8 suggests that an absolute annual increase of 5 per cent for the non-U.S. members would produce somewhat more than if NATO continued to devote a constant 5 per cent of its growing GNP; while 10 per cent of the annual increment in GNP would yield still a larger amount—about the equivalent of a constant 6 per cent of GNP. In the absence of any major shift on the international scene, but assuming a gradual reduction in the East-West conflict, the middle possibility of an annual increase—enough to take care of inflation and provide some modernization—seems the most politically feasible.

Undoubtedly some pressures for reductions will develop; but the momentum of an on-going defense establishment, and the need to maintain NATO's considerable investment in it, must be reckoned with. To the extent that easing tensions permit some arms reductions, those countries which have long been doing more than their share would seem entitled to the first benefits. The United States,

TABLE 9

Actual Defense Expenditures of NATO Countries, 1949-1962

(In millions of national currency unit)

Country	*Currency Unit*	*1949*	*1950*	*1951*	*1952*	*1953*	*1954*	*1955*
Belgium	B. Frs.	7,653	8,256	13,387	19,965	19,815	19,925	17,067
Canada	Can. $	372	495	1,220	1,875	1,970	1,771	1,819
Denmark	D. Kroner	360	359	475	676	889	885	920
France	New Frs.	4,787	5,591	8,811	12,531	13,865	11,710	11,020
Germany[a]	DM	—	—	—	—	6,195	6,287	7,383
Greece	Drachmae	1,630	1,971	2,615	2,655	2,767	3,428	3,688
Italy	Lire (milliard)	301	353	457	521	480	543	551
Luxembourg	L. Frs.	112	170	264	436	488	566	614
Netherlands	Guilders	680	901	1,060	1,253	1,330	1,583	1,699
Norway	N. Kroner	370	357	572	831	1,067	1,141	953
Portugal	Escudos	1,419	1,516	1,553	1,691	1,975	2,100	2,224
Turkey	Liras	556	599	652	725	827	936	1,077
U.K.	£s. Strlg.	779	849	1,149	1,561	1,681	1,571	1,567
U.S.A.	U.S. $	13,580	14,559	33,398	47,852	49,621	42,900	40,518
Area								
Total, Europe[b]	U.S. $	4,825	5,445	7,627	10,231	12,403	11,746	11,828
Total, N. America	U.S. $	13,952	15,054	34,618	49,727	51,591	44,671	42,337
Total, NATO[b]	U.S. $	18,777	20,499	42,245	59,958	63,994	56,417	54,165

Figures are based upon the NATO definition of defense expenditures and represent payments made or to be made in the calendar year indicated. Military aid expenditures are included for the U.S. and Canada, but are not included for recipient countries.

[a] Before it acceded to the North Atlantic Treaty Organization (May 1955), the Federal Republic of Germany contributed to the defense budgets of certain NATO countries by the payment of occupation costs; moreover, it bore certain other costs which also fall within the NATO definition of defense expenditures. The total given in the column for 1953 represents the expenditures made under these various heads for the fiscal year 1953-54 (1 April-31 March).

TABLE 9 (*Cont'd*)

Actual Defense Expenditures of NATO Countries, 1949-1962

(In millions of national currency unit)

Country	*1956*	*1957*	*1958*	*1959*	*1960*	*1961*	*1962*[c]	*1963*
Belgium	17,065	18,356	18,312	18,686	19,161	19,561	21,111	22,461
Canada	1,888	1,829	1,740	1,642	1,654	1,711	1,810	1,745
Denmark	936	1,012	988	986	1,113	1,180	1,551	1,598
France	14,690	15,600	16,569	17,926	18,940	19,932	21,460	21,570
Germany[a]	7,211	8,962	6,853	11,087	12,115	13,175	17,233	19,779
Greece	4,939	4,477	4,469	4,735	5,110	5,034	5,102	5,535
Italy	584	611	647	667	710	749	861	970
Luxembourg	395	439	429	402	263	290	355	388
Netherlands	1,854	1,845	1,656	1,505	1,728	2,013	2,186	2,250
Norway	967	1,049	1,024	1,107	1,058	1,179	1,371	1,493
Portugal	2,297	2,391	2,485	2,820	3,023	4,922	5,744	6,066
Turkey	1,159	1,266	1,470	2,153	2,405	2,614	2,980	3,297
U.K.	1,615	1,574	1,591	1,589	1,655	1,709	1,814	1,944
U.S.A.	41,773	44,548	45,503	46,614	46,545	49,417	52,382	53,243
Area								
Total, Europe[b]	13,137	13,814	12,925	13,385	14,215	15,264	17,263	18,589
Total, N. America	43,661	46,377	47,243	48,256	48,199	51,128	54,097	54,857
Total, NATO[b]	56,798	60,191	60,168	61,641	62,414	66,392	71,360	73,446

[b] The totals for Europe and for NATO do not include defense expenditures of the Federal Republic of Germany for the period prior to 1953, and for this reason they are not directly comparable to the totals for the following years.

[c] Forecast expenditures. Figures since 1961 are subject to revision in the light of final expenditure data.

Source: NATO Letter (Paris: NATO Information Service, January 1963 and January 1964).

TABLE 10

Comparative Defense Efforts, European NATO Nations

Country	Calendar Year 1962 GNP (Factor cost, $U.S. billions)	Calendar Year 1962 Defense Expenditures ($U.S. millions)	Per Cent of (Factor) GNP for Defense		Men Under Arms 1962	
			1962	1956	Per Cent of Population	Total No. (Thousands)
Belgium	12.2	416	3.4	3.6	1.2	107
Denmark	6.3	223	3.5	3.4	1.0	47
France	56.7	4,206	7.4	9.2	2.0	921
Germany	72.1	4,094	5.7	4.3	.7	399
Greece	3.3	168	5.1	7.1	1.9	163
Italy	33.4	1,351	4.0	4.5	.7	367
Luxembourg	.46	7	1.6	2.1	1.2	2
Netherlands	11.9	596	5.0	6.3	1.2	142
Norway	4.6	191	4.2	4.0	.8	30
Portugal	2.4	211	8.8	4.5	1.4	128
Turkey	5.4	330	6.1	5.2	1.6	466
United Kingdom	69.0	5,001	7.2	8.8	.8	425
Non-European						
Canada	31.0	1,646	5.3	7.1	.75	131
United States	506.7	54,452	10.7	10.8	1.5	2,704

Source: U.S. Congress, Joint Economic Committee *Fact Book*, 88th Cong., 1st sess., 1963.

rightly or wrongly, believes itself to be in that position as compared to Europe, particularly in view of balance-of-payments considerations. It seems appropriate therefore to focus the discussion mainly on the European defense effort. There appear to be three requirements for placing the "political economics" of NATO's defense on a sound footing: first, a sounder relationship between forces, budgets and strategy; second, procedures which will permit a fair sharing of the defense burden; and third, an amelioration of balance-of-payments problems.

Strategy, Forces and Budgets

For the peoples, parliaments, and politicians of NATO Europe to vote even the modest funds projected above will require better answers to the age-old questions, how good a defense do we need and against what? Some will argue that Secretary McNamara and his U.S. colleagues have done a disservice to the alliance by pointing out that the Russians cannot have the overwhelming ground power traditionally credited to them. It is said that only a somber view of "the threat" (such as opens all military staff papers) can generate the political will to meet it. But this attitude is a two-edged sword. The traditional definition of the threat in Central Europe stems from the days when only American strategic power stood between the Russian forces and the channel, and it has convinced many Europeans that nothing can be done about it, except to rely upon the deterrent of massive thermonuclear warfare. And if deterrence fails? Thermonuclear retaliation might of course be invoked, especially as long as Western counterforce superiority remains meaningful. But such a course is unlikely to look as promising at the brink as it does in the abstract. If the unthinkable dilemma became real, there might well be a rush for what has unkindly been called "pre-emptive surrender."

The argument is sometimes heard in Europe—fortunately with decreasing frequency—that preparing to defend one's interests at the lower rather than highest levels of violence detracts from the credibility of the nuclear deterrent. But it appears equally convincing to argue that an ability and willingness to resist forcibly at any level heightens the relevance of the ultimate deterrent.

As we saw in Chapter 5, NATO has mesmerized itself by focusing on the very worst, and least likely, of all possible forms of aggression. This is the "some Sunday morning" surprise attack by the entire Soviet Army across the East-West border in Germany. Except as an outgrowth of a long period of tension, with build-ups on both sides, this attack is simply not very credible. And Europe's man in the street does not believe in it enough to make sacrifices for it.

But other contingencies or threats to vital NATO interests are not so unlikely or so difficult to meet. The enclave of Berlin is an obvious case in point; so are other vulnerabilities such as Hamburg, Northern Norway, and Thrace. And in many of the likelier contingencies something can be done. Even the worst case may be more manageable than it first appears, if one assumes strategic warning and a sound base for rapid NATO augmentation.

A circular relationship exists between the over-all strategy of the alliance, the political will to generate resources to support it, and the actual force posture created. Inadequate forces circumscribe strategy, even though strategy should tailor forces; lack of confidence in strategy engenders lack of will and denies resources—and so on. Yet NATO's plans and institutions have not taken these interrelationships into account. In practice, military leaders develop a strategic concept based upon an extremely generalized political directive. The major NATO commanders then generate force requirements; the politico-economic specialists consider how to meet them; and then the member countries supposedly provide the forces. But the history of the alliance has been one of continuing shortfalls between force goals and actual forces, which inevitably impaired confidence in the utility of the strategy.

It was for this reason that a promising forward step was taken at the Ottawa Ministerial Meeting in the spring of 1963. The NATO Forces Planning Exercise, known journalistically as the Stikker Study because of the personal initiative taken by NATO's Secretary-General at the time, has been described as the "first genuine attempt at a cohesive examination of the military strategy and force requirements of the Atlantic Alliance . . . to bring every government from Ottawa to Ankara face to face with the hard questions."[6] For the first time, the interdependent variables of forces, strategies, and budgets were to be approached simultaneously rather than seriatim. Existing country plans for the members' defense forces were to be taken into account in developing a strategic concept for the late 1960's.

[6] See *The Washington Post*, July 15, 1963, p. A7.

Unfortunately, the novelty of this approach to defining NATO's long-term strategic needs led to opposition, notably from the French. They objected to any revisions in existing NATO strategy but especially to any adjustment which might undercut the rationale for Gaullist defense policies and the *force de frappe*. There was also some suspicion on the part of NATO military leaders of any enhanced role for the civilian international staff and the use of outside experts.[7] Consequently, the international approach so far has been limited to a series of data-gathering exercises and studies on how to get a larger return at the margin from funds invested in defense, rather than the over-all strategic reconciliation which had been originally contemplated. At this writing, it is still unclear what prospects this study retains for providing a broader perspective on NATO's posture.

NATO had made fairly good progress with its "Annual Review" procedures, inaugurated in 1952, which were put on a three-year basis in 1962. The members have exchanged—and continue to do so—detailed information on their military and economic programs through the Annual Review mechanism. Military recommendations from the major NATO commanders form the basis for evaluation of the country replies to the annual questionnaires. The military authorities and international staff participate in detailed examining sessions, leading to suggested modifications in national programs, which ultimately become NATO's planning or provisional goals for each country's forces. The review does make an assessment of accomplishments and shortcomings, both as to the alliance as a whole, and for individual countries. The final report of the Annual Review Committee also takes into account economic capabilities and limitations in the various members, but "without seeking . . . mathematical judgments in this respect."[8]

[7] For a discussion of the initial difficulties encountered, see *The Washington Post* article of July 26, 1963 entitled "Stikker's NATO Plan is Vetoed by France."

[8] A good account of the Annual Review procedures is contained in Ch. 9, pp. 93-98, of *NATO—Facts About the North Atlantic Treaty Organization* (Paris: NATO Information Service, 1962).

But notwithstanding the utility of this procedure, it basically treats NATO as an aggregate of separate national components, rather than as a whole, and reaches its judgments arithmetically rather than geometrically. Because NATO is a coalition, and not a supranational entity, actual decisions about forces and budgets will continue to be made by the countries themselves. But the over-all planning concepts could be brought into a much better focus on the alliance as a whole if a procedure such as the one advocated by former Secretary-General Stikker could be followed. We shall explore some possible organizational and procedural devices for moving in this direction in the final chapter. For the moment, let us assume that NATO's strategy, forces, and budgets have somehow been brought into a better balance. This would still leave problems in allocating the common defense effort among the various members with their widely disparate sizes and economic potential.

Sharing the Burden

It is increasingly evident that economic aid to other countries and defense spending are complementary aspects of the over-all alliance effort. The foreign aid is mainly concerned with what I have called task two: building a stable world order; while the defense expenditures are associated with the first, or Atlantic security task. Because of differences in efficiency and other economic variations, the real costs of a given amount of economic aid or military expenditure may differ markedly from country to country. The domestic and international political influences and effects are also obviously different. Therefore, only rough approximations are possible, and no precise equivalency can be established. Nevertheless, as a matter of general principle, both NATO and OECD take into account both types of activity. Some comparative aid figures are contained in Table 11.

It may well be that the desire of the United States to lighten the heavy load it has been carrying can best be met by shifting more of the economic aid responsibility to its European partners. Clearly, there is an interrelationship, which argues for closer and

TABLE 11
Aid from NATO Countries to Countries in the Course of Economic Development
(Actual Disbursements in Million U.S. Dollars)

	1956	*1957*	*1958*	*1959*	*1960*	*1961*	*1962*	*Percentage of Donor's 1962 GNP at Factor Cost*
Belgium	$20	$20	$23	$79	$101	$92	$97	0.78
Canada	29	48	92	60	75	62	50	0.15
Denmark	3	2	5	14	6	7	9	0.14
France	648	819	884	832	837	943	996	1.6
Germany	149	300	278	337	324	589	427	0.58
Italy	36	155	45	43	55	66	66	0.2
Netherlands	48	23	39	49	47	69	86	0.72
Norway	8	8	—	4	10	9	1	0.02
Portugal	3	3	1	17	37	30	37	1.45
United Kingdom	205	234	276	375	402	441	417	0.60
United States	1,996	2,083	2,388	2,310	2,817	3,493	3,606	0.71
Total, NATO Countries	3,145	3,695	4,031	4,120	4,711	5,801	5,792	0.71

Notes:

1. The figures are on a disbursement basis and cover all nonmilitary grants and loans from the public sector exceeding five years. Grants and loans from the private sector are not included.
2. The share of grants (and grant-like contributions) in the figures above varies substantially from country to country. Percentage-wise, it amounted in 1962 to 96.9% in Belgium, 69.8% in Canada, 100% in Denmark, 89.1% in France, 48.8% in Germany, 80.6 % in Italy, 95.0% in the Netherlands, 100% in Norway, 86% in Portugal, 61.0% in the United Kingdom, and 81.0% in the United States.
3. Countries which do not have significant economic aid programs are not included in the above table.

Source: OECD, Report by the Chairman of DAC, July 1963.

more formal links between the economic and military organs of the Atlantic alliance, represented respectively by OECD and NATO.

The details of military burden-sharing are a statistical thicket in which even trained economists sometimes get lost. The science of "costing" military forces—their research and development, procurement, supporting bases, and other capital investment, and their manpower, administrative, and similar "operating" costs—is at a very rudimentary level for most countries. The problems of international comparisons are also formidable. One pioneering effort with respect to national products was done under OEEC auspices in the early 1950s. It found that comparison on the basis of exchange rates "very substantially understates the position of all the European countries in comparison with the United States and gives distorted relationships among the Europeans themselves." By analyzing the purchasing power of the various currencies, Gilbert and Kravis derived price weights to produce two quantity indexes at the respective prices for countries being compared which could then be averaged geometrically.[9]

Thus these authors point out that in 1950, the U.S. spent $14.6 billion on defense compared with $5.4 billion for Britain, France, Germany, and Italy combined, when converted at exchange rates. When the European spending was valued by quantity at U.S. prices, however, their total amounted to $11.4 billion.[10] The price disparities are now less, of course, and more recent studies have further improved our ability to compare the true costs of various defense efforts; but there is still no basic official data base on which to make realistic international financial comparisons. It would therefore appear to be worthwhile for NATO and OECD to collaborate in preparing the necessary statistical materials.

A third difficulty is that there is no single economic criterion by which burden-sharing capacity can be evaluated. Gross national product is the commonly accepted over-all measure of an economy's output. And per capita GNP is an even better indicator of a population's wealth. But taxation, prices, and other factors distort real income. Actual "ability" to pay can be adversely affected by many considerations ranging from balance-of-payments diffi-

[9] Milton Gilbert and Irving B. Kravis, *An International Comparison of National Products and the Purchasing Power of Currencies* (Paris: OEEC, 1954).

[10] Same, p. 43.

culties to problems of employment and the degree of utilization of resources.

There have been a number of efforts to find a sound economic guide to apportioning the shares of an international activity. The United Nations and its specialized agencies, the OECD, and NATO have all arrived at a working scale of assessments. In the U.N., the United States, for example, pays slightly over 30 per cent, while Belgium pays 1.2 per cent. In OECD, the latter country is assessed nearly 3 per cent of the total, while the U.S. share is about 25 per cent. And in NATO, Belgium pays over 4 per cent of the infrastructure program but less than 3 per cent of the military headquarters and agency budgets, while the United States currently has a cost share of about 30 per cent and 24 per cent, respectively. Depending on the formula used, the appropriate U.S. share of the total NATO defense spending ranges from a low of about 60 per cent (under a complicated real-income GNP formula, modified for unemployment and with a $300 per capita exemption) to a high of 78 per cent (according to a formula based on U.S. income tax rates applied to GNP per capita computed via exchange rates).[11] In fact, it is actually paying about 75 per cent of the total defense outlay of the NATO nations, so that any formula which takes into account *real* income, and all but the most progressive exchange-rate formula, would lead to some American reduction.

NATO has a common definition of what constitutes defense expenditures, but it is really based upon total national outlays under the heading of defense, without regard to their relevance to the needs of the alliance. Thus, Europeans can argue that a substantial part of the U.S. forces are maintained for contingencies in parts of the world that have no relationship to NATO as such. On the oth-

[11] Among the valuable sources on burden sharing are Hitch and McKean, cited, and Lincoln Gordon, "Economic Aspects of Coalition Diplomacy, the NATO Experience," *International Organization*, Vol. 10, pp. 530-540, 1956. I am also indebted to John A. Pincus of the RAND Corporation and of the State Department, who has done some valuable analysis on cost sharing, for giving me his views and for making available some working papers on the subject.

er hand, Americans point out that almost all of the U.S. nuclear forces contribute to the over-all deterrent against the Communist bloc, and that the majority of U.S. "general purpose" forces are assigned to NATO directly or as strategic reserve.

In sum, each country tends to argue for the definitions, economic base, and formulas which work to its advantage. The cost-sharing methods actually employed therefore represent political bargaining rather than economic analysis. Each country also measures its interests in a particular alliance activity from its own point of view. From time to time Americans are heard to argue that the only way to equalize the NATO burden is to bring home one or more of our divisions. Such threats might have a limited bargaining value; but if they were carried out, and if the Europeans did not increase their own efforts to make up the loss, the American interest in European security would suffer as much as any.

Measured against these complexities, NATO's cost-sharing program for "infrastructure" has been remarkably successful. NATO borrowed this term from the French railroads, where it was used to describe bridges, tunnels, and the like. In military parlance it has come to include all of the fixed installations—airfields, communications, pipelines, headquarters,—necessary for peacetime training or wartime support of NATO forces. Each member, of course, is responsible for the installations needed for its own national forces. The "common" infrastructure, so-called, involves installations in one country used by the forces of one or more allies or existing for their support.[12] As of 1961, the twelve "slices" (annual construction programs) had financed over 200 airfields, 27,000 miles of communications, 5,300 miles of pipelines, and numerous naval, storage, radar, missile, air defense, and ammunition facilities, to cost over $2 billion. And by 1964, the accomplishments were even more impressive. (For historical reasons, which need not be explored

[12] The NATO fact book, cited, devotes an entire chapter to infrastructure and describes the program and the procedures involved in considerable detail; see pp. 121-129.

here, NATO developed a separate program for its thirty-odd military headquarters and technical and staff agencies. There are thus two different cost-sharing formulas and sets of financial procedures. The United States is currently among those allies seeking to combine them—and particularly to lower its total contribution.)

The special nature of this infrastructure program has made it necessary to develop a cost-sharing formula which takes into account not only ability to pay (GNP), but also the advantage gained by the using country and the benefits to the host nation (the country which provides the land and eventually will inherit the residual value of the installation; meanwhile it may gain various economic side benefits, including a boost to local employment). The benefits of construction work or procurement, however, are shared by means of competitive international bidding on NATO-approved specifications.

The actual cost-sharing percentages agreed upon are listed in Table 12. The system has at times proved cumbersome, slow (with actual construction often years behind schedule), and conducive to much wrangling. Nevertheless, it has produced hundreds of essential installations for NATO forces which otherwise might not have existed. And it may offer some useful experience upon which to build. For example, the principle of benefit to host or user might be adapted to common financing of a broader range of NATO projects, with special subsidies scaled to the size of a country's participation. Financing by NATO as a whole would, in effect, replace the incentive to national defense efforts formerly provided by the U.S. military assistance program, now largely eliminated for most of NATO Europe. A country would then be able to vary the extent of its participation in projects in accordance with its desire to bid on construction or procurement or its need for the goods or services involved. Such an arrangement would offer both flexibility and an efficient use of resources.[13]

Still another possibility would be to develop common financing

[13] Mrs. Doris Iklé, formerly of the Stanford Research Institute, has developed some interesting ideas along this line in an informal staff paper of May 1962, "A Financial Plan for Strengthening NATO."

TABLE 12
Approved NATO Infrastructure Cost-Sharing Formulas

Country	Slice Programs		
	II-VIIa[1] *1951-56*	VIIb[2]-XI *1957-60*	XII-XV *1961-64*
Belgium	5.462%	4.39%	4.24%
Canada	6.021	6.15	5.15
Denmark	2.767	2.63	2.87
France	15.041	11.87	12.00
Germany	0.000	13.72	20.00
Greece	0.750	0.87	0.67
Iceland	0.000	0.00	0.00
Italy	5.681	5.61	5.97
Luxembourg	0.155	0.17	0.17
Netherlands	3.889	3.51	3.83
Norway	2.280	2.19	2.37
Portugal	0.146	0.28	0.28
Turkey	1.371	1.75	1.10
United Kingdom	12.758	9.88	10.50
United States	43.679	36.98	30.85
Total	100.000%	100.00%	100.00%

[1] Cost-sharing percentages represent a weighted average as agreed upon by the North Atlantic Council.
[2] Slice VIIb was entirely devoted to Germany, which paid 50 per cent.

for special military forces, such as SACEUR's mobile "fire brigade" force discussed in Chapter 5. The availability of "NATO" funds would give the alliance important leverage in meeting requirements of an unusually international character. But present NATO procedures do not provide for such funds. Even the infrastructure and headquarters programs are handled between the alliance and the host country, with the secretariat-international staff acting merely as a bookkeeping agency or clearing house for national accounts. But if NATO is to move forward institutionally, it may be necessary to evolve in the direction of international control and disbursement of funds, which is authorized by the international agreement establishing NATO's juridical personality. If the multilateral force comes into being as a specialized joint venture with its own budget and funds, it may pave the way for other NATO programs.

The Balance of Payments Problem

In recent years American defense programs have encountered a special kind of economic constraint popularly known as the gold-flow problem but more accurately described as a continuing adverse balance of payments. In the early days of the alliance, the major financial problem was the so-called dollar gap, which led the United States into extensive off-shore procurement in Europe to supply its own forces, and into major military assistance and defense support programs for its NATO allies. However, beginning early in 1959, the United States government and public gradually became aware that the adverse balance of international payments had started to run steeply in the other direction, resulting in a substantial outflow of U.S. gold—nearly $7 billion during 1958-62, bringing the reserves down to about $16 billion. This trend reflected a decline in the postwar dominance of the dollar as weaker currencies, particularly in Europe, gained in relative strength.

In very broad terms, over the five-year period 1958-1962 the United States had a favorable balance of merchandise and service exports over imports totalling about $30 billion. Long-term capital transfers reduced this by about $11 billion, and private remittances and miscellaneous transactions by $5 billion, leaving a favorable balance of roughly $14 billion. Nonmilitary governmental loans and grants totalled $16 billion, leaving a net deficit of about $2 billion. The addition of nearly $13 billion of military expenditures in excess of receipts helped to change a manageable five-year deficit into a problem of serious proportions.[14]

[14] The favorable export and services balance excludes military sales but *includes* earnings on capital and some loan repayments which partially offset the large adverse figures on capital and governmental transfers. This data

Thus, the United States faced a dilemma. The burdens of governmental and private financing of foreign economic development, of military assistance, and of troop deployments abroad were the natural result of the U.S. postwar emergence as the primary leader of the non-Communist world. Continuing these programs was essential to the global responsibilities associated with that role. Yet the drain in gold and dollars which they entailed appeared to be undermining the international confidence in the dollar itself, which had come to play a key role in international commerce and financial reserves.

Financial interdependence and the relationship between international payments and domestic prices and employment made it difficult to adopt such classical measures as devaluation of the dollar or restricting the capital outflow. Massive retrenchment in foreign aid and defense programs was obviously also undesirable. Yet allowing the adverse balance to go unchecked could equally damage the international position of the United States and hence injure its allies.

Many combinations of techniques can be used to bring a deficit down to manageable levels. But any action by the United States must affect other countries if it is to be effective. The measures chosen inevitably represent a selection among various competing policy objectives. Moreover, most transactions are interrelated in the sense that a deficit item may be generating the dollars abroad which are essential for some other country to pay for U.S. exports. Several aspects of the over-all payments problem deserve mention in order to place the military aspects in perspective.

First, the continuing short-term difficulty is the need to settle international deficits. A large part of the American problem concerns Europe, although Japan is also an important contributor to the U.S. deficit. The $600 billion U.S. economy and the $300 bil-

---

is taken primarily from Walter S. Salant and Associates, *The United States Balance of Payments in 1968* (Washington: Brookings Institution, 1963), Appendix Table 1. The primary source is the statistics published by the U.S. Department of Commerce (Office of Business Economics) in *Survey of Current Business*, June 1963 and June 1964.

lion economy of Europe both increase annually in amounts larger than the cumulative payments deficit. Thus, the underlying financial health of both "debtor" and creditors is good. But to finance the over-all 1958-1962 deficit of $15.7 billion it has been necessary to decrease American gold reserves by $6.4 billion, increase liquid liabilities to foreign central banks and governments and the International Monetary Fund (IMF), and make settlements of $3.6 billion with other international institutions and commercial banks. The Treasury has negotiated "swap" arrangements for currency, sought prepayment of loans, and tried to induce foreigners to increase their holdings in the U.S., rather than to withdraw gold and dollar assets.[15] But short-term measures to finance the deficit may merely complicate the long-range problem by postponing a more lasting solution. This highlights the importance of such possibilities as increasing world currency reserves, perhaps through an expansion of IMF resources, so as to develop an international mechanism for financing of payments deficits.

Although the technical aspects of any longer-term restructuring of the international financial community are outside the scope of this discussion, the challenge is important for the Atlantic Community as a whole. The theoretical possibilities range from an Atlantic payments union, through removal of restrictions on international financial transactions, up to a common currency and supranational banking institutions. The practical—and political—difficulties are numerous, however. In any case, because of the closely knit structure of international economic cooperation, where a major reserve currency like the dollar is involved, other countries automatically have a strong self-interest in seeing its strength preserved. Thus international cooperation can be assumed both to relieve short-term payments strains, and to help strengthen the international financial structure.[16] The rapid "rescue" operation for the

[15] See "Financing the U.S. Payments Deficit" in the *Federal Reserve Bulletin* for April 1963, p. 421.

[16] For a comprehensive analysis see Henry G. Aubrey, *The Dollar in World Affairs* (New York: Harper & Row, for the Council on Foreign Relations, 1964).

pound, undertaken late in 1964, reveals the soundness of the assumption.

Secondly, there is the long-term trend to consider. Psychology plays a larger role perhaps in international banking than in many other forums of human judgment. Evidence that a payments deficit is likely to be corrected over time, either by special measures or by the normal working of the international economy, can keep a potential crisis from becoming an operative one. The various measures taken to date have reduced America's over-all deficit from $3.7 billion and $3.9 billion in 1959 and 1960, respectively, to $2.4 billion in 1961 and $2.2 billion in 1962. It rose again to $2.6 billion in 1963, and, despite a favorable first quarter, showed signs of rising again in 1964.[17] In any case, the past three U.S. administrations have displayed a determination to maintain the dollar's position, which should be reassuring in itself. As far as the United States is concerned, the emotional concern generated by the loss of gold may be more important politically than economically, for some experts advocate removing the gold backing from U.S. currency entirely.

As to the future, a detailed study by the Brookings Institution suggested that by 1968, other things being favorable, U.S. payments might well be back in balance—due largely to inflation in Europe (which should further increase the competitive advantage of U.S. exports) and to repayments on capital investments.[18] Economists who challenge these optimistic conclusions point to the likelihood of wide annual fluctuations and note that favorable prospects depend on continued U.S. efforts. But a majority would agree that the over-all trend is toward improvement, if only because, as Seymour Harris has pointed out, the classical medicine of surplus

[17] *Survey of Current Business*, cited, June 1964, pp. 9-21.

[18] Salant, cited. The Brookings group projected an improvement in the basic balance of $2.7 billion by 1968 as against 1961, leading to a surplus. Alternative and less optimistic assumptions gave a projection of a $600 million deficit—about the same as the 1961 "basic" balance, i.e., excluding special and military transactions.

funds bringing higher prices and benefiting deficit areas is at work.[19]

The economic and fiscal complexities involved in the balance-of-payments problem make it extraordinarily difficult to judge whether the United States has shifted to the Defense Department too much of the burdens of defending the dollar as well as the country. As a major contributor to the deficit, the Defense Department has properly been charged with eliminating all nonessential overseas expenditures and continuously evaluating those that remain against major security objectives.

Private overseas investment has generally been in the same order of magnitude as military expenditures abroad—and the latter have contributed considerably less to the deficit than the so-called "service" imports such as tourism. Of course, controls on capital or tourism would raise their own separate problems. Consequently, no single villain can be pointed out as the major cause of the payments deficit. Also, the United States has by no means limited its actions to the defense and foreign policy field. Major programs of export promotion and foreign tourism in the United States have been started; the interest equalization tax has been aimed at reducing the flow of new portfolio investment abroad; grant aid has largely given way to loans; and foreign assistance has been tied to U.S. purchases.

Nevertheless, it is worthwhile to examine the defense aspects more closely. Table 13 shows that the defense expenditures contributing to the net adverse balance were down from more than $3 billion in 1958 to about $1.7 billion for fiscal 1963. The principal items are: procurement, hiring of foreigners, and spending by servicemen and their dependents overseas. The military deficit has been reduced about $1 billion during the past two years by such

[19] U.S. Congress, Joint Economic Committee, "Factors Affecting the United States Balance of Payments," Committee Print, 87th Cong., 2nd sess., 1962, p. 20. Professor Harris' paper on "The Problem and Its Solution" is an excellent over-all summary. The Joint Committee also held hearings in December 1962, "Outlook for United States Balance of Payments," which contained testimony by a number of top U.S. officials.

TABLE 13
U.S. Defense Expenditures and Receipts Entering the International Balance of Payments
(In Millions of Dollars)

	Fiscal Year 1963 (Estimated)
Expenditures:	
U.S. Forces and Their Support:	
Expenditures by U.S. Military, Civilians and Dependents	787.2
Foreign Nationals (Direct Hire[a] and Contract Hire)	432.0
Procurement:	
Major Equipment	76.1
Construction	96.5
Materials and Supplies	556.7
Contractual Services	500.6
Sub-Total	2,449.1
Military Assistance Program:	
Off-shore Procurement	120.8
NATO Infrastructure	89.3
Other	103.8
Sub-Total	313.9
Total Expenditures	2,763.0
Receipts	1,326.2
Net Adverse Balance (Dept. of Defense)	1,436.8
Other Expenditures (AEC and Other Agencies included in NATO Definition of Defense Expenditures)	248.1
Net Adverse Balance (NATO definition)	1,684.9

[a] Includes expenditures for goods and services by nonappropriated fund activities.

Source: Joint Economic Committee, *Fact Book*, 88th Cong., 1st sess., 1963.

measures as: voluntary individual savings; procurement in the U.S. for use overseas; cutbacks in overseas construction, contractual services, and local employment of foreigners; restrictions on military assistance (very little of which actually affects the payments balance) and a major effort to sell U.S. equipment to its allies.[20] In the last-named category, Germany's agreement to offset U.S. defense spending in Germany, primarily by U.S. forces stationed in its territory, through equivalent military procurement in America, has saved over $600 million per year in dollar outflow since 1961. Major military sales arrangements have been or are being negotiated with Italy and other countries. Over the years, such sales abroad have made a substantial contribution to the favorable export balance.

But there are potential political and military—as well as economic—costs for all of these measures. Troop morale can be injured by too many restrictions. President Eisenhower's politically courageous but unpopular limitation on dependents accompanying U.S. forces overseas was soon lifted by the Kennedy administration for morale reasons. "Buying American" has averaged nearly a third more in actual expenditures than cheaper procurement nearer to the point of consumption. Heavy pressures on allies to buy U.S. equipment can have unfavorable political repercussions, while cutting back bases and logistic support, or over-reliance on air-deployment capacity can hamper military effectiveness in a crisis. And perhaps hardest to measure, but nevertheless of the greatest importance, the essential political objectives of American deployments in Europe can be jeopardized by constant rumors about possible further reductions.

Under the leadership of Secretary McNamara, Defense has cut much of the fat from its overseas structure. Any sizable further redeployments may cut into the military muscle and cause political trauma quite out of proportion to the savings gained. Germany is particularly sensitive to any implication that De Gaulle may be right in his predictions of an eventual American withdrawal from Europe. And having agreed to offset the American expenditures there, Germany has every reason to be sensitive.

[20] Joint Economic Committee, *Fact Book,* 88th Cong., 1st sess., 1963. For a full discussion of the effects of defense transactions, see Salant, cited, Ch. VII.

Since the problem is of concern to several countries it might be worthwhile to explore the possibilities of a NATO-wide principle that no country should suffer in its balance of payments because of overseas deployments in the common defense. Canada, Britain, and a few other countries, as well as the United States, would benefit from such an arrangement. Local costs of foreign forces could be reimbursed by the host country promptly, thereby gaining a long-term credit on which to draw for procurement in the country concerned. This would overcome the problem that overseas spending tends to enter the balance immediately, while the compensating procurement may have a long lead-time, delaying payment and complicating the accounting. Payment of interest on the credits, or special discounts on purchases, could be used to make the scheme attractive to the creditor nations (chiefly Germany) and shift some of the cost to the domestic account. The pros and cons of the multilateral plan would have to be carefully weighed against the benefits already being obtained through specially tailored bilateral arrangements such as the United States is now pursuing.

But whether such a multilateral scheme proved workable or not, it seems clear that defense programs should do their part, but only their part, in trimming the payments deficit. We have seen that the long-term trend is favorable, and that significant strides have already been made. Given continued efforts to insure against a return to the adverse trend of the late 1950s, the disequilibrium should be manageable if the creditor nations remain cooperative.

In the end, the balance-of-payments dilemma comes down to a question of timing. As long as a small continuing deficit can be financed in a favorable economic climate without serious fiscal consequences, the political considerations should be dominant. And in the mid-1960s, while NATO is in a transition of uncertain dimensions, the implications of any lessened American determination to maintain its forward deployments should be avoided. It would indeed be unfortunate if the arbitrary ceiling on defense spending, which was a feature of some earlier periods, was replaced by a similar constraint because of the balance of payments. Happily, indications both past and present are that this development can be avoided.

8

The Reform of the Alliance

It is well to reiterate that NATO is not a supra-national organisation and does not possess mandatory powers over national governments.

NATO, Facts about the North Atlantic Treaty Organization

True statesmanship is the art of changing what is into what ought to be.

APHORISM

The publication of a revised and extensive fact book about NATO has made it unnecessary for scholars to encumber their works on this subject with historical and statistical details. In its narration of the development and workings of the alliance, the fact book is more frank about shortcomings than might be expected in an official publication of the NATO Information Service.

Several of its chapters start with the admonition to the reader that NATO is an international and not a supranational entity. There is almost a petulant note in the reiteration of this theme—due perhaps to the fact that the alliance is often publicly measured against the standard of what might have been accomplished if, in fact, it had been endowed with supranational authority. Thus viewed, the shortcomings are many and far-reaching. But measured against the true standard of its inherent limitations, the alliance has made far greater progress in the past fifteen years than most people realize, or indeed than its founders could have anticipated. NATO, that is, the organization created pursuant to the

Treaty, is an entity with juridical personality and can hold funds and own property. It has worked out an intricate "status of forces" and an international headquarters agreement to cover the legal problems of the alliance; and it has thus overcome a number of conceptual and legalistic obstacles.[1]

The history of NATO can be divided roughly into three periods. The first, or organizational phase, covered the period from the inception of the alliance in 1949 through the winter of 1951-1952 when the first Temporary Council Committee—better known as the "Three Wise Men"—[2] reported on the economic capacity, military build-up and organization of the alliance. The report of the Temporary Council Committee paved the way for the Lisbon meeting in February 1952, which set the Korean War force goals of fifty divisions, and recommended the reorganization of the Atlantic Council and its civilian agencies and the establishment of what became the Annual Review procedure.

A second phase ended with the heads of government meeting of the NATO members in December 1957, at which a number of important military decisions were taken, notably to deploy nuclear weapon systems. A year previously, another Committee of Three had been appointed to focus on political consultation, one of NATO's major perennial problems, and it made a number of significant recommendations.

NATO is now at the end of its third phase, marked by the new defense concepts of the Kennedy administration on one hand, the growing intransigence of France within the alliance, and the preoccupation of over half the members with intra-European rather than Atlantic integration.

The period ahead to the twentieth anniversary in 1969 will be a

[1] The Status of Forces, International Military Headquarters, and Status of the Organization agreements are reprinted in *NATO—Facts about the North Atlantic Treaty Organization* (Paris: NATO Information Service, 1962), Appendices 7, 8 and 9. The last-named, known also as the Ottawa Agreement of 1951, provides for juridical status—an attribute which is not widely known—and for privileges and immunities.

[2] Averell Harriman of the United States, Jean Monnet of France, and Sir Edwin Plowden of Britain. See pp. 24-25 of the NATO fact book.

fourth phase in the history of the alliance. There is a widespread but wrong impression that the treaty is in some way due to expire in 1969. The Charter merely provides that the parties may review the treaty after ten years (which was done on a rather cursory basis and without modification in 1959) and that it may be denounced by any party after it has been in force for twenty years. Since 1959 any party has had the right to request consultation for the purpose of reviewing the treaty. France has made no secret of its desire to reform the organization either on a *de facto* or a *de jure* basis; but it has never put forward any concrete suggestions. While according to the treaty itself, France would have to wait until 1969 to give formal notice of its intention to "cease to be a party" one year later, De Gaulle's government has already so watered down its participation that, if the present trend continues, formal withdrawal would probably be unnecessary.

France is the geographic heartland of the North Atlantic alliance. Paris is the site of the NATO headquarters building and SHAPE, as well as a number of subsidiary bodies such as the NATO Defense College. Much of NATO's line of communications and supply system operates through France, the link between the central region of the alliance and the Mediterranean and Southern Europe. Nevertheless, it may not be premature to raise the fundamental question of whether the alliance could survive without France—or with France remaining only in the "alliance" (in which abstraction De Gaulle professes to believe) but absenting itself from the organization which alone gives reality and meaning to NATO's peacetime existence.

It is unlikely that France would seek to withdraw completely; and such a development, should it occur, would be highly undesirable, to say the least. But the bargaining that will go on within the alliance between General de Gaulle's conceptions and those of other countries will inevitably be conducted against the backdrop of this "ultimate" question. If, for example, the other members refused to accede to De Gaulle's desire to back down from such limited progress as has been made toward international integration of military forces, or if he pursues the concept of some sort of triumvirate executive committee (an arrangement which France has long sought as a matter of parity with Britain and the United States), this question might become more than academic. For if France threatened either to discontinue such cooperation as remains, or indeed to formally sever its ties, it could very effectively continue to obstruct and veto any forward progress whatever, unless the other members were prepared to go ahead as best they could without it. Although at first blush a NATO without France appears to make little sense, politically, militarily, or economically, a second look reveals that French abdication need not cause the complete rupture of either the alliance or its structure. Cost-effectiveness and balance-of-payments considerations have already dictated the closing down of some line of communications installations in France. Those that remain could be shifted to Belgium and the Netherlands, even though the supply line to U.S. forces in Bavaria would then run parallel, rather than perpendicular, to the assumed line of engagement. But this was in fact the situation that existed for several years after the war.

Since the bulk of the forces for forward defense are provided by Germany, the United States, and Britain, in that order, the French contribution exists essentially to secure the rear area of the central front, which is France itself. France would hardly go so far as to invite a Russian military presence in its country, and would therefore maintain the same security without a NATO label as with it. Thus the concepts discussed in Chapter 5 of a more decentralized system of supply depots and a combination of ready reserves, divisions of the "forward defense" type, and defended barriers, could well make possible a defense against the more likely categories of threat even within the narrow defensive zone available in Germany. If Spain were subsequently to join the alliance, the entire Iberian peninsula would then be available for training areas and logistic installations, from which peacetime supplies could be moved by sea. The headquarters of the alliance could be shifted to any of several capitals—possibly to London, or if a location on the Continent were deemed important, to Brussels or even to Rome or Bonn.

Although NATO might be able to survive such an unpleasant development as French withdrawal (whether formal or not), NATO should bend every effort to avoid it. But depending on French actions, the members of the alliance might be forced to decide whether an alliance in name only *with* France served their combined interests better than the more cohesive and politically effective one which could be evolved without it.

Let us turn from pessimistic assumptions about the future and examine the possible areas of reform within NATO's present terms of reference. A good case can be made that the alliance has come about as far as it can without some more formal delegation by the members of supranational authority. But even apart from the problem of French attitudes, none of the members has been exactly eager to give up its defensive sovereignty in matters of substance. This applies equally to the United States, although we shall want to examine in a moment whether the concerns that motivated this attitude in the 1950s should remain applicable to the late 1960s.

NATO's structure is, to put it mildly, extraordinarily cumbersome. Both its civil and its military components have experienced a vast proliferation of committees; and the officers and civilians of its professional staff reflect the inevitable immobilism of 13- to 15-member participation in all activities. (Iceland and Luxemburg, because of their small size, often do not take part unless they are directly concerned.) The organization is made to order for obstruction. Frustration has been the almost universal experience of everyone who has really tried to get something done quickly within the NATO environment. It is no small tribute to the Secretaries-General and other top officials that the record shows as much accomplishment as it does.

Political Consultation

Contrary to the impression conveyed in many writings about NATO, the North Atlantic Council has proved a reasonably effective forum for political consultation in the sense of exchanging information. It meets regularly (weekly) at the ambassadorial level; annually with the foreign, defense, and often the financial ministers, in Paris in December; and at the defense and/or foreign minister level in the spring at various capitals. It also has met once at the heads of government level. The permanent representatives are in frequent contact, and their political and economic advisers hold regular discussion meetings. There is thus considerable flexibility in the Council's operation. The United States in particular has made it a point to inform the other allies about troublesome situations in other parts of the world, of the actions it is contemplating or changes in its policies, and about the progress of any contacts with the Soviet Union, such as trade talks or disarmament negotiations.

The members with special responsibilities for Berlin have also used the Council to keep NATO as a whole informed during the periodic crises there as well as on the more routine aspects. The Council has not, however, proved especially effective in obtaining the views of the allies at an *early* stage of policy—what the American Congress in its complaint about the Executive sometimes calls the "take off as well as the crash landing." The fault here lies on both sides of the Atlantic. On several of the relatively rare occasions when the United States has discussed a dilemma frankly and asked for advice, it has more often than not been greeted with an embarrassed silence. Although a few of the other countries, particularly the larger ones with global responsibilities such as Britain, have followed the United States' lead, the others have for the most part used the political consultation machinery as a device for advancing particular claims or interests—for example, defending colonial positions or seeking greater economic assistance.

Two inescapable facts of life affect the progress of political consultation within the alliance. The first is the preponderant power and responsibility held by the United States.[3] This reality cannot

[3] In a recent article in *Figaro,* Raymond Aron described French policy as seeking "the glory derived from showing her indifference to the susceptibili-

be changed by organizational tinkering, although its divisive effects may be mitigated. The second is that a Council of fifteen permanent representatives, each of whom must either have advance instructions or wire his capital for guidance before making any major policy statement, does not lend itself to dramatic diplomatic accomplishment. On the other hand, the Council does have the advantage that the weight of allied objection can be multiplied by numbers. The combined effect of several expressions of disapproval in the Council may be more effective in dissuading a member from a particular course of action than several unilateral communications from individual countries. And as in most quasi-legislative organizations, much of the actual work is done behind the scenes, through private discussions in the cloakrooms and in committees rather than in plenary session.

It should be recalled that NATO's second task is concerned with the evolution of a stable *world* order. It is probably too much to expect that NATO as an institution could or would develop coordinated plans for non-NATO matters—in which only a few members would have either an interest or a responsibility. But the alliance should not therefore shy away from playing an active role in developing a consensus among those of its members who are necessarily going to have to provide the leadership in this task.

To facilitate the increasingly important economic coordination there are possibilities of improving NATO-OECD collaboration—and perhaps building a broader political framework around both organs—which I shall discuss at the conclusion of this chapter. But in the political-military field alone there are several trends and problems which could well profit from joint research, analysis, and discussion. The evolution in Eastern Europe towards greater national independence is one; possible arms control and disarmament initiatives might be another; and the ominous presence of Communist China looms ever larger on the world stage. The work of the quadripartite groups in Washington and other

ties and preferences of an ally whose major error is that it is in possession of the reality of power." Quoted in *The New Yorker,* March 21, 1964, p. 157.

capitals which have successfully concerted allied policy on Berlin matters might be paralleled by other groupings of NATO countries concerned with contingencies in the Middle East, Africa, or Far East. The Atlantic Policy Advisory Group could be developed into a permanent international policy planning mechanism. More use could be made by the NATO Council of specialized *ad hoc* committees to examine and report on specific issues and problems.

The actual choice of machinery—and indeed the substance of the work to be done—may be less important than the decision to step up the tempo of political collaboration and extend the range of intergovernmental contacts. Because of the difficulty of getting unanimity in the fifteen-member Council, the alliance might have to accept the principle that NATO could institutionally bless and assist any project of the foregoing type which three or more members wished to pursue, without requiring the consent of all. A country could object in principle if its interests were involved; but otherwise, nations not wishing to take part would be expected to abstain. The only requirement should be that membership in various *ad hoc* groupings be theoretically open to all NATO countries, and that the Council as a whole be informed periodically about the activities involved.

Notwithstanding the limitations, NATO early recognized the importance of the principle of effective consultation; and after the Suez misadventure dramatized the consequences of not adhering to it, a special committee on nonmilitary cooperation in NATO (the Committee of Three) focused its report accordingly.[4] Among the recommendations later put into effect were an annual political appraisal, and a special committee composed of the political advisors of each delegation, which continues to do useful coordination on such matters as diplomatic notes to the Soviet Union.

A subsequent development has been the creation of an informal

[4] The Committee of Three was established in May 1956, and completed most of its work in September. Its report, however, was not submitted until after the Suez fiasco, and was approved by the Council on December 13, 1956. The full report is printed as Appendix 11 in the NATO fact book, cited.

Atlantic Policy Advisory Group which holds periodic meetings of the senior foreign ministry officials who specialize either in policy planning generally, or in regional affairs. Getting together the officials of the NATO governments who specialize in say, Latin American or African affairs, provides a valuable opportunity to take soundings, exchange notes, and keep abreast of the thinking that lies behind policy. This sort of consultation is hardly sensational; but as the bread-and-butter work of the professionals, it may be more effective in the long run than dramatic visits by special emissaries for "crisis" briefings. When Dean Acheson flew to Paris to brief General de Gaulle on the Cuban missile crisis, the latter was presumably appreciative; but he is reported to have said: "I consider that I have been informed. I have *not* been consulted."

A final possibility for improving NATO's existing machinery deserves mention. This would involve an up-grading and expansion in the alliance's consultation, policy research, and contingency planning. NATO might recommend that its permanent representatives (now ranked as ambassadors) should have cabinet status, perhaps as deputy foreign ministers, in their governments. The individual quality of the ambassadors to NATO has been quite high for all countries; but several of them have commented to me that a cabinet rank or equivalent status in their own governments would improve their access, simplify coordination with their capitals, and generally upgrade the level and authority of NATO discussions. Such a move would not change the geographic fact that decisions are made in home capitals, not in Paris. But it could lend somewhat greater weight to the counsels originating at the seat of NATO.

Other Areas of Cooperation

On the economic side, NATO has evolved a complicated procedure for arriving at an agreed infrastructure program and cost-sharing formula. Moreover, it has provided the framework for a number of cooperative production arrangements, such as for the Hawk and Sidewinder missiles and the G-91, F-104, and maritime patrol aircraft. It has established a NATO pipeline system, a maintenance supply services system for spare parts, and made some progress on military standardization. It has made a few innovations in harnessing the scientific and technical talent of its members through AGARD and the SHAPE Air Defense Technical Center.

Finally, although none would qualify as having set the world on fire, the alliance has mounted several modest programs in the field of cultural cooperation, studies, fellowships, and public information activities.

The machinery is there. Were the alliance to generate the will necessary to utilize its resources to maximum efficiency, the existing structure could be reorganized so as to work fully *as well as the member governments desire*. Consequently, it would appear to make more sense to expand on existing patterns of cooperation than to tear down the organization in the hope that it could be rebuilt. But in present circumstances, the improvements likely to be adopted would appear to be minor repairs having a marginal effectiveness in most areas.

There may be a few exceptions to this general observation. One concerns the mechanism for arriving at an alliance consensus on the interrelationships of strategy, forces, and budgets. Here, greater provision might be made for close day-to-day working relationships between the civil-political-economic side of NATO and its military staffs—principally that at SHAPE. The NATO Forces Planning Exercise discussed in Chapter 7 is one example, although as we have seen, national attitudes, particularly the objections of France, have strongly hampered this activity.

Another area might be the expansion of the infrastructure program to include some operative military forces, such as the embryonic NATO mobile force, and a greater degree of common funding of construction, procurement, and research and development projects. In the last area, particularly, it might prove possible to reduce (one can never entirely eliminate) the cut-throat competition among national suppliers which inevitably influences the selection and design of weapon systems. Rather than having individual manufacturers and governments seek to tailor NATO's basic military requirements for equipment to suit their products, NATO could be injected much earlier into the cycle. If the alliance machinery started to function with basic and applied research and system concepts, detailed specifications might be developed multilaterally so that competitive bidding could begin earlier. If each country were to subscribe to NATO a certain percentage of its national expenditures on military research and development (perhaps through the infrastructure program), the alliance could then award contracts specially suited to alliance rather than national needs. The Mutual Weapons Development Program is a step in this general direction, but it is primarily a coordinating and exchange mechanism, rather than an independent source of concepts and funding.

But in these, as in other areas of possible improvements, the outer limits are set by the basic *political* attitudes of the members toward the concept of supranationalism. It is almost inconceivable that any order of magnitude increase in NATO's effectiveness as an alliance can be obtained until its members are much more willing than heretofore to subject themselves to decisions over which they do not have a veto. To leave aside France, a major stumbling block has been the attitude of the United States, and to a lesser degree, that of Great Britain. The two other major members, Italy and Germany, lost their claim to be world powers through their defeat in World War II. For the most part, they have developed their forces and defense concepts purely from the standpoint of NATO missions. The smaller members, by virtue of their limited resources, have already found themselves strongly affected by decisions of the alliance—or at least its larger members like the United States. They would therefore appear to have relatively little to lose and perhaps something to gain by agreeing to a greater supranational functioning of NATO.

American attitudes stem in part from the initial postwar period when the effect of any such action would have been to subject the

United States to even greater claims upon its resources—which were already being devoted to a large extent to allied defenses. For example, had NATO not adopted the early principle that logistics were a national responsibility, the United States might well have found itself in the business of furnishing the logistic support for virtually the entire forces of the alliance.

A somewhat related factor was that the United States, as a global power, could have become involved in two separate logistic systems, one geared to Europe, and the other to its national forces designed to meet commitments in other parts of the world. However, under the Military Assistance Program, NATO's rearmament took place largely on the basis of American equipment; and even as the other members developed their national weapons, sufficient standardization has probably occurred so that this would no longer be an insuperable obstacle.

A second, and perhaps more basic objection, is that as long as the United States has the *de facto* responsibility for carrying the main burden of defense, not only of NATO, but of SEATO, CENTO, and the OAS alliance systems, plus key individual nations such as Korea and Taiwan, it seemed neither prudent nor appropriate that its decisions should be subjected to scrutiny and influence, if not a veto, by other countries who often lack either the responsibility or the resources to help if needed. This brings us squarely to the question to which this book is addressed: whether from the standpoint of its own long-term interests, the United States stands more to lose than to gain by giving up some of its freedom of action. If we accept the basic assumption formulated in Part I that the United States and Europe must work together, and that neither alone can meet the challenges of the future, perhaps the time has come for a searching reappraisal of closer involvement with our European allies. The alliance is already an entangling one—perhaps a greater source of informal constraints upon U.S. policy than is commonly realized.[5] The possible disadvantages of making NATO a more

[5] Robert Osgood has some interesting comments on this point in his aptly-named book, *NATO: The Entangling Alliance* (University of Chicago Press, 1962).

supranational body (in which the constraints could become more formalized) must be balanced against the potential gains in European sharing of the defense burden, and a greater sense of joint responsibility for the twin tasks of securing the Atlantic area and developing a stable world order.

I am not here suggesting a truly supranational government in which the "common defense" would be the responsibility of a NATO Secretary of Defense with wide powers. For this would inevitably involve a degree of Atlantic political unification which, as we have already seen, is impractical for the present. What I am talking about is an American willingness to take the lead in abandoning the sacred principle that NATO is an "international rather than a supranational" organization, and delegating to alliance officials greater authority in specific areas. These might be narrowly limited, especially at first; but the details are less relevant than the basic act of will involved. If the United States did take such a lead, Britain would be quite likely to follow as would most, if not all of the other countries, except for France. Such an act by the United States could sufficiently transform the prospects of the alliance so that France would find it extremely difficult to maintain its posture of aloofness. Or, after De Gaulle, when hopefully the French nationalist orgy may have passed, France might again become a willing and cooperative partner. It may be that strategic or tactical multilateral forces, discussed in Part II could pave the way for NATO as a whole.

On the assumption that the rather gloomy picture outlined above would then no longer apply, let us examine what might be done to reform the alliance. Three specific areas offer interesting possibilities: structural reform, force planning, and centralized production and logistics.

Structural Reform

At present, NATO's planning and operations are sharply divided along political and military lines. At the top of the civil organization, the Secretary-General has no military staff of his own, nor any mechanism for meshing political, military, and economic factors. As Alastair Buchan pointed out in one of the Adelphi papers of the Institute for Strategic Studies:

> As weapons become more lethal and more costly, as manpower and military budgets rise, and as research and development become more complex, so the area of purely military consideration diminishes . . . one reason why Ministers of Defense, who are a constitutional innovation of the last 20 years in all NATO countries, have become such important political figures.[6]

NATO may well find it appropriate to parallel, insofar as possible, the evolution of national defense organizations in which combined staffs of military and civilian officials wrestle with the tough policy choices. To use the United States as an example, NATO is still in the pre-1947 pattern in which "purely military" force requirements are submitted for review by political officials who lack any means for considering alternatives. NATO's "civilian control" also follows what might be called the U.S. Navy's "vertical" structure, rather than the "horizontal" pattern of the Army or Air Force.[7] As illustrated in Fig. 2, there are seven major components of NATO's over-all organization.

First, there is the North Atlantic Council itself—the highest political authority in the alliance. This is basically an international committee, whether it meets in full ministerial session or with the Permanent Representatives. Then there is an elaborate structure of Council committees, currently totaling thirteen, of which one, the Senior Civil Emergency Planning Committee, has eleven specialized committees under it. This is the area where much of the actual work of the Council organization is done. The third area is

[6] A shorter version of this paper appeared in the January 1962 issue of *Foreign Affairs*. Belgium, Canada, and Britain are among the NATO members who have recently reorganized their defense establishments along more centralized lines.

[7] See generally Timothy W. Stanley, *American Defense and National Security*, (Washington: Public Affairs Press, 1956), especially Ch. XI.

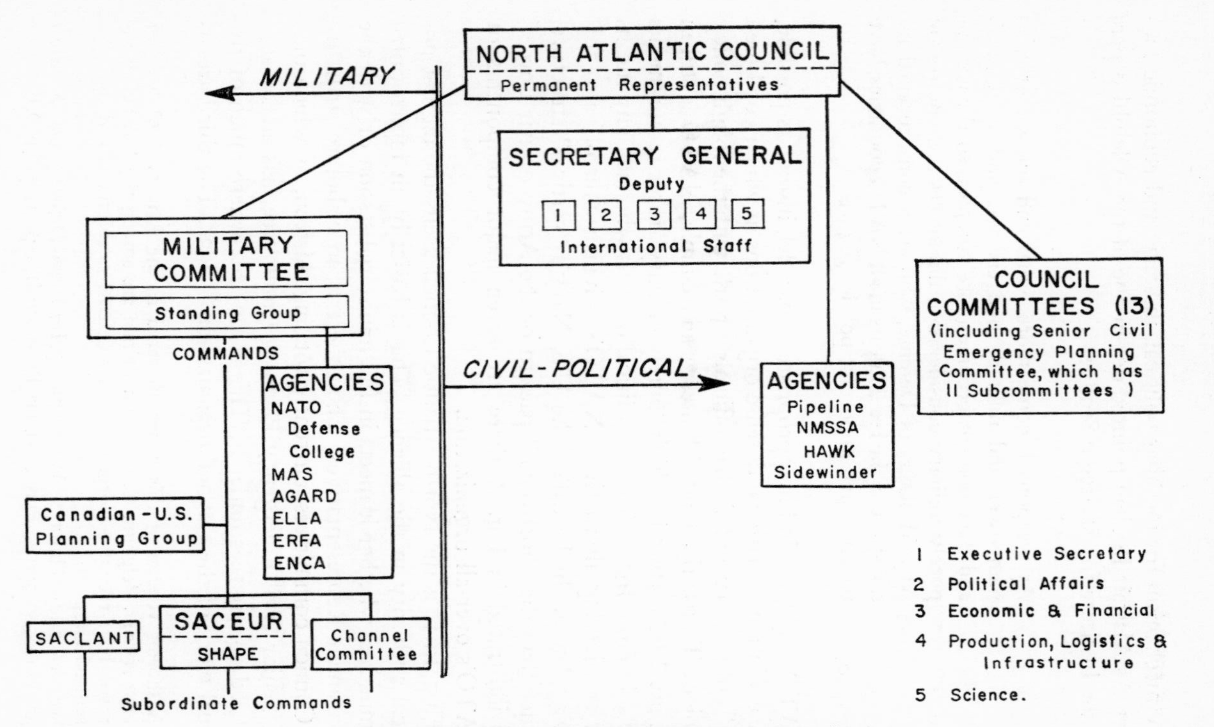

Fig. 2. Schematic Chart of NATO's Present Organization

that of the Secretary-General and the Staff Secretariat, which is divided into five major functional subdivisions. A fourth grouping on the civilian side consists of such agencies as the NATO Maintenance Supply Services Agency (NMSSA), the NATO Pipeline Agency, and the Hawk and Sidewinder production organizations.

On the military side, the top organ is the Military Committee (a chiefs-of-staff counterpart to the Council, to which it is responsible) and its executive committee, the Standing Group, located in Washington, and composed of representatives of the Chiefs of Staff to the United States, Britain, and France. SHAPE (just outside Paris) is actually the dominant center of military planning; and under General Norstad as SACEUR, it attained a high degree of independence from national views. Then there is the actual military command structure subordinate to SACEUR and SACLANT (plus the Channel Committee). Finally, there are half a dozen agencies responsible to the Standing Group, such as the NATO Defense College, standardization and communications agencies, and an aeronautical research group.[8]

A first requirement for rationalizing this cumbersome organization is to do away with the complete separation of military and nonmilitary planning. Secondly, a Secretary-General may be the "optimum" senior post for the United Nations, but an operating and policy making organization needs an Executive formally recognized as such. He might be a single man of outstanding stature, or it might be necessary to proceed along the "Commission" lines

[8] This proliferation of organizations with undecipherable abbreviations almost puts the Pentagon to shame. One who glances down the long list in the NATO fact book can hardly be blamed if he perpetrates such whimsical horrors as,

ELLA needs AGARD ENCAse
her SHAPE makes men
forget ERFA ACE.

The capitalized abbreviations stand for, respectively, European Long Lines Agency, Advisory Group for Aeronautical Research and Development, European Naval Communications Agency, Supreme Headquarters Allied Powers Europe, European Radio Frequency Agency, and Allied Command Europe.

followed by the European communities. In any case, the Executive, whether single or plural, requires an integrated civilian-military planning staff, as is now the case in most national ministries of defense. Thirdly, the "three-power" Standing Group ought to be reorganized along more international lines and revitalized so as to become both the major military planning center and the source of strategic direction for the forces of the alliance. Along with its parent Military Committee, the Standing Group probably should also be located together with the rest of the NATO organization, whether this remains in Paris, or is shifted to Washington or elsewhere.

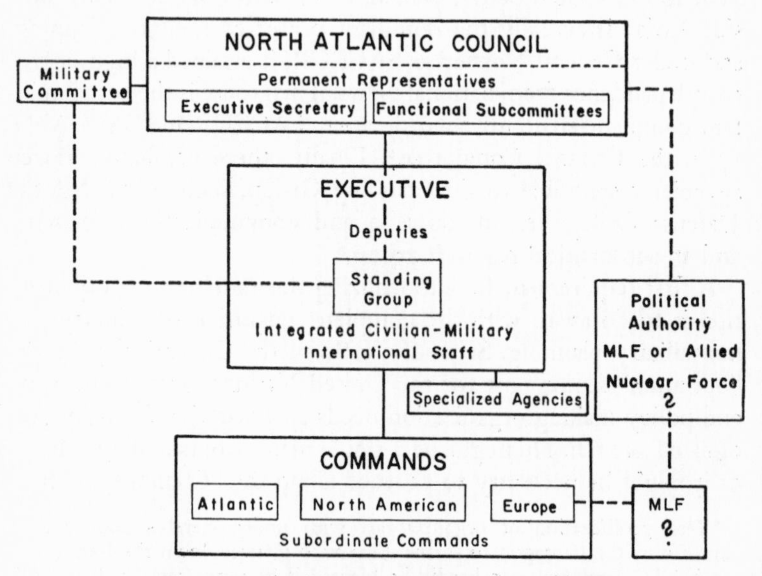

Fig. 3. A Possible Reorganization of NATO

Fig. 3 suggests one of several possible ways in which this might be accomplished. The North Atlantic Council should remain as an international body, but one having the essentially "legislative" functions of guidance, review and approval rather than executive prerogatives. The Military Committee would continue to function, as an advisory body to the Council, and as the senior focus for *national* military advice even as the U.S. Joint Chiefs of Staff represent the points of view of their respective services. The Standing Group would, however, become an international interservice planning and operational staff and the primary source of international military advice to the Executive, analogous to the U.S. Joint Staff and the chairman's staff group. Its membership should be enlarged to include other larger countries in the alliance, perhaps on a rotating basis, and it should work closely with an integrated civilian-military staff under the Executive and his deputies—which would, in effect, be a merger of the SHAPE planning staffs and the International Staff. The dozen miscellaneous organizations would be regrouped under appropriate directorates of this staff. Finally, the command line would run from the Executive, who is under the general guidance of the Council, through the Standing Group, to the several commands. Some changes may also be needed in the command structure, e.g., bringing NORAD directly into the NATO picture, instead of the present tenuous link via the Canada-U.S. planning group, adjusting the residual SACEUR and SACLANT staffs, and providing for a separate command for any allied nuclear force or MLF that is created.

It should not be thought that such structural changes could be made easily or without some sacrifice in what has been achieved under the present organization. In addition to the normal factors of inertia which resist change in any bureaucratic entity, the interrelationships of NATO's command organization with that of the United States would have to be taken into account. These are important for many reasons, but especially because the availability of nuclear weapons for NATO forces is closely tied to the two-hatted arrangement which exists in many key spots. Thus General Lemnitzer is both U.S. Commander in Chief Europe (CINCEUR) and Supreme Allied Commander Europe (SACEUR). The senior U.S. Army commander in Europe is also the NATO commander of ground forces in the central region. While such duality could be retained under a more streamlined organization, there are strong political factors at work in the assignment of commands among nations. The Channel Command for example was set up separately, paralleling SACEUR and SACLANT, to give the British an appropriate role. The further down into the command structure one goes, the more troublesome become international (and sometimes interservice) rivalries. The present balance has been achieved laboriously; but it appears to work reasonably well.

I have criticized the political-military separation in NATO's structure as unsuited to the present era of interlocking political, economic, technical and military factors. But this very institutional isolation has meant that effective military cooperation has for the most part *not* been blocked by frequent political disagreements. If prospects for an intergovernmental consensus on major strategic issues are judged to be poor, it is fair to question the net value of a reorganization which would involve the military planners even more in international political disputes. On the other hand, as presently structured, NATO may never be able to balance its forces, strategies, and budgets to meet the real needs of the late 1960s along the lines suggested in earlier chapters. We are discussing organizational change only in the assumed context of a decision by the leading NATO countries to get the best possible collective defense from available resources. In such a context, I believe the risks and difficulties of reorganization are outweighed by the prospective gains.

Force Planning and Budgets

Given a more centralized and streamlined planning and management organization, what functions might reasonably be performed by the revised structure and the NATO executive authority through increased delegation from the members?

There would seem to be no reason why the combined political-military-planning staff, drawing upon recommendations from the major commanders, should not develop a NATO-wide defense posture and force plan tailored specifically to alliance requirements. Then, by the addition of a sophisticated force-costing mechanism within the international staff, it should be possible to develop a

"NATO" defense budget comprising all of the forces and supporting elements necessary for Atlantic defense, much as is now done within national ministries of defense. Then if the NATO and OECD staffs could collaborate to produce reasonably accurate and equitable measures of comparative economic potential, possibly utilizing a revision of the Gilbert and Kravis *real* income tables, a formula might be devised for assigning to individual countries a reasonable allocation of the common defense burden.

This allocation would create, in effect, a paper debt to the organization on the part of each member country. Then credits would be given for forces which met NATO criteria (which would have to be sharpened considerably) as to their organization, location, readiness, quality, and mission. Thus, for example, if the master defense plan called for thirty D-Day divisions on the central front, the United States, Germany, Britain, and other countries maintaining forces which helped meet the requirement would receive an appropriate credit. Whether the credit should be the *actual* costs involved, or a theoretical cost figure for a NATO standard division, would have to be negotiated in working out the scheme. Admittedly, however, costing on other than an actual expenditure basis would pose formidable problems.

Let us suppose, hypothetically, that the over-all Atlantic defense budget, including strategic nuclear forces, totaled $75 billion, of which the United States' share was, say, $50 billion. The United States would receive credit for that portion of its "strategic retaliatory forces" which the international executive believed served alliance rather than purely national purposes. Taking into account the global nature of the alliance's task, U.S. military aid to certain underdeveloped areas, and Britain's forces east of Suez might also qualify for NATO credits. The excess of amounts due over credits received could in time become a charge upon which NATO could draw, either to reimburse countries (particularly from a balance-of-payments standpoint) which were providing more than their share, and to give NATO some common funding for such programs as infrastructure and research and development.

Such a procedure would produce strong incentives to tailor forces to NATO rather than purely national requirements, so that they would be eligible for credits; conversely, it would discourage the maintenance of expensive national forces which duplicated the missions of existing alliance forces. This would also provide a mechanism for comparing more realistically than in the past the true magnitudes of the relative defense efforts, and it could permit balance-of-payments compensation to countries having substantial forces stationed abroad.

It must be recognized at the outset that any such scheme would give unprecedented authority to the international decision-making levels of the alliance. It might be necessary to provide for some kind of an appeal mechanism through which countries which felt that they were being unfairly treated could have a review by specially qualified senior officials from countries not directly involved in the particular issue. Moreover, it would be necessary to develop a staff of career specialists, civilian and military, whose advice to the NATO executive was based upon loyalty to the alliance as a whole rather than to their parent service or country. The parallel between developing a supranational authority in an alliance of fifteen members and the relationship of a Minister of Defense to three or more services within a single country cannot be stretched too far. But it can be instructive in some respects. For example, in the United States, the requirement that any officer must have served on a joint, combined, or international staff before promotion to general or flag rank has been helpful in reducing parochialism. A similar requirement for NATO staff service on the part of the member countries could create strong incentives for the better professional officers to put in such a tour. If the efficiency reports affecting future promotion were made by international officials evaluating the individual on the basis of his service to NATO, rather than as a national representative, it should be possible to develop over time the same kind of objective staff advice which the Secretary of Defense now gets from officers of the various services—even when they are called upon to comment on proposals adversely affecting the interests of their own service.

A demonstrable requirement for "top drawer" talent in international service could permit a badly needed upgrading in the quality of NATO's international schooling and its Defense College, and contribute to the development of a group of specially qualified NATO specialists within each of the member countries. A recent article by a former faculty member at the NATO Defense College reveals the gap between the standards which the alliance would need under any growing supranationalism and the present reality. Language, diversity of rank and experience, and the need to balance country representation among the faculty and student body all contribute to the difficulties. The men who attend the institution do benefit from exchanges of views and an intangible sense of allied solidarity.[9] But they are too far along in their careers for maximum impact. To implement the concept under discussion might require cross-training in operational assignments, at junior officer courses, and even in service academies. At present, such training is limited mostly to the attendance of foreign officers at selected U.S. military schools.

Related to the education and training area is an imaginative proposal by Donald Brennan of the Hudson Institute.[10] He suggests that a strategic consensus within the alliance might best be advanced by the assignment of highly qualified specialists from NATO countries to key staff assignments in other countries, much as the U.S. Departments of State and Defense have created an exchange program to improve their coordination and mutual understanding. The administrative and security obstacles might make such an international exchange impractical; but if feasible, it could contribute to the development of a NATO staff corps fully qualified to act effectively and impartially as international civil and military servants.

[9] Col. Richard Stillman, U.S.A., "NATO Defense College," *Military Review*, January 1964, p. 32.

[10] Mr. Brennan's proposals on "staff integration" have been circulated privately as individual "think pieces."

Research, Production and Logistics

As suggested earlier, there is no reason why the principle that logistics are a national responsibility could not gradually be modified. The foregoing "common budget" scheme would provide both the authority and the funds for the development of requirements on a NATO-wide basis and their allocation to individual industries through competitive bidding. This process would have to begin gradually, but over time might evolve in the direction of a truly common NATO logistic system.

At present, NATO is even minimally involved in only 5 or 6 per cent of the total defense production of the members. If arrangements were made for the common budgeting procedures discussed above, the financial obligations of the member countries toward the alliance could be modified to take into account special benefits received from matériel procurement through the award of contracts to a particular country. Countries with economic slack could take it up in this way, which would combine the infrastructure "advantage" principle with the incentive aspects of such common production arrangements as the F-104G and Hawk consortia. NATO funds would in effect be used as incentives for greater alliance spending on the common defense in the same way in which American offshore procurement, military assistance, and Mutual Weapons Development Program funds have been used in the past. There would seem to be no reason why NATO involvement in production of weapons could not grow from the present nominal level to a third or even a half, or more. The availability of sizable research and development funds could also advance interallied scientific and technical cooperation and promote the maximum utilization of research talent, which would have important economic and political side effects.

The Atlantic Alliance

Thus far we have been treating NATO as an organization without reference to the broader connotations of the Atlantic alliance of which NATO is a symbol as well as the military embodiment. The Organization for Economic Cooperation and Development (OECD) provides an economic counterpart. While functional in scope, both organs are "political" in the broadest sense of the term. Yet there is no institutional political framework for the Atlantic community as a whole.

The central thesis of this book is that the Atlantic alliance is in transition from a regional security mission to the task of providing leadership in building a viable world order. This broader purpose suggests that the defense and economic elements represented by NATO and OECD should be welded into a sturdier political framework which can give meaning to the concept of Atlantic partnership.

Although they have differing functions and membership, NATO and OECD serve companion purposes and are organized on somewhat similar lines. There seems little reason why a new charter could not be drawn which would create a combined ministerial body concerned with both economic and military affairs. The North Atlantic Council, it should be recalled, meets at least annually in full ministerial session with foreign, defense, and finance ministers in attendance. For regular working purposes, the new entity, which might be called an "Atlantic Political Council," could subdivide into a Defense and an Economic Council which would meet through permanent representatives (preferably having cabinet status) much as the North Atlantic Council now does for NATO.

Subordinate to the Political Council could be a steering body composed of the Secretaries-General of NATO, OECD, and EFTA, and perhaps the Commission of the EEC, to coordinate the work of the various bodies. The executives of OECD and NATO would supervise the international staffs and would be responsible to the Council for their respective organizations. Both would presumably continue to operate much as at present, although some merging of staffs and services should be possible; and the resulting additional economic competence could be very beneficial to NATO.

The principal objection would be the so-called "neutrals" problem, that is, those countries which are members of OECD but not NATO. Of the five countries in this category, Spain and Ireland reflect special political situations which might be modified in time. Sweden and Switzerland are voluntary neutrals by tradition, while Austria's neutrality was the price of its independence from Soviet occupation. One solution would be to leave them out of the new organization entirely if they could not or would not change their status. In this case, provision might be made for special consultation on matters of interest to them. Another solution would be to provide for an associate category of membership (restricted to participation in nonmilitary affairs) which could be designed to prevent any "contamination" of neutrality. Japan, as an important but non-Atlantic nation first developed special ties with the OECD through membership in its Development Assistance Committee and is now a full member. The obstacle of the neutrals may therefore loom larger in theory than in practice.

To provide further political depth to the Atlantic community, arrangements should be made for a parliamentary assembly. This possibility has had considerable discussion and has been recommended by a number of individuals and groups.[11] Here also, the problem of the neutrals would arise, but could be met through special arrangements for limited participation in the nonmilitary activities of the assembly.

A more basic objection is that already a number of parliamentary bodies are active on an international basis. The European Parliament, established by the Treaty of Rome, serves as the legislative branch of the European communities. Both Western

[11] The Declaration of Paris proposed that "the NATO Parliamentarians Conference be developed into a consultative Atlantic Assembly . . . to receive reports . . . raise questions . . . debate and review the work of all Atlantic institutions and make recommendations to other Atlantic bodies and governments on questions of concern to the Atlantic community." Some of the many works on the general subject of Atlantic "community" are cited in the notes to Ch. 3. In addition, Frank Munk's *Atlantic Dilemma* (New York: Oceana Publications, 1964) contains a useful summary on parliamentary assemblies, pp. 137-139.

European Union and the Council of Europe have consultative assemblies, which, while useful, are primarily debating societies.[12]

Strangely enough, despite this plethora of activity in Europe there are no official parliamentary bodies serving an Atlantic purpose.[13] The OEEC had an informal arrangement with the Council of Europe whereby the latter's assembly served as the former's parliamentary mechanism. However, this approach became less applicable as OEEC lost the purely European aura of the Marshall Plan days and became the OECD—in which the United States and Canada are active members. (This transition, incidentally, might have been the best time to consider a merger of OECD with NATO; but the opportunity has not been lost by any means).

NATO has an active Conference of Parliamentarians who meet regularly. This body has, however, remained in a semi-official status notwithstanding its own recommendations for achieving a more formal standing. The Parliamentarians' political committee, noting that "the Atlantic nations are now served by a multitude of separate international organizations of differing memberships," commented that "two assemblies and only two are in fact needed, namely a European Parliament and an Atlantic assembly."

Such streamlining is, to be sure, much easier said than done. But the WEU assembly has, as explained in Part I, lost some of its original purpose, and since its membership is entirely included within the Council of Europe—and, except for Britain, in the European Parliament—the question of its disposition or retention should not pose too great a problem. The latter organ, however, represents only the Six; and pending enlargement of the EEC membership, it might be necessary to draw upon the Consultative Assembly of the

[12] Benelux and the Nordic Council also have consultative mechanisms involving parliamentarians, but they are of such limited regional scope that they need not be considered here.

[13] I am indebted for valuable background on this subject to a Council on Foreign Relations discussion group on an Atlantic Assembly, and particularly to the working papers prepared for it by Mr. Judd Polk of the Council staff.

Council of Europe as well as the European Parliament in providing the European delegates to an Atlantic assembly.

The United States already participates in inter-parliamentary activities with a number of countries, including Canada and Mexico, and has occasionally sent observers to Commonwealth and Council of Europe meetings. The Citizens Commission on NATO, which represented the United States in the Atlantic Convention and helped draw up the Declaration of Paris of January 1962, was actually created by an act of Congress passed in 1960.

Enough experience has been generated on both sides of the Atlantic to solve the organizational and procedural problems should the countries involved feel it worthwhile to create an Atlantic Assembly. To opponents of the idea, such a group could have no real role to play, might make divisive efforts at "back-seat driving," and would merely waste the time and add to the frustrations of the participants. But the experience with other organs suggests that extensive parliamentary contacts can generate considerable pressure on balky governments, as well as educating national legislatures and public opinion.

Moreover, there would be no reason why the Secretaries-General of NATO and OECD and perhaps NATO's senior military commanders as well could not submit to an international equivalent of Britain's "question time" in an Atlantic Assembly. Its purpose would therefore be consultative, as well as informative; and its reports would almost certainly command the attention of the Atlantic Political Council and the international staffs, as well as the member governments.

Should NATO evolve in the direction of supranational control of certain funds and activities, as suggested above in this chapter, the Assembly could provide the necessary democratic checks and balances. In the meantime, the mere fact of an Atlantic Assembly would provide valuable links to the several component bodies politic.

For the immediate future at least, selection would have to be indirect, i.e., by the participating parliaments. But an eventual possibility of direct popular election need not be ruled out, should the developing Atlantic community acquire quasi-legislative powers in selected areas.

Other features of an Atlantic community might be grafted on to the central trunk, comprising the high international council, two executive bodies (NATO and OECD) and a consultative assembly. Suggestions have been made for a Court of Justice, various advisory groups of elder statesmen, for cultural and scientific commissions, and even for operative research agencies, possibly in the field of space technology.[14]

My own view is that it is better to start on as simple a basis as possible and add other functions only when experience has shown that the organs involved could play a truly useful role. One key advantage of placing an Atlantic institutional structure around existing organizations would be that an official forum would exist for examining the merits of further steps and helping them evolve. The Atlantic Institute, established in Paris in 1961, serves as a useful clearing house and a source of studies with an international focus.[15] Although reorganization and expansion would be needed, the Institute could provide the Atlantic Assembly with a source of staff competence analogous to that which the U.S. Legislative Reference Service furnishes Congress.

The steps that would have to be taken to establish the proposed structure are small ones, for all of the essential organs exist in one form or another. The benefit from providing an over-all framework would be as much psychological as practical—although functional improvements might result in a number of areas. But politics is, after all, an exercise in group psychology. Every facet of the present alliance—political, economic, and military—would benefit from a clear demonstration that America and Europe have established not just a defensive arrangement, but a true and lasting partnership.

[14] Two European organizations are already active (and are receiving some U.S. technical help) in launches and satellite development, so that this might well be a particularly useful area for more formal Atlantic collaboration.

[15] The Institute's *Atlantic Studies* is a valuable register of research planned and in progress. The first edition was published in April 1964.

Once such a "community" had been operating for several years, the subtle chemistry of collaboration might make possible a greater supranational functioning of NATO and even permit steps toward a true federation on an Atlantic or even wider basis, which now seems beyond the bounds of political reality. Whether this was the end result or not, the creative act of political will involved in even the simplest over-all Atlantic framework would be worthwhile in itself. For in this way, the NATO nations could capitalize on their already impressive achievements. It would be ironic and tragic if, by failing to do so, they freely handed the Soviet Union the division between America and Europe which world communism has been at such pains to bring about, with so little success.

Conclusion

NATO, as the book's title asserts, is in transition. I have tried to answer the obvious questions of "from what" and "to what" in terms of the central relationship on which NATO's past rests and without which its future is meaningless. It is, of course, the relationship between North America and Western Europe. The adjustment which must be made is from a marriage of military necessity to a partnership of common political and economic purposes vis-à-vis the rest of the world.

That world, however, is in flux, with both East and West undergoing far-reaching changes; but the Communist challenge remains. For the immediate short term, the Soviet Union seems likely to be preoccupied with the problems posed by Communist China to Russia and to the world Communist movement. For the more distant future, there are encouraging signs that the Soviet Union may come to acceptable terms with the free world. A comparable evolution within Communist China, however, appears to lie in an even more distant future. The critical time period for NATO's future therefore falls in the middle years, extending into the 1970s. Here, there may be several abrupt shifts in Soviet leadership and policies. The worldwide effects of the Russian contest with the Chinese for influence threaten to aggravate the world's inherent instability.

Against this background, the Atlantic alliance must make a transition from its traditional mission of preserving the security of the Atlantic area, to a second task: leading the way toward a stable and relatively peaceful world order. Even though we cannot foresee with any precision the character of such a global system, it must be flexible enough to accommodate the changes which are inevitable, and thus be progressive in the literal sense of the word. These two tasks will require America and Europe to work in harmony, complementing rather than opposing each other.

From the political standpoint, the influence, experience, and common interest of Europe and the United States can best be brought to bear in the second task by fully cooperative efforts—certainly not by a return to some form of exclusive "spheres of influence." The magnitude of the economic task of building a viable world trade pattern, geared to the needs of both industrialized and underdeveloped areas, and of insuring an adequate pace of development will surely tax the combined resources and technology of both America and Europe. And such broad missions can only be undertaken from a secure base, namely, the entire Atlantic Treaty area.

As for the still vital security task, Europe cannot defend itself against all likely dimensions of threat in the future without an intimate association with the United States. Nor can the United States maintain an effective global deterrence against the Communist bloc without being equally involved in the defense of Europe. The major portion of this book therefore has dealt with the defense of the Atlantic area. Although this is a job that is being fairly well performed, all things considered, it is still a task only partially completed. The purpose of perfecting NATO's defenses is much less one of staving off an attack, since none appears imminent, than of denying the Communist bloc any profitable political returns from renewed adventuring. Such denial can hasten the transformation of Soviet policies toward the West which is already underway.

In the chapters on strategy in this book I have emphasized three themes. First, President Johnson's figure of speech that nuclear was is "impossible" expressed the indisputable fact that nuclear war is no longer a rational way of advancing national interests, if it ever was. But however unlikely or undesirable it may be, such a war is *possible*. Therefore, as long as the basic interests of the nuclear powers remain incompatible, nuclear weapons will remain indispensable. These upper rungs on the escalation ladder are the ultimate deterrent to aggression, as well as the umbrella over possible conflicts at lower levels of violence.

Second, notwithstanding the declining feasibility of a counterforce strike which would "disarm" an enemy of his retaliatory power, and the fact that the West would resort to a first use of nuclear weapons only under extreme provocation, quantity as well as quality of nuclear systems remain extremely relevant. For its strategic superiority provides NATO with an option of selective and controlled attacks which is not available to the Soviet Union. This advantage preserves an essential deterrence and some coercive value for the West. The strategic "stalemate" which has been so widely publicized is therefore only a relative condition. Paradoxically, the three-or four-to-one ratio favoring NATO in strategic nuclear power is not necessarily destabilizing. The Soviet Union may feel that its legitimate security requirements are met by a much smaller number of invulnerable second-strike missiles, and that, since it cannot afford to redress the balance, it will accept the military status quo—which the West can also accept.

Third, the Soviet Union's formidable military capabilities and the imperatives of non-proliferation mean that there are no solutions to the problem of managing NATO's nuclear power which are both militarily sound and politically feasible. The minimum European nuclear "independence" from the United States that would be militarily meaningful might be enough to require America to declare *its* independence from Europe. And many military, technological, geographic, political, and economic factors combine to render Europe incapable of effective self-defense except in partnership with the United States. Without that partnership, dangerous risks and a tempting politico-military weakness will result in Europe. But even if there is no ultimate answer to the nuclear-control dilemma of triggers and safety catches, there are methods, such as the proposed multilateral force, of giving Europe a greater role in the determination of the alliance's strategy and the management of its forces.

I have not dealt in any detail with the issue of control of nuclear power *within* the U.S. government, which was raised during the 1964 election campaign, for I agree with General Lemnitzer who described the matter as extraordinarily complex, highly classified, and not suited to public discussion. Purely from the standpoint of military readiness, it would be theoretically desirable to have as many nuclear weapons as possible dispersed and immediately available to responsible commanders. From the standpoint of over-all security, safety, and political control, one might seek to make it physically impossible for a nuclear weapon to be detonated without the express direction of the President—and perhaps even with congressional sanction.

Obviously, the solution lies between these extremes and must take into account communications, survivability, and command relationships. Technology can help through such devices as permissive links; but it still cannot eliminate continued reliance on military discipline and human integrity. The precise arrangements inevitably represent the kind of compromise that reasonable men must make in balancing mutually inconsistent criteria. After two decades of the atomic era the American record would seem to warrant continued confidence in the judgment of its leaders.

By stressing the strategic nuclear power of the alliance, I have not intended to minimize present gaps in non-nuclear defenses, but rather to highlight the sound military and economic base which already exists for the primary task of preserving the security of the Atlantic area. There are no economic constraints which would prevent the alliance from attaining *conventional* as well as nuclear superiority over the Warsaw Pact countries if the NATO powers so wished. Just by bringing strategy, forces, and budgets into a better balance, and by making such simple adjustments in its defense as are readily available *without substantial cost increases*, NATO could, within the next five years, achieve a virtually invulnerable posture throughout the spectrum of deterrence.

The gap between present military realities and this optimistic prospect is caused by *political* factors, rather than by economic or military limitations. And these same political issues (best symbolized by, but by no mean exclusive to, President de Gaulle) also affect the prospects for American and European cooperation in the second task of leading the way toward a stable and relatively peaceful world order. But if we look beyond the quarrelsome present to the middle future, the arguments for Atlantic partnership become overwhelming. Those who see in present difficulties an end to the NATO alliance fail to face up to the likely result: a world characterized by a neo-isolationism in America, an inward-looking Europe dominated by Gaullist-type nationalism, competing Chinese and Soviet Communist ambitions, and conflict between the industrialized northern hemisphere and the "have-nots" of the south—all compounding the world's familiar turbulence and instability.

On the assumption that common sense prevails over short-term pride and prejudice, much can be done to provide the political framework for a sound Atlantic relationship. A stronger alliance can be built without smothering Europe's emerging internal unity. Nor need it be premised upon an eventual Euro-American political confederation. But rededication and reconstruction of an Atlantic partnership to accord with the realities of the 1960s can no longer await the creation of the "single and equal" European partner, which was the key to President Kennedy's grand design. Rather, it is essential to create a working partnership of the many, within which the European element can coalesce at its own pace. In short, the framework of political, economic, and military cooperation on an Atlantic basis must be strengthened *now* so as to be consistent with—but not dependent on—Europe's tortuous evolution toward unity.

I have concluded that the relatively simple act of political will necessary to merge NATO and OECD into a common framework, perhaps under a single Atlantic Political Council and with a parliamentary assembly, could provide the necessary impetus to reform the alliance for its redefined tasks. The many defects in NATO—not least of which is the structural separation between military and civil components—stem largely from the fact that it is an international and not a supranational organization. There are, and will remain, clear limits on the extent to which greater supranational operation will be permitted by the members. But as with all evolutionary organisms, small steps can be significant. One specific military step which could pave the way for reform in the alliance as a whole would be a multilateral nuclear force—because such a U.S.-European joint venture would be *internationally* owned and operated. And there are a variety of political steps which could be taken to help mold a consensus within NATO on global problems.

French attitudes constitute at present an effective bar to reform of the alliance. But if other members lead the way, the alliance may be able to contain and isolate the negative effects of Gaullism, hopefully inducing some trimming of nationalistic sails while preserving France's place in the alliance. History may well credit De Gaulle with having saved France from itself; and with the health of the body politic sufficiently restored, the French statesmanship exemplified by Schuman, Pleven, and Monnet can again play a constructive role in Europe. But should this not be the case, the alliance has too much at stake to permit itself to be immobilized by France—even if it has to go along without one member for a time.

What I have called NATO's central relationship arises from historical, cultural, and geopolitical factors common to North America and Europe. It is reinforced by current political, economic and military necessities. Yet there is another dimension, too often slighted in this pragmatic world. Man's moral and spiritual evolution has increasingly led him to ask "why" as well as "how." The Western world has no monopoly on man's quest for understanding; if only because it has the physical power to do so, it must continue to lead in defining as well as in helping to realize humanity's long-term goals.

This is perhaps the essence of the transition. For the NATO relationships, initially cemented by fear, have now registered enough accomplishment to evolve into a partnership based on hope.

Index

Index

Index

Council on Foreign Relations

Publications of the Council on Foreign Relations

FOREIGN AFFAIRS (quarterly), edited by Hamilton Fish Armstrong

THE UNITED STATES IN WORLD AFFAIRS (annual). Volumes for 1931, 1932 and 1933, by Walter Lippmann and William O. Scroggs; for 1934-1935, 1936, 1937, 1938, 1939 and 1940, by Whitney H. Shepardson and William O. Scroggs; for 1945-1947, 1947-1948 and 1948-1949, by John C. Campbell; for 1949, 1950, 1951, 1952, 1953 and 1954, by Richard P. Stebbins; for 1955, by Hollis W. Barber; for 1956, 1957, 1958, 1959, 1960, 1961, 1962 and 1963, by Richard P. Stebbins.

DOCUMENTS ON AMERICAN FOREIGN RELATIONS (annual). Volume for 1952 edited by Clarence W. Baier and Richard P. Stebbins; for 1953 and 1954, edited by Peter V. Curl; for 1955, 1956, 1957, 1958 and 1959, edited by Paul E. Zinner; for 1960, 1961, 1962 and 1963, edited by Richard P. Stebbins.

POLITICAL HANDBOOK AND ATLAS OF THE WORLD (annual), edited by Walter H. Mallory.

REMNANTS OF EMPIRE: The United Nations and the End of Colonialism, by David W. Wainhouse.

The European Community and American Trade: A Study in Atlantic Economics and Policy, by Randall Hinshaw.

The Fourth Dimension of Foreign Policy: Educational and Cultural Affairs, by Philip H. Coombs.

American Agencies Interested in International Affairs (Fifth Edition), compiled by Donald Wasson.

Japan and the United States in World Trade, by Warren S. Hunsberger.

Foreign Affairs Bibliography, 1952-1962, by Henry L. Roberts.

The Dollar in World Affairs, An Essay in International Financial Policy, by Henry G. Aubrey.

On Dealing with the Communist World, by George F. Kennan.

Foreign Aid and Foreign Policy, by Edward S. Mason.

The Scientific Revolution and World Politics, by Caryl P. Haskins.

Africa: A Foreign Affairs Reader, edited by Philip W. Quigg.

The Philippines and the United States: Problems of Partnership, by George E. Taylor.

Southeast Asia in United States Policy, by Russell H. Fifield.

UNESCO: Assessment and Promise, by George N. Shuster.

The Peaceful Atom in Foreign Policy, by Arnold Kramish.

The Arabs and the World: Nasser's Arab Nationalist Policy, by Charles D. Cremeans.

Toward an Atlantic Community, by Christian A. Herter.

The Soviet Union, 1922-1962: A Foreign Affairs Reader, edited by Philip E. Mosely.

The Politics of Foreign Aid: American Experience in Southeast Asia, by John D. Montgomery.

Spearheads of Democracy: Labor in the Developing Countries, by George C. Lodge.

Latin America: Diplomacy and Reality, by Adolf A. Berle.

The Organization of American States and the Hemisphere Crisis, by John C. Dreier.

The United Nations: Structure for Peace, by Ernest A. Gross.

The Long Polar Watch: Canada and the Defense of North America, by Melvin Conant.

Arms and Politics in Latin America (Revised Edition), by Edwin Lieuwen.

The Future of Underdeveloped Countries: Political Implications of Economic Development (Revised Edition), by Eugene Staley.

Spain and Defense of the West: Ally and Liability, by Arthur P. Whitaker.

Social Change in Latin America Today: Its Implications for United States Policy, by Richard N. Adams, John P. Gillin, Allan R. Holmberg, Oscar Lewis, Richard W. Patch, and Charles W. Wagley.

Foreign Policy: The Next Phase: The 1960s (Revised Edition), by Thomas K. Finletter.

Defense of the Middle East: Problems of American Policy (Revised Edition), by John C. Campbell.

Communist China and Asia: Challenge to American Policy, by A. Doak Barnett.

France, Troubled Ally: De Gaulle's Heritage and Prospects, by Edgar S. Furniss, Jr.

The Schuman Plan: A Study in Economic Cooperation, 1950-1959, by William Diebold, Jr.

Soviet Economic Aid: The New Aid and Trade Policy in Underdeveloped Countries, by Joseph S. Berliner.

Raw Materials: A Study of American Policy, by Percy W. Bidwell.

NATO and the Future of Europe, by Ben T. Moore.

African Economic Development, by William Hance.

India and America: A Study of Their Relations, by Phillips Talbot and S. L. Poplai.

Japan Between East and West, by Hugh Borton, Jerome B. Cohen, William J. Jorden, Donald Keene, Paul F. Langer and C. Martin Wilbur.

Nuclear Weapons and Foreign Policy, by Henry A. Kissinger.

Moscow-Peking Axis: Strength and Strains, by Howard L. Boorman, Alexander Eckstein, Philip E. Mosely and Benjamin Schwartz.

Russia and America: Dangers and Prospects, by Henry L. Roberts.

Foreign Affairs Bibliography, 1942-1952, by Henry L. Roberts.